Pamela

Pamela Tiffin

Hollywood to Rome,
1961–1974

Tom Lisanti

McFarland & Company, Inc., Publishers
Jefferson, North Carolina

LIBRARY OF CONGRESS CATALOGUING-IN-PUBLICATION DATA

Lisanti, Tom, 1961–
Pamela Tiffin : Hollywood to Rome, 1961–1974 / Tom Lisanti.
p.   cm.
Includes bibliographical references and index.

ISBN 978-0-7864-9661-7 (softcover : acid free paper) ∞
ISBN 978-1-4766-2016-9 (ebook)

1. Tiffin, Pamela.   2. Actors—United States—Biography.   I. Title.

PN2287.T485L48 2015   791.4302'8092—dc23   [B]   2015031628

BRITISH LIBRARY CATALOGUING DATA ARE AVAILABLE

Front cover: Publicity photograph of Pamela Tiffin, 1963

Printed in the United States of America

*McFarland & Company, Inc., Publishers
Box 611, Jefferson, North Carolina 28640
www.mcfarlandpub.com*

Acknowledgments

My deep appreciation to the following people who contributed to this book starting with those who worked with Pamela Tiffin over the years: actor Jed Curtis from *Straziami, ma di baci saziami*; actress Niki Flacks from the Broadway play *Dinner at Eight*; actors Peter Gonzales Falcon, Larry Hankin, and Eldon Quick from *Viva Max*; actor Franco Nero from *Giornata nera per l'Ariete* and *Deaf Smith & Johnny Ears*; actor Martin West from *Harper*; writer-producer John Wilder from TV's *The Survivors*; and assistant director Tim Zinnemann from *The Hallelujah Trail*. Thank you for permitting me to share with readers your anecdotes and memories.

A huge thank you to writers-historians Dean Brierly, Roberto Curti, Howard Hughes, Paolo Mereghetti, and Ed Robertson for their intelligent insights and expert opinions on Pamela Tiffin's performances in film and/or TV; her stature in cinema history; and her movies, especially the Italian kind.

A special nod to Roberto Curti (a fellow McFarland author) for his immense help, from providing information on Pamela Tiffin's Italian movies that I could have never found here in the States, to recruiting Paolo Mereghetti for this book and then translating his comments into English.

Thanks to the very talented writer-blogger Shaun Chang for making the connection to John Wilder and for his continued encouragement and friendship; writer-editor Lee Pfeiffer of *Cinema Retro* magazine (www.cinemaretro.com); TV historian Stephen Bowie for use of his interview with TV producer Richard DeRoy; and to Camilla Fluxman-Pines for making the connection to her client Franco Nero. As always, thanks to Jim McGann, my web master. I will forever be your servant.

Thanks to my family, friends, and fans of sixtiescinema.com for their continued support with a special shout-out to Alan Pally, Peter Vigliarolo and David Hermes.

I couldn't have written this book without using the vast collections of the National Film Information Service at the Margaret Herrick Library in Beverly Hills, the General Research Division at the New York Public Library, and the Billy Rose Theatre Division at the New York Public Library for the Performing Arts, with a special thanks to librarian Jeremy Megraw and photographer Peter Riesett.

A Medal of Honor to Ernie DeLia for putting up with my obsessions with Pamela Tiffin; Carol Lynley; sixties starlets; beach movies; *Ryan's Hope*; *Real Housewives*; Ilene Kristen; *Land of the Giants*; and *The Poseidon Adventure*.

And last, but surely not least, a gracious thank you to the Danon family for their support.

Table of Contents

Preface

Why a book on Pamela Tiffin? There are more famous actresses of the sixties who deserve to be written about, true. But Tiffin is one of the most beautiful and talented actresses of her time and she left an indelible impression on movie fans. For my money, she is prettier than Raquel Welch, funnier than Jane Fonda and more appealing than Ann-Margret. Yet they all became superstars and Tiffin did not. This book will help explain why Tiffin, gifted with comedic ability, did not achieve mega-stardom (due in part to contract obligations and her self-imposed exile in New York and later Rome), though she remains a cult sixties icon.

I first saw Pamela Tiffin in the colorful travelogue *The Pleasure Seekers*, which was broadcast on *WABC*'s *The 4:30 Movie* sometime in the mid-seventies. I was already a huge Carol Lynley fan, having seen *The Poseidon Adventure*, and would seek out her other movie appearances. I had heard of co-star Ann-Margret but was not familiar with the handsome brunette Tiffin, the third member of the movie's romance-seeking trio. I recall being unimpressed with Ann-Margret, though I thought she did swell performing the title song. I did love Carol Lynley in the film, but I was beguiled by Pamela. She took the typical naïve ingénue role and made it funny, touching and sexy. I was only 13, but even at that age I knew Pamela had a certain something the other two did not. Soon after, I began seeking out Pamela's movies and *The 4:30 Movie* came through with *For Those Who Think Young* and *The Lively Set*. I was hooked and could not understand why she was not as big a star as Ann-Margret or Carol Lynley.

I began researching Tiffin's career only to discover that she practically disappeared from the silver screen after 1966, with a few Italian movies popping up thereafter. My determination to learn more about her culminated in an interview with her at her New York City home in 1998 for a series of short magazine articles and a chapter in my first book. She was elegant and charming with that same whispery voice. We stayed in contact for a brief period, but then I stopped hearing from her though my devotion to her never ceased. This book is, I hope, the definitive look at her career.

Pamela Tiffin once described her entrée into Hollywood "as a kind of Cinderella story."[1] And it truly was. A model and cover girl, she was discovered while on vacation having lunch at the Paramount Studios commissary. She won critical acclaim for her first two films, *Summer and Smoke* (1961) and the Billy Wilder comedy *One, Two, Three* (1961). In the latter, she gave a wonderfully amusing performance as a southern belle who sneaks into East Berlin and marries a communist, to the chagrin of her guardian in Germany. Everyone from Wilder to James Cagney to Jose Ferrer praised her acting ability, especially her knack for comedy.

While most sixties starlets were playing the fame game in Hollywood, Pamela refused to relocate, remaining in New York taking college classes and modeling between acting gigs. Though it's commonplace today for movie actors to live outside of Los Angeles, it was unheard of then. Movie roles kept coming though through her contracts with Hal B. Wallis, 20th Century–Fox, and the Mirisch Brothers, but nothing equal to her first two films; Hollywood type-cast Pamela as the naïve, marriage-minded ingénue in a string of campy romantic comedies aimed at the drive-in crowd beginning in 1962, with the musical *State Fair*, co-starring Pat Boone and Bobby Darin. She next played a novice stewardess in *Come Fly with Me*, followed by a surfing coed in *For Those Who Think Young*, a coed determined to land a racecar driver in *The Lively Set* and a tourist in Madrid who falls for a Latin playboy in *The Pleasure Seekers*.

With her seductive soft voice, Pamela Tiffin imbued her romance-seeking characters with a wide-eyed naïveté and endearing flightiness, but also a sexiness that her contemporaries could not match. She made these movies better than expected. But her comedic abilities put her above the competition, including Sandra Dee, Connie Stevens, Shelley Fabares, Deborah Walley, and Hayley Mills. For boys and young men, it was not very cool to admit to being a fan of these actresses. But it was hip to dig Pamela Tiffin. Though all had played the innocent virgin, Pamela exuded sex appeal far beyond the others. She was the sex kitten masquerading as the girl next door and male moviegoers were able to see through the chaste façade Hollywood had foisted on her. It wasn't until the bikini-clad actress jiggled the diving board as the love-starved Miranda in *Harper* opposite Paul Newman that she left the ingénue far behind.

What is ironic about Pamela Tiffin was that off-camera she was known as being a demure, intelligent, serious-minded woman and not someone you would expect to be funny on screen. But she had the rare talent to play comedy so well as demonstrated in *One, Two, Three* and *Come Fly with Me* especially. This ability though may have hampered her in getting the dramatic roles she craved. And to her disappointment comedic parts that she should have landed went to less talented but more famous actresses. It is no wonder that she became frustrated with Hollywood.

It was at this pivotal junction that a major change happened in Tiffin's career. A chance to become Marcello Mastroianni's first American leading lady in the three-part *Oggi, domani, dopodomani* took her to Italy where she was required to bleach her hair blonde and act the vapid sexpot, taking her overtly sexy image one step further. She never looked back. The new, sensuous, fair-haired, curvaceous Tiffin should have then taken Hollywood by storm. Instead, she made her Broadway stage debut in *Dinner at Eight* and then, unhappy with her marriage, ran away to Rome to start anew in 1967.

Italy welcomed Tiffin with open arms, pairing her with some of the country's most popular leading men, including Ugo Tognazzi, Nino Manfredi, and Vittorio Gassman. She was perfectly suited for sexy Italian comedies such as *L'arcangelo*, playing a seductive vixen with murder on her mind, and *Il vichingo venuto dal Sud*, playing a Danish coed who moonlights as a porn actress. Back in the States, she entertained as a mini-skirted activist coed with hay fever who sides with a Mexican army general (Peter Ustinov) who has retaken the Alamo in the comedy *Viva Max*. Returning to Italy, she gave standout performances in a pair of movies with international star Franco Nero. In the underrated giallo *The Fifth Cord*, Tiffin played the sexy, playful girlfriend to his murder-investigating alcoholic reporter and

Publicity photograph of the iconic Pamela Tiffin in *Harper* (Warner Bros., 1966).

in the entertaining spaghetti western *Deaf Smith & Johnny Ears* she was a feisty whore to his amorous gunslinger. Unfortunately for American moviegoers, most of her Continental films were either not released in the U.S. or received limited distribution. As early as 1972, her fans were writing to movie magazines asking, "Whatever became of Pamela Tiffin?"

Tiffin's beauty, warmth, comic ability, and charisma lingered with movie fans for years. She is such a cult sixties pop icon in part because she is an enigma. The sultry brunette disappeared from Hollywood just when she was on the verge of superstardom and left moviegoers craving more. Very few of the newly blonde Tiffin's Italian movies reached the U.S. so it became a treat when they did and had her fans thinking what may have been if she had stayed in the States. She quit acting in 1974 and kept a very low profile even to this day. You won't spot Pamela Tiffin hawking her autographed photos at celebrity fan conventions or find her on Facebook sharing clips of her work with her "friends." All Tiffin fans are left with are her Hollywood movies, her hard-to-find Italian films, and limited TV appearances.

In 2007 author Chris Strodder named Tiffin one of the 1960s' grooviest people in his book *The Encyclopedia of Sixties Cool.* You won't find in it Sandra Dee, Carol Lynley, or demure brunettes of the time similar to Tiffin such as Janet Margolin, Millie Perkins, Ina Balin, Susan Strasberg, or Diane Baker, whose icy screen persona leaves this moviegoer cold fifty years later. Described by Strodder as "one of the most stunning young actresses of the '60s,"[2] Tiffin is included because she was the darling of the drive-in movie crowd beginning with *Come Fly with Me* through *The Pleasure Seekers,* and cemented her coolness with *Harper.*

Today there is a website devoted to the actress, *Pamela Tiffin: A Toast to Tiffin* (http://pamelatiffintribute.blogspot.com/) and fan pages about her at *Brian's Drive-In Theater* (www.briansdriveintheater.com) and *Glamour Girls of the Silver Screen* (www.glamourgirlsofthesilverscreen.com). You can find many video clips in tribute to Tiffin on YouTube. In 2003 an Italian punk rock band called themselves the Pamela Tiffins in honor of the actress. The music of this duo, consisting of Scanna and a pretty long-haired blonde named Alpe, is the opposite of what you would expect. As described on Soupy Records' website (www.soupyrecords.net) they are "in the style of the Jesus and Mary Chain, punk-garage attitudes and pure art surround the band with gloomy atmospheres"—nothing like the whispery-voiced, effervescent Tiffin.

This book is not a biography so there are no interviews with family members or friends. There are also no racy stories about Pamela's love affairs as found in some recent memoirs by a few of her sixties contemporaries. Instead, it is a career retrospective focusing on her body of work, with behind-the-scenes anecdotes and expert opinions.

Pamela Tiffin unfortunately could not contribute to the book. All quotes from the actress are from published sources (including my own interview with her) and from transcripts of interviews she gave to the publicity people at 20th Century–Fox. Also included are quotes from film historians specializing in Italian or sixties cinema, and from actors, directors or producers who worked with her. These come from either brand new interviews I conducted or from other published sources.

1

In the Beginning

Pamela Tiffin Wonso was born on October 13, 1942, in Oklahoma City. She is of Russian, British, and Scottish decent. Her father, Stanley Wonso, was a successful architect and her mother was named Grace Irene Tiffin. The family soon relocated to the well-to-do town of Oak Lawn, Illinois, outside of Chicago, where she attended grammar school in Oak Park. As the town grew the school system kept changing and Pamela—Peppy Wonso as she was known then—had to keep switching schools even though she still resided in the same house, which was unpleasant for her.

Pamela's first sign of talent was dancing. Her parents enrolled her at age four in classes at the Gertrude Morgan School where she studied tap and interpretive dancing. The Wonsos provided their daughter the encouragement children need when embarking on a new venture. They didn't push her for professional reasons but to broaden her horizons and to learn rhythm, grace, and poise. Pamela enjoyed dancing a lot because she loved music. She attended the school on and off until she was about eleven years old.

It was Pamela's looks, not her dancing, that received the most attention. A neighbor named Mrs. Graber suggested to Grace Wonso that her photogenic daughter would be ideal to model children's clothes. Pamela's mother thought Pamela, at age six, was too young and wanted her daughter to have a normal childhood filled with fun. She did not want her to have to always concentrate on her looks and clothes, not to mention being carted around town for interviews. About six years later they ran into Mrs. Graber in downtown Chicago. When she heard Pamela was not modeling, she insisted they stop in at the Models Bureau nearby. On an impulse, Pamela agreed and asked her mother to take her there. She was signed on the spot. Her first modeling job was for the soft drink 7-Up: She held up a can of soda looking at it as if eager to drink it. She earned $70 for the day.

Pamela confessed she only modeled during her free time during high school in Blue Island, nearby her home in Oak Lawn, because she wanted to save up for her college tuition. However, to make her learn the value of money, Pamela had to cover all her own expenses (i.e., phone charges, transportation, clothing, etc.) and pay back her parents for any money they laid out. While she enjoyed modeling, she had no interest in acting and declined to join her school's drama department because the other girls were really competitive for roles. Pamela preferred to spend her time studying and modeling. Most of her shoots were print ads in which she stood in front of a record player or something. She also had a steady gig posing in the newest clothes for the *Chicago Tribune* and did high school and church runway fashion shows.

Pamela graduated from high school in only three years by doubling up on junior and senior work with a straight-A average. She relocated to New York with her mother in June

1959, missing out on attending her high school graduation, while her father moved his business to Chicago. She began taking night classes at Hunter College, studying advanced algebra, French, and English literature, and worked with a private French tutor from the Language Guild Institute while continuing to pursue her modeling career.

Though she was almost 5'7" with chestnut brown that fell below her shoulders, hazel eyes, a round face, and a glowing, porcelain-like complexion, the New York modeling world did not immediately embrace her. She registered with the Frances Gill Agency and quickly learned that working in New York was much different and more difficult than in Chicago. She needed a portfolio of new photographs. This could only be accomplished by testing with different photographers and meeting with various advertising agencies. Pamela found this process frustrating, as it was time-consuming, tiring, and boring. She didn't get her first New York modeling job until three months later and after she had switched to the Plaza Five Agency in August.

Tiffin also did not like to be at the beck and call of some photographers whom she described as being "childlike in their impulsiveness."[1] Some rejected her initially, but later hired her repeatedly, while others fawned over her but never used her in a shoot. It wasn't until January of 1960 that she finally began getting immersed in New York's modeling world with a proper book and getting steady work thanks to Plaza Five.

The busy career gal was sought after by all the top photographers and chic magazines of the time. Soon she was making $60 per hour and earning up to $1,500 a week. During various shoots, people would talk highly about a photographer named Philippe Halsman. One day, coincidentally, she found herself in the same building as his studio and dropped in on him without an appointment. His wife answered the door and, seeing this gorgeous brunette, quickly rushed her inside to meet her husband. He reviewed her photographs and promised he would hire her. Pamela appeared in a number of ads photographed by him for a stationery line.

Halsman was very influential for Pamela and piqued her interest in modeling. She respected him greatly and he encouraged her when she needed it most.

Pamela also introduced herself to photographer Lloyd Fromm, who immediately told her she should be in motion pictures. She declined, explaining that she was only interested in modeling and her school studies. Fromm would not take no for an answer and insisted she head straight to Paramount Studios' New York office to meet with Boris Kaplan, their East Coast casting director. Kaplan really wanted to sign her to Paramount; Tiffin insisted that she had no interest in becoming an actress and thanked him for the offer. Two weeks later he called her into his office to read some Cornelia Otis Skinner for him. After they let the theatrical conversation die, talk turned to other things. Kaplan was intelligent and knowledgeable and helped Pamela appreciate her algebra class, which she was finding tedious.

Pamela seemed to be drawn to intelligent men and enjoyed conversing with them so it is no surprise she remained friendly with Kaplan. When he invited her to his office the third time, they were joined by director Sidney Meyers and two men from the Rockefeller Foundation. They were seeking a girl to play an Irish miller's daughter in their documentary about Colonial Williamsburg. Coming directly from a photo shoot, Pamela was still made-up and looked quite mature. Though they liked her, they thought she was too sophisticated and wanted someone closer to the girl in an Irish Airlines print ad they had seen in the

Sunday *New York Times* magazine. When one of the men pulled it out of his pocket, it was Pamela, *sans* makeup. Realizing that Tiffin really looked young, they offered her the part, which required no acting. After checking with her modeling agency to make sure she did not have any conflicts, she accepted because she wanted a new adventure, and this required very little acting. Kaplan must have realized that despite her protestations, there was a small part of Pamela that wanted to give acting a try and that is why he kept pushing. This opportunity was a baby step.

As the adage goes, when it rains it pours, and just as Pamela was preparing to go on location, she received a call from the editors of *Vogue*, the epitome of high fashion magazines, to come in for a meeting. Two Italian photographers immediately fell in love with her look and asked to photograph her, but Pamela's sitting quickly took a wrong turn. "I posed in the proverbial 'little nothing' black dress," she recalled:

> A plank fell on my foot—it was one of the props—it hurt too much even to cry. It hit the nerve in the arch and the foot swelled up. I had very high heel shoes on and really couldn't get a firm foothold to pose because the foot was swollen. A model needs to be comfortable when she stands in order to hold her pose or shift her weight to the position the photographer wants. I couldn't stand it, so it was postponed and we continued the sitting a later day.[2]

Vogue was delighted with the photos of Pamela from the second sitting and used one of them in the magazine.

Music of Williamsburg was directed by Sidney Meyers, most remembered for his 1960 docudrama *The Savage Eye*. In the film, Pamela wore a 17th-century costume and was the main figure used to tie together the scenes demonstrating how music played a major part in the daily lives of 18th-century citizens of Williamsburg. Afterward, Pamela remarked, "It was just a lovely simple experience. I wasn't even nervous in front of the camera."[3]

When she returned to New York, *Vogue* came a-calling again, wanting to do a feature on Tiffin with photos by Fred Pleasure for their 1960 Beauty Book. She worked for the magazine frequently, which gave her a lot more exposure. So much so that while riding the bus one day she was spotted by Bert Stern, the self-described "mad man photographer" known for shooting some of the world's most beautiful women, including Marilyn Monroe and Audrey Hepburn. She debarked before he could speak with her, but noticed the letter she was reading was addressed to Pamela. He went through all the composites of the models in New York until he found her. She then began modeling for him at *Vogue*.

Others pursued Tiffin including legendary fashion photographer Horst P. Horst, who once had a difficult time shooting Pamela holding a compact while wearing false fingernails that kept falling off. Another well-known photographer was Mark Shaw, who worked for *Life* magazine and was the personal photographer of President John F. Kennedy and his family while he was in the White House. Shaw photographed Pamela for many Ivory Soap print ads plus a TV commercial that never aired.

Pamela eventually burst out from the interior pages to the covers of such publications as *Red Book*, *Glamour*, and the *New York Post* magazine section, among others. She loved doing photo shoots and explained that modeling was more than just standing still in front of a camera. And she had the bruises to prove it. Clad in a nightgown, she was jumping on beds with three other models for a *Glamour* magazine layout when the frame collapsed, sending the ladies flying and rendering her black and blue from the fall. For another *Glam-*

our shoot, she was wearing elegant high-heeled shoes on the slimy rocks along the shore of a Central Park lake. She recalled, "With new shoes you can't get a foothold. There were several models in the picture. I slipped and the model in back of me caught me.... [T]he picture is very funny because all of us were holding on like mad so we wouldn't slip into the lake."[4]

A Career Is Launched

Summer and Smoke

Thanksgiving 1960 was fast approaching and the busy model and part-time student was looking forward to the holiday. She was craving some time off to spend with a few friends who owned horses in the Los Angeles area. Before leaving New York for her mini-vacation, Pamela spoke with her casting director friend Boris Kaplan. He arranged for her to meet a writer friend on the Paramount lot. It was not for professional reasons; he simply thought she would enjoy meeting him since he was a wonderful conversationalist. Kaplan may have also had an ulterior motive, knowing that the stunning girl would not go unnoticed and that somebody would bring her to the attention of the studio heads.

Pamela considered herself a tourist, so she made a date to visit Paramount Studios the day after Thanksgiving to meet Kaplan's friend and also because she wanted to see the sets and watch them shoot movies. She never had an inkling of being discovered while she lunched at the studio commissary talking about Latin, books, and cinema. Up to this point the highlight for her was spotting the sauntering John Wayne.

Kaplan's writer friend then introduced Pamela to Paul Nathan, an associate of producer Hal B. Wallis. Nathan immediately whisked the befuddled young girl away to meet his boss. Was it just an accident that Nathan was accessible that day or did a mischievous Boris Kaplan set the entire series of events in motion? Whichever, it is ironic that Pamela was discovered lunching since the name Tiffin is British slang for "lunch."

Producer Hal Wallis was just about to go into production for *Summer and Smoke*, based on the play by Tennessee Williams. The role of Nellie, the young girl—a "Dixie flirt," as described in *Life* magazine—who steals the doctor away from the spinster lead character, was coveted by Dolores Hart, one of Wallis' more recent discoveries. (Others included Shirley MacLaine, Dean Martin, Jerry Lewis, and Charlton Heston.) Hart craved the role because she wanted to prove to Wallis and Hollywood that she was capable of more than just playing Elvis Presley girls (she co-starred with the singer in *Loving You* and *King Creole*). The producer agreed to let Hart test for the part, even though he felt she was too young. Hart took that to mean that she wasn't sexy enough. After viewing the test, the film's director, Peter Glenville, thought Hart too old for the part, which she again took that to mean she wasn't sexy enough.

It was reported that Hart was still in consideration for the role until Pamela Tiffin wandered onto the Paramount lot. The rest of that day played like a frenetic comedy in the vein of *One, Two, Three*. Wallis and Nathan bombarded her with questions. Did she have any stage experience? Did she ever take acting lessons? She answered no to all. When Wallis asked if she wanted to be an actress, she gave a firm no—she was content being a student and model. She explained that she didn't have any training as an actor and didn't want to embarrass herself.

The undeterred Wallis insisted Tiffin audition for him then and there. Handing the *Summer and Smoke* script to her, he instructed Pamela to go outside and take as long as she needed to prepare. Nathan helped her with a scene and fifteen minutes later they were back with Wallis. Tiffin's natural acting ability, coupled with her fresh beauty, wowed the producer. He offered her a contract on the spot and told her to call her agent. The problem was, she did not *have* an agent and was overwhelmed by what was happening. Her parents were home in Chicago and her friends were waiting for her outside. Pamela told the men she could not make such an important decision without consulting her family. Wallis agreed, and also felt that she should meet director Peter Glenville before they went any further. Pamela was taken aback; Glenville's Broadway production of *Becket* was all the rage in New York.

While Wallis was trying to track down the director, an overwhelmed Tiffin was busy trying to connect with her parents. Glenville was harried that day, but took the time to meet with Wallis. He was polite, but only spoke a few words to Pamela before she read the part of Nellie for him. Glenville, who was having a hard time finding the right actress for the role, was so pleased with her reading that he wanted to do a screen test immediately. Everything was happening so quickly for Pamela that she declined, as she had prior commitments with her friends and was just so awed by the director. Pamela explained, "I wasn't being coy about not doing the screen test that day.... I was too astonished at the progress of events and particularly meeting Peter Glenville, an idol. It's a very exhausting thing to meet an idol unexpectedly. Excitement is exhausting."[1]

Wallis then had to convince the reluctant Pamela to extend her stay in California so they could screen test her on that Monday. She had a modeling assignment and, it being a holiday weekend, knew it would be too difficult to change. When Pamela finally relented, Wallis had studio personnel make umpteen phone calls before finally getting through to somebody at Tiffin's modeling agency. "There's a certain electricity about a day like that," she revealed shortly after. "I was so excited, so bewildered. They were awfully nice to me that day."[2]

Events continued to get even more bewildering. She was to screen test with the scene in which Laurence Harvey's doctor first meets Nellie when he accidentally opens the door to her room and finds her in bed wearing a nightgown. Wanting to make sure her old-fashioned costume fit just right, Pamela was whisked away to meet with Academy Award–winning costume designer Edith Head. After the fitting, she was sent to Wally Westmore for a makeup test. Finally, an exhausted Pamela was sent home to relax over the weekend until her big day that Monday.

Pamela awoke at 5:30 a.m. the day of her screen test since her friends' home was quite a distance from Hollywood. "When we arrived at the studio, everything was all set up," recalled Pamela:

> I was made up, dressed, and pushed in front of the cameras. Three people made me feel very comfortable—Peter Glenville, who directed my test; Charles Lang who photographed it; and Mr. Nathan was there. I don't even remember the man I did the test with. I forgot to take my hose off and I was sliding around under the sheets until I realized that I better take the stockings

Promotional poster art for *Summer and Smoke* (Paramount, 1961).

off if I wanted to be comfortable—and it's very difficult to do with about twenty men standing around, but I managed. We got it on the first take, and then they changed my wardrobe—they called me "one-take Nellie" and I was so thrilled. Then they had me change to one of my own dresses, and we did a straight interview. Mr. Glenville asked me questions about myself and I answered. Peter and I got along very well.

After the test was over the lights immediately went out and people scattered. No one said a word. No one said it was good, bad or indifferent. The wardrobe girl helped me undress, and I just went home. No one even said we'll let you know later or call you. They just walked off and left me. Peter did hold out his hand, shook hands with me and said politely, "It was nice working with you," but that's all.[3]

During the prep for the screen test, Glenville mentioned in passing that he had just purchased a building in New York and in a really odd coincidence it was the one where Pamela and her mother lived. Remembering that she had some leaking pipes in the kitchen and bathroom, the director-actress bond was broken for a moment, as Pamela morphed into the unhappy tenant informing her landlord about the problem and insisting that the pipes be fixed. Taken aback, the director said it was not the time or place for that discussion. Pamela felt he got a bit annoyed with her despite the fact that he brought the building up.

After Pamela returned to New York, her mother asked if she got the part. Tiffin answered that she wasn't sure, but said that she did bring up with Peter Glenville their leak problem. Due to the silence that followed her test, the fledging actress did not expect to get the role, but she wrote thank-you notes to all the people who helped her. Putting the screen test out of her mind, she returned to her daily routine.

A few weeks later, Pamela was thrilled to learn that she not only got the role in *Summer and Smoke*, but that she would also be getting new faucets and pipes for her home. Looking back on her test, Tiffin admitted to Tennessee Williams scholar W. Kenneth Holditch that she really was confused about the whole process and was surprised it turned out well. She remarked, "I guess ignorance is wonderful; not knowing and naïveté is good sometimes."[4]

After landing the part, Tiffin received a phone call from Martin Baum, the president of the talent agency General Artists Corporation. He explained that he had been on the Paramount lot the morning of her screen test when Glenville recommended that he represent her. Baum was busy meeting with the head of the studio and not that hurried to meet this "Pamela Tiffin." He was distracted by the girl he had spotted in a *New York Times* lingerie ad that was published just before Pamela headed off to California and had ordered his staff to "Find that girl in the slip!" Unbeknownst to him, Pamela Tiffin *was* that girl.

Photographer Bert Stern chose her to do that Chemstrand lingerie ad, posing in a petticoat. Back then, "good girls" did not pose in lingerie, even though the hourly fee was double. Stern felt Pamela was perfect for his concept and she finally relented due to the respect she had for him. However, the condition was that only one photo would run and not a series of photos as the client originally wanted. The print ad featured the sultry model posing on her knees wearing a white form-fitting petticoat, eyes closed, with a side pony tail. It was an eye-popping shot but was not released in the scheduled *New York Times* issue or the one after. Pamela presumed the ad campaign was scrapped because of Stern's new high art concept in presenting a woman's slip was not right for the client. She forgot about it and did not realize that it finally ran in that week's newspaper.

On Pamela's behalf Baum took it upon himself to negotiate a contract with Wallis for $1,000 a week with an eight-week guarantee, as well as one with 20th Century–Fox. Tiffin was not certain, but she thinks Fox studio heads saw her test, though Wallis claimed he locked the film up and would not let anyone else see it. Under the terms of the pact negotiated by her new agent, Tiffin would make one picture a year for $8,000 with the studio having the right to option her for three additional movies during the seven-year period. She now joined the starlet-eat-starlet world at Fox that included such ambitious young actresses as Ann-Margret, Tuesday Weld, Carol Lynley, Diane Baker, Barbara Eden, Juliet Prowse, Millie Perkins, and Julie Newmar. Wallis' other contract player Dolores Hart also had a picture deal with Fox.

Pamela was thrilled to land *Summer and Smoke*, but unsure about the contracts. As a model she experienced a life of independence and felt nervous about being tied down. She eventually came around and signed the contract with Wallis, which stipulated she was guaranteed one picture a year with an option for a second. Wallis had to approve all loanouts, but Baum negotiated for Pamela to receive 25 percent of the fees paid to the producer by other studios for Tiffin's services. Most newcomers weren't able to get any percentage of loanout fees, so the fact that Baum was able to get this was a financial advantage for Tiffin and proved how much she impressed the veteran producer.

Contracts aside, going from in-demand model to aspiring actress by the age of eighteen was quite an achievement for a young girl from the Midwest. Pamela now had a new adventure to tackle—acting. The assured young woman was surprisingly not scared as she had complete trust in Peter Glenville to help her with her acting and in costume designer Edith Head.

Despite the confidence in her acting talent, Pamela was just not ready to give up her modeling career per Wallis' request. She enjoyed modeling, especially when the agencies gave photographers and models an opportunity to be creative in their work. Also, it would keep her busy between motion picture assignments while living in New York. The newcomer had no intentions to relocate to California and was determined not to play the Hollywood fame game. This meant no arranged dates with actors for fan magazine pictorials and no Hollywood parties. She confessed to being a homebody and was not interested in that part of being an actress. Her agent even negotiated that all her travel expenses would be picked up by the studios. Pamela proved to be a trailblazer. Not many aspiring actors had the fortitude and confidence to live outside of Los Angeles during that period of time.

When asked what it was about Pamela Tiffin that drew him to her, Wallis replied, "Upon seeing Pamela for the first time I was struck by an elusive regal quality as rare as it is difficult to define. She is that fascinating combination of poise and the unpredictable encountered, once in a great while, in a lovely girl hovering between her teens and twenties."[5]

For a big-time producer, Wallis seemed very patient with Pamela and did not force her to sign anything against her will. Even after she was under contract to him, he seemed to allow her to make her own choices with a number of film projects. Pamela felt there were two Hal Wallises: the one in Hollywood being all-business, and a charming and jolly Wallis when visiting New York.

Pamela was the envy of many actresses in Hollywood, making her film debut in a Tennessee Williams movie directed by Peter Glenville. The actress did admit that she was not familiar with *Summer and Smoke* when she landed the role but she certainly knew about the playwright, having seen his *Sweet Bird of Youth* on Broadway the year before. This was only Glenville's third movie (he previously directed *The Prisoner* and *Me and the Colonel*)

Publicity photograph of Pamela Tiffin in *Summer and Smoke* (Paramount, 1961).

but he was considered one of the most acclaimed theatrical directors of the time and directed the London stage production of *Summer and Smoke*. Pamela knew how lucky she was to enact Nellie, one of Williams' well-defined female characters, while guided by such a talent as Glenville. It was a part many a Hollywood starlet longed for.

The newcomer was also thrilled to be working with such an esteemed cast. Academy Award nominee Geraldine Page was reprising the role as Alma which she played on stage at the Circle in the Square in New York to rave reviews. The leading man was the brooding Englishman Laurence Harvey, red hot after his Academy Award–nominated performance in *Room at the Top* in 1959, followed by such popular films as *Expresso Bongo*, *The Alamo* (his first movie playing a Southerner) and *BUtterfield 8*. Other cast members included Rita Moreno, Una Merkel, and Thomas Gomez.

In the turn-of-the-century tale, Nellie is the sweet young thing who innocently steals the heart of a carousing, handsome doctor who has been secretly loved by his prim and uptight neighbor Alma. "Nellie is not the typical Tennessee Williams woman," opined Pamela at the time. "She is more poetic than most. She grows up in the picture. I'm sent away to school and when I come back I capture Laurence Harvey."[6] Pamela also felt a kinship to the setting that Williams created due to her years growing up in similar small towns in Illinois.

Before filming began, the cast and director met each day for a week. Per Pamela, "There was a rehearsal, often at other people's homes. Geraldine Page's home, Peter Glenville's home … it was just sort of 'home hopping' for about a week reading the play. I found myself amongst a serious group of people who were recreating a world."[7]

The *Summer and Smoke* screenplay was by James Poe (who won an Academy Award for co-writing *Around the World in Eighty Days* and successfully adapted Tennessee Williams' hit play *Cat on a Hot Tin Roof*) and Meade Roberts (who worked with Williams on the screen version of his play *The Fugitive Kind*). Shooting took place afternoons and nights. Rehearsing made it easier for the novice actress to make the progression to filming, as did the talents of Academy Award–winning costume designer Edith Head. "As we put on costumes, it was no problem," reflected Pamela. "They were the clothes of the characters, they weren't costumes. Because Edith Head did it, it was so right that you didn't have to become accustomed to anything."[8]

Since *Summer and Smoke* was a heavy drama, it was reported that the producers closed the set to all visitors including reporters and even Laurence Harvey's miffed girlfriend. Pamela liked this rule as it represented to her real commitment by all to make a beautiful motion picture. She commented years later, "There was a great deal for concentration, and we literally created that Tennessee Williams world for two months on the sound stage. That was an extremely privileged way to make a film, because in later films, sometimes all hell would break loose. Silly things would go on, or it would be more 'show biz,' and so I always treasure that."[9]

Pamela had nothing but kind words about her castmates. She respected their intelligence and remarked, "They were people who cared about the human voice."[10] She particularly praised her leading man. "I had the delightful experience of kissing Laurence Harvey," she exclaimed, "and he was so nice to me all during the picture. He is … so warm and intelligent—a very entertaining man."[11]

Pamela also revealed that there was a fun, mischievous side to Harvey, who liked to play practical jokes on the set. She remembered that they were doing a scene where the actor had to open a door and then close it after saying his lines to Geraldine Page. There was a prop man on the other side to catch the door so it wouldn't make too much noise and drown out the dialogue. As a joke, Harvey held on to the doorknob and the prop guy was pulling like mad. He did it just for laughs and it quite amused his young co-star.

Harvey wasn't the only man on the set giving Pamela the giggles. She had to do a surprise laugh in one scene near the end of the day and with the cast and crew tired, director Peter Glenville wanted it in one take. After calling action, he crept up behind Tiffin and tickled her, getting the surprised reaction he needed. She then chased him around the set in retaliation.

She too only had admiration for her "charming" and "devastating" director and continued, "I would work for Peter Glenville if I had to sign my life away. He symbolizes so much for me. He made me feel comfortable and confident and always extended every possible courtesy to me. I will always be grateful to him and will always admire him."[12] Glenville was such a perfectionist that he not only concentrated on the performances of his actors, but their looks as well. Per Tiffin, before the cameras rolled, he would pull out wisps of her hair, to make the hairdo slightly disheveled. He felt her hair not being perfect made Nellie more enticing. He also had nicknames for his leading ladies—"Geraldinola" for Page and "Pameloren" for Tiffin because he knew she studied Latin.

Pamela was also lucky to have her first film shot by Academy Award–winning cinematographer Charles Lang. He won for *A Farewell to Arms* in 1932 and his other films included *Sudden Fear*, *Sabrina*, *Separate Tables*, *Some Like It Hot* and *The Facts of Life*. Reflecting on Lang's approach to his work, Pamela opined years later, "Like all good professionals [he] knew when to be present and absent on the set. It's only less talented people whose voice is heard above the others. Talented people are usually very modest, very careful, very discreet."[13]

During the first few days of shooting, Pamela quickly learned that there was a lot of down time on a movie set. It was not like the quick modeling sessions she was used to. To keep occupied, the *Vogue* fashion model sewed. Somehow between her modeling gigs and classes she found time to take sewing lessons in New York and was determined to create her own designs. She admitted that she didn't like the clothes sold off-the-rack in shops or those created by fashion designers. She was determined to become fully proficient with a needle so she could create her own wardrobe.

Wearing fashions designed by the incomparable Edith Head must have given her motivation as well. "I loved my clothing on *Summer and Smoke*," remarked Tiffin. "I really appreciated dresses I could move in and I certainly appreciated Edith Head's costumes. She has a fine sense of style that is equaled by her sense of movement in clothes."[14]

Pamela revealed that sometimes after seeing the rushes of the previous day's filming, Geraldine Page and Laurence Harvey would ask for re-shoots and not because they were being prima donna actors. She explained, "A few things were re-shot with Geraldine and Laurence because they knew they wanted to bring out other qualities…. It wasn't 'Oh, my God we have to re-take this,' it was an effort to be as close as possible to Tennessee Williams' writings. As I look back on this … it was exceptional. All films should be like that, but they're not."[15]

All and all, *Summer and Smoke* was a very pleasant experience for the first-time actress. The only problem for her arose on her last day of shooting, on the village square set. She developed a terrible head cold and was in excruciating pain. "I tried very hard to keep my head about me," Pamela recalled. "If [this scene] wasn't good, the whole continuity would have been broken. It was my hardest day on the picture, but because I wasn't bleeding, no one thought I was sick. Only Charles Lang understood how miserable I felt."[16] Pro that she was, she played the scene beautifully and most were unaware of her discomfort.

Summer and Smoke was shot entirely on soundstages on the Paramount lot, unlike Pamela's future movies that took her to locations throughout the U.S. and the world. Being a novice, Tiffin liked the comfort of this way of moviemaking with the actors on a lit set and everything beyond in darkness. She felt shooting this way put the concentration on the dialogue and that the cinematographer served the story, unlike with today's movies where CGI effects dominate.

When the shoot ended, Pamela revealed that she was extremely impressed with her hands-on director and producer: "Mr. Glenville and Mr. Wallis took particular pride in the picture as a whole and wanted to see personally every detail of emotion, dialogue, props, costumes, etc."[17]

Summer and Smoke was only Geraldine Page's second movie after making her film debut in the 1953 John Wayne western *Hondo* for which she was nominated for a Best Supporting Actress Academy Award. When asked why she waited so long to make another, she revealed that she had a fear of filmmaking: "I never had a moment's stage fright, but these cameras and lights make me terribly nervous. I couldn't quite reason why until Pamela Tiffin … summed it up beautifully. She said that 'moviemaking is like eating a big dinner with the waiters taking away the plates before you've finished the course.'"[18]

Two days after Pamela wrapped her role in *Summer and Smoke*, she was back in New York modeling. She had prior obligations she had to keep despite Wallis' request that she drop out of the modeling world. However, many of these assignments were with agencies and magazines that accommodated her leave to make the movie, so she felt obligated to fulfill these commitments.

Tennessee Williams never visited the set due to his working on his play *The Night of the Iguana*, but Pamela met him briefly in a Chicago theater after being cast in the movie. A few years later, when married to editor Clay Felker, the actress would encounter the playwright a few times at social events. She described him as "a graceful man. I remember his twinkling eyes, his sidelong glance, a playfulness and sense of humor (which few people have), and yet a strength. [He] had a courtly, cavalier charm. It was real, it wasn't party manners, and yet there was this cordiality and graciousness."[19]

Looking back on her first motion picture over thirty years later, Pamela reflected, "I never thought I would have done any at all, or acted in any way, and yet, the seriousness and respect for [the] efforts of everyone made it something like a dream. It was the ideal working conditions and that is unusual, as we know."[20]

Summer and Smoke opened in late 1961. The "smoke" in the title refers to "the elusiveness of the spirit." Highlighting the tawdry to lure moviegoers, the poster art proclaimed, "There is a haze, a smoke in summer … from the smoldering fire in this, the season of her longing…." Pamela received "Introducing" credit for the movie and was described on the poster art as "The Young One … a girl past seventeen can be just so sheltered…." This was in contrast to Rita Moreno, who was called "The Wild One…. 'Can we never make love without you biting or scratching me?'"

Pamela bursts on the screen as Nellie Ewell when Dr. John Buchanan, Jr. (Laurence Harvey), goes looking for the restroom at a casino and accidentally enters the room of Nellie, the proprietress' nubile daughter. Prodigal son Dr. John has returned to the family homestead after spending time away drinking, gambling and womanizing instead of concentrating on his career. His childhood friend and next door neighbor Alma Winemiller

Alma (Geraldine Page) frets while her teenage piano student Nellie (Pamela Tiffin) gushes over meeting "Dr. Johnny" in *Summer and Smoke* (Paramount, 1961).

(Geraldine Page) is thrilled but apprehensive about his homecoming due to her deep-seated feelings for the rogue. Uptight Alma loves the sinner, but hates the sin.

In her room, Nellie reminds John that she is a patient of his father (John McIntire) and they met once at his office a few years prior. John recalls their meeting and comments on how she is "sweet sixteen," but she corrects him and says she is seventeen. She then confides in him that her mother was too shy to tell her about the facts of life, so she asked his father who recommended a stuffy book. A giggly Nellie asks "Dr. Johnny" why she gets funny feelings when around "not so much boys, but men—especially handsome ones." He tells her to stop by the office to discuss this further and recommends to her mother (Lee Patrick) that she send Nellie to boarding school to get away from the low-lives that frequent her establishment.

A music student of Alma's, exuberant Nellie rushes over to share the good news that because of "him" her mother is sending her off to finishing school. She rehashes what happened the night that led up to it, including asking about the facts of life. When Alma realizes that Nellie is talking about Dr. John, her excitement for Nellie turns to jealousy—especially when the young girl reveals that Dr. John was there with Rosa (Rita Moreno), known for her sexual exploits. Alma scolds Nellie for peeking out the window to watch Dr. John wash his car. Alma's mother (Una Merkel) enters the room and cruelly taunts Alma about her spying on the boy next door and her secret love for him. Alma becomes upset. Nellie makes a hasty exit while mother and daughter have it out.

Nellie returns from school a year later. The brazen girl still flirts with the doctor, who is now on the straight and narrow since the killing of his father by a drunken Papa Zacharias (Thomas Gomez); the tragedy was indirectly caused by a jealous Alma's meddling. Surprised by Nellie's maturity, John remarks, "High heels, feathers, and paint." Nellie corrects him that her cheeks are flushed due to excitement about being home from school. She confesses that she feigned ignorance about the facts of life in her room that night and apologizes before kissing him on the mouth and professing her love for him. Dr. Johnny is taken aback, and sends the impetuous girl on her way. Not taking no for answer, she promises to be back.

John tries to make amends with the depressed Alma, who he blamed for his father's death, but he is turned away by the Rev. Winemiller (Malcolm Atterbury). A few months later, Nellie finds the reclusive Alma underneath the stone angel fountain in the park and gives her a Christmas present. Unaware of Alma's true feelings toward John, Nellie chatters on about the doctor, who only has nice things to say about Alma and credits her for his redemption. A hopeful Alma runs off before Nellie can reveal her big news. Alma immediately goes to John and tells him the reserved Alma no longer exists—that she has come around to his way of thinking about enjoying the sins of the flesh. As John begins to let her down easy, Nellie bursts in and announces their engagement. The doctor admits he has come around to Alma's way of thinking and believes there is a soul so he has decided to settle down with the young girl. Trying to hide her bitter disappointment, Alma slinks off. She meets a stranger in the park near her fountain, a salesman named Archie Kramer (Earl Holliman). Alma goes off with him.

To Hal Wallis' surprise, *Summer and Smoke* received mixed reviews from the critics not so much for the performers (though a number of reviewers felt Laurence Harvey was miscast) or Peter Glenville's direction, but for Tennessee Williams' story where he once again dipped into the same well about odd-behaving folks in the Deep South. Most critics raved about Geraldine Page's superb performance as Miss Alma. When Pamela was mentioned, it was usually along the lines of the reviewer in *Variety* who remarked, "Pamela Tiffin … adds a pro flair to dazzling youthful beauty to rate plenty of future attention." The actress' rival for the role, Dolores Hart, wrote years later that she thought Pamela was "very good in the part."[21]

Pamela's beauty and performance did not impress every critic. Pauline Kael, writing in *Film Quarterly*, was especially vicious in her criticism and described Tiffin as having "a face as soft and dimply as a baby's bottom—and just as expressive. Couldn't the stork take her back?"

Kael's opinion aside, Tiffin was just lovely in the movie. Her beauty astounds the moviegoer from the first moment she is seen on screen sitting upright in bed wearing a nightgown, but there was more to her than that. She takes the film's only real innocent major female character, which could have come across as perkily annoying or as a selfish brat, and makes her extremely engaging and likable. This alone makes her stand out from the tortured Alma and hardened Rosa. In *Tennessee Williams and Company: His Essential Screen Actors*, author John DiLeo remarked, "Tiffin … is fresh and bubbly (Page and Moreno don't stand a chance), and she brightens the picture considerably at just about the point it needs it most."

Tiffin's infectious performance truly makes the viewer believe her Nellie is naïve and totally oblivious to Alma's longing for Dr. John. She has a schoolgirl crush on the doctor and that is all she is aware of. Like most self-indulgent teenagers, she is only concerned with her own feelings; however, there is nothing malicious in her actions. Tiffin successfully imbued in Nellie a youthful exuberance and charm, so much so that when she finally wins over the good doctor you could not be mad with her despite the hurt it caused Alma.

Summer and Smoke did not fare very well at the box office despite the accolades won by Geraldine Page. She received an Academy Award nomination for Best Actress (she lost to Sophia Loren in *Two Women*) and copped the Golden Globe for Best Actress in a Drama and the Best Actress award from the National Board of Review. *Summer and Smoke* accumulated three additional Academy Award nominations: Una Merkel was nominated for Best Supporting Actress and its color art direction/set decoration and original musical score by Elmer Bernstein also received nods. The screenwriters, Charles Lang and, most surprisingly, Edith Head were not recognized for their contributions.

Poof, She's a Star

One, Two, Three

Tiffin thought she would be working for director Peter Glenville again in her next movie, *Devil in Bucks County*. It was based on the sensationally lurid Edmund Schiddel novel about city folk who flock to the rural community oasis, bringing sin and scandal with them. However, the movie never came to be.

Unbeknownst to Tiffin, while she was making *Summer and Smoke*, director Billy Wilder had also spotted her in that notorious lingerie ad in the *New York Times Magazine* and had his agent trying to track her down. Commenting about why he was drawn to the fresh-faced model, Wilder exclaimed, "Pamela Tiffin is a thing of such beauty that, my God, I can't stand it. I first saw her … and I couldn't believe it. She looked good enough to eat."[1]

Wilder was quite surprised to find that Tiffin had been in Hollywood and now was back home. He wanted to meet with her to discuss playing the All-American, materialistic teenage Scarlett Hazeltine in his new film *One, Two, Three*, a satire on capitalism and communism set in Germany. He and his writing partner I.A.L. Diamond (they had just won the Academy Award for Best Original Screenplay for *The Apartment*) based their script on a French play by Ferenc Molnár. In the original set in 1920s Paris, the teenage daughter of a powerful Scandinavian industrialist elopes with a Socialist cab driver while she is the houseguest of an ambitious banker. He has only a few hours to change the groom to become acceptable to his new father-in-law.

Wilder and Diamond had been working on this screenplay for a few years. From the get-go, they knew they were not going to use the title and Molnar's dialog since they wanted to update the play and make it current. At one point it was to star Marilyn Monroe as an American film star who gets brainwashed by a handsome Communist while attending the Berlin Film Festival. Among the titles tossed around were *The Hot Breath of the Cossacks* and *Dead Herring in the Moonlight*. The movie now focused on C. R. MacNamara (played by the great James Cagney) whose boss sends his scatterbrained daughter Scarlett to Europe on a whirlwind vacation. While under MacNamara's care in Germany, she sneaks over the border to East Berlin and marries a Communist whom she just met. Trying to save his career, a frantic MacNamara first tries to end the union and then has to reunite the lovers when Scarlett's flu turns out to be a pregnancy. Due to Wilder's success with *The Apartment*, this was one of the most anticipated movies of 1961.

According to I.A.L. Diamond, the title *One, Two, Three* represented the speed at which Cagney's Coca-Cola executive transforms the East German Communist into a Capitalist suitable to marry the daughter of a conservative Southern businessman. He added that Wilder took it one step further and made speed the keynote of his direction. Scenes and dialog moved at lightning pace once the race was on to fool the boss. It's no wonder Cagney later remarked, "It's the talkingest part I've ever had."[2]

Also signed for *One, Two, Three* were respected stage actress and TV personality Arlene Francis as Cagney's long-suffering wife; Swiss actress Lilo Pulver as MacNamara's shapely secretary (reportedly Audrey Wilder saw her at a party at Curt Jurgens' home and told her husband that the actress would be perfect for Ingeborg); and Horst Buchholz as the East German Communist who steals Scarlett's heart. Dark-haired and brooding, Buchholz was the "It Boy" for a short period during the early sixties. He had six films under his belt from his native Germany when he was cast as a lovesick killer in the British film *Tiger Bay* (1959), co-starring Hayley Mills. The film brought him international attention. The Mirisch Brothers brought him to Hollywood for a star-making role in the hit western *The Magnificent Seven* (1960). He just completed his next movie *Fanny* (1961), directed by Joshua Logan, before being cast in *One, Two, Three*. It was reported that the actor was being considered for *Lawrence of Arabia*, probably in the role of Prince Ali that eventually went to Omar Sharif, but chose this instead due to the many filming delays on *Arabia*. This pleased Wilder considerably since he revealed that he and Diamond wrote the part of Otto Ludwig Piffl with only Horst in mind to play it.

Jack Lemmon was slated to play a cameo role. It was reported that he would be making a "guest appearance" in the movie as a favor to Wilder, who directed him to Best Actor Oscar nominations in *Some Like It Hot* and *The Apartment*. He did not appear in *One, Two, Three*. Lemmon most likely would have played the brief role ultimately given to Red Buttons, who did not receive billing, as the corporal searching for the man in the polka-dotted dress.

The only main role left to be cast was Scarlett, whom Wilder envisioned as a blonde. Tuesday Weld, who impressed the critics playing sexy, outgoing teenagers in the comedies *Rally 'Round the Flag, Boys!* and *High Time*, desperately wanted it, but Wilder was not sold on her. One Thursday while Pamela was working in New York, she received a phone call from Martin Baum, who told her to hop on the next plane because Wilder and Diamond were interested in her for a role in their new comedy. She couldn't leave until Friday night due to modeling jobs. After some flight delays, a tired Pamela staggered into Wilder's office Saturday morning after stopping at her hotel to freshen up. Wilder felt that Tiffin was a bit too sweet in appearance for the role, but he asked her to audition anyway. She read the scene where Scarlett debarks from the plane and meets the MacNamaras for the first time in the Berlin airport. According to Pamela, after she finished reading she just waited for a reaction. She recalled, "The first thing Mr. Wilder said was, 'My wife Audrey will meet you in New York to shop at Bergdorf's for your wardrobe.'"[3] Tiffin was astonished that he cast her immediately after stating that she did not have the right look. Choosing her over Tuesday Weld was a daring move since Weld had proven acting talent, but it turned out to be a winning gamble.

There were two problems with the casting of Tiffin. One, she had already agreed to do *A Pocketful of Miracles*. Hal B. Wallis honored director Frank Capra's request to borrow Pamela to play the debutante daughter of a street peddler played by Bette Davis. Makeup artist Wally Westmore brought the newcomer to the esteemed director's attention and he cast her on the spot.

Wallis, who had script approval before Pamela could work on any other movie, had to first give his permission for her to do *One, Two, Three*. He did and in a generous move allowed the actress to keep all the money paid to borrow her services. Then she had to bow out of *A Pocketful of Miracles*. According to Pamela, "Mr. Capra was very happy for me and said, 'That's all right. You'll have the female lead in *One, Two, Three*.' He understood and was very sweet about it."[4] She was replaced in *A Pocketful of Miracles* by Ann-Margret, who was making her film debut.

Tiffin's second hurdle was that she had to sign a contract with the Mirisch Brothers, which she did in March 1961. The deal was not just for *One, Two, Three*: It included an option for an additional movie per year with script approval by Wallis.

As ordered, Pamela met with Wilder's wife in New York to pick out her movie wardrobe. They had a problem finding just the right outfits and settled on many pink dresses, even though the actress disliked the color and had never worn it in her life. But since the movie was going to be filmed in black and white, it didn't matter as much. What was more troubling is that Pamela learned from Mrs. Wilder the dreadful news that she had to be a blonde in the movie. She thought she could wear a wig, but Mrs. Wilder told her that she had three weeks before the start of production to dye it. Pamela was torn because nice girls from the Midwest like herself didn't bleach their hair.

Just before Pamela was to depart to Germany, *Esquire* magazine arranged for her to be photographed by Bert Stern and then coupled with Hal B. Wallis and Billy Wilder for a major article they were doing on her. "Mr. Wallis came to town … with his son Brent," she said, recalling that day:

> In the morning Mr. Wallis and I were photographed…. I had my portrait sitting in the afternoon, then came home to dress for dinner. That was the night we went to Danny's Hideaway [a steakhouse frequented by many celebrities]. It was my first time. I was very excited because Danny [owner Dante Stradella] loves Mr. Wallis and Mr. Wallis' pictures were all over the restaurant. Mr. Wallis and Brent are very talkative people…. I really had a marvelous time, and the food was so good.[5]

Pamela had to gulp down her dessert because they had front row center seats to see the Broadway play *Becket* starring Laurence Olivier and Anthony Quinn. Due to pouring rain, their car got stuck in traffic and it took them forty-five minutes to get to the theater. "We could have walked it in seven minutes," Pamela recalled:

> We came in late … it was so embarrassing. I feel it is terribly discourteous to be late to a performance, and Mr. Wallis was worried too. But Olivier and the others didn't expect us, and they all glared when we came in late to see who the sinners were. I didn't blame them really. But then they saw it was Mr. Wallis and the performance perked up.[6]

The latecomers were forgiven because Wallis had purchased the screen rights to *Becket*, and Olivier (as Thomas Becket) and Quinn (as Henry II) no doubt wanted to reprise their roles in the movie version. Alas, they were replaced by Richard Burton and Peter O'Toole.

Pamela departed New York to Munich, Germany, in June 1961. After being greeted by the film's assistant director with a big bouquet of flowers, the actress and her mother were whisked away to the Five-Star Bayerischer Hof Hotel where they would be staying when not in Berlin. Her luggage and her film wardrobe were temporarily lost, then delivered to the hotel at midnight after she had dined with the Wilders, the Diamonds, and an executive from United Artists' European division.

The next day when Pamela saw Wilder, she got the good news that he had acquiesced and decided to let her play Scarlett with her natural brown hair. This was weighing hard on the actress and now she was able to depart for Berlin for exterior shots in much better spirits.

Pamela's hair color was the least of Wilder's worries. Though Horst Buchholz spoke fluent English, he had a British accent since he learned the language in England before filming *Tiger Bay* with Hayley and John Mills. This annoyed Wilder, who gave the young actor three days to lose it. By the time shooting began in Berlin, Horst had succeeded and his director was pleased. However, Horst would soon draw the ire of Wilder for other reasons.

During filming, to keep *One, Two, Three* as topical as possible (the East-West Berlin situation was escalating), Wilder and co-writer Diamond would listen to Armed Forces Radio every morning and read the international edition of the *New York Times* when they returned to their hotel to keep abreast of the Berlin state of affairs. A brigadier general in charge of the U.S. forces in Berlin was transferred, so his name had to be excised from the script. Nikita Khrushchev announced Russia's Twenty-Year Plan, so a joke about it was hurriedly added. Anti-Communist jokes from behind the Iron Curtain were also added after the writers grilled a Radio Free Europe reporter who visited the set one day.

Berlin was familiar territory for Wilder. Pre-Hitler, he worked as a newspaper reporter and at night danced as a gigolo at a hotel to earn extra money to take a playwriting class. When shooting began in Germany, Wilder was in constant negotiations with the East Berlin authorities to obtain permission to film through the Brandenburg Gate and up to thirty yards onto their side of it. This was the scene where Buchholz's East German beatnik

Publicity photograph of James Cagney and Pamela Tiffin in *One, Two, Three* (United Artists, 1961). Billy Rose Theatre Division, The New York Public Library for the Performing Arts, Astor, Lenox and Tilden Foundations.

rides his beat-up motorcycle from West Berlin back to his home in the East unaware that there is a large yellow balloon attached to his exhaust pipe that, when blown up, said in big black letters, **Russki Go Home!** A camera was mounted onto a truck that followed him. Inclement weather moved in and Wilder was not able to finish shooting the sequence. The East Berliners wanted to read the screenplay before they allowed any more filming and Wilder refused, declaring, "I wouldn't even let President Kennedy read my script!"[7]

That night East Berlin diplomats met Wilder at his hotel and invited him to the East Berlin premiere of his movie *The Apartment*. The director agreed to go if he could have another day filming at the Brandenburg Gate. Permission was granted.

It was reported that the next day when the director spotted clearing skies he yelled, "Okay! Get your steel helmets everybody. We're going back to the Gate."[8] He hopped into his car and led the procession of autos and trucks, with cast and crew aboard, back to the site near the Brandenburg Gate. But when they arrived, the Soviet side was teeming with armed uniformed police officers. Wilder received the bad news that the East Berliners had withdrawn their cooperation after catching the message on the balloon. He was now only allowed to film up to the boundary line. He tried in vain to get them to change their minds, but they refused. Wilder reportedly joked in frustration, "I wonder if they'll let me shoot there if I have the musical score written by Irving East Berlin."[9]

Exasperated, Wilder filmed on the West Berlin side, getting the East Berlin police into the shots. He tried to use this as a negotiating tactic, claiming the world would view East Berlin as a police state. This almost worked and it looked as if he would be allowed to film on their side of the Gate. But when the Communists insisted on reading the script, Wilder balked. The director's balloon joke cost him $200,000, as he had to construct his own full-size replica of the Brandenburg Gate on the back lot at the Bavaria studio in Munich. The crew nicknamed the set "Billy's Folly."

Wilder had the last word about the East Berliners: "Those people over there have no sense of humor. That's their trouble. So now we'll get back at them. Just wait and see what we shoot on the other side."[10] He wasn't bluffing. East Berlin was represented by some of West Berlin's most blighted areas containing gutted buildings and debris (such as the Anhalter railway station), that weren't touched since the Nazi regime collapsed. To make West Berlin far more attractive, Wilder shot only the restored and rebuilt areas and buildings including the actual Coca-Cola bottling plant.

Pamela's first scene was in a car where she had to shout "Otto!" out the window. For the rest of the picture, she usually called him "Liebschen." She recalled, "Mr. Cagney would mock-imitate me because I had to say 'Liebschen' with a Southern accent."[11] This amused the veteran actor greatly.

Pamela wasn't needed much in Berlin and spent most of her time sightseeing and eating in fine restaurants. Cagney took an immediate liking to his young co-star and she found him to be "a delightful person."[12] They would spend a lot of time together off-camera. The actor and his wife would take Pamela and her mother touring Berlin (and later Munich) in his bright green Bentley. They also spent time visiting museums and attending concerts. Tiffin commented, "Mr. Cagney was so kind to me. Mother and Mrs. Cagney struck up a real friendship.... And we had some great times together."[13]

Cagney socialized with Tiffin off-camera but kept refusing Wilder's invitations, to the chagrin of the director. Years later, Wilder told Cameron Crowe, "I would invite him to a restaurant in Munich or Berlin, wherever we were. No, he would rather be with his wife. I would say, 'Your wife comes along too.' But he would say *blah-blah-blah*."[14]

Interiors were shot at Munich's Bavaria Studio. Built for Pamela was a very beautiful flower-filled dressing room with blue carpet; white walls and ceiling; white wood French cabinets with pink inlaid embroidery in the drawers; and a very huge mirror. Wilder also had the crew build a leaning board for her. This was routine in Hollywood where the costumed actors could rest standing up without wrinkling their clothes between takes. "They had never seen one in Germany," said Pamela. "It was custom-made, just my size, but so comfortable that I hardly ever got on it—everyone else was always leaning on it."[15]

It wasn't all fun and games with Cagney, who shared his moviemaking knowledge with the novice actress. The actor revealed in his autobiography that before they did their first scene together, he approached her about talking it through since there was a lot of back-and-forth dialog between the two. "As we worked on the scene I noticed she just couldn't look me in the eye. Self-conscious, ill at ease, I wanted to help a bit."[16] He asked her if she wanted to take some advice from an old man. When Pamela readily said yes, he instructed her to "walk in, plant yourself, look the other fella in the eye, and tell the truth. So may I say, bless her, she did just that, never wavering for a moment."[17]

However, in another scene Cagney caught Tiffin's eyes wandering from his left eye to his right in Ping-Pong fashion. This time he suggested she look in the downstage eye (the one nearest to the camera). Cagney also shared his philosophy on acting with her: "I told her that for me acting begins with an awareness that the *audience* [knows] why I am doing what I am doing. I am acting for them, not myself, and I do it as best I can."[18]

As much as Cagney loved Pamela, he disliked her on-screen romantic interest Horst Buchholz. At first, Horst's clowning around bemused the cast and crew. According to Pamela, Wilder would try to contain his laughter, but would sneak behind screens to let it out, and Diamond could be seen with a grin on his face. Horst also loved teasing Pamela about her character Scarlett being from Atlanta, Georgia. He would steal a line from the movie and groan, "The South—that's Siberia with juleps." Tiffin soon began to feel wary as the young actor was starting to get carried away and angering his director and especially Cagney. The veteran actor hadn't encountered such a maddening scene-stealer since he worked with S.Z. Sakall in *Yankee Doodle Dandy* (1942). Cagney recalled, "Horst Buchholz tried all kinds of scene-stealing didoes, and I had to depend on Billy Wilder to take some steps to correct this kid. If Billy hadn't, I was going to knock Buchholz on his ass, which at several points I would have been very happy to do."[19]

Pamela knew too what Buchholz was doing with his tricks and that Cagney didn't like his style, but she was more bemused by her handsome co-star than angry. She attributed his behavior not to arrogance but to enthusiasm. And she opined that any director would appreciate someone that eager.

The one thing all the actors had trouble with was saying the lines as exactly written. Wilder would not allow any deviations from the script no matter how minor. This was particularly difficult for Cagney since he had to deliver his lines at lightning speed in some scenes and would invariably stumble over the words. He reached his breaking point when he had to bark out orders to people around him to buy a complete wardrobe for the transformation of Otto from beatnik Communist to son of a grand lord. Wilder would not allow any changes to the dialog or paraphrasing, which frustrated the actor. He kept stumbling over a line during one particular long sequence of dialog, "Where's the morning overcoat and striped trousers?" Also, a frustrated Wilder was reported to be walking behind the camera giving Cagney direction to "take it a little slower"; "bear down on those words 'alligator, tassle'"; and "slow down, we need to hear every word."[20] When Cagney finally got through his dialog to Wilder's satisfaction, the take was blown by an extra who entered too late. The director exploded but "a second later he was sweet-tempered as ever."[21] It took over fifty takes for Cagney to get through this scene, exhausting the actor.

Wilder explained his directorial decisions regarding Cagney's line deliveries to Cameron Crowe. "He really had the rhythm, and that was very good," Wilder remarked, adding:

> It was not funny. But just the *speed* was funny. The speed was very good, how Cagney figured it out. The general idea was, let's make the fastest picture in the world.... And yeah, we did not wait, for once, for the big laughs. We went through the big laughs. A lot of lines that needed a springboard, and we just went right through the springboard.[22]

Though a newcomer, Pamela respected that Wilder and Diamond had written the script and you could not change a word despite the pace. Gut instinct led the newcomer to know and understand a written article and preposition had to be that one.

Horst Buchholz, however, was always trying to improve on the script. For instance, he added an "Oh, well" in one scene because he felt that is what someone would say in real life. Wilder took him to task, telling his actor that he worked with Diamond for eight months on the script and if they had thought of one "Oh, well," they would have written it down. Ironically, after casting the young German actor, Wilder boasted that the real Horst Buchholz would shine on the screen since he had previously played a Polish sailor, a Mexican gunslinger, and a Frenchman. Perhaps Buchholz's personality was *too* real for Wilder's taste.

As for Pamela, she described their director as being "a very witty man, a sophisticated man, very quiet, but purposeful."[23] She made sure not to get involved with any disagreements between Wilder and Buchholz and just minded her own business like she was taught by her parents.

Pamela only had one mishap during the shoot. In one scene she had to run across the very slick floor of MacNamara's office. The take was perfect and Wilder yelled, "Cut!" It was a print. Pamela tried to come to a complete stop, but due to how fast she ran, she slipped and fell, landing on her ankle and twisting it. She was in excruciating pain for five days.

On another day, Hedda Hopper came to town to report on the making of one of Wilder's most controversial movies. The columnist was one of the most powerful in Hollywood. If she requested an interview, you agreed—especially if you were a newcomer. Pamela joined Hopper and actress Jessie Royce Landis for lunch in Munich. The sweet-natured girl quickly won over the powerful journalist, who gushed, "Pamela has a special quality of freshness and beauty that has to be seen to be believed—green eyes, brown hair, a piquant, intriguing face, and perfect figure."[24] Hopper would extol the virtues of Pamela in many columns to come.

Very nearsighted, Pamela once wittily quipped, "I don't make contact without my contacts."[25] She owned six sets of contact lenses tinted three different shades to compliment her wardrobe—romantic green, surrealistic blue, and earthy brown. Her contacts caused quite a stir when shooting her next movie *State Fair*. One day a gust of wind blew her right lens out of her eye. Cast and crew were on their hands and knees looking for it because the actress did not bring an extra pair to the location. She even lost one lens during filming *Come Fly with Me*. Her contact lens came up in many of her early interviews and fascinated journalists of the day.

When Pamela wasn't spending her "down time" lunching with gossip columnists or studying Latin, she was designing her own clothes. On *Summer and Smoke* she got into sewing, but took it to another level only a few months later. She designed a suede wardrobe consisting of suits, coats, and dresses, which she had made by a shop in Munich. Regarding her fashion taste, Pamela said, "I like clothes that are classic. I like to be able to wear something long enough to have memories with it."[26] This was not a statement you expect to hear from a Hollywood starlet of the time, but Tiffin was proving she was no typical starlet.

The last *One, Two, Three* scenes to shoot were on the recently constructed studio set of Templehof Airport. Two days before shooting, an inebriated Buchholz was injured when he totaled his new white Cadillac outside of Munich and couldn't finish the picture. The set had to be recreated in an airplane hangar in Hollywood. A few weeks later, after he had recuperated, Horst joined the cast in California to complete the movie. Finally *One, Two, Three* wrapped and went into post-production. Pamela did not have time to catch her breath as she immediately reported to the set of her third motion picture, *State Fair* for 20th Century–Fox.

Just before *Summer and Smoke* and *One, Two, Three* were released, *Esquire* magazine did a major feature on Pamela, touting her as one of the finds of the year. They were able to get producer Hal Wallis and director Wilder to pose with her in photographs shot by Bert Stern. The Wallis photo was classy with the duo standing next to each other laughing for the camera, but the one with Wilder had a very creepy Lolita-ish feel to it with a messy-haired Pamela with a sexy glint in her eye sitting on the director's lap.

Wilder was quoted in the article praising Tiffin: "She's going to become a very big star," he exclaimed:

> We brought her to Germany, in some ways a mistake because Pamela wasn't used to the ways of making movies. She expected us to be as fast as those guys she works with when making fashion layouts in New York, and she hadn't much patience which, believe me, you need in this business. So whenever she wasn't working she was lobbying to go somewhere, like Zurich or Rome, and instead of being her director I suddenly became her guide, philosopher, and booking agent. But every now and then we did manage to sneak her into the picture and I am happy to say that her performance was unimprovable. She's another Audrey Hepburn … she comes off on the screen even better than she looks and in this case that is saying a lot.[27]

Pamela had the highest respect for Wilder. She knew that she was extremely lucky to have had the chance to work with the Academy Award winner so early in her career and that he got a performance of a lifetime out of her. The grateful actress' esteem for the director never waned. A few years after completing *One, Two, Three* she was quoted as saying, "It's a sign of distinction—it means something very important for an actor or an actress to be able to say 'I have worked for Wilder.'"[28] The downside for Pamela is that once you are directed by one of the best in Hollywood, you can get spoiled and it is hard not to compare and get frustrated when working with someone pedestrian. She would never again work with a director of his caliber.

Wilder and Cagney's relationship was another story. Years later Wilder was still praising Cagney ("a wonderful actor"[29]), but admitted there was no friendship. "Not anything mean was said, not anything demeaning, not any question with the script," Wilder commented to Cameron Crowe. "But he was a very peculiar, peculiar man. We said goodbye on very good terms. But it was a big distance of thinking between us. We were not just especially designed for each other."[30]

One, Two, Three was released on December 15, 1961, with movie poster art designed by Saul Bass featuring one of his most creative drawings: a black-gloved girl holding three balloons over her breasts. Pamela as impetuous Scarlett Hazeltine makes an auspicious entrance as she exits her Pan Am flight clad in a mink coat and squealing in a flirty manner with the male crew members fawning over her. The 17-year-old has been sent by her father Wendell Hazeltine (Howard St. John), the head of Coca-Cola in the U.S., on a European tour to keep her away from her latest fiancé Choo Choo Babcock, whom she met while stuffed in a campus phone booth trying to set a world record. Now in West Berlin, she is to stay with the reluctant C.R. "Mac" MacNamara (James Cagney) who is in negotiations with three Russian representatives to get the soft drink distributed throughout the Soviet Union. If the deal goes through, Mac thinks this will help get him a promotion to head of European Operations based out of London. This is to the chagrin of his homesick wife Phyllis (Arlene Francis), two smartaleck children, and a seductive blonde secretary named Ingeborg (Lilo Pulver) who gives him "German lessons" on the weekends and doesn't want to lose her fringe benefits.

Stepping onto the tarmac where she is greeted by the MacNamaras, Scarlett asks Mac for his hat and throws pieces of paper with their names into it. Phyllis then picks Lucky Pierre the navigator as the winner of a date with Scarlett, which is quickly shot down by Mac. After accusing him of being a company man and an old poop, she bemoans, "Europe! What a drag! I've done the Coliseum bit *and* the Mona Lisa bit, but they never take me to those marvy places, like the Lido and the Crazy Horse and La Sexy." Mac and Phyllis know it is going to be a long slog with Scarlett, who describes all the women in her family as hot-blooded.

When Scarlett comes down with German measles, her two-week stay turns into two months. Her parents fly in to bring their daughter back with them. Mac is relieved until he finds out from Phyllis that the girl is missing, prompting him to declare, "I'd rather be in Hell with my back broken." He soon learns that for the last month his chauffeur has been driving the girl to the Brandenburg Gate every night after eleven and picking her up early the following morning—but on this day she never returned. A panicked Mac is sounding the alarm to find her when Scarlett comes sauntering in as if nothing has happened. She cops to sneaking out, but explains that she has exciting news: She met a boy in East Berlin named Otto and that they got married six weeks ago. When Mac exclaims, "You married a Communist," Scarlett responds, "He's not a Communist. He's a Republican—comes from the Republic of East Germany." An exasperated Mac retorts, "Why you dumb, stupid little pop. Do you realize what you've done? You've ruined me … all on account of you and your hot blood."

Scarlett yells down to Otto (Horst Buchholz) to come upstairs. His looks alone antagonize Mac, as he enters wearing sandals, ill-fitting pants, and a bulky sweater with his longish jet black hair under a cap. It gets worse when he opens his mouth, insulting the

U.S. and mocking capitalism. The couple then announces that the next day they will be moving to Moscow so Otto can attend school. When Mac asks what he is supposed to tell Scarlett's parents, she responds defiantly, "You just tell Daddy that I am on my way to the U.S.S.R. That's short for Russia."

While on the phone filling in Phyllis about Scarlett's shenanigans, Mac hatches a plan. He wishes the couple well, giving them his cuckoo clock as a wedding present. As Scarlett returns home to fetch her things, an oblivious Otto heads back to East Berlin on his motorcycle with a balloon saying, **Russki Go Home!** attached to his exhaust pipe by Mac's right hand man Schlemmer (Hanns Lothar). This attracts the attention of the East German police who pull him over. When the clock goes off and Uncle Sam pops out, they arrest the innocent boy for spreading propaganda. Trying to break him, his captors torture him by repeatedly playing the American pop song, "Itsy Bitsy Teenie Weenie Yellow Polka Dot Bikini."

After giving her second mink coat to the MacNamaras' maid, dim-witted Scarlett shares her happiness with Phyllis and coos excitedly, "Do you realize Otto spelled backwards is Otto?!" She then asks Mac's wife if she ever made love to a revolutionary, she confides that Otto is "the wildest—no contest" and she should know after having been engaged four times. A jubilant Mac comes home with that news that Otto has been arrested and an unmarried Scarlett will be returning to Atlanta the next day. The poor girl faints in what they think is in despair but it turns out she "is going to have puppies," as the MacNamaras' daughter Cindy translates to her parents the diagnosis of the German doctor.

Knowing he cannot give a pregnant unwed Scarlett back to her parents, Mac has an idea to free Otto from prison and to get him back to West Berlin. He enlists the aid of Schlemmer, Ingeborg, and his chauffeur to pull it off as they all head to East Berlin to negotiate with the three Russians. The dinner scene at their hotel is one of the film's many high points, brilliantly using composer Aram Khachaturian's "Sabre Dance" to enliven the pacing as Mac sets his plan in motion. The Russians' desperate counter-offers to make a deal without having to get Otto out of jail come faster and faster as the music's tempo and Ingeborg's dance gyrations on a tabletop quicken. Finally a swap of Otto for the curvy secretary is arranged with the entranced trio, but Mac dupes them: Schlemmer dons Ingeborg's polka-dotted dress when the switch is made on the street.

With Otto back in his hands, Mac decides the only course of action is to turn him into the perfect capitalist son-in-law. Of course Otto protests mightily, but reluctantly goes along with prodding from Scarlett. Though he learns that she will receive 20,000 shares of Coca-Cola stock on her eighteenth birthday, he vows that he won't be "a gigolo" living off his wife. Proud Otto tries to fight everything from wearing underwear and striped pants, to getting his hair cut and nails manicured, to pretending to be the adopted son of a down-on-his-luck baron now working in a hotel men's room. After refusing to raise his son as a capitalist, Scarlett responds, "When he is eighteen he can decide for himself if he wants to be a capitalist or a rich Communist." Teaching Otto table manners proves most difficult as he uses his hands to eat his chicken and swigs red wine out of the bottle. Mac grabs it out of his hands as an exasperated Scarlett proclaims, "He's right, darling. Always white wine with chicken!" After the baron "officially" adopts Otto for a bribe of 4,000 marks, Mac tells Otto and Scarlett they are now the Count and Countess von Droste Schattenburg. Scarlett squeals in delight, "Countess! That means everybody has to curtsy to me … except maybe Grace Kelly."

Mac, Scarlett, Otto, Schlemmer, a tailor, and more then crowd into Mac's limo as they race through the streets of West Berlin to the airport to meet the Hazeltines with the "Sabre Dance" once again used as musical accompaniment. As the tailor stitches up a tear in Otto's striped pants, Scarlett tries different hats on Otto, deciding on a black bowler. They get to the airplane just as her parents debark. A fumbling but charming Otto makes such an

A pregnant Scarlett (Pamela Tiffin) comforts her husband Otto (Horst Buchholz), who has just learned he cannot return to East Germany, in a scene from *One, Two, Three* (United Artists, 1961).

impression playing capitalist that his father-in-law gives him Mac's desired job as head of the London Office. Tossing his umbrella to the boy, Mac wishes him luck as Scarlett runs over to kiss him and says, "I just adore you." Mac does get a promotion: He is "kicked upstairs" as vice-president of procurement in the Atlanta office. He intercepts Phyllis and the kids who were leaving him. After a vote of two to one, they decide to take Mac back.

For the most part, *One, Two, Three* was a critical darling. The comedy was hailed as the "Year's Best" in *The Chicago Defender. Variety* exclaimed, "Billy Wilder's *One, Two, Three* is a pause that refreshes; a fast-paced, high-pitched, hard-hitting, lighthearted farce crammed with topical gags and spiced with satirical overtones. Story is so furiously quick-witted that some of its wit gets snarled and smothered in overlap. But total experience packs a considerable wallop." Ben Kubasik of *Newsday* called the movie "another comedy bulls-eye" from Wilder and Diamond, predicting that moviegoers will "witness a series of furiously paced situations calculated to explode at any second—into laughter." Mae Tinee of the *Chicago Daily Tribune* raved that *One, Two, Three* was "far-fetched, frantic and very funny." She went on to compliment the screenwriters for their equal opportunity in drubbing "Russian arrogance, German heel-kicking and American enterprise."

Hedda Hopper, with her own crass style of writing, called the movie "a glorious spoof of the commies. It's a laugh riot." She predicted come Oscar time, *One, Two, Three* would be a serious contender. Philip K. Scheuer of the *Los Angeles Times* thought otherwise, and though he called the Coca-Cola tied-in film a "wacky farce" he added, "You have to be pretty thirsty for laughs to find it as funny as the preview audience seemed to think it was; I had a bellyful, personally, long before it was over." He went on to say the cast performs "nimbly if broadly."

One of the most introspective reviews came from Bosley Crowther of the *New York Times*, whose balanced piece commended *One, Two, Three* for being a very funny satire on the Berlin crisis peppered with "sharp political jokes." But he also criticized the screenwriters for trivializing the matter, which was much more serious than the mere wedding of a Communist boy to an American girl.

Cagney won almost universal raves for his rapid-fire, comedic performance. Due to the expert direction by Wilder and helped by Cagney himself, Pamela won kudos as well. *Variety* remarked, "Pamela Tiffin scores with a convincing display of mental density." Crowther of the *Times* found her to be "very good"; Paul V. Beckley of the *New York Herald Tribune* called her "a bright young actress"; Hedda Hopper found her "delightful to behold"; and *Los Angeles Times*' "Around Town" columnist Joan Winchell described Pamela as "frantically funny."

Pamela's winning performance was even acknowledged by film great Norma Shearer. After seeing *One, Two, Three*, she remarked that Pamela "is one of Hollywood's most exciting newcomers. She has a wonderful, refreshing beauty with a sense of humor that radiates thru her eyes."[31]

Pamela truly excelled in the movie. The scenes where Scarlett announces her marriage plans and introduces Otto to MacNamara are some of Pamela's best ever on film. She plays dumb so sincerely that you cannot help but laugh. Her lilting Southern drawl coupled with her slow delivery (compared to Cagney's fast sharp-tongued comebacks) make her performance even more humorous, as dim-witted Scarlett seems to be in a world of her own, oblivious to everything around her. She makes a wonderful foil to Cagney's frustrated businessman, partly due to her natural talent and partly because she was guided by two greats, Wilder and Cagney. She rightly listened and learned from both of them. She not only followed Wilder's acting suggestions, but kept to his script word for word (unlike Buchholz). And she was extremely lucky to have an old pro like Cagney. Because she followed all his suggestions, Cagney praised her to the hilt. No doubt being a college student outside of the world of show business helped Tiffin absorb all the new screen tricks and acting methods Cagney shared. She used them effectively, delivering an energetic, funny performance and makes what could have been a strictly shrill, selfish character charming and fun to watch— so much so that when Scarlett is off-screen, the viewer begins to miss her. Unfortunately in the movies to follow, Tiffin never worked again with such helpful, distinguished talents as Wilder and Cagney.

Pamela left such an indelible impression on Cagney that twelve years later he was still praising her to the press. Interviewed in 1973, Cagney extolled the talent of the current crop of actors and thought them to be "great kids,"[32] singling out Tiffin and how they worked so well together in *One, Two, Three*.

Though *One, Two, Three* was a hit with the critics for the most part, it disappointed at the box office. It ranked #38 for the Top 50 Rentals of 1962, grossing an estimated $2.4 million against a budget of $3 million. It earned close to the same as the Troy Donahue-Connie Stevens romantic sudser *Susan Slade*; the Elvis Presley musical drama *Kid Galahad*; and, ironically, *A Pocketful of Miracles*. The infamous Berlin Wall was being constructed by the time of the film's release. Perhaps that undermined the satire's chances with audiences who felt it was too serious a situation to satirize and laugh at at a time when the public was gripped by war panic. *The New Yorker* was not surprised by its less-than-stellar grosses and commented that the filmmakers "pitched their circus tent on grounds that threaten to become a cemetery." Screenwriter Abby Mann, who wrote the same year's *Judgment at Nuremberg*, found *One, Two, Three* so tasteless that he apologized for it at the Moscow Film Festival. Co-screenwriter Diamond conceded, "At the time we started writing the script, people were making jokes about Khrushchev pounding his shoe at the United Nations, and Castro plucking chickens in his hotel room. As the political climate changed, however, certain subjects that the public had once laughed at suddenly ceased to be funny."[33]

Pamela was perplexed on why it wasn't a bigger hit. She viewed it many times and said, "I keep finding new things to laugh at."[34]

After the release of *Summer and Smoke* and *One, Two, Three*, Pamela Tiffin began being hailed as one of the most promising newcomers of 1961. *Films and Filming* chose her as 1962's first "Person of Promise." *Screen World* and *The Saturday Evening Post* both proclaimed that she was destined for superstardom. Hedda Hopper chose her as one of fourteen newcomers for her column "I Pick These to Star in 1962" and she was hailed, along with Jane Fonda and Ann-Margret, as one of the top three new actresses. Hopper declared, "She has that legendary look of roses and moonlight seldom seen today."[35]

It was also noted by some of these publications that Pamela was more than just a pretty face and was very bright, unlike her ditzy screen characters. After she posed for *The Saturday Evening Post*, Gjon Mili, a longtime freelance photographer for *Life* magazine, called her "the most *aware* child I know."[36] Others extolled her for studying Latin and for reading books by Plato, Chaucer, Keats, Hemingway, or James Joyce between takes on movie sets. One publicist didn't believe her and investigated because he thought it was a publicity ruse.

But she proved she had actually read every title mentioned. Another publicist was shocked when, asking Pamela what she did on a free day from shooting, she replied that she browsed around a Pickwick Bookshop and purchased an old Latin textbook to keep her busy on the set between takes. While girls her age were listening to Elvis Presley and Fabian, Pamela preferred classical music and a bit of jazz.

When award season began in early 1962, Pamela's name came up frequently. *Photoplay* was one of the most-read movie magazines of the time and every year it bestowed the Photoplay Gold Medal Awards for Most Popular Film; Most Popular Male Star; Most Popular Female Star; and Most Popular Male and Female Newcomers, as voted by its mostly female readership. Mail-in ballots were included in copies of the magazine and readers would select their choices from a list of nominees assembled by the editors. Pamela was a strong contender for Most Popular Female Newcomer for 1961, but lost out in a tie to Paula Prentiss in *Where the Boys Are* and Deborah Walley in *Gidget Goes Hawaiian*. That year's Most Popular Film was *Splendor in the Grass* and the Most Popular Male and Female Stars were Troy Donahue and Connie Stevens.

Tiffin received two Golden Globe nominations—one for Best Supporting Actress for her performance in *One, Two, Three* and the other for Most Promising Newcomer—Female. She lost both. Rita Moreno took the Supporting Award for her fiery turn as Shark Girl Anita in *West Side Story*. The other nominees were Fay Bainter as the rich dowager who spreads the lies about two teachers being lesbians in *The Children's Hour*; Judy Garland as a German forced to recall her "friendship" with a Jewish man on the witness stand in *Judgment at Nuremberg*; and Lotte Lenya as a courtesan and provider of male escorts in *The Roman Spring of Mrs. Stone*. All would go on to receive Academy Award nominations. The fifth slot was filled by her *Summer and Smoke* co-star Una Merkel.

A possible reason why Pamela missed out on an Oscar nomination was an overcrowded field. The Mirisch Brothers had four movies that were strong contenders for Oscar consideration: *West Side Story*; *One, Two, Three*; *The Children's Hour*; and *Town Without Pity*. United Artists, the distributor of the Mirisches' films, also had a strong contender with *Judgment at Nuremberg*. It was decided to promote *One, Two, Three* for Best Picture; Best Actor; Best Director, and Best Screenplay. United Artists decided to push Rita Moreno, Fay Bainter, and Judy Garland for Best Supporting Actress and all three were nominated. The lack of UA support killed Pamela's Oscar chances; if she *got* the push, she may have gotten the nomination. Una Merkel slipped in, no doubt buoyed by sentiment for she was a beloved figure in Hollywood since the early thirties.

As for the Golden Globe for Most Promising Newcomer, Ann-Margret, Jane Fonda, and Christine Kaufmann won out over Tiffin and Cordula Trantow. What's a Cordula Trantow? This category was really odd. First, Jane Fonda did not appear in a movie in 1961. Her debut was the prior year in *Tall Story*. Her second movie *Walk on the Wild Side* was not released until February 1962. Pamela Tiffin was the only nominee to be singled out in another acting category, which right there should have propelled her to the top of the list. If you just compare Tiffin in *Summer and Smoke* and *One, Two, Three* with Ann-Margret in *A Pocketful of Miracles*, the brunette makes more of an impression. Tiffin plays sweetly naïve in *Summer and Smoke*, then is a comedic standout in *One, Two, Three*. That performance is even more memorable than Jane Fonda's in *Tall Story*. As for Christine Kaufmann in *Town Without Pity*, the Hollywood Foreign Press always liked to honor a foreign actress deserving (Anita Ekberg in 1956; Hayley Mills and Nancy Kwan in 1960) or not (Bella Darvi in 1954; Linda Cristal in 1958; Janet Munro in 1959). Kaufmann belongs to the latter category of winners. To show how quirky the Foreign Press was that year, George Chakiris was named Best Supporting Actor for his role as Puerto Rican gang leader Bernardo in *West Side Story*, but he lost out in the Most Promising Newcomer—Male category to co-star Richard Beymer, Warren Beatty in *Splendor in the Grass* and Bobby Darin in *Come September*.

In fairness, you could say the Foreign Press got it right as undoubtedly Ann-Margret and Jane Fonda became superstars and Pamela Tiffin did not. However, based on the merits of their 1961 performances, Tiffin deserved the win. The Golden Globe would not be the only prize Pamela lost to Ann-Margret. The popular redhead won the Laurel Award for Top Female New Personality. This award was voted on by film buyers across the U.S. and Canada. There was no actual ceremony, but winners and also-rans were published in the *Motion Picture Exhibitor*. Pamela placed third in the poll behind Connie Stevens and ahead of Diane McBain, Carol Lawrence, Deborah Walley, Vicki Trickett, Stella Stevens, Sharon Hugueny, and Genevieve Page.

Hedda Hopper proved to be no fortune teller as *One, Two, Three* was snubbed by the Academy Awards in all the major categories and received only a single nomination for Daniel L. Fapp's black and white cinematography. He lost to Eugene Schufftan for *The Hustler*.

One, Two, Three is perhaps one of the most underrated comedies of the sixties. Coming on the heels of Wilder's Academy Award–winning *The Apartment*, the movie couldn't rise from its shadow. The timing of its release just as the Berlin Wall was being constructed also hurt it. However, years away from that situation, it has rightly received the recognition it deserves, especially for Cagney who delivers one of the funniest and most fast-paced performances of all time. His rapid-fire delivery astounds.

Wilder always liked *One, Two, Three* and was greatly satisfied that it was finally fully appreciated even in Germany: Re-released there after the Berlin Wall came down, it was a sensation.

When *One, Two, Three* was shown at New York City's revival house the Film Forum in 2006, *The Village Voice* praised the comedy, calling it "a Cold War poltergeist, rattling chains in the vanished spook house that was West Berlin." It went on to say, "At once hysterical and ironic, sophisticated and vulgar…. *One, Two, Three* celebrates as it satirizes American cultural imperialism." It is Pamela Tiffin's best movie, containing her most outstanding performance.

4

It's a Grand Night for Singing … Well, Maybe Not

State Fair

Pamela began her third movie before her first two were even released. *State Fair* was a 1962 remake of the 1945 Rodgers and Hammerstein musical starring Dick Haymes, Jeanne Crain and Dana Andrews, which itself was a remake of the 1933 movie starring Will Rogers, Janet Gaynor and Lew Ayres. Changes were made to give it an updated, "hip" 1962 feel, beginning with the shift in setting from Iowa to the more modern Texas State Fair, and the addition of new songs by Richard Rodgers. Despite the presence of Pat Boone, Bobby Darin, Tiffin, and Ann-Margret, the new film is mostly remembered for the infamous scene where a farmer sings to his pig.

The musical was offered to a number of directors by producer Charles Brackett, but all passed. Walter Lang, who directed the 1945 version and other hit musicals (most notably *The King and I*), accepted, but at the last minute withdrew. With the shooting start date fast approaching, Brackett was now desperate for a director. Academy Award–winning actor José Ferrer had just directed the sequel, *Return to Peyton Place*—another film a lot of established directors wouldn't touch—and agreed to tackle this project as well. However, Ferrer did not consider this movie a remake: "This is entirely a new treatment of a classic. So I don't believe there is any chance of a comparison with a memory or nostalgia."[1] The critics would disagree once the movie was released.

Brackett was excited to entice former Fox star Alice Faye out of her sixteen-year retirement to play Tiffin's mother opposite the wonderful comic actor Tom Ewell as her husband.

A number of actresses wanted to play the role of Margy made famous by Jeanne Crain. Ann-Margret was initially cast as Margy, but Brackett could not make up his mind and had her test in various hair colors. Eventually, he thought she came across too sexy and seductive and would make a better Emily, the role played by Vivian Blaine in 1945. Barbara Eden came very close to securing the role of Margy and would have brought a whole new perspective to the part. Being a few years older than Tiffin, her screen test (opposite singer Andy Williams, auditioning for the role won by Bobby Darin) portrayed a saucier, sexier Margy. Fox and Brackett, however, decided Margy should be a more naïve teenager and chose Pamela instead.

Pamela was still filming *One, Two, Three* in Germany when she learned that she would be playing Margy in *State Fair* without even an audition. She knew that Wilder and Brackett were friends and speculated, "Mr. Wilder probably told him about me. We do know that Mr. Jose Ferrer went to see some test of me—we are not sure whether it was *Summer and Smoke* or the screen interview I did for Mr. Wallis. Halfway through he said, 'That's the girl. That's Margy.' That's what we were told."[2]

Pat Boone headlined the cast as the race car–driving farm boy who falls for a pretty entertainer. During the mid– to late fifties, Boone was the All-American wholesome crooner in contrast to the rock 'n' rollin', hip-shaking Elvis Presley. Hence, Boone's films such as *Bernardine, April Love, Mardi Gras*, and *Journey to the Center of the Earth* were box office hits and he had a number of #1 records including "Ain't That a Shame" in 1955 and "Love Letters in the Sand" in 1957. Boone's popularity began to wane a bit in the early sixties, especially after the King returned from the army and they toned down his rebel persona for the silver screen, making him more acceptable to parents and their kids. While Elvis' movies were raking in the dough, Boone flopped with *All Hands on Deck*. Fox was hoping *State Fair* would return Boone to box office glory.

Bronx-born singer Bobby Darin positioned himself as another Frank Sinatra. For awhile, the Grammy winner ruled the record charts with a string of hit records beginning in 1958 with "Splish Splash" and most notably "Mack the Knife" in 1959. He made his film debut in the Rock Hudson comedy *Come September* (1961) for which he won a Golden Globe for Most Promising Newcomer—Male and found love with his co-star Sandra Dee. He went dramatic to good reviews in his second film *Too Late Blues* (1962) playing a jazz musician caught between his band members and a beautiful would-be singer. As with Pamela, *State Fair* was his third movie.

Despite landing this musical film without a reading or an audition, Pamela was not very enthused about making it. She hadn't seen the original and thought it was pointless to do another *State Fair*. Not only didn't the part of Margy thrill Pamela, but she was not very excited that Darin was going to be her leading man. Fox was insistent, so she had no choice in the matter.

The one thing Tiffin was looking forward to was the chance to vocalize on screen, as she demonstrated her singing ability first over the long-distance phone from Munich. She then was requested to make a tape of her singing "It Might As Well Be Spring." However, this was easier said than done. "We couldn't find the lyrics, the music, or the musicians who knew it or had a free day to do it in," recalled Pamela. "We finally made it in the theater where we saw the rushes. They moved the studio piano in and built a whole stage. We had a German musician, a concert pianist who didn't speak English, transcribe the record, which we had bought at a PX, to sheet music for himself. He transcribed note by note by listening to the record over and over again."[3]

All this trouble was for naught, as the mailed tape arrived in Hollywood ten days later, which was the same day Pamela got there in person. Associate music supervisor Ken Darby liked Pamela's voice. That day she was also rushed for fittings with costume designer Marjorie Best. Edith Head at Paramount had sent her colleague Tiffin's measurements, so alterations only had to be done on a few of the dresses. While she was in wardrobe, Pamela met her producer and director. She was happy to hear from him that he had a new vision for the role of Margy. Pamela said he wanted to make her "a contemporary believable Margy, instead of a marshmallow farmer's daughter…. By letting Margy be a combination of girl, woman and female, a new Margy may evolve, who knows."[4] Ferrer's new interpretation for the character and the fact she would be singing, helped increase Tiffin's enthusiasm for the movie.

With a multi-million budget, *State Fair* was shot on location at the Dallas State Fair grounds during its off-season except for the racing scenes which were filmed at the Oklahoma State Fair Raceway. Pamela's first day of shooting was at the Swine Pavilion. It was an overnight shoot with her on-screen family of Boone, Ewell, and Faye and winds gusting to fifty miles an hour outside due to the passing Hurricane Carla. Shooting began at 7:30 p.m. and lasted to 5:30 a.m. "I'd come from the racy, political *One, Two, Three* and there I was sitting in the drafty cold with the hogs," said Pamela proving that Hollywood was not all glamour and glitz. "I hadn't brought a warm enough coat. I was cold, sleepy, bewildered, and the hogs did not enchant me, not even Blue Boy."[5] The shoot was not starting off well for the actress and she longed to be back in Munich with Billy Wilder shooting *One, Two, Three*.

Boone had attended college near the Dallas State Fair, so for him the experience was like old home week, but this time surrounded by legions of fans. The production needed about 2,000 extras. On some days they had 15,000 to 20,000 folks milling around the State Fair grounds. It was a madhouse filming as a lot of these were bobbysoxers who flocked to the location to see Boone and Darin. The two stars had to be escorted back and forth to the shooting locations. Police officers and phone operators were recruited to keep fans from disturbing the actors as they tried to get much-needed sleep at their hotel. Darin also had a few minor troubles to handle. His agent valiantly tried to reach him to renew expiring insurance policies and he had to take care of his visiting pregnant wife, Sandra Dee, who became very upset when the duo were mobbed by fans while shopping at Neiman-Marcus.

Though this was Pamela's third movie, her previous films had not been released when she filmed *State Fair*. It is understandable then that neither she nor Ann-Margret, who was making her second movie, were mobbed by the crowds. However, the newcomer turned heads wherever she went and the eyes of Texas were upon her. People stopped in their tracks to see the pretty brunette and could be heard asking, "Who is she?"

The mobs of fans did come in handy when director Ferrer needed extras to fill the seats at a band shell for a scene. A newspaper item was placed promising that Boone would sing for them after the takes were completed. An estimated 3,000 people showed up and Boone led the crowd in singing "The Eyes of Texas."

Richard Rodgers contributed five new songs to this remake: "This Isn't Heaven"; "Willing and Eager"; "Never Say No"; "More Than Just a Friend"; and "It's the Little Things in Texas." They joined favorites from the original such as "It Might As Well Be Spring" and "It's a Grand Night for Singing." All the leads did their own singing except for a disappointed Pamela, who said, "When I arrived on the set, I was told that because of the time that would be required to re-record my voice until it was perfect, a professional singer would have to do it. I was a little upset."[6] Vocalist Anita Gordon was chosen to dub Pamela on the Academy Award–winning "It Might As Well Be Spring" and other songs.

Despite this disappointment, Pamela prepared for shooting the scene at the Wilkens Farm forty miles from Dallas. "I'm eager to do that scene," she exclaimed the week before shooting:

> I've never done anything like that before. I've been practicing synchronizing with the record. I have my own portable record player with me, which runs on batteries. I always take my record player and a few of my records with me. At the studio, Mr. [Ken] Darby was thrilled the second

Promotional poster art for *State Fair* (20th Century–Fox, 1962).

time I did it. He thought I lip-synched very well. But doing it with lights and people is another thing, of course.[7]

That scene went off beautifully; however, some others were less successful. Charles Brackett in Hollywood would send his director notes after viewing the rushes. He was not initially pleased with the scene where Margy first meets Jerry. He wrote, "Pamela is dangerously close to being too naïve. Watch this. Give her a little spiz."[8]

On the DVD audio commentary track for *State Fair*, Boone described Pamela as being "very sweet and very real. A good actress ... perfect to play the naïve, innocent farm girl." She returned the compliment, finding him very likable and a comfortable fit for his role.

Darin, on the other hand, was the kind of actor Pamela felt very uneasy around. After the movie was completed, she remarked that *State Fair* "was a bit of a letdown after *One, Two, Three*. I mean, after you've worked opposite Laurence Harvey and Horst Buchholz, it's not exactly a thrill to get Bobby Darin. And, wouldn't you know, all the longest love scenes were in *State Fair*."[9]

Since Pamela acted the professional while shooting, Darin never knew of her true feelings. If he did, he may not have come to her rescue. The actress revealed that as a child she only liked going on the merry-go-round and avoided all the other rides at amusement parks. The pair had to do a scene on a Tilt-A-Whirl. Her Margy gets into one of the seats followed by Darin's character in a disguise; he is supposed to scare her until she sees it is him and not a stranger. The ride begins and the look of fright on Pamela's face was real. "I began to slip off the seat and screamed," she recalled. "I wasn't acting. I was terrified. Bobby thought I was just being animated for the scene. He said, 'That's all right.' And I said, 'No, I'm really falling.' The gravitational force kept me from sitting and I fell to the bottom below the seat."[10]

Ferrer finally yelled *cut* and they had to reshoot the scene. Pamela once again began to slip off, but this time Darin had his arm around her shoulders. He grabbed her so tightly, though, she wound up black and blue. Then Ferrer gave her the bad news that she had to do a scene on a roller coaster next. It would be her first time on one. Needless to say, Pamela did not enjoy shooting these scenes and Darin's association with them may have contributed to her discomfort working with him. Years later, Pamela was contrite about dissing Darin: "He was a wonderful singer and actor. But at the time I thought he was just a tough, cocky guy from New York.... I decided I just didn't like Bobby Darin. *Who in the world was I not to like him*? He was friendly and I wasn't as friendly as I should have been."[11]

Pamela got along better with Tom Ewell, whom she described at the time as being "so nice. He's funny and easy to get along with."[12] Another older gentleman Pamela may have liked a little too much was her director, as reported by the gossip mongers during filming. Per Pamela, the Fox publicists planted these stories to drum up press for *State Fair*. Ferrer fueled the flames with his over-the-top compliments when speaking about her. He raved about Tiffin's beauty and talent. He thought her performance in *State Fair* sheer perfection and compared her talent to Greta Garbo's. Pamela is beautiful here and projects a sweet essence, but calling her the next Garbo was a big stretch. Obviously, some misconstrued his over-praising of her acting ability for something more.

At the time, Pamela had nothing but admiration for Ferrer. She admitted that he was one of her favorite actors after seeing him six times on the big screen in his Oscar-winning title role in *Cyrano de Bergerac* and as Toulouse-Lautrec in *Moulin Rouge*. The pair talked on the phone a lot after filming wrapped, mostly about the picture. Pamela described her director as "so nice. He's very gracious ... considerate ... [and] a very versatile artist."[13] She especially admired his determination to do something different with his *State Fair* and not make a carbon copy of the original musical.

With the gossip getting out of hand hinting at a romance between the two, Pamela set the record straight in the press and stated, "I'd like to add that there was nothing to any of those rumors linking Jose Ferrer and me. Mr. Ferrer was a perfect gentleman and we were never together except under camera lights."[14]

State Fair's most infamous scene had poor Tom Ewell singing to his hog Blue Boy. Boone also admitted on the DVD commentary track that the cast at the time knew how ridiculous this was. He revealed that he and Ann-Margret stood around laughing at the absurdity and feeling sympathy for poor Ewell. Blue Boy, however, was treated like a star. He was given a daily bubble bath and rubbed down with perfume to make him smell especially nice for the cast and crew, especially since the filming of his scenes was done in the middle of a heat wave.

The pig even had the distinction of being in Alice Faye's first scene shot since her retirement sixteen years prior. It is when she walked down the aisle of the swine pavilion

Publicity photograph of Pamela Tiffin in *State Fair* (20th Century–Fox, 1962).

looking for her husband. Not seeing him, she looks at Blue Boy and asks, "Where's your father?" Faye admitted that she was nervous, but got through the take like the pro she was. She even quipped, "Making my re-debut with 80 other hams!"[15]

Unbeknownst to Pamela while she was shooting the movie on location, David I. Zeitlin, the motion picture correspondent for *Life* magazine, was touting the actress for a feature spread in the magazine. In a memo dated September 28, 1961, he mentioned the good word-of-mouth she has been receiving for the yet-to-be-released *Summer and Smoke* and that "I have heard that the girl, who is only 18, already has been signed to play along with Olivier in *Camelot*. If this be true, Pam is the female counterpart of Warren Beatty in these parts."[16] He ended the letter with a big push for a story: "I ask if you don't think we should be trying a full-fledged intimate look and take-out on this slim, lovely, but apparently very, very talented girl...."[17]

According to a response memo dated October 2, 1961, to Zeitlin from an editor at *Life*, "Tiffin will be lost to Page in the *Summer and Smoke* story"[18] and that *One, Two, Three* was covered in a piece the magazine was publishing about Horst Buchholz. They were willing to do a story on Tiffin "around the time she starts work with Olivier in *Camelot*."[19] That never came to be and neither did a piece on her in *Life* magazine.

During and after filming wrapped, Pamela had to endure the 20th Century–Fox publicity machine. Posing for photographs and doing promotion for motion pictures is part of the job for actors, but Pamela found the staff at Fox particularly distasteful. "They were so cynical," she remarked:

> When I heard them discuss Donald O'Connor, Gene Kelly, and Marilyn Monroe in pejorative terms, I felt like I was on enemy territory and I was next. Instinctively, I thought, "I don't want to get too involved here because they're just going to throw me out too." That bothered me that they were so disloyal. They were denigrating actors who I admired since I was a child. Who were these people? You became cagey and mistrustful of them.[20]

20th Century–Fox was so happy with the performances of Pamela and Ann-Margret that it was announced that the actresses would be reunited in *Love in a Cool Climate* by Frederick Kohner, who was most noted for writing *Gidget* and its sequels. They weren't, but they would be in another Fox feature.

State Fair was released in March 1962. Pamela, as daughter Margy, is conspicuously absent in the rousing opening number. Brother Wayne (Pat Boone) roars through the dirt country roads in his red sports car with his girlfriend Betty Jean (Linda Heintich) sitting at his side. Betty Jean refuses to attend the Dallas State Fair because she doesn't want to watch her beau race, fearful that he will be killed. This doesn't deter Wayne in the least and he bids her goodbye. As he drives home, the opening credits begin with a chorus singing the title song "Our State Fair" before segueing to Wayne singing while driving; his father Abel (Tom Ewell) singing while tending his hog; and his mother Melissa (Alice Faye) singing while baking pies.

Melissa is nervous about entering her mincemeat pie into the competition, while Abel is confident his 750-pound hog Blue Boy will be named prized pig. Calling out for Margy, Melissa finds her sitting on the dock with her feet in their pond. She tells her daughter to stop moping and finish packing. Looking adorably cute, Tiffin's Margy gets up and begins singing the musical's most noted tune, "It Might As Well Be Spring." Margy laments her humdrum life on the farm and yearns for more in song with beautiful vistas of rolling hills and the Texas prairie, complete with grazing cows, behind her.

Margy's practical boyfriend Harry (David Brandon) drives up on his scooter to say goodbye before she heads off to the Fair. The frugal penny-pincher doesn't want to waste money on just having fun, and Margy quips, "I guess that is the trouble with fun—it's gone."

Both Wayne and Abel find Melissa's mincemeat lacking brandy, which she refuses to add. Separately, they both sneak some in. Melissa reneges and adds the rest of the bottle, unaware that her mincemeat was already spiked twice. The family drives off to the Texas State Fair with Blue Boy and Wayne's racing car in tow while singing a refrain from "Our State Fair."

The family settles in at a trailer park nearby. The next morning, everybody deserts Melissa to get to the Fair including Margy, who wants to wander the grounds alone. The camera follows the farm gal as she tours the Fair exploring the many attractions, including a futuristic monorail. She stops to watch a fast-talking, slick local TV announcer named Jerry (Bobby Darin) who immediately plucks her from the audience to come on stage. After bantering for the cameras about her being from a small town, he takes her aside to get her address. A wide-eyed Margy then begins asking him questions about his work and he tries to impress her with phony stories, from covering the war in Algeria to being on assignment in Rome. Despite her interest, Margy turns down his dinner invitation. Jerry says if she changes her mind, she knows where to find him.

Wayne scores high in the time trials for the big race and is required to take some publicity photos with pretty entertainer Emily Porter (Ann-Margret, sexily clad in yellow tight-fitting shorts) who Wayne goes gaga over. The farm boy makes his move and the two hit it off. Meanwhile, Blue Boy is blue and just lays in his pen to Abel's dismay. He croons the song "Sweet Hog of Mine" to lift Blue Boy's spirits in the film's most ridiculous and embarrassing moment. The song doesn't do the trick, but a sow named Zsa Zsa, brought in nearby, perks ol' Blue Boy up.

The family hits the Fair at night and Margy notices the KTVT television truck outside the auditorium. She ventures inside and tries to get Jerry's attention as he is hosting a weightlifting competition. Afterwards, he rushes out with a curvy blonde to grab a beer. Saying good night to the camera crew in the truck, he spots Margy on one of the monitors. He goes back inside to find her, but she has already left. He ditches the fair-haired dame and races after Margy, who he finds wandering around the Midway. After going on one of the rides, they head off to a cocktail lounge for a drink. Realizing she is underage after her poor attempt to act older, he orders her a soft drink and a double vodka for himself, which he then uses to spike Margy's beverage. She marvels how different Jerry is from the boys back home while he speaks of strippers in Paris and geishas in Japan that he has met in the course of his travels.

Jerry and Margy are strolling the grounds when Jerry steals a kiss on the cheek. Seeing her pull back, he guesses correctly that she has a boyfriend back home and intends to marry him. She responds with sadness in her voice, "I guess so. Everybody else in Banning does." Realizing he has a chance with her, Jerry kisses her hard on the mouth, causing Margy to flee into the night.

A crestfallen Margy returns to the trailer park. She confides to her mother about the boy she met and how he kept trying to steal kisses. Margy states firmly, but unconvincingly, that she has decided not to see him any more. Wanting Melissa to agree, she is surprised when her mother doesn't. Melissa then sings the song "Never Say No to a Man" written especially for this remake.

The next day is the big mincemeat competition with Jerry hosting for local TV. Melissa's mincemeat is a hit and takes first prize (thanks to that triple shot of brandy that gets the judges soused). Jerry gets the assignment to cover the drag races that will be beamed to Chicago. He then takes a new approach with Margy and invites himself to her trailer to meet her parents. Emily on the other hand is just out for a weekend of fun and keeps reminding Wayne that nothing serious can exist between them.

That night Jerry and Margy are dancing at a pavilion and Wayne and Emily are on a Ferris wheel as they sing the film's most joyous song, "It's a Grand Night for Singing." And all agree that they think they are falling in love. Later, back at Emily's place, Wayne proves it by giving her an engagement ring. Overwhelmed, Emily accepts the ring and looks at it longingly. A more sensible-thinking Margy knows once the Fair is over, Jerry will be back on the road and she will return to Banning. Despite his invitation to join him and his crooning "This Isn't Heaven" to her, she knows that it will never work out. However, when he professes his love, Margy has a surprising change of heart and kisses him back passionately for the first time. This takes Jerry aback and he pulls away, telling her that she should be getting back home. He promises to meet her the next night and as she walks away she says, "I can never marry Harry. How could I when I love you so much?"

After Blue Boy wins the hog contest, the family gathers to watch their son's championship car race and Emily overhears them talking about Wayne meeting a girl who probably is "trash" and hoping it is just a fling. Wayne wins, but a dejected Emily slinks off without making her presence known.

That night, their last at the Fair, an excited Wayne and Margy race around primping for their dates with Emily and Jerry. Wayne appeases his mother and says he will spend the night with Margy, but the second they hit the fair the pair split up. Wayne finally catches up with Emily, who ends their affair. Jerry meanwhile was offered a national broadcasting gig and chooses it over Margy, standing her up.

Shortly after, the Frake family begins their drive back to Banning with two forlorn youngsters in the backseat. After arriving home, a dejected Margy receives a phone call from Jerry who, feeling pangs of guilt, decided to pass up the job offer to be with her and is lost in town. They are reunited, as are Betty Jean and Wayne, who seems to have gotten over Emily rather quickly and acts as if nothing happened at the Fair. Wayne turns out to be the film's unintentional real cad.

State Fair was highly anticipated due to its cast, especially the return of Alice Faye to the big screen, but once the critics got to see it their enthusiasm quickly waned. While they felt empathy towards Faye and Tom Ewell, they did not for the movie or its younger leading players. Though a good review popped here and there (for example, Joan Winchell in the *Los Angeles Times* called it "a fun-film welcome in these days of downbeat flicks"), many more critics felt *State Fair* was too folksy, old-fashioned or conventional, offering nothing new despite adding car racing and on-location photography at the Texas State Fair. Moira Walsh of *America* stated, "The whole approach in the new movie is inane, tired and perfunctory." The *Variety* reviewer quipped, "*State Fair* is still as American as mom's apple pie, but the pie is stale after seventeen years in the pantry." Many attributed its failure to Ferrer, who they felt was not suited to direct such a light, wholesome piece of Americana. His forte was more melodramatics as exemplified by some of his prior directorial efforts such as *The Great Man* and *Return to Peyton Place*. Due to him, the film lacked a flow with the

Wayne (Pat Boone), Melissa (Alice Faye), and Margy (Pamela Tiffin) cheer after Blue Boy the hog wins the blue ribbon in a scene from *State Fair* (20th Century–Fox, 1962).

songs being mere inserts stopping the action and then resuming when they are finished. John Cutts of *Films and Filming* in particular trashed Ferrer's direction and opined, "On this outing his style is completely off-key—heavy, mechanical stuff, inclined to be more plain organization and methods than creative film direction proper."

Pamela weighed in with her opinion about *State Fair*. Regarding *Summer and Smoke* and *One, Two, Three*, Tiffin felt all the actors were in the moment and became their characters. She remarked, "I was there. I said the lines. I understood the scripts."[21] However, it was not the case with *State Fair*. Halfway through filming she noticed that "something was going wrong. I became aware that everyone was acting. I said, we are acting—not we *are*. It was an artificial situation."[22]

Paul V. Beckley (*New York Herald Tribune*) agreed with Pamela's assessment that everything rang false in *State Fair* particularly, he noted, the performances of Boone and Ann-Margret. He commented, "The whole thing has an air of something made by people who can't believe a bit of it; it is no remarkable consequence, then, that those of us who might have been willing to indulge in a little innocent illusion are left with a feeling of emptiness."

Pamela received mixed reviews with some critics surprised that the effervescence she brought to *Summer and Smoke* and *One, Two, Three* was lacking here. That may be due to the direction she received from Ferrer. Brendan Gill, in *The New Yorker*, said Tiffin "gives an impression of being a direct descendant of Little Miss Muffet." Mae Tinee in the *Chicago Tribune* described her as "cute." The *New York Times*' Bosley Crowther found her to be "merely bland and vacuous in the role," while *Variety* said, "Pamela Tiffin's range of expression seems rather narrow." *Time* magazine bemoaned, "There is too much sugar in Tiffin." On the other hand, Marjory Adams in the *Boston Globe* raved that Pamela is "young, lush and adorable." Her fans would agree.

Pamela was visually perfect in the role of the naïve innocent farm girl—all serious and doe-eyed—and plays her very demurely with a bit of sophistication to make her an atypical farm gal. For Pamela's fans looking for another comedy tour-de-force from her *à la One, Two Three*, it is a letdown since Margy was the ultimate romantic ingénue role. Pamela does fare better though than Ann-Margret, who was much too wholesome at this point in her career to play the "bad" girl. It was a role she probably would have handled better a few years later. As usual, Ann-Margret's best moments are musical, particularly when performing the song "Isn't It Kind of Fun?"

Pamela's best scenes are when her Margy is itching for some excitement and wants to experience life. Here she projects her discontent quite well, injecting the character with some spunk, particularly at the beginning of the scene with her frugal boyfriend and at the end when Boone as Wayne is supposed to spend the last night of the Fair with her. He hands Margy three dollars to go off by herself so he can be with Ann-Margret's Emily. She takes it and replies she was going to give him two so she could go off alone. The latter scene especially has Pamela channeling *One, Two, Three*'s Scarlett if only for a flashing moment.

Pamela and Bobby Darin don't really connect as a couple. Perhaps Tiffin's unease about working with him carried over into their scenes. Their best work together is where Darin's cocky city slicker brings her to a club and realizes that she is under twenty-one. Margy tries unsuccessfully to act older and urbane. Seeing through her ruse, Jerry doesn't call her out on it, but instructs the waiter to leave the liquor out of her drink. Pamela is able to portray her character's trepidation and insecurity about being with a more worldly kind of guy who is so different than the small town boys she is used to dating. It has been obvious that Jerry was attracted to her physically, but now begins to fall for the sweetness in her—an attribute that he may not have experienced much with city women. Darin and Tiffin play this scene quite well, as his brashness meshes so well with her fresh innocence. Here maybe Pamela's discomfort with the singer played to her advantage and made the scene believable. Though the two are reunited by the film's fade-out and most likely headed for matrimony, touching the heart of every romantic in the audience, this was not considered a happy ending for all. Moira Walsh of *America* wittily opined, "Darin makes the character such a convincingly cheap and worthless little 'punk' that the girl's future as his wife may easily be a fate worse than death."

Boone especially liked Pamela and Bobby's scene in the bar. He remarked on the DVD, "It is interesting that he married Sandra Dee during this period. He brought her to the set while we were filming. She was exactly the kind of girl that Pamela Tiffin was."

Tiffin's outstanding scene is at the beginning with her lip-synching "It Might As Well Be Spring." It was beautifully photographed, juxtaposing the fresh beauty of Pamela's restless Margy yearning for a new experience far away from farm life with the wide open spaces of the Texas prairie. It is a truly stunning piece of film and arguably the visual high point in the movie. Producer Charles Brackett and director Ferrer knew immediately after seeing the rushes that they nailed it. The editors of *Musicals: Hollywood and Beyond* called this scene "the most poignant moment in the film where the actualities of the fair and the boy scarcely match the dream of transmogrification expressed in the lyrics and the visuals of Tiffin's solitary walk through rolling American hills and open plains." It is too bad that the other musical segments could not come close to this.[23]

Though the critics were not impressed with *State Fair*, the star wattage of Boone, Darin, Tiffin, and Ann-Margret brought the audiences, particularly the younger folks, into the theaters. The film was by no means a smash hit, but it did rank #23 for the Top 50 Rentals of 1962, grossing an estimated $3.25 million, and turned a small profit. Come awards time, the movie received a Writers Guild nomination for Best Written American Musical for Richard L. Breen. (It was slim pickings that year as one of the other nominees was *Hey, Let's Twist!*) The prize went to *The Music Man*.

Proving it really was a lean year for musicals, Ann-Margret surprisingly won a Laurel Award for Top Female Musical Performance, beating out Natalie Wood and Rosalind Russell in *Gypsy*; Shirley Jones in *The Music Man*; and Connie Francis in *Follow the Boys*. Pat Boone was nominated in the Top Male category. Bobby Darin and Pamela Tiffin were ignored.

Today, this *State Fair* is still is not well-liked by fans of Rodgers and Hammerstein. In the definitive look at their career *The Rodgers and Hammerstein Encyclopedia*, musical theater and film scholar Thomas S. Hischak opined, "Jose Ferrer's clumsy direction, the television-special—like dancing by Nick Castle, and the garish widescreen photography—seemed to be making a mockery of what the first film was all about."

Soaring Into the
Wild Blue Yonder

Come Fly with Me

After *State Fair* wrapped, the press had a field day speculating what Pamela's next movie would be since she was in such high demand. There was talk that she would co-star opposite Laurence Olivier in the film version of the hit stage musical *Camelot*. Though her singing voice was dubbed in *State Fair* due to time constraints, producers were impressed with her vocal ability. Alas, *Camelot* was not made at this point in time.

Pamela made only one movie in the almost two-year period after finishing *State Fair*, despite the praise she received from directors extolling her acting talent and other virtues. She got along well with them because she was at ease taking direction due to her modeling experience. There was no temperament there, and directors liked actors who were pleasant to work with and who followed direction. They also adored spending time with her. Despite her young years, she was a model of sophistication and class. Pamela opined at the time that producers may not have known what to do with her because at age twenty she was no longer a teenager and not quite a mature woman.

Producers were further perplexed on how to cast Pamela because of her comedic abilities. Pretty ingénues were not supposed to be funny and usually just played the romantic interest. Humorous roles were either the tall gangly girl who finds it hard to attract a man and laughs at herself *à la* Paula Prentiss or the buxom, dumb sexpot *à la* Stella Stevens and Jill St. John. Tiffin did not fall into either of these categories.

Around this time it was reported that Alfred Hitchcock considered Pamela along with blondes Sandra Dee, Carol Lynley, and Yvette Mimieux for *The Birds* until Tippi Hedren came to his attention via a TV commercial. Pamela was announced to play a nymphomaniac in *A Rage to Live*, based on John O'Hara's bestselling novel, but it was postponed (Suzanne Pleshette starred three years later). Even more offbeat was when the press revealed that she was signed by producer Hal Wallis to play, in a ludicrous, politically incorrect casting decision, a Japanese woman in *A Girl Named Tamiko*, directed by John Sturges. This was not just publicity; Tiffin was actually ready to shoot this movie, which would have reteamed her with Laurence Harvey as a half–Chinese, half–Russian photographer living in Japan and caught in a love affair with a U.S. Embassy official (Martha Hyer in a role originally meant for Dolores Hart) and a sophisticated Japanese girl named Tamiko. Pamela was supposed to play Tamiko! Though she spent hours in makeup and did look Japanese, she thought the whole thing rather ridiculous. Wallis and Sturges finally came to their senses and got France Nuyen (who was half–Vietnamese and half–French) to replace her.

Wallis then offered Pamela a chance to work with Elvis Presley in *Girls! Girls! Girls!* (1962), which she turned down. Surprisingly, the producer didn't force this movie on her when he could have due to Tiffin's contract. The role intended for her was that of a rich girl who hides her wealth from poor-but-proud fisherman Elvis, who also moonlights as a nightclub performer. Pamela would have been perfect for this part as it called for someone to act sophisticated but playful, though it would not have tapped her comedic abilities in any way. And despite its title, there were only two major female roles unlike Elvis films to come that had him surrounded by a bevy of beauties. After Dolores Hart and Pamela said no, Wallis decided to find an unknown for it. Coincidentally, he discovered another fashion model to play the part: Laurel Goodwin, making her film debut.

Luckily for Pamela, her modeling assignments and studies were keeping her busy. With the whirlwind of three back-to-back movies over, Pamela had time to reflect how quickly her life had changed. She admitted to being apprehensive about acting because she was happy modeling and attending night school in New York. She wasn't prepared to become an actress, and prior to that everything else she did was planned by her. However, Pamela was glad she took the chance and admitted it was exciting being selected from the crowd to work in motion pictures. She felt acting was more of a challenge than modeling and at the end of the day it gave her a feeling of accomplishment.

Pamela followed in the footsteps of Suzy Parker, one of the most photographed and highly paid models of the fifties, who went to Hollywood in 1957. After making her film debut in 1957's *Funny Face* with Fred Astaire, she followed with such films as *Kiss Them for Me*; *Ten North Frederick*; and *The Best of Everything*. Tiffin only met Parker a few times socially, but admitted to being in awe of her triumphs in the modeling and acting fields. Most felt Pamela was on the way to equal or perhaps surpass Parker's success.

Pamela was home in New York City when she got the call that Hal Wallis was loaning her and Dolores Hart to MGM for her next movie *Champagne Flight* (the working title for *Come Fly with Me*). Though Pamela was taking college classes and modeling, her life had changed again. A number of Hollywood's established columnists had hailed the actress as a role model. She was free of scandal (unlike, say, Tuesday Weld); traveled to film locations with her mother; dressed fashionably but demurely; and was an intellectual. And unlike other starlets who would show up at social functions on studio-arranged dates just to get their picture printed in *Modern Screen* or *Photoplay* or *Screen Stories*, Pamela was quietly dating thirty-something journalist Clay Felker and staying out of the Hollywood limelight. The divorced Felker was a former sports writer, then political reporter for *Life Magazine*, before joining *Esquire* as a features editor in 1957.

The actress met him through a friend while they were lunching at the Museum of Modern Art. After *Esquire* did a pictorial on her in 1961, Pamela went to their offices to obtain a copy of one of the photo negatives shot by Bert Stern. She saw Felker and told him how much she liked the story about her, unaware that he wrote it without credit. They went to dinner shortly thereafter and continued to see each other regularly. She felt that the six-foot-tall, blondish, brown-eyed Felker resembled both John Wayne and Robert Mitchum—two of her favorite actors at the time.

Columnist Earl Wilson reported that Pamela and Felker ran into her former co-star

Publicity photograph of Lois Nettleton, Karl Boehm, Pamela Tiffin, and Dolores Hart in *Come Fly with Me* **(MGM, 1963).**

Laurence Harvey and his date one night at the ultra-private New York hot spot Le Club. The overwhelmed actress was quoted as saying, "What more could I want? Clay on one side, Laurence on the other. I didn't know which way to turn. Laurence is so romantic, so gallant, so abandoned."[1]

Champagne Flight (which briefly was to be called *Over the Rainbow* but obviously it conjured up confusion with the classic song) was a lightweight romantic comedy about three flight attendants, or air hostesses as they were referred to back then, looking for love in the air. It was part of that long line of "Three Girls" films such as *Three Bad Sisters, Three Daring Daughters, Three Little Girls in Blue* and *Three Coins in the Fountain* and could have easily been titled *Three Air Hostesses with the Mostest*.

Champagne Flight was based on Bernard Gemsler's 1960 novel *Girl on a Wing*. It was the story of Carol Thompson, who abandons her Greenwich Village life and heads to Miami where she becomes an air hostess trainee for Magda International Airlines. She becomes romantically involved with the company's psychologist and a notorious gambler who could ruin her chances for employment. She befriends four other air hostesses and gets involved with their romantic entanglements as well. Two have unhappy endings, but Carol helps the fourth land a millionaire while she passes on the bad boy and winds up with the good doctor.

MGM bought the rights to the book and assigned writer-producer Anatole de Grunwald to give it a more polished international flavor. He had begun working for the studio in 1959 with *Libel* starring Dirk Bogarde and Olivia de Havilland followed by *I Thank a Fool* (1962) with Susan Hayward and Peter Finch.

William Roberts, who had scripted the hit western *The Magnificent Seven* (1960), received sole screenwriter credit. Five lead characters were unwieldy so it was cut to four. But even that was thought to be too much for the audience to follow, so the fourth air hostess practically disappeared. Also excised were the book's more tawdry aspects involving sex and booze. This left smoking as the only on-screen "vice" these fly girls could display.

With MGM British producing, interiors were shot in London and exteriors on location in New York, Paris, and Vienna. Veteran Henry Levin was hired by de Grunwald to direct. Never considered a great director, Levin had that light touch perfect for this schoolgirl fantasy. He worked at Columbia Pictures in the forties and fifties, mostly in lower-budget movies. Once he broke free, he was able to get work at 20th Century–Fox, MGM, and Universal specializing in light, frothy, medium-budgeted comedies such as *April Love* (1957), *The Remarkable Mr. Pennypacker* (1959), *Holiday for Lovers* (1959), and *If a Man Answers* (1962). One exception during this period was Fox's very successful big-budget fantasy film *Journey to the Center of the Earth*. It was both a critical and box office success so no doubt this led MGM to hire him for another epic fantasy film, *The Wonderful World of the Brothers Grimm* (1962). Another big hit for him was MGM's *Where the Boys Are* (1960), about four college coeds looking for fun and romance, and descend on Fort Lauderdale, Florida, for spring break. The studio no doubt felt that Levin had the expertise to direct another comedy about three girls looking for love, this time in Europe.

British cinematographer Oswald Morris was hired to shoot his movie. He was known for his innovative use of color. His acclaimed movies included *Moulin Rouge*, *Moby Dick*, and *The Guns of Navarone*. He would go on to win an Academy Award for *Fiddler on the Roof* (1971). Morris told *Films and Filming* that for *Champagne Flight* he was aiming for a texture with a visual lushness completely different from his last two movies, *Term of Trial* and *Lolita*. However, he refused to ape director Levin's last cinematographer Russell Metty, who poured diffused colored lighting over everything in the Sandra Dee-Bobby Darin comedy *If a Man Answers*.

Originally Dolores Hart, Pamela Tiffin, Ann-Margret, and Mariette Hartley were announced as the film's leading ladies. However, after deciding to narrow the film's focus, it was adieu to Ann-Margret.

Hart, who was topped billed in MGM's big hit *Where the Boys Are*, was tapped to headline the cast. No doubt Levin, who had directed *Where the Boys Are*, had a hand in casting Dolores as the hard-edged Donna Stuart in *Come Fly with Me*. On *Where the Boys Are*, MGM wanted Jane Fonda to play Merritt, but Levin championed Hart to producer Joe Pasternak who agreed.

Hartley was cast as the more pragmatic, older Bergie. She was a stage actress who studied with Eve Le Gallienne and was now under contract to MGM. The unconventionally pretty blonde actress made an auspicious film debut as a young woman who needs saving in the classic Sam Peckinpah western *Ride the High Country* (1962) starring Randolph Scott and Joel McCrea. This was her second film assignment.

Handsome blond German actor Karl Boehm was being groomed by MGM for stardom, so he was cast as Hart's romantic interest, a baron who turned to jewel smuggling once his family's fortune was depleted. He began acting in his native country in 1952, but didn't get noticed in the U.S. until 1960 with his starring role as a serial killer in the British horror movie *Peeping Tom* (1960). He then signed with MGM, who tried to turn him into a more conventional leading man in *The Four Horsemen of the Apocalypse* (1962) and *The Wonderful World of the Brothers Grimm* (1962).

Academy Award–winning character actor Karl Malden was cast in an atypical romantic role as the rich, frugal tycoon visiting Europe shortly after the death of his wife and falls for Bergie. Virile Hugh O'Brian, fresh off his six-year TV run in *The Life and Legend of Wyatt Earp*, was cast as a carousing flyboy juggling his married girlfriend with enticing stewardess Carol.

With their common theatrical backgrounds drawing them together, Hart and Hartley began rehearsing with Malden at his Brentwood home. Just before filming was to commence, a devastated Hartley was forced to withdraw from the picture due to illness (she was misdiagnosed as having hepatitis, but once the mistake was realized it was too late). She was replaced by Lois Nettleton, who only a week prior had signed a contract with MGM. She had made a major impression on the studio with her supporting role in the Jane Fonda comedy *Period of Adjustment*, based on the play by Tennessee Williams. She was sent to the Paris location after filming had begun. She revealed in *The Ear of the Heart* that she had not even time to pack correctly, and Hart would loan her clothes during the first week until she could buy some more of her own.

Before heading to Europe, Hart and Tiffin took courses at Grace Downs Airline School in New York to help them be more convincing as air hostesses. Hart remarked, "Pamela and I bonded quickly."[2]

The next time she was in the air, Pamela paid especially close attention to the plane's flight attendants and was amazed with their routine, declaring it very hard work after going through the training herself. Hart concurred and said that she learned a number of things from taking that course. "The stewardess' first function is to project a Mother Image," she shared. "The theory is that people aren't used to being a mile up in the sky and what that they instinctively want is reassurance. This Mother Image is achieved very subtly, the smile which greets each passenger as he (or she) steps into the plane, the conscious effort being to make each one feel he (or she) is the ONLY one Mother is devoting all this attention to … you know, like getting coats hung up and seat belts fastened."[3] Hart went on to expound about how flight attendants should not take steps larger than eight inches because it would make Mother appear to be strident and it would swivel the hips, shattering the Mother Image. When asked what she thought of this doctrine, Hart replied, "As an actress playing a stewardess I believe the whole thing, but as a passenger I must confess I think it's a perfect hoot."[4]

Dolores got to put her training to the test the first day of shooting at the airport in Paris. An elderly woman who missed her flight to New York took her wrath on the pretty brunette when she mistook her for a real stewardess. When Hart explained she was a movie actress working for MGM, the woman reportedly snapped, "I don't care what company you fly for, you're incompetent—and wearing too much makeup."[5] Following the airline doctrine, this passenger found all her troubles were Mother's fault and she needed to fix it now. Exasperated, Hart escorted the passenger over to the airline counter to speak with a real employee. The clerk recognized Dolores, so to pacify the woman he bawled Hart out and fired her on the spot, making for one happy customer.

Levin also hired a consultant to help the actresses be as realistic as possible playing flight attendants. Her name was Valerie Imbleau and the director met her when she was the purser on his Pan Am flight from Istanbul to London. He contacted MGM and they were able to arrange for the airline to give her a leave of absence to work on the movie. She and Hart became very close during the production and formed a spiritual connection. Imbleau would remain good friends with Dolores even after the movie wrapped.

While shooting in Vienna, Hugh O'Brian wrote to columnist Hedda Hopper (in a letter dated July 5, 1962) that he was so enjoying making *Champagne Flight*, which was quite a change of pace from the westerns he was doing prior. The cast was staying at the famous Bristol Hotel and the actor's suite overlooked the Ringstrasse, described by O'Brian as "one of the most beautiful and colorful avenues in the world."[6] He went on to talk about a Fourth of July party that he threw for the cast and crew as well as the cast from Disney's

Acerbic Donna (Dolores Hart) and flighty Carol (Pamela Tiffin) are air hostesses flying from New York to Paris in *Come Fly with Me* (MGM, 1963).

The Miracle of the White Stallions, also filming in Vienna. Then he got down to business and wrote, "We will be here for two weeks and then back to Paris for two days filming and on to London where we will finish the picture the end of August.... Our picture ... promises to be a winner from all the reports on the rushes seen so far.... My part is a welcome change of pace being light comedy, and I get to kiss the girl and keep her for a change, which in this case is even more pleasant because the girl is Pamela Tiffin, a doll. This will be the first film in which I get a chance to play love scenes and kiss a girl—after six years on a horse I'm having a ball."[7]

Years later, O'Brian's feelings about making this movie had not changed and he still only had praise for Pamela. "She was one of the nicest and sexiest leading ladies I ever had," O'Brian exclaimed. "Pam was so much fun to work with—we had a lot of laughs. She was so respectable. I bet even today if you gave her a hug for me she still would blush."[8]

Of the remaining cast, the one who stands out for O'Brian was Dolores Hart. "Dolores was the greatest," he remarked. "She was a beautiful and special lady ... *and I mean lady*! A great gal—so was Pamela."[9] Pamela recently remarked, "It was only my fourth film, and Dolores was so experienced. I looked up to her. She was decent and sensible—and a bit of a smart aleck, which I liked. She was so helpful to me, not the least bit competitive or jealous."[10]

Pamela also revealed that the two had many serious and spiritual conversations about life in general. Dolores shared her misgivings about her engagement and her recurring thoughts about entering a monastic life. Pamela admitted that she couldn't understand Hart's decision at that time.

Hart had the same warm feelings about Pamela and Lois Nettleton. She loved working with them because "they act from the heart" and she had fun off-screen as well with them, remarking, "[T]he company was probably the happiest I had ever worked with."[11]

Clay Felker also made the shoot quite enjoyable for Pamela. While she was filming in London, Paris or Vienna, he was on business in Helsinki and would fly in to wherever she was for the weekend. Though her mother accompanied her again to Europe, Felker and Tiffin alone would sightsee; attend the theater; dine; or just stroll the streets in whatever city they were in together. When she had a week off, Pamela jetted down to Rome and fell in love with the city and professed a desire to live there. It was a prophetic statement.

Though Pamela was enjoying her time with the cast and seeing parts of Europe, she was beginning to annoy director Levin due to her different color contact lens and a Southern accent that wouldn't go away. "The other day I forgot and wore my blue eyes on the set," said Pamela, whose character was green-eyed.

> The director has also been upset with me because I have been slipping a little too much of magnolia and peach blossoms into my voice. If he has said it once, he has said it ten times, "Please, Pamela, you're speaking with too much of an accent." But I just can't help it. I've been a Southern girl in every picture so far—deep south. But this is just medium south—more north, if you know what I mean.[12]

Matters got worse when Tiffin accidentally left four cases of green-colored contact lens in a taxi cab. Despite posting a reward in the *London Taxi News* (contact lens were much more expensive in 1962 than they are today), they never were returned

Pamela not only took home memories of making *Come Fly with Me* on location in Europe, but also a number of antiques to add to her collection. She and Felker both had a fondness for the Tudor and Medieval periods reflected in the design of their living and dining rooms at the time. While filming in London, Tiffin bought a very expensive 1598 Tudor tester bed made from solid carved oak, which she had glimpsed in Woolsey's store window while driving by it one day with Dolores Hart. "We stopped and I knew I must have it," the determined actress explained at the time:

> But I was working and couldn't get to Woolsey's when it was open. I spoke to this marvelous prop man who helped me get it. For a while it looked as though I wouldn't because the president of Pan-Am wanted it and there was a possibility we'd have a tie-in with Pan-Am. [MGM eventually decided to go with a fictitious airline name.] The prop man got it for me at a studio discount, which was lucky for me because … the bed and canopy are so heavy I had to have it sent home by ship; the dock and storage charges were astronomical. It was the only bed of its kind left in England, and I think is the only one of its kind in the United States.[13]

Two weeks after *Champagne Flight* wrapped, Pamela married Clay Felker. The ceremony took place at the Riverside Church in New York City on October 6, 1962, one week before her twentieth birthday. The Rev. Gordon Gilke officiated. A reception followed at the home of Felker's close friend, journalist Peter Maas. Tiffin's romantic life was never fodder for the movie columnists, unlike some of her contemporaries, so her wedding came as a complete surprise to most in Hollywood. Pamela didn't play the starlet publicity game so there were no multi-page photo spreads in *Photoplay* or *Modern Screen*, just small news items picked up by the major newspapers.

Marriage to Felker changed the actress. Due to his position as journalist and editor, Felker was a regular on New York City's social scene attending the sort of parties and functions which Pamela avoided in the past. She credited him for helping her feel more comfortable mingling and meeting new, interesting people and expanding her world beyond modeling and acting. Where her taste in music and literature was based in only the classics, her new husband helped her appreciate jazz and twist music and contemporary fiction.

Being married to a beautiful movie star also helped Felker, who had left *Esquire* and was now an editor at the *New York Herald Tribune*. Tom Wolfe, author of many books including *The Bonfire of the Vanities*, worked for Felker at the newspaper during this time of transition. Writing years later about this period, Wolfe declared in *New York* magazine (founded by Felker in 1967) that the former Midwestern boy from Missouri lived in an opulent duplex apartment on East 57th Street complete with 22-foot-high windows, a vast fireplace, and a staircase leading from the elevator down to the living room. He went on to say that guests were lucky when Mrs. Clay Felker was at the bottom to greet you. Wolfe described Pamela as having "a fair white face smooth as a Ming figurine's. She was gorgeous. She had something else, too, a career that was taking off so fast she had not one but two personal managers, Irwin Winkler and Robert Chartoff. She could afford them and two more like them…. For a man on the beach, Pamela Tiffin was a lovely helpmate to have. Clay Felker was broke."[14] That would not be the case for long, but may explain why he encouraged his lovely wife to work unlike other men of that generation who expected their wives to abandon their careers for a life of domesticity.

During post-production of *Champagne Flight*, MGM decided the title had to go and changed it to *The Friendliest Girls in the World*. Then they soured on that new title, no doubt because it sounded more like a movie about a bunch of hookers than airline stewardesses. They finally settled on the more appropriate *Come Fly with Me*, stealing the title from the hit Frank Sinatra record written by Jimmy Van Heusen and Sammy Kahn. MGM was too frugal to pay for the rights to his song, so they hired Frankie Avalon to re-record it for the movie. Despite Avalon's popularity with the teenage set, it was not a hit record for him.

Come Fly with Me was released with the tagline "Join the Jet Set! A wild spree in Paree! A love affair in every airport!" The film opens with a point-of-view shot of a cab on the way to Idlewild Airport. Stewardess Carol Brewster (Pamela) jumps out of the taxi late for her first day on the job at Polar Atlantic Airlines. She scurries through the terminal and barely makes it to her Paris-bound flight. Finally on board, she explains matter-of-factly with a big smile to the steward and her fellow air hostesses, "I'm late. Wanted to especially be here on time—my first trip. Gotta make a good impression, but I locked myself in the bathroom and couldn't get out. Pretty dumb, isn't it?" Bergie (Lois Nettleton) finds Carol amusing, but Donna Stuart (Dolores Hart) does not. Things get worse for Carol, who closes the aircraft's door with half the cockpit crew still outside. When the officers ask for her name, she replies, "Mud." During the trip, flight engineer Teddy Shepard (James Dobson) tricks her into thinking the plane needs stabilizing and it is up to her to run back and forth between forward and rear bathrooms to flush the toilets. Donna and First Officer Ray Winsley (Hugh O'Brian) help Carol get even. Winsley then asks her to dinner during their layover in Paris.

Golddigger Donna agrees to a date with first class passenger Franz Von Elzingen (Karl Boehm) only after learning that he is a baron. Bergie, back in tourist class, is rescued from a drunken flyer by kind Texan Walter Lucas (Karl Malden), a frugal millionaire and recent widower. At the airport, Carol is behind Ray Winsley in Customs. When the agent asks her if she has anything to declare, she responds, "Yes I have. If this company had any sense, he would be captain before he'd know it." Ray disappoints the stewardess: Before they even leave the Paris airport, he and Franz bail out on their dates (Ray's excuse is to meet an old friend, while Franz receives a telegram to fly on to Austria). Bergie says yes to dinner with Walter.

Excited to be in Paris for the first time, Carol rides most of the way to the hotel standing up with her head sticking out of the taxi's sun roof. After Donna and Carol set Bergie off with Mr. Lucas, they bump into Katie Rinard (Dawn Addams), who is looking for Ray Winsley's room. Carol points her in the right direction and is infuriated that the pilot lied to her about why he broke their date. She fumes, "'Old friend! Call of duty'—some duty!" When the gals return from dinner, Katie's furious husband (Maurice Marsac) is in the lobby. While Teddy tries to stall him, Carol races to the room to warn the lovers. Katie rushes out while Carol jumps on the bed to take her place. Ray opens his door only to get socked in the jaw by Rinard, who is surprised to find that his wife is not there. He stumbles over an apology and makes a quick exit. Carol then gives Ray a piece of her mind for his lack of a moral code. He tells the high-and-mighty air hostess that he is just human and makes mistakes. Carol refuses to have dinner with him in Austria, but then he gives her a long kiss. She floats away and says, "I'll think about it."

In Vienna, while Donna goes to meet Franz and Bergie goes sightseeing, Carol orders dinner for two in her room. Ray is very late because the airline's persnickety rep in Vienna, Oliver Garson (Richard Wattis), tells him in the hotel's lobby that he is being transferred due to a complaint from Rinard. Carol finds Ray and berates him for standing her up in front of Garson, not realizing he works for Polar Atlantic Airlines. Ray introduces the embarrassed air hostess as "Miss Mud" and whisks her back to her room before she can cause more trouble for him. She leaves Ray in the hallway, wailing that she is tired of waiting for him to fulfill his obligations. He lets himself into her room and, after he calms her down, the pair dines together. Thinking they can move forward, Carol breaks down in tears when Ray tells her that he is flying to Cairo the next day and not back to Paris with her and the crew.

As the air hostesses sign in for their return flight to New York, Carol tries to convince Bergie to help her get through to Donna that her attitude about wanting wealth and being part of the "in crowd" can get her into hot water. She then spots Mr. Garson staring at her. As he approaches the counter, she ducks out of sight and begins crawling away pretending to be looking for her lipstick. When two pilots join her on the floor and ask what it looks like, she replies, in a disguised husky voice, "Gold outside and red inside. Cost me a dollar. Hate to lose it." She then makes a dash to the airplane, as Garson yells after her, "Pleasant trip, Miss Mud."

Donna flirts with the Idlewild crew scheduler to make sure the trio gets to work the same flights to Paris and Vienna the following week, so she can see Franz again. However, she has no idea she is his dupe in a smuggling ring. When the trio checks into their Vienna

Carol (Pamela Tiffin) shares a tender moment with co-pilot Ray Winsley (Hugh O'Brian) only to learn that he has been transferred to another flight crew in a scene from *Come Fly with Me* (MGM, 1963).

hotel, they get a shock when they are taken to a penthouse suite. Donna assumes it was her "tinhorn baron nobleman welcoming them to the city of love and laughter" in a jab at Carol for doubting him. A contrite Carol responds that some of her best friends are tinhorns. However, they soon learn that Lucas is the one who made the arrangements, to Bergie's displeasure. After quarrelling with the millionaire, she makes the gals change rooms.

Carol is surprised that Ray has returned to the crew for their flight back to the States. He is delighted to see her. He then placates an upset little boy traveling by himself to New York; a touched Carol gets the impressed passengers to write to the airline on Ray's behalf. Her good mood sours when she runs into Katie with Ray at the airline's airport offices where she is trying to get him to quit his job. Katie lets "co-conspirator" Carol know that she was able to get her husband to drop the charges against Ray because she found proof of his infidelities and that he agreed to a divorce with a big financial settlement as well. As Carol exits, she hands Ray back his handkerchief, which she will not need any more, and says to Katie, "Wonderful seeing you again—a real kick in the head."

Donna once again uses her wiles with the crew scheduler to get the gals back to Paris and Vienna. Carol confronts Ray on the flight about Katie. When he admits he has not made a decision, she takes him to task. A peeved Ray responds by ridiculing her attitude about life's morals and ideals, and calls it "cornball juvenile hogwash." She follows him back into the cockpit and tells him off. However, Carol's faith is restored in Ray when he comes to Donna's defense when she is caught with smuggled stolen diamonds in a cigarette carton that she was bringing to her baron at his request. The police agree not to put Donna in jail as long as the airline vouches for her. She then rushes over to meet Franz, who is steely-eyed and cold-hearted with her. As she runs off, she sees detectives waiting and realizes that Franz turned himself in.

The movie ends with Bergie agreeing to marry Lucas who has charted the entire plane and Carol agreeing to go out on a dinner date with Ray. Despite Ray buckling her into a seat and gagging her with his handkerchief, Carol still gets the last word and says, "First thing I do, if we get married, is go to the president of the airline. If that man doesn't make you a captain, I will give him such a blast." As for Donna, the tear-stained air hostess is left holding a present from Franz and the audience wonders if she will wait for him or not as the plane takes off. The title tune is sung over the end credits roll.

As expected, a movie of this type received mixed reviews. When it was not criticized for being "formulaic," "familiar," "tired," or "weightless," the romantic comedy received some positive notices. It was called "delightful," "dreamy," "highly engaging," "a laugh-filled comedy," "frisky and fancy and fun," and "colorful and occasionally comical." Across the pond, Cecil Wilson of the *Daily Mail* remarked, "The pleasure of this undemanding comedy lies in the likability of all its characters, male and female." The film was best summed up by Bosley Crowther of the *New York Times*: "Right out of the wild blue yonder of schoolgirl romantic dreams, travel-advertisement fancies and true-confession clichés, this dear-diary log of the activities of three good-looking cloud-land pillow-maids still comes across as a substantial and, indeed, cute divertissement."

Come Fly with Me proved to the critics that Pamela's expert comedic performance in *One, Two, Three* was no fluke. Even in a teenage-girl fantasy romance like this, Pamela was a standout for the critics due to a truly well-balanced performance. *Variety* raved, "Sometimes one performance can save a picture, and in *Come Fly with Me*, it's an engaging and infectious one by Pamela Tiffin." After then bashing the movie due to its "frail, frivolous, and featherweight storyline," the reviewer added, "Fortunately for the Metro release, Miss Tiffin is around to bail it out almost every time the going gets too bumpy for passenger comfort. It's a performance that will generate word of mouth, particularly among teenage girls always on the prowl for screen stars to emulate."

Most other reviewers praised Pamela as well:

"Pamela Tiffin … begins to look like a new Audrey Hepburn—and that's no discredit to either one…."—Bosley Crowther, *New York Times*

"The girls, Miss Tiffin particularly, have the requisite sparkle."—Philip K. Scheuer, *Los Angeles Times*

"It is Miss Tiffin, with her natural gift for comedy, who comes across strongest. She is the prettiest young comedienne in years…."—James Powers, *The Hollywood Reporter*

"The girls are a lively trio, especially Pamela Tiffin."—Raymond Durgnat, *Films and Filming*

"Pamela Tiffin … is not only adorable here but a clever comedienne."—Hazel Flynn, *Hollywood Citizen-News*

"Both Pamela Tiffin and Dolores Hart are distinctly engaging and it is rather fun watching Lois Nettleton being turned into a kind of poor man's Joanne Woodward."—Richard Roud, *The Guardian*

Pamela deserved all the raves she received. She was funny, sweet and touching and hit all the right notes as the flighty flight attendant who falls for a carousing pilot. She draws the audience in from the moment she appears on screen, careening through the airport in her air hostess uniform to make her flight. Pamela is then energetic and amusing as the out-of-breath flight attendant makes her excuses for her tardiness. Among her standout scenes is when she runs into Ray's room and warns him and his paramour that her irate husband is on his way. She is just wonderful as she masterfully runs the gamut of emotions from funny (making a wisecrack after Ray is socked by the husband), to mad (berating him for lying to her and for having an affair), to tenderly weeping because she really liked him and is disappointed in his behavior.

Another standout moment for Pamela is in the hotel where Carol and Ray have dinner. She is just charming as she once again shows a range of emotions. The character could have come off whiny and preachy, even unsympathetic in the way she scolds Ray. However, Pamela successfully balances those harsher moments with her natural sweetness and comedic abilities.

The only minor disappointment with the movie in regards to Pamela Tiffin is her styling. MGM arguably had the best hair stylists and makeup artists in the business. When actresses did films for the studio, they were almost guaranteed to look the best they ever did on the big screen. Unfortunately, this was not the case here with Pamela. The British team (Joan Johnstone, hair stylist, and Tom Smith, makeup artist) did a nice job with Dolores Hart, but excelled with Lois Nettleton who looks simply radiant in practically every scene. Arguably, she never looked more glamorous on the silver screen. Pamela, on the other hand, is saddled with a less than flattering hair style. It was parted in the middle and worn in a sort of bun most of the movie. Pamela is such a natural beauty that even with hair styled like a schoolmarm, she still is more attractive than most.

Though *Come Fly with Me* was a hit with teenage girls, it failed to appeal to a wide audience. In its opening week it finished seventh at the box office. Overall, grosses were disappointing across the U.S. but the film did better than average business in Boston, New York, and Portland, Oregon, per *Box Office* magazine.

At the end of 1963, Quigley Publications released its yearly Stars of Tomorrow poll. The ten most promising actors of the year based on their box office clout were voted by theater owners throughout the country. Pamela placed fifth behind George Chakiris, Peter Fonda, Stella Stevens, and Diane McBain. Rounding out the Top Ten were Patrick Wayne, Dorothy Provine, Barbara Eden, Ursula Andress, and Tony Bill. All had respectable movie careers; however, none of them became superstars of the silver screen.

Though Pamela received the best reviews then and is still amusing now, Dolores Hart and Lois Nettleton shine as well. Hart makes the audience like the wisecracking Donna despite her being a golddigger because Hart is able to let us see that underneath Donna's tough exterior is a sweet girl looking for love. Lois Nettleton has never looked lovelier on screen and her character is atypical for this type of movie. Superficial qualities mean nothing to Nettleton's more pragmatic and wiser Bergie, who falls for the older gentleman who is just plain nice and polite to her. Even when she cruelly breaks it off with him because she thinks she is only a replacement for his dead wife, you feel empathy for her. And you can't help but smile when she winds up the big winner at the end with not only a marriage proposal from a nice man, but a millionaire to boot. Nettleton is quite sweet in the role and her chemistry with Karl Malden, so good as the awkward smitten widower, is wonderful.

In June 1964, shortly after *Come Fly with Me* was released, Dolores Hart officially left her Hollywood career and entered the Regina Laudis Abbey to become a cloistered nun. Pamela and Lois Nettleton didn't know anything about it and wondered where the actress was when they were scheduled to do a personal appearance for the movie. The film's publicist nonchalantly informed them. Tiffin said that at the time she couldn't understand Dolores' decision, but does now. Nettleton remarked in Hart's memoir, "I was totally shocked at first, but very soon everything slipped into place. I always thought of her as being very close to God."[15]

Almost fifty years after *Come Fly with Me* was released, ABC-TV picked up a TV pilot called *Pan-Am* (created by Jack Orman for Sony Pictures Television) about four flight attendants (Christina Ricci, Karine Vanasse, Kelli Garner, and Margot Robbie in the Pamela Tiffin role as the fumbling newbie) working for Pan American World Airlines in 1963. Though most of the characters and plots did not ape *Come Fly with Me*, the old movie had a great influence on the production design, the styling of the actresses and the clothes they wore. Watching the four actresses in their tight blue Pan-Am uniforms with white gloves marching through the airport terminal immediately recalled *Come Fly with Me*. Though the debut episode received strong ratings despite mixed reviews, the show did not catch on and ratings thereafter began to tumble. ABC cancelled the show in mid-season before all completed episodes had aired. Though *Pan-Am* was a failure in the U.S., it was a hit overseas.

6

No, Films Is Where
She'd Rather Stay

The Fugitive (TV)
Three on an Island (TV pilot)

After *Come Fly with Me* was released, Pamela Tiffin made her TV acting debut, receiving "Special Guest Star" billing on the hit new series *The Fugitive*, where she played, once again, a stewardess.

The series starred David Janssen as Dr. Richard Kimble, a man wrongly convicted for the murder of his wife and sentenced to death. On the way to prison, his train crashes, allowing him to escape. He goes on the run, with the police in hot pursuit, to try to clear his name and ensnare the real killer, "the one-armed man." The series was produced by Quinn Martin in conjunction with United Artists Television. The actress had a picture deal with the studio via the Mirisch Brothers, which probably explains her *Fugitive* appearance.

"The Girl from Little Egypt" was directed by Vincent McEveety and written by Stanford Whitmore. The "Little Egypt" in the title referred to an area in Illinois. In Whitmore's original script, Tiffin's character Ruth Norton was a Puerto Rican hooker who shelters a delirious Kimble, suffering from pneumonia. Quinn Martin demanded changes. He wanted the hooker turned into a stewardess because his wife used to be one. And he wanted Kimble to be hit by her car instead of him suffering from an illness caught while on the run. Whitmore reluctantly obliged.

In the episode, Pamela looks as if she literally stepped right out of *Come Fly with Me* onto the *Fugitive* set, as she is first seen in her airline hostess uniform. Her pinned-up hairstyle is almost identical as well. In an interview for *The Fugitive Recaptured: The 30th Anniversary Companion to a Television Classic*, Whitmore remarked that when David Janssen heard who his leading lady was going to be, he quipped, "'What's a Pamela Tiffin?' He wasn't familiar with her. We said, 'She's your romantic interest while you're dying and you go into the flashback.'"[1] Though Tiffin was still a relative newcomer, she did have three movies in release and was one of the hottest young actresses of the time. It is very strange that Janssen had not heard of her by then.

This episode differed from most in the series' long run. After thirteen weeks on the air, viewers finally got to see flashbacks to Kimble's life with his wife (Diane Brewster) leading up to her murder and what happened directly afterwards with his trial and sentencing.

His chief pursuer Lt. Philip Gerard (Barry Morse) only appears in the flashbacks and is not in pursuit of him here in the present, as he was in many other episodes.

As Ruth Norton, Tiffin has just received the news from her paramour Paul Clements (Ed Nelson) that he is married. Distraught, she leaves the restaurant and drives away. On a deserted curvy San Francisco roadway, she runs down Kimble, who is standing on the side of the road. At the hospital, Kimble goes in and out of consciousness accidentally revealing his past to Ruth and that his name is not George Browning, which he told the police. Knowing the truth, Ruth decides to keep it a secret and help him, since he saved her from suicide and lied to the police (he claimed the accident was his fault because he stepped in front of her car).

Pamela Tiffin, ca. 1963.

The rest of the episode has Kimble pretending to be Ruth's brother. He acts like it too, as he tries to convince her that she is too good a person to be a man's mistress, despite Paul's efforts to keep her in his life. Seeing that Ruth is torn, Kimble takes a drastic step: Knowing that the Clementses are throwing a party, he escorts a shocked Ruth to it to see Paul's family life up close. It does the trick as the girl, shocked by his cozy home and two sons, ends the relationship. Later Kimble bids Ruth farewell and says, "I never thanked you for running me down." Teary-eyed, she responds, "The pleasure was all mine."

An episode that was truly core to the series and filled in the entire back story of Richard Kimble aired without much fanfare on December 24, 1963. In regards to his feelings about "The Girl from Little Egypt," Whitmore opined, "Well, the whole thing simply turned out dreadful, and I remember that I called Quinn after it aired, and said, 'Quinn, I want to thank you for showing it on Christmas Eve, when no one saw it,' because it really came out lousy. I don't know why, but everything went wrong with it."[2]

According to Ed Robertson, Whitmore never singled Pamela out for its failure during their interview. (Some avid fans do in the blogger sphere.) Robertson added, "For what it's worth, I did not think Pamela Tiffin was all that bad, and that she and Janssen had a decent rapport."[3]

Playing Ruth stretched Pamela's dramatic abilities. Her Ruth is distressed, sullen, or worried throughout and never gets to show a trace of humor or happiness. Pamela is at her best when the character shows flashes of strength, trying to break it off with her married lover.

Making *The Fugitive* was a new experience for the actress—one she was not satisfied with. This being her first foray into episodic television, she was not used to the fast pace of filming. Pamela admitted at the time, "I think I'm just too slow-paced for television. I'm slow in life. I take time to read. I love long lunch hours. I talk slowly. My husband calls it dawdling."[4]

TV directors cared more that you hit your marks and knew your lines than trying to massage a performance out of the actor. To be fair, these hard-working directors only had one week to produce an hour episode while movie directors had the leisure of one to three months (sometimes more) to create a two-hour motion picture.

Casting Pamela in "The Girl from Little Egypt" gives the episode a bit of extra cachet since she did not do much television. It really holds the interest and incorporates the flashbacks very effectively. Despite criticism from the episode's writer and some fans, Ed Robertson says it "is one of the most popular episodes of the series because it gives the fans what they want: the background story. The episode has many great moments...."[5]

Pamela's next TV excursion was a pilot for a proposed sitcom called *Three on an Island*, originally titled *The Brownstone*, from 20th Century–Fox. Co-starring were Julie Newmar (fresh off the cancellation of her TV sitcom *My Living Doll*), Monica Moran (Thelma Ritter's daughter), and Jody McCrea (everyone's favorite dumb surfer in *Beach Party* and its sequels). It was Fox's first venture into television after a short hiatus that was probably due to the havoc the budget overruns of *Cleopatra* caused the studio. The sitcom was created by Hal Kanter, an Emmy-winning writer of TV variety shows during the early fifties; he then turned to screenwriting for a bit before returning to television in the mid-sixties. The director was the prolific and respected Vincent Sherman, whose films included *Mr. Skeffington*, *Adventures of Don Juan*, *The Hasty Heart*, *The Young Philadelphians* and *Ice Palace*.

Though set in New York City, the pilot was shot on the Fox lot. Pamela and her husband were moving into their new two-story, eight-room apartment in Manhattan when the studio summoned her to star in this projected TV series. Pamela only agreed to do this when Fox promised to let her out of their contract after one more movie. Though she was outfitting her new home with expensive period pieces, she abandoned her movers, painters, and cleaners to fly off to Hollywood. She confessed, "Now that I am married, when I do come here [Hollywood] to make a movie I either want to do something very good or make lots of money...."[6] It was also agreed that if the show was picked up as a series, it was arranged that it would be shot within a fourteen-week period and she would be paid the same as if making a movie. It would not cut too much into her time in New York with her husband.

During the shoot, Pamela injured her back and neck due to a careless co-star. She revealed, "I had one scene where I had to teach Jody McCrea boxing and he didn't pull his punch so he hit me. It didn't do a lot of damage—but it did hurt. He hit me right in the mouth. It was very upsetting to me. He's completely insensitive!"[7] Words must have been exchanged between the two as Pamela wondered to Hedda Hopper, "I still can't understand why the other men on the set couldn't have said to Jody, 'You don't talk to a lady like that!'"[8] This sounds quite plausible as a few actresses who worked with McCrea in the *Beach Party* movies found him disrespectful of women; Linda Rogers got into a fight with the "grabby" actor on an airplane while on a promotional tour.[9]

That incident with McCrea, plus a short filming schedule, had Pamela bemoaning, "I've been getting up at 5 a.m. and coming home at 8:30 p.m. for the last two weeks. I've never worked so hard in my life—I'm so tired I'm numb.... Making this pilot really wore me out. When I was doing my last movie I became impatient because I'd have such long waits between scenes—now I can't wait to get back into a movie to have those long periods just to sit around.... I wish I had the magnificent vitality of Julie Newmar."[10]

In this pilot, Pamela played the cutely named Taffy Warren, a sculptress who shares her brownstone with statuesque Kris Meeker (Newmar) and wisecracking Andrea Franks (Monica Moran). Taffy accepts half-ownership in glass-jawed boxer Jules Sweetly (Jody McCrea) in exchange for payment for one of her works. He wants to give up life in the ring, but she does her best to prevent it until she can complete her statue of him. Taffy and her roommates nickname him "Bulldog" to toughen up his image. Her sculpture is entered into a competition about the same time as his next bout, with surprising results.

Three on an Island was not received very enthusiastically from the networks despite its pedigree. Pamela also did not care for it: "*Three on an Island* ... wasn't like *Gilligan's Island*. It was worse."[11] Lucky for her it was not picked up as a series. *Three on an Island* was broadcast, along with a number of other unsuccessful pilots, on the summer TV series *Vacation Playhouse*.

Pamela disliked doing television and this would be her last TV show for almost four years. Her lack of enthusiasm for the small screen made her distinguishable from a number of her contemporaries who delved into the medium to play varied roles. Most felt their TV appearances made them known to a wider audience and gave them the opportunity to play more challenging roles that the ones being offered in motion pictures. In the first half of the decade Tuesday Weld, Carol Lynley, Diane McBain, Connie Stevens, Shirley Knight, Suzanne Pleshette, Susan Oliver, Anjanette Comer, Diane Baker, Stella Stevens, and others were popping up all over the small screen in anthology series such as *The Alfred Hitchcock*

Rare pin-up photograph of Pamela Tiffin, ca. 1964.

Hour, Alcoa Premiere, Kraft Suspense Theater, Bob Hope Presents the Chrysler Theatre and any number of episodic dramatic or western series. Some even were stars of their television shows.

But some starlets felt that doing TV would cause overexposure and diminish their "movie star" status. You rarely found the likes of Ann-Margret, Jane Fonda, Sandra Dee, or Sue Lyon guest starring on *Burke's Law* or *Ben Casey*. Pamela fell into this latter camp, but not for that reason. It was the aforementioned fast shooting schedule that she disliked.

Also by this time, most TV shows were filmed in Hollywood. Pamela's decision to remain in New York could have also contributed to the shortage of her TV work. She may have not wanted to jet off to Hollywood for only one week's work; and as the saying goes, "out of sight, out of mind."

Whatever the reasons, perhaps Pamela should have overcome her discomfort with working on TV and directed her agents to get her meaty small screen parts especially since she was so unhappy with the movie roles offered. By venturing into episodic television, particularly those anthology series popular at the time, she could have shown producers and directors that she could play more dramatic parts well if given the chance. There were even a number of outstanding drama series filmed in her hometown of New York (such as the Emmy Award–winning *The Defenders, Naked City* and *East Side/West Side*) that could have offered her opportunities to display her dramatic talent.

The one positive thing she gained by not doing more television was that it made her even more of a cult movie star. Her body of work available to see is much less than most starlets of the day and it becomes a real treat when you get to watch the gorgeous actress on film or in a rare TV appearance.

For Those Who Think Pamela

For Those Who Think Young

Pamela Tiffin deserved—but never *got*—a leading role opposite a major comedy actor, such as a Jack Lemmon or a Peter Sellers or a Jerry Lewis. She proved with *One, Two, Three* and *Come Fly with Me* that she had comedic talent. Perhaps it never came to be because she was hampered by her studio contracts. Hal Wallis' film output was trailing off except for the yearly Elvis Presley movie. He offered Pamela another chance to work with the King in *Fun in Acapulco* (1963), which she declined due to advice from Dolores Hart. Though she felt obligated to do these films, Wallis left it up to her. And despite her warm feelings toward Elvis (whom she met), she listened to others and passed on working with him. The ironic thing was that every time she turned down an Elvis movie, she was forced to co-star with a Pat Boone or a James Darren. No wonder Pamela regrets her decision to this day.

Due to major cost overruns on the epic *Cleopatra*, 20th Century–Fox was in dire financial shape. They let go many of their contract players and slowed down its production. There was one comedic teenage role Pamela coveted, but Fox gave it to a non-contract actress. The film was *Take Her, She's Mine* based on the hit Broadway comedy. The studio bought the film rights to the play. Henry Koster was set to direct with James Stewart signed to play the befuddled father who keeps having to rescue his rebellious teenage daughter who goes off to college and then Europe. Pamela felt she would be perfect for the part and wanted to work with Stewart, but Fox honchos decided on Sandra Dee, who was riding high at the box office, and borrowed her from Universal Pictures. Financially, casting Dee helped propel the movie to become a major hit. Creatively, the studio arguably made a mistake going with the petite blond who just delivered her usual perky, sometimes verging on whiny, performance. Close your eyes and it could have been Tammy or Gidget who went off to college. Pamela would have brought a more sexy sophistication coupled with a charming naïveté to the part of the protesting coed, making her more believable and memorable. Her sparring with James Cagney in *One, Two, Three* was hysterical and she no doubt would have made a more formidable antagonist for James Stewart here.

On the dramatic front, the Mirisch Corporation dangled their screen version of Lillian Hellman's Broadway play *Toys in the Attic* in front of Tiffin and in a number of interviews at the time Pamela claimed the movie would be her next. Instead they went with Yvette Mimieux. Mirisch also had a picture deal with Elvis Presley and one wonders if Pamela was offered *Kid Galahad* (1962). She would have been a nice fit in the role played by Joan Blackman, that of boxing promoter Gig Young's sister who falls for the King. At Columbia Pictures, Pamela also had a nerve-wracking audition for producer-director Otto Preminger for the role of priest Stephen Fermoyle's ill-fated sister Mona in the lavish production *The Cardinal*. She vied with Ann-Margret, Dolores Hart, Shirley Knight, and Carol Lynley for the role. The nervous actress could not give "Otto the Ogre" (as some actors nicknamed him) what he was looking for and Lynley got the part.

Through Clay Felker, Pamela met author Richard Condon, who wrote *The Manchurian Candidate*. He had just completed a screen adaption of his satirical novel *A Talent for Loving: Or The Great Cowboy Race* and told Felker he wanted Pamela to star. The role he had in mind for her was that of a wealthy rancher's virginal daughter, the victim of a long-ago family curse making her sexually insatiable once she experiences physical love even if just in the form of a kiss. Condon was hoping Tiffin's *Summer and Smoke* co-star Laurence Harvey would play opposite her. The movie was postponed due to Harvey's film commitments and then cancelled. It did not get made until 1969, and then from a screenplay by Jack Rose and with Caroline Munro in the role of the daughter.

Despite her rising popularity with teenagers, especially of the male kind, a more forthright Pamela began voicing her disappointment about losing out on these film roles and not working with a James Cagney again, but having to work with James Darren in her next movie. Due to comments like this, she began receiving some backlash in fan magazines aimed at the youth market. Some teenage girls may have taken this as being snooty and felt that Pamela was biting the hand that feeds her. It was the teenage market after all which she was most popular with. While reviewing new monthlies, the *Los Angeles Times* reported that *Teen* magazine took the actress to task rather harshly: "Pamela Tiffin still acting stuck-up to small people on the set. Color her nothing."[1] Here is probably a perfect example of how Pamela preferring to read the classics and study Latin for her college classes, rather than socializing with her cast mates and the crew, was taken as snobbery. Or was it just these publications were lashing out at her for not kissing up to them by participating in arranged photo shoots and interviews? Pamela was notorious for refusing most publicity pinup photo requests and was dubbed "Lady Pamela" by some.

She may have also received that nickname because Pamela admitted that she was reserved when meeting people for the first time. It was a type of behavior she preferred and owned up to because "I like a choice of relationships. I like to feel that people seek one another out instead of forcing relationships with immediate familiarity."[2]

Pamela also defended herself when statements from her first year in Hollywood about acting came back to haunt her such as "I don't know how I'll feel a year from now, but at the moment I can take it or leave it."[3] Some members of the press called her indifferent and perhaps even unappreciative for the film career that practically fell into her lap. She responded, "This isn't so. I am just as grateful as anyone. I am happy to be in the movies and I enjoy it. I must tell you, however, that if it all came to an end tomorrow I would not be despondent about it."[4] This honest admission was due to the fact that Tiffin had other fulfilling things going on in her life and she was not a slave to Hollywood despite what some folks there felt should be the case. She was a wife, model, and student, as well as an actress.

Putting aside what was being said about her, Pamela only wanted to make good movies like *One, Two, Three*. However, it seemed youth-oriented movies were only in her immediate future, much to her chagrin. Contractual obligations forced her to co-star opposite handsome teen idol James Darren twice, in the *Beach Party* knock-off *For Those Who Think*

Publicity photograph of James Darren and Pamela Tiffin in *For Those Who Think Young* (United Artists, 1964). Billy Rose Theatre Division, The New York Public Library for the Performing Arts, Astor, Lenox and Tilden Foundations.

Young and the juvenile hot rod flick *The Lively Set*. *For Those Who Think Young* was for United Artists, but she had no idea which of the three loaned her to Universal Pictures for *The Lively Set*. The two movies made Pamela Tiffin one of the teen queens of the drive-in movie set.

James Darren was among the most talented young actor-singers of this period and one of the best-looking to boot. And like Pamela, he too was fighting to get more mature movie roles. The Pennsylvania native began his acting career at Columbia Pictures in 1955 after being discovered by talent scout Joyce Selznick in New York (where he studied with Stella Adler, just as Pamela would). He appeared in a few movies, but did not hit it big until he landed the role of surfer Moondoggie opposite Sandra Dee in *Gidget* (1959), where he also warbled the title song.

Before his teen idol persona completely overshadowed his acting ability, Darren was able to land dramatic roles in *The Gene Krupa Story* (1959) starring Sal Mineo, the Korean War drama *All the Young Men* (1960) starring Alan Ladd, and *Let No Man Write My Epitaph* (1960). In the latter, he arguably gives his finest performance as the problem-plagued son of Shelley Winters, trying to rise out of a life of crime and drug dependency. Though all three films received positive notices, not one was a major hit at the box office. Nineteen sixty-one turned out to be a banner year for Darren. He played the important role of Pvt. Spyros Pappadimos in the Academy Award–winning *The Guns of Navarone* and critics took notice of how he held his own as a Greek soldier against such acting stalwarts as Gregory Peck, David Niven and Anthony Quinn. His teenage fans, however, preferred his All-American boy-next-door persona and flocked to see him reprise his Moondoggie role in *Gidget Goes Hawaiian* co-starring newcomer Deborah Walley in place of Sandra Dee. They also began buying up his single "Goodbye Cruel World," propelling it to #3 on Billboard's Hot 100 chart.

In 1962, Darren was ridiculously cast as a full-bred Hawaiian native boy in love with white girl Yvette Mimiuex, the sister of bigoted land baron Charlton Heston, in *Diamond Head*. He then reluctantly reprised his Moondoggie role for a third time opposite yet another new Gidget. With Deborah Walley pregnant, actress Cindy Carol took over as the surfing sweetie, who abandons the sunny shores of California for romantic Italy in *Gidget Goes to Rome* (1963). He complained that when considered for more dramatic roles, he was dismissed because of the stigma brought on by the *Gidget* movies. Needing the work and following the age-old adage "if you can't beat 'em, join 'em," Darren headed back to the shore when paired with Pamela in *For Those Who Think Young* and then to the race track for *The Lively Set*. As with Pamela, he did not relish either movie though their fans loved the pairing of the two charming actors and made each movie a hit.

For Those Who Think Young was developed by Frank Sinatra's Essex Company for distribution by United Artists. Former Warner Bros. executive William T. Orr had built a dynasty for the studio's television division; at the height of its success, they had eight series on the viewing schedule. Orr and his assistant Hugh Benson eventually left Warner Bros. to work on feature films with Howard W. Koch at Essex. As director, busy TV helmsman Leslie H. Martinson was hired by Koch, who knew of Martinson's body of work and respected his talent. Since this was going to be a rushed production, his expertise would be an asset.

The working title for *For Those Who Think Young* was *A Young Man's Fancy*. The title was changed when Sinatra's company signed a deal with the Pepsi-Cola Bottling Company to promote and advertise the movie. Hence, the name was changed to *For Those Who Think Young* to cash in on the soda company's slogan at the time. A huge Pepsi dispensing machine is featured prominently in several scenes.

In *One, Two, Three* Pamela played the daughter of a Coca-Cola executive and here the equal opportunity actress was pushing Pepsi. Martinson has no knowledge of the deal between the soft drink company and the producers but did confirm that the company was not at all involved in the making of the film. Frank Sinatra was not either, though Koch would report back to him and show him the dailies, which he was pleased with.

To reach a wide audience, the producers surrounded Darren and Tiffin with a supporting cast of veterans and exciting new faces. Bob Denver, playing Darren's idolizing buddy, was fresh off the cancellation of the successful sitcom *The Many Loves of Dobie Gillis*. Film star Tina Louise, playing a stripper with a high IQ, had been living in New York studying Method acting. This was filmed before both were stranded on *Gilligan's Island* but because they were never in the same scene together, the two actors never met during filming.

Comedian and TV game show host Woody Woodbury, who at one time was considered for the job of Jack Paar's replacement on *The Tonight Show*, was seen performing his stand-up act in Florida by Sinatra, who offered him the role of Tiffin's uncle. He not only was excited about landing the movie, but that Jeanne Crain was signed to be his love interest. For whatever reason (perhaps she read the script?), Crain dropped out and was replaced by Ellen McRae (soon to be rechristened Ellen Burstyn).

Paul Lynde, cast as Tiffin's other uncle, had a banner 1963 appearing in the hit films *Bye Bye Birdie* and *Under the Yum Yum Tree*. Newcomers included Nancy Sinatra, Claudia Martin (Dean's daughter), dancer Lada Edmund, Jr. (later of *Hullaballoo* fame), and Susan Hart. To give the movie that *Beach Party* feel, producer Koch was able to convince James H. Nicholson of American International Pictures to loan out some of his beach boys. Surfers Mickey Dora, Mike Nader, and Ed Garner (inexplicably listed as "Byron Garner" in the credits) appeared as part of the beach and college crowd.

Trying to ape *Beach Party* even more, Darren and Tiffin perhaps were paired because they were dark-haired and similar in looks to that film's young leads Frankie Avalon and Annette Funicello (though Pamela couldn't compete with the former Mouseketeer in the bosom department). Darren played a rich, brash surfing playboy who falls for poor, headstrong college coed Tiffin, who has two overprotective uncles trying to pay her tuition by working in a nightclub. But at least here her virginal heroine doesn't want to nab a husband, like her other movie characters at this time. Instead her character wants to stay in school and graduate before marrying.

The movie was given a 21-day shooting schedule and included musical numbers and exterior location shooting. It was then cut to eighteen days and director Martinson learned he would have only one day on the shore to shoot all the beach scenes. The director thought it would be a challenge, but knew he could pull it off despite worries about the shortened schedule. He shot about eighteen minutes of cut film including the "Surf's Up" musical number and some surfing scenes. Dialogue scenes were saved for nightfall.

Martinson was a good choice to bring *For Those Who Think Young* to the screen, especially since the movie had to be completed in less than three weeks. He directed a number of features in the mid-fifties including his first movie *The Atomic Kid* (1954) with Mickey Rooney, which was shot in twelve and a half days. After joining Warner Bros., Martinson built up a solid reputation as a proficient director who was able to deliver professionally shot television episodes on time. He worked on all the top series including *Cheyenne, Mav-*

erick, *Lawman*, *77 Sunset Strip*, *Hawaiian Eye*, *Surfside Six*, etc. On the big screen, he had just completed directing *PT 109* (1963) starring Cliff Robertson as John F. Kennedy. He was used to shooting fast, which was an asset for him in getting the job.

   For Those Who Think Young was a typical shoot in the sense that scenes were filmed on location at Malibu Beach and Occidental College as well as on a soundstage. Producers

Candid photograph of Pamela Tiffin during the filming of *For Those Who Think Young* (United Artists, 1964).

usually barred the public from the set but fans were encouraged to watch the filming as Hugh Benson welcomed visitors to create word of mouth about the movie. As reported in the *Los Angeles Times*, "Hundreds of invited guests have dropped into this most open of open sets. On a make-believe beach inside stage eight it was impossible to tell the players from the passerby. Visitors swarmed over the sands like ants at a picnic."[5] According to Benson, there were a total of 6,774 visitors who watched some portion of the movie being filmed.

The film also had a number of product tie-ins other than Pepsi: clothiers Jax, Peter Pan Swimwear, and Wembley; the food chains International House of Pancakes and Baskin-Robbins; sunscreen maker Coppertone; and car manufacturers Honda and Buick. The most expensive prop used for the film was a Buick Riviera that was custom-made at a cost of $18,000. In return for their product placement, these companies were contracted to promote the movie in their ad campaigns.

To keep the anticipation level for the movie high, the cast posed for numerous publicity stills and granted interviews to all the movie fan magazines. In between scenes, they were required to participate in a television making-of featurette being produced in hopes of getting viewers off their couches and into the theaters.

Though Pamela and Darren were in the beach scenes, they were on the periphery. The main focus was on Bob Denver and Nancy Sinatra. Martinson liked Denver and adored Nancy, whom he found to be delightful. Pamela also liked Frank's little girl a lot.

James Darren was juggling filming *For Those Who Think Young* while performing twice a night at a Las Vegas nightclub. The busy actor would hop a flight at 4:30 p.m. to Vegas, perform his two shows, then take a sleeping pill and be chauffeured via ambulance back to the studio. Sometimes he would go via ambulance both ways.

Not apparent to the cast and crew was the unhappiness of leading lady Pamela Tiffin. She admitted that she only connected with Nancy Sinatra, who was also a newlywed missing her husband. Not only was the beautiful actress feeling lonely, but she also had to contend with a co-star whom she found to be flirty, making her very circumspect around him. Darren, on the other hand, liked Pamela and told *Seventeen* in 1964 that they "get along really well; it's fun working with her."[6] Co-star Ed Garner remembered it being that way also and said, "James Darren was a really nice guy. It seemed to me that he and Pamela Tiffin were enamored equally with each other."[7]

Tiffin was a professional and kept her unhappiness hidden. Not even Martinson was aware, but he did know that she was feeling lonesome and would invite her back to his home after a day's filming. The director remarked:

> I found James Darren to be a very pleasant fellow, but I can't say enough about Pamela Tiffin. In fact, my wife Connie [host of the longtime talk show *Connie Martinson Talks Books*] and I became very friendly with Pamela. We had dinner at my home with her a number of times. She was just a delightful, beautiful young woman—one of the prettiest of her day. In fact, I was driving her back from the studio to have dinner with Connie and me one early evening. The harsh setting sun coming through the windshield could be very tough on the loveliest of ladies, but it made Pamela look even more beautiful. I never told her that. She was like spring rain, but as gorgeous as she was, Pamela was terribly bright. Connie was very impressed with her.[8]

When asked about working with Tiffin by *Movieline* magazine in 1992, Tina Louise remarked that she "was beautiful and very smart."[9] A few years later Tiffin returned the compliment: "Tina Louise was one of the most beautiful females I've ever seen in my life. Her beauty was unearthly and just a miracle of nature."[10]

Surprisingly, the one explosive incident that happened during filming did not involve Tina, known for being a bit difficult to work with, but soft-spoken Pamela. Lada Edmund, Jr., was a New York dancer who had just appeared on Broadway in *Bye Bye Birdie* and the revival of *West Side Story*. She came out to Hollywood and landed a minor role as one of Pamela's sorority sisters. One day the novice actress' inexperience on a movie set got her in trouble with the female lead. "Since this was a beach movie, Pamela was getting her whole body painted," recalled Lada. "I didn't realize it when I opened up her trailer door by accident. She was supposed to be this sweet quiet little girl, but you couldn't believe the curse words that came out of her. I had never heard half of them in my whole life. I had worked on stage for years and was not a sheltered kid either."[11]

The story did not end there. When filming was completed, Lada hightailed it back to New York where she landed a regular slot on the new NBC-TV music series *Hullaballoo*. It featured a number of male and female dancers, but Lada quickly became the breakout star due to her shimmying and shaking in a cage. The show was shot on a soundstage above where Johnny Carson hosted *The Tonight Show*. She became a favorite guest of his. One night, he asked Lada how she liked working with Pamela Tiffin in *For Those Who Think Young*. Desperate to say something, Lada told Johnny that Pamela was "absolutely stunning" and then reiterated the trailer story. She didn't stop there and, to her forever regrets, made things even worse. "I don't know why she was so upset because it was an accident," she told Johnny. "And quite frankly, Johnny, from the waist down she looked like Sophia Loren and from the waist up she looked like Roddy McDowall."

Years later, Edmund said, "I knew I should never have said it immediately after I did. It came out like toothpaste out of a tube. Johnny laughed. During the break he leaned over and said, 'I love you.' Of course it was in every column the next day and for a month afterwards. I am sure to this day if you ever mentioned my name to Pamela Tiffin she'd cringe."[12]

Despite the few minor incidents with the cast, *For Those Who Think Young* turned out to be one of director Leslie Martinson's favorite projects. "I sound like a Pollyanna but it was a delightful experience," commented the director. "This cast had a lot of respect for me since I had done a lot of television so that always helps the director too. The set was always comfortable. The crew was excellent—very fast and professional."[13]

For Those Who Think Young was released in June 1964 just in time for the start of summer and vacationing students. Any movie that opens with the gorgeous Pamela Tiffin showering, you know can't be all bad. Her character, coed Sandy Palmer, is called away from her morning toilette when she receives a phone call from Gardner "Ding" Pruitt III (James Darren). Her sorority sisters (including Nancy Sinatra as Karen, Claudia Martin, Lada Edmund, Jr., and Susan Hart) are jealous. Right off the bat you know Ding is a rich playboy since he is driving a souped-up Buick Riviera complete with *two* car phones. His friend Kelp (Bob Denver) acts as his assistant, even making the initial call to Sandy. He also has an overprotective grandfather, Burford Cronin (Robert Middleton), controlling the purse strings. To the bewilderment of her fellow coeds, Sandy turns down a date with Ding, who wants to know what makes him so resistible to her. She replies, "Aside from the fact that you are irresponsible, incorrigible, intolerable, impossible, and insane, I can't think of a thing." Ding responds with his feelings about her, but when he gets to "opinionated and mule-headed," the miffed coed hangs up on him. This makes Ding even more determined to win her over.

Ding rushes over to the sorority house and, with a surfboard to shield him from the house mother, sneaks up to Sandy's room. To get rid of him, Sandy agrees to a date later that night. Making his escape, Ding slips down the stairs and, with his surfboard, takes out the same "old man" he stole a parking space from. He turns out to be Sandy's Uncle Woody (Woody Woodbury), a piano-playing comic who performs in a seedy nightclub called the Silver Palms along with Sandy's Uncle Sid (Paul Lynde) and exotic dancer Topaz McQueen (Tina Louise). As her guardians, Woody and Sid are paying Sandy's way through school. Woody tells her that she cannot come see him perform at the club.

A determined Sandy makes Ding take her to the Silver Palms anyway for their date. After arriving, Woody gets them thrown out for being under age. Ding then suggests that they go to "Ding-a-Ling's hideaway—no uncles there." A mischievous Sandy asks, "Your fabulous apartment? I've heard a lot about it—soft lights; music to supper by; two sleepy people alone on a cloud. Take me home." Horny Ding says, "Right," to which a smirking Sandy then says, "*My* home." Unbeknownst to the youngsters, they are being spied on by Ding's houseman Clyde (Sammee Tong), hired by Cronin. The old man is determined to break up Ding and Sandy even before they become a couple due to her déclassé background.

Sandy's uncles get sacked from the Silver Palms. Performing for what he thinks is the last time, Woody starts making up humorous lyrics to songs and telling jokes aimed at the few college kids in attendance. They love it and he is a hit. The club then morphs into Surf's Up with Woody, complete with graduation cap and gown, as the star attraction.

The next day on the beach, Sandy mocks Ding for how easy it has had it all his life. Ding defends himself and insists that his eager assistant Kelp actually uses *him* for status. Sandy almost comes around until a blonde beauty named Maggie (Amedee Chabot) interrupts them, thanking Ding for her new bathing suit. Sandy runs off just as the big waves roll in. A lifeguard shouts, "Surf's up!" The surfers and their girls do a tribal-type dance to "Ho Daddy" sung by Kelp, who is buried in the sand. Ding, Sandy, and the other surfers grab their boards and head for the ocean to ride the waves. Lying on their surfboards in the ocean, Ding tries to get Sandy to believe that she is the only girl he wants. She asserts that she could care less about what Ding does with Maggie or any other girl and that her main concern is to get an education.

At the local Baskin-Robbins, Sandy feels sorry for Ding, who corners her on crutches limping from a surfing accident (in reality he just borrowed them from another injured surfer). She reluctantly admits her attraction for him and says (in some of the silliest dialogue in the movie), "I'm not immune. I've caught the Pruitt infection." To which he replies, "Then why don't we run a temperature together?" Sandy still won't budge on another date. When she realizes his injury is just a ruse, she splits—and surprisingly disappears from the movie for about fifteen minutes as the focus shifts back to Woody Woodbury whose comedy and music act has become a huge hit with the college crowd. Cronin plots to sabotage them with help from Dr. Pauline Swenson (Ellen McRae), but his plan goes awry when Woody proves to her that the club identifies all underage patrons and that Topaz moonlights as a math tutor.

A pig-tailed Sandy finally reappears on screen after too long an absence. She watches Ding and some of the beach gang dancing on the shore. At first telling her friend Karen that she is "only treading water" with Ding, Sandy becomes a bit jealous of the beach babes dancing with him and announces that she is going to make her move. She cuts in and accepts Ding's invitation to his 21st birthday party at his apartment. When Karen informs her that she is the only guest, Sandy admits that she already knows that. The wily girl plays along with Ding's charade and surprises the lothario by putting the moves on him. Guilt-ridden, Ding admits to setting a love-trap for her. Sandy takes his heartfelt confession as a sign that he truly loves her and they kiss. The mood is interrupted when Sandy catches Clyde photographing them and gets the wrong impression. After his houseman confesses that Ding's grandfather has been paying him to spy, Ding takes Sandy to confront the old man, who admits to everything, In front of his grandfather and mother, Ding proposes to the dumbstruck Sandy, who accepts. Cronin congratulates Sandy and says, "Just what this family needs, a nice new strain of bad blood" and goes on to insult her lineage. As an irate Ding and Sandy go to make their exit, his mother begs him to be patient with his grandfather because he has a reason. Ding replies, "Hitler thought he had one too."

The next night Cronin gets his cronies to work at Surf's Up to make sure the place is closed down for serving alcohol to minors. The plan succeeds. Sandy is ready to give up Ding to get Cronin to drop the charges against Woody, but he will not hear of it. Watching

Ding (James Darren) and Sandy (Pamela Tiffin) head for the shore after some surfing in *For Those Who Think Young* (United Artists, 1964).

television, Sid views old newsreel footage that reveals B.S. Cronin as former mobster Nifty Cronin during Prohibition. Sid, the college kids, and the dean converge on Cronin's house after seeing the clip about the former gangster. Pressured, Cronin has a change of heart and drops the charges while welcoming Sandy into his family.

Beach movies were never popular with the mainstream press so of course with a title like *For Those Who Think Young*, the critics had a field day coming up with quips to put it down: "*For Those Who Think Young* are for those who think stupid" (Judith Crist); "If *For Those Who Think Young* has an audience it would be for those who are too young to think" (Wanda Hale, *New York Daily News*); "*For Those Who Think Young* borrows a popular soft-drink slogan, but carelessly omits the fizz" (*Time*); "Anyone who thinks over '16' will be bored stiff" (Mae Tinee, *Chicago Tribune*), and "You have to think very young to dig this picture, or better, not think at all" (William Wolf, *Cue*).

The film was received better overseas. The critic for *The Times of India* called it a "summer sparkler … sun and sand, youth in full form create mere frivolity that helps beat the heat."

It didn't matter what the critics said because the youth audience *For Those Who Think Young* was aimed at did not pay attention to reviews. The film was a hit, earning approximately $1.6 million (it was reportedly one of the few movies from Essex Company that turned a profit). Its success was due to the timing of its release just at the beginning of the beach party movie craze and the attraction of its lead players James Darren and Pamela Tiffin.

For Those Who Think Young is a pleasant, colorful diversion peppered with nice-looking young people and some old pros. The film really comes alive when Pamela and James Darren are on screen. Unfortunately, too much attention is paid to the amiable Woody Woodbury and his nightclub act. This film is a perfect example of just how the major studios didn't understand what made the Frankie and Annette pictures so successful. Instead of rock groups, there are parents! Rather than lots of beach scenes and surfing footage, there are way too many studio-bound interior shots.

The film doesn't come near the zaniness of the *Beach Party* movies and the shortened shooting schedule really hurts as there is not enough time spent on the shore for a beach movie. Darren sings a catchy opening song, "For Those Who Think Love," over the credits (though why the lyrics don't match the film's title *For Those Who Think Young* is a mystery), but it is Bob Denver who steals the show performing the tribal surf stomp "Ho Daddy, Surf's Up." He sings the song while buried in the sand with only his inverted mouth showing, with a cartoon face painted on it upside down; beach boys and girls dance around him. This is definitely one of the best musical dance sequences from any beach movie. *For Those Who Think Young* could have used more of that and less nightclub scenes.

Despite only one day shooting on the beach, the surfing footage is impressively shot and features a number of real surfers including legendary Mickey Dora, who naturally gets the most wave action. These segments are nicely scored and excellently photographed. What is not notable is the scene with the two leads on their surfboards in the ocean. This is obviously filmed in a tank on the studio lot and is what made these movies odious to real-life surfers. Not only were they irritated about the phony lifestyle Hollywood was perpetrating about them, but sometimes they cast actors who barely would get wet or carry a surfboard let alone really surf. Tiffin and Darren were prime examples.

Girl watchers may be disappointed since there is nary a bikini in sight. All the actresses wear one- or two-piece high-waisted bathing suits. Another no-no for a beach movie is to have its leading lady disappear from the screen for almost fifteen minutes, as Pamela does here. Annette Funicello was never off-screen that long. Even in *Beach Party* when Robert Cummings dominated the action, he was at least on the sandy shore for a good portion of it.

Darren and Tiffin, however, more than make up for the film's minor offenses. They are charming together and make a striking pair though this is Pamela's movie and one most fans recall fondly. The actress is ravishing as she wears her hair down in various styles. She is costumed wonderfully with the standout being the tight white dress with a green pattern that she wears to Ding's faux birthday party. Also, she is just not all looks and gives Sandy a bit of sophistication, despite her poor upbringing, and imbues her stereotypically head-strong ingénue with some witty line readings and comical facial expressions to make her character a bit more comedic than was written. Also, it is refreshing for the period that her Sandy only agrees to wed *after* she graduates from school. *For Those Who Think Young* is one of the reasons Pamela Tiffin is remembered as an iconic cult sixties actress to this day.

Though the movie is no doubt lightweight fluff and helped expand Pamela's popularity, at the time it left a bad taste in her mouth. A year after making it, she revealed, "I never saw that one, I just couldn't."[14] It wasn't that the actress was averse to seeing her own movies. She admitted to loving *One, Two, Three* and saw it at least eight times in theaters. Her tastes ran to more sophisticated fare than a teenage beach movie. Pamela, like many other actors who toiled in those genres such as Darren, Linda Evans, and Deborah Walley, was embarrassed by the movies at the time. Yes, they were frivolous and not classic cinema, but they were fun and entertaining. There was no reason for Pamela to be ashamed, as she does quite well in it.

Of the non–AIP beach movies, *For Those Who Think Young* ranks as one of the most popular due to the pairing of Pamela and James Darren. Years later the movie became a TV favorite and was heavily rotated in syndication including four airings on WABC-TV's *4:30 Movie* from 1974 through 1978. Nowadays it is a staple of Turner Classic Movies.

Start Your Engines

The Lively Set

Universal Pictures liked the chemistry Tiffin had with James Darren in *For Those Who Think Young*, so they reunited them in the college hot rod flick *The Lively Set* (1964). This was this studio's response to AIP's *Beach Party* movies, with dragsters replacing surfboards and the college kids acting more maturely. When telling columnist Hedda Hopper about this movie, Tiffin said with a sigh, "Universal sent me a script for one of those 'young' pictures—it will be done in January some time."[1] Again, contractual obligations forced Tiffin to do another film opposite Darren. She had nothing personal against the charismatic Darren (though she made an unflattering comment in *Newsday*, "There's a difference, acting opposite a Jimmie Darren or a James Cagney"[2]); but she was striving to appear in important motion pictures. She really wanted to do more Tennessee Williams and work with Billy Wilder again.

Darren made it be known that he didn't want to do any more *Gidget* movies and was not happy about having to appear in *For Those Who Think Young*. However, at the time, he was a bit more enthused about *The Lively Set* because he felt the role of a cocky driver who designs a gas turbine engine and builds an experimental car had more bite to it. Many years later, Darren lamented making this as well. Seems he had the same career problems Pamela had: knowing he had the talent to play more challenging roles, but not the ability to obtain them due to contractual obligations.

In contrast to *For Those Who Think Young*, *The Lively Set* had Tiffin's character as the pursuer out to trap herself a man and Darren playing hard-to-get as a reluctant college student who prefers building and racing cars to girls. However, when the hunter is as someone as beautiful as Pamela Tiffin, you soon become the willing game.

The Lively Set was produced by William Alland, who also co-wrote the story; the screenplay was by Mel Goldberg and William Wood. Its director Jack Arnold was mostly known for his classic fifties science fiction movies including *It Came from Outer Space*, *Creature from the Black Lagoon*, *Tarantula* and *The Incredible Shrinking Man*. Alland was now working at the studio on a picture-by-picture basis and recruited his friend Arnold to direct *The Lively Set*, their seventh collaboration.

To attract the teenage audience, Alland also cast popular young star Doug McClure (from TV's *The Virginian*) and the recording industry's Joanie Sommers, a sort of poor man's Connie Francis, who just had a Top 10 hit with the song "Johnny Get Angry." For the older folks in the audience, screen veterans Marilyn Maxwell and Charles Drake were cast as Darren's parents. Maxwell was a former platinum blonde sex siren of the forties and

Promotional poster art for *The Lively Set* (Universal, 1964).

fifties and still was a curvy knockout, causing Darren to comment, "I look at her—and I can't call her mom."[3]

Playing the movie's vixen and spoiled girlfriend of the villain was a beautiful green-eyed blonde named Carole Wells. Formerly a busy child actress, she blossomed into a very attractive young woman and was signed by MGM in 1960. After appearing in the western *A Thunder of Drums* (1961) starring George Hamilton, Luana Patten, and newcomer Richard Chamberlain, she switched to television and for two seasons played the older sister to Lori

Martin on *National Velvet*. A bad experience with a studio executive caused her to leave MGM in 1962; then all her scenes as Tony Bill's girlfriend were cut due to running time from the 1963 Frank Sinatra comedy *Come Blow Your Horn*. Her spirits picked up when Universal signed her to a contract a short time later, and *The Lively Set* was her first movie assignment from them.

Singer Bobby Darin composed the musical score for the movie (his first) and wrote five original songs including the title song sung by James Darren and "Boss Barracuda," with lyrics by Terry Melcher, which was a minor hit for the Surfaris. To give the movie a realistic feel, five of the nation's top drivers appeared as themselves: Mickey Thompson, James Nelson, Duane Carter, Billy Krause, and Ron Miller, the latter doubling as technical advisor.

The film's "real" star was a futuristic racing car propelled by a gas turbine engine developed and assembled by Chrysler Corp. Hailed as "revolutionary," the experimental auto was accompanied to the studio by its real-life inventor, Chrysler's executive engineer George J. Huebner, Jr. The car was used to promote the movie. When it was parked in Hollywood for a press event, it was reported that crowds mobbed it to get a peek and one stranger offered to buy it right then and there for $50,000. According to Carole Wells, the turbine engine really worked and they let the actors test drive the cars for about six months. Carole was even scheduled to testify at a hearing for the automaker in Sacramento. However, she was married to Edward Laurence Doheny IV of the fabulously wealthy Doheny family and was pressured by her oil man father-in-law *not* to participate.

All the racing sequences were shot on location at the drag strip in Pomona, California; the Salt Flats in Bonneville, Utah; and Death Valley National Park, which was the scene of a tri-state endurance stock car race from California to Utah. For the scenes of the cast watching Darren competing in the hot rod time trials at Bonneville, art director Walter Simonds created a Salt Flats set using thirty tons of white sand hauled onto one of the studio's largest soundstages.

A number of scenes featured mint-looking racing cars. Having a studious, artistic mind, Pamela became intrigued with hot rods as a sort of folk art. She explained at the time, "I always thought hot rods were the old wrecks you see in juvenile delinquent films— but the ones we used were painted, chromed, tufted and upholstered. Some of these boys put together parts of old cars found in dumps and made them into really individual, fantastically beautiful cars. It was interesting watching them create."[4]

Also interesting to learn is that the sound guys did not have a problem with the racing scenes but with a segment shot in a nightclub where Joanie Sommers performs. The dance floor was crowded with about twenty-five couples doing the Twist and the Watusi to a song belted out by the pretty vocalist. Their gyrations produced loud scraping noises that played havoc with the sound men as it drowned out Sommers. To rectify this, all the dancers were made to wear soft felt booties over their shoes.

As with the making of *For Those Who Think Young*, Pamela was once again feeling lonely and missing her spouse back in New York. She befriended co-star Carole Wells who was also newly married. "Pamela definitely was not a happy camper during the making of *The Lively Set*," recalled Wells. "I loved her and we stayed friendly for a long time. Pamela was darling, but I think she wanted to be home with her husband. When she wasn't with him, she was unhappy. Also, everybody was hitting on her—actually the world was hitting on Pamela!"[5]

Jack Arnold (left) gives direction to Pamela Tiffin and James Darren during rehearsal for a scene in *The Lively Set* (Universal, 1964). Billy Rose Theatre Division, The New York Public Library for the Performing Arts, Astor, Lenox and Tilden Foundations.

The Lively Set was released in late October 1964 with the tagline "Romance and racing are in their blood … and the faster the action … the more the fun!!!" As the film opens, coed Eadie (Pamela Tiffin) is juggling her school books accompanied by her brother Chuck (Doug McClure) who gets sidetracked when he sees a roadster. It belongs to 22-year-old freshman Casey Owens (James Darren), a racing car builder and driver who just entered college after serving two years in the army. Casey challenges Chuck to a drag race despite Eadie's protestations. The race is a draw, but they get ticketed for trespassing and Chuck's hot rod breaks down. Eadie blames Casey and calls him a monster. Without a car, Chuck realizes he can't meet his fiancée Doreen (Joanie Sommers) later. Eadie suggests they double date with Casey. Confused because she just insulted him, Eadie replies to Chuck with a mischievous grin, "Of course I did. But he just happens to be very attractive."

Eadie soon learns that Casey would rather play with engines than dolls. He practically ignores her at the nightclub where Doreen is performing, instead sharing his engine design with her brother. The next day she tries to get Casey to concentrate on her, but he is miffed that his professor felt his design was off the mark.

While taking a shortcut through a park, Eadie tries to persuade Casey to pull his car over but the preoccupied boy doesn't take the hint. Eadie then purposely lets her scarf fly off and demands he stop. As he searches for it, she pours two cups of root beer into the gas tank to get some alone time with him. The car conks out as she planned. Not able to start it, Casey goes off to find a pay phone while a satisfied Eadie pretties herself up. When he returns, he apologizes and says they will have a long wait. She's ready to start making out with him, but Casey instead tries to figure out what happened. Exasperated, Eadie fesses up and, to prove she knows a thing or two about cars, drains the fuel pump. Casey is impressed, but she storms off because that seems to be the only thing he cares about. He stops her and calls her sensational. She agrees to go to the movies with him later that night, which turns out to be watching old racing footage of him at the Bakersfield Drag Strip in his father's garage. After agreeing to accompany him to his next championship race, Casey begins working on his car, leaving poor Eadie stuck making coffee for her man.

At Bakersfield, Eadie continues taking a backseat to the turbine engine and decides "if you can't beat 'em, join 'em." She dons a pair of mechanic's coveralls and tries to pitch in. This not only attracts Casey's attention, but a marriage proposal from him as well. Soon after his invention comes to the attention of millionaire racing enthusiast Stanford Rogers (Roger Mann) who offers to hire him to build the engine for a car he wants to race at Bonneville. Eadie and his parents encourage Casey to accept the offer though it means his moving to San Francisco for nine months. A self-sacrificing Eadie puts their marriage plans on hold so Casey can achieve his dream.

A few months pass when Eadie, with her hair pinned up in a hideous bun making it the least flattering hairdo Pamela Tiffin ever sported on screen, pays a surprise visit to an overworked Casey. While he cleans up, Eadie finds a photo of him and a beautiful blonde named Mona (Carole Wells). While picnicking at Golden Gate Park, Eadie confronts Casey about it and he says it was posed for publicity purposes. They come close to making love and though they are engaged, it is still 1964, and Eadie insists they wait until marriage. With his excited state no doubt subsiding in his pants, Casey suggests they go back to his trailer. As he takes a shower, Eadie cooks eggs. When he doesn't respond to her, she finds him asleep in the tub and storms off into the bedroom. Is she mad because he was sleeping or because she got a peek at his fine naked body? The question is left unanswered as the tuckered-out boy falls asleep on the couch (clad in a bathrobe, of course) and Eadie heads back to LA.

At a test run, Casey continues being pigheaded, not heeding anyone's advice and taking Eadie for granted. She declares, "I can't live like this and I won't," before she goes stomping off. Rogers is happy with Casey's showboating performance and cajoles him to try to break the record the following day. But, when Casey cracks up the car while trying to attain high speeds, Rogers fires him and sells the engine to a junk dealer—or so he thinks.

Casey's family, with the help of friends, secretly buys the turbine engine back. Now seeking the advice of his former professor, Casey builds a car around the engine. He and Chuck enter the Tri-State Endurance Race where Rogers is their chief competitor. For the remainder of the film, there are mostly reaction shots of Pamela's Eadie as she and others watch the race on a TV screen in the Owens' garage or as she dreams of Casey's car careening off a cliff. In a panic she has her father call him only to hear a drunken woman on the other end of the line. He hangs up before Casey can explain it is Doreen, who had a fight with Chuck when she caught Mona in his room. In the end, Casey wins the race and decides to return to school. The newlyweds set up house in a trailer park for married students and their neighbors are a reunited Chuck and Doreen. As an exhausted Casey heads for the shower after studying into the wee hours of the morning, Eadie once again scrambles egg for a late night snack. Thinking he has fallen asleep again in the shower, she goes to check on him, but this time he pulls his wife in to join him as the movie ends.

Reviews for *The Lively Set* ran the gamut. The critic of *The Times of India*, who liked *For Those Who Think Young*, also liked this movie and commented, "Unexpectedly racing cars and peppy music do blend well." Some of the wittier pans came from Joseph Gelmis in *Newsday* who called the car racing film "a drag" and added, "The oh-so breathless Pamela Tiffin and co-stars James Darren and Doug McClure bore along full speed…." Margaret Harford in the *Los Angeles Times* quipped, "*Lively Set* anything but that." Mixed reviews, however, were not surprising for this type of youth-oriented movie.

The four leads, when praised, were described as "wholesome, exuberant youth" (Bobb., *Variety*), "spirited" (Mandel Herbstman, *The Film Daily*), and "pleasant" (Jon McInerney, *Motion Picture Herald*). Pamela was singled out by James Powers in *The Hollywood Reporter*

Eadie (Pamela Tiffin) and Casey (James Darren) share a tender moment in *The Lively Set* (Universal, 1964).

who described her as being "pretty and funny, a young actress with a rare combination of sex and humor."

The film was well-directed by Jack Arnold and meticulously produced (though scenes with the actors at the Bonneville Flats were filmed on some of the phoniest-looking sets built on a sound stage). The film's production team garnered the best reviews. The *Variety* critic remarked that the racing scenes were "some of the most exciting shots seen in a long time." However, it was the sound editors in particular who were singled out come award season. In December of 1964, Universal Pictures executive Robert L. Bratton described how the sound effects were achieved in a letter to the Academy of Motion Picture Arts and Sciences. For the sound of the turbine engine, the sound effects team used tracks from an extended takeoff of an English Viscount Turbine prop plane. For the sound of the super stocks during the cross-state race, they recorded Ford, Chevy, and Plymouth super stocks at the Pomona Race Track.[6] *The Lively Set* would go on to receive an Academy Award nomination for Best Sound Effects (it lost to *Goldfinger*) and the Golden Reel Award for Best Sound Editing for a Feature Film from the Motion Picture Sound Editors.

The Lively Set was more serious than the beach party movies of the period, so it may have turned off a number of younger viewers looking for something goofier. Here college boys were still clean-cut and wore letterman sweaters and ties to school. Coeds wore knee-

Publicity photograph of Pamela Tiffin in *The Lively Set* (Universal, 1964).

length skirts and majored in holding onto their virginity until marriage. Compared to other films of its ilk, though, *The Lively Set* was definitely above average due to its high production values. It was well acted, outside of Joanie Sommers, and contained some nifty songs composed by Bobby Darin including the jazzy theme song sung by James Darren. Pamela is simply ravishing with her long brown hair feathered back, revealing her exquisite facial features. She plays her scenes really well, especially where she sabotages Casey's car engine so her frustrated Eadie can get some quality time with him. She and Darren once again make a charming couple and really do have screen chemistry. The actor connects with Tiffin more so than with most of his other leading ladies.

The Lively Set was received more positively than *For Those Who Think Young* and holds up well though there are flaws starting with Joanie Sommers. She was similar in looks and voice to Connie Francis, but did not have her appealing screen charisma. She comes off very annoying and whiny here though she sings well. The fact that McClure's character chooses Sommers over stunning blonde Carole Wells leaves you scratching your head in bewilderment. Not surprisingly, this was Sommers' last big-screen appearance.

If you are not a racing fan, the continuous talk about turbine car engines with lots of technical jargon and lengthy car races become a drag. The *Lively Set* is also very chauvinistic in its treatment of women. Though Pamela's Eadie is a college student, we never learn what she is majoring in. The minute she meets Casey, her academic career seems tossed out the window. She is seen making coffee; picking out drapes; watching him tinker with engines and drag racing; laying out his pajamas; and scrambling eggs. Not once do we see Eadie studying or hear anything about her desires other than marriage. She becomes subservient to her man and his engine design. At least in *For Those Who Think Young* Pamela's character insists she will not wed until she has a degree in hand and is more of an equal to Darren's playboy college student.

The Lively Set did quite well, pulling in older car racing fans as well as youths, proving there was an audience for this type of movie. The following year saw the release of Howard Hawks' medium-budgeted racecar drama *Red Line 7000* starring James Caan and Marianna Hill, followed in 1966 by MGM's all-star Academy Award–winning epic *Grand Prix*.

The popularity of *The Lively Set* and *For Those Who Think Young* were enough for Tiffin and Darren to be nominated for the *Photoplay* Gold Medal Award for Favorite Actress and Actor of 1964. They lost, respectively, to Ann-Margret and Elvis Presley. Though these films helped make Pamela popular with moviegoers, they also began to typecast her as a sort of brunette Sandra Dee for the teenage set.

Looking back on *The Lively Set* and *For Those Who Think Young*, Pamela remarked that when you are young you have your own taste and predilections. They were just not to her liking back then though she was happy they were well-liked by young people. Today, however, she is proud of these movies and her work in them, and is charmed by their innocence.

9

It's a Starlet-Eat-Starlet World

The Pleasure Seekers

In February 1964 it was announced that Jean Negulesco had agreed to direct Ann-Margret and Carol Lynley in *The Pleasure Seekers*. It was a remake of his 1954 Academy Award–winning film *Three Coins in the Fountain* for the same studio, 20th Century–Fox, but with the locale shifted from Rome to Madrid. The definitive sixties three-girls-out-to-trap-themselves-a-man movie, it follows the typical pattern where girls get boys, girls lose boys, and girls reunite with boys for a happy ending. Unlike its predecessor, the camp quotient is revved due to some bad dialogue, lively musical numbers *à la* Ann-Margret, and actors who would rather be making any movie but this. Despite its flaws, *The Pleasure Seekers* is well produced, with gorgeous, overly made-up gals and handsome stiff guys in front of beautiful Spanish scenery accompanied by a bouncy musical score, making it one of the sixties most underrated camp fests.

Without *Three Coins in the Fountain*, there would be no *Pleasure Seekers*. The hit movie, based on a novel by John H. Secondari, was the story of three girls who find love and romance in Rome. It was produced by Sol Siegel and beautifully shot on location in Italy in CinemaScope and De Luxe Color by Milton R. Krasner. Negulesco, who scored a big hit the year before with *How to Marry a Millionaire* (1953), about golddiggers (Betty Grable, Marilyn Monroe, and Lauren Bacall) who set out to trap rich husbands, was selected to direct based on the wonderful rapport he had with actresses and the success he had shooting in CinemaScope. He was able to get 20th Century–Fox to let him shoot *Millionaire* in the new process even though the film told a simple story unlike the epic *The Robe*, the first to be shot in CinemaScope. Prior to this, his most famous movie was *Johnny Belinda* (1948) where he directed Jane Wyman as a deaf mute who is raped and becomes pregnant. She won the Academy Award for Best Actress.

Three Coins in the Fountain focused on three women looking for romance in Rome. Anita (Jean Peters), thinking she can land a husband easier in the U.S., is soon to depart her job at a U.S. government agency, pretending she is engaged even though she is attracted to translator and struggling student Giorgio (Rossano Brazzi). Her replacement Maria (Maggie MacNamara), newly arrived in Italy, falls for Prince Dino Cessi (Louis Jourdan) despite the warnings about his womanizing. The least likable of the trio, she then devises an underhanded plan to snare the sympathetic prince by finding out his likes and feigning interest in them as well. Loyal secretary Frances (Dorothy McGuire) pines for her aristocratic though pompous writer boss John Frederick Shadwell (Clifton Webb).

Three Coins in the Fountain was a huge critical and financial success. It went on to receive three Academy Award nominations for Best Motion Picture and winning for Best Color Cinematography and Best Original Song, "Three Coins in the Fountain" by Jule Styne and Sammy Cahn.

The formula of three girls looking to trap themselves a man was not Negulesco's last before *The Pleasure Seekers*. He directed *The Best of Everything*, based on the bestseller by Rona Jaffe, about a trio of young single working women (Hope Lange, Suzy Parker, and Diane Baker) living and loving in Manhattan. Negulesco felt it was time again to revisit the women's romance picture with three simultaneously running plots. He opined, "The multiple-story technique is, I feel, peculiarly suited to today's frenetic pace. At the same time, sentiment has been absent from the American screen for too long a time. Women's stories have been terribly neglected."[1] Hence, he felt it was a perfect moment to update *Three Coins in the Fountain* for a more modern audience. Negulesco seemed to be dismissing (or was oblivious to) *Come Fly with Me*, released the year before. It too had three girls finding romance in beautiful European locations.

Negulesco insisted in the press that *The Pleasure Seekers* was not going to be a remake. He said, "Instead of Rome, this picture is set in Madrid. And instead of three girls and three men, I'm using four. Naturally the problems of American girls living in Madrid are similar to those in *Three Coins*, but this is 1964, so we'll have more difficulties."[2]

David Weisbart was tapped to produce and Edith Sommer wrote the screenplay. (Sommer already had experience with the three-girls-looking-for-romance movie as she scripted *The Best of Everything*.) Weisbart began his career in Hollywood as a film editor and worked as Negulesco's cutter on *Johnny Belinda*, which earned both Academy Award nominations. He began producing at the young age of thirty-six for Warner Bros. in 1951 before joining Fox. Mostly aimed at the younger audience, his films included four with Elvis Presley, *Love Me Tender*, *Flaming Star*, *Follow That Dream*, and *Kid Galahad*. He also previously worked with Carol Lynley on her first Fox movie *Holiday for Lovers* (1959) where she played the hip-talking teenage daughter of Clifton Webb and Jane Wyman.

To take the movie as far as he could from *Three Coins in the Fountain*, Negulesco spent time in Madrid discovering the feel of the city and had Edith Sommer join him to observe and capture the Spanish way of life in her script. "Fortunately or unfortunately, *Three Coins in the Fountain* was such a hit, and so closely identified with a European capital city, that everyone is tempted to make it a convenient point of reference," remarked Negulesco. "But times have changed, and no two cities have the same character or feel."[3]

He continued, "Everything that happens to our three amorous young ladies will be intimately knitted, I hope to an authentic feeling for the Spanish people and their country. If I succeed, *Three Coins* will not be around like Banquo's ghost, to invoke comparative memories."[4] To help achieve that end, Negulesco had Sommer keep the secretary character, but here she is torn between her boss (now a married wire service bureau chief) and a handsome playboy reporter on staff. The newcomer to Madrid is now the secretary's former college roommate and, following *Three Coins*, she falls for a rich womanizing cad though here he is not a prince. The other story plot about the government worker girl was jettisoned. Instead, a singer-dancer, in a chance meeting, falls in love with a poor doctor visiting Madrid from Costa del Sol. This subplot would add a number of songs to the movie, differentiating the film even more from *Three Coins*.

Negulesco was very happy with the screenplay and commented, "Edith Sommer has

Promotional poster for *The Pleasure Seekers* (20th Century–Fox, 1964).

provided us with a script in which the characters are different, the situations are different and the backgrounds and customs are different. The activity takes place in a different moral climate. To be sure, boy meets girl, etc.—but it would take more sophistication than I possess to employ any other basis for a film romance."[5]

Originally announced for *The Pleasure Seekers* in one of Hedda Hopper's columns were Ann-Margret as Fran the performer; George Chakiris, recent Academy Award winner for *West Side Story*, as Andres the proud doctor (Chakiris claims that he never knew he was considered for this and that his representatives at the time never mentioned it[6]); Carol Lynley as Maggie the secretary; and James Darren as Pete the reporter. Soon added to the cast were Paula Prentiss as Susie the newcomer to Madrid; Tony Franciosa as Emilio the cad; Efrem Zimbalist, Jr., as Paul Barton the editor; Dina Merrill as his wife Jane Barton; and Isobel Elsom as Emilio's sophisticated dowager mother.

Eventually, Chakiris, Darren, Zimbalist, and Prentiss (a great comedic talent but not right for the role of naïve Susie) were no longer being touted as part of the project. Perhaps the reason was that none had picture deals with Fox unlike Ann-Margret and Carol Lynley.

Academy Award nominee Tony Franciosa was the best known of the young male leads at the time. He had just completed the Fox western *Rio Conchos* for *Pleasure Seekers'* producer David Weisbart. Newcomer Andre Lawrence from Montreal, Canada, was cast as Andres. The actor had one film to his credit, playing the lead role of Diomedes in the French-Italian co-production *Seven from Thebes*.

Also cast in minor unbilled roles as Pete and Emilio's dates were a number of nubile starlets including Irene Tsu, Warrene Ott, and Shirley Parker. The only one to receive on-screen credit, however, was Shelby Grant, billed as "American Girl." She appears at the party where the married men take their mistresses, but does not have any lines. Obviously, her scene was cut but since Fox was trying to build her up, they left her billing as is in the credits. She would go on to have many lines as one of Derek Flint's (James Coburn) girlfriends in the hit spy movie *Our Man Flint* (1966).

Still not cast were the roles of Pete the reporter and Susie Higgins. Fox wanted to populate these roles from the ranks of its contract players. It pursued the extremely handsome Gardner McKay for the role of Pete. The heartthrob had just wrapped three seasons on the studio's hit TV series *Adventures in Paradise*. He was one of the most popular actors on television and one of the most difficult, walking away from the series in 1962 but still under contract. He turned down a hefty salary to star opposite Marilyn Monroe in *Something's Got to Give* despite the sex symbol's reportedly personal pleas to work with him. McKay didn't say no outright to *The Pleasure Seekers*, but didn't agree to it either. He kept the studio wondering and waiting.

Shortly after, in early May, Fox announced Adam West for Pete the reporter and newcomer Donna Michelle for Susie. West had co-starred with Robert Taylor on the TV series *The Detectives* during its last season (1961–62) and had just completed a supporting role as an ill-fated astronaut in the cult science-fiction movie *Robinson Crusoe on Mars*. Michelle was *Playboy* magazine's Playmate of the Year for 1964 and just signed a contract with Fox. She film-debuted playing a swinging party guest on a yacht in the studio's comedy *Goodbye Charlie* with Tony Curtis and Debbie Reynolds.

Neither actor, however, made it into the movie. Gardner McKay, after waffling for weeks, finally agreed to play Pete and Fox sent Pamela Tiffin from New York to meet with Negulesco. The director thought she was just perfect for the part of Susie. Pamela had other ideas: She didn't want to do the frivolous *Pleasure Seekers*. Threatened with suspension by Fox, the actress gave in. Obviously Pamela had no choice if she still wanted to work in movies, so she packed her bags and headed to Spain where she would reunite with her *State Fair* co-star Ann-Margret. After almost working together in *Come Fly with Me*, they got the chance to co-star in a different three-girls-looking-for-romance picture instead.

However, the dynamic was different now. While both were relatively unknown when they made *State Fair*, both were currently quite popular.

Busy stage and TV actor Brian Keith filled in for Efrem Zimbalist, Jr., as the older married boss whom Carol Lynley's Maggie pines for. Just prior, Keith had appeared in a series of popular movies for Walt Disney including *The Parent Trap* and *Savage Sam*. Zimbalist got his chance to romance Lynley in her next movie *Harlow* for Electronovision, playing a disguised William Powell to her thirties sex bomb, Jean Harlow.

With the casting complete, gossip maven Louella Parsons weighed in and cattily remarked, "I must say that my young friend, Richard Zanuck [20th Century–Fox's studio head], is a brave boy for he has set Carol Lynley, Ann-Margret, and Pamela Tiffin—all in the same picture. Doesn't Richard know how ambitious this trio of cute dolls is? While the exteriors will be done in Spain, interiors will be done in Hollywood. I personally think the attempt at scene-stealing will go on all over the place. The free-for-all—or film, if you insist, starts right after the first of the year."[7] How right this prediction turned out to be.

Hollywood in the mid-sixties was a starlet-eat-starlet world. Casting Ann-Margret, Lynley, Pamela Tiffin in the same movie without expecting any competition was just naïve and foolhardy. All were on the verge of superstardom and even competed against each other prior to this for other roles. All three were jockeying to hold onto their status or improve it. Pamela was frustrated with making teenage movies and let it be known, putting down James Darren in an interview and even refusing to make *The Pleasure Seekers*. Carol Lynley left her husband after having a baby because he claimed she wanted stardom and would sacrifice her marriage for it. And Ann-Margret was already playing the diva, refusing to do certain publicity promotions with her co-stars. So it is no wonder friendships did not form on this picture, unlike on *Come Fly with Me*.

Negulesco decided to shoot on location in Madrid, Barcelona, Toledo, and the Costa del Sol with his six leading players. Only Brian Keith and Dina Merrill stayed behind as they did not have any exterior scenes. Interiors would be shot in Hollywood. Living in Spain for a few years, Negulesco had come to appreciate immensely its distinctive beauty and customs and hoped to do justice to the country. He remarked that he hoped that, after seeing his movie, those who never had been would want to visit and those who had would want to return.

Days after his western *Rio Conchos* wrapped, producer Weisbart was working on *The Pleasure Seekers*. Just before filming began, he commented on what the shoot would be like. "We have six weeks of interiors on Fox sound stages … but in most instances, we are establishing the scene and highlighting the background here. This means two to four different locations a day in Madrid and you know what it means to get the first shot of a new scene more than once a day. It is a pretty harrowing experience for the entire unit, but everyone agrees it is worthwhile."[8]

As the cameras began to roll in Spain, the actors' frustrations and unhappiness began to immediately emerge. Most of the major players were contractually bound to appear in the movie and showed up to fulfill their obligations and collect their paychecks. Most went on record with the press regarding their negative feelings towards the script. With attitudes like this, it's no wonder friendships were not forged. To be fair, Tiffin too did not want to make this movie and voiced her discontent with the screenplay. It was only the threat of a suspension, preventing her from doing *any* film work, that made her change her mind.

Pamela had a friendly relationship with the powerful Hedda Hopper, who never wrote a disparaging remark about the actress as she had with others including Ann-Margret and Carol Lynley. So when the columnist asked Pamela to keep a journal about her time shooting in Spain, she agreed. The actress was discreet and kept any negative feelings toward her co-stars out of her piece.

According to Pamela, once the company arrived in Madrid, the first order of business was for costumer designer Renie to get busy. Renie won an Oscar for her design contributions to *Cleopatra* in 1963 and received Academy Award nominations for *The Model and the Marriage Broker*; *The President's Lady*; and *The Big Fisherman*. Renie was known for costuming her actors in elegant creations, so she decided to incorporate clothes from Spanish designers for her three leading ladies. "Carol Lynley and Renie began the hunt for a party dress, which successfully ended at Balenciaga, much to Carol's delight," wrote Pamela:

> Carol plays the part of an international wire service secretary in love with her married boss. The black- and flesh-colored lace dress was to be worn in a glamorous sequence, in which Carol finds herself at a "mistress" party.
>
> Although much of the women's wardrobe was bought from Madrid couturiers, director Jean Negulesco decided that I should wear a red linen dress for the bullfight sequence with Tony Franciosa.
>
> Renie and I selected Mitzou, the beautiful young French-Spanish designer, to do the dress. Mitzou is attracting more and more attention because of her unique ability to use suede.... Since I play the part of an art history major visiting my girl friends in Spain on a budget, red linen rather than red suede was chosen. Red, or any color of suede seems hard to imagine, but all of Mitzou's suede is dyed to order from Barcelona, and only the youngest, softest lamb skins are used, instead of cowhides, so familiar to Americans. I was so impressed with the colors and flattering softness that I bought an entire wardrobe there in green, red, blue, black, and fuchsia.
>
> As Ann-Margret plays an American entertainer working in Spain, her wardrobe had to be more casual, save for her fabulous flamenco costume.... Renie and Ann were careful to select simple, but appropriate, dresses for the type suited to the energetic young woman she plays.[9]

Negulesco was able to convince the board of the Prado Museum to permit one night's shooting of some of their masterpieces. He appealed to their desire to attract more tourists to the country explaining that the more people saw what Spain had to offer in the film, the more they would want to visit to experience first-hand the wonders of the country. The Prado agreed; it was the first time in almost eight years that the museum allowed a film company inside. One condition was that a museum official would be constantly present with a thermometer to make sure the arc lights did not raise the interior temperature above ninety degrees, the maximum allowed by the Prado.

Pamela, Tony Franciosa, and an unidentified actor playing Jose, a friend of Emilio's, were filmed admiring the artwork. "After five o'clock on a Friday evening, the entire crew filed quietly and quickly past the guards at the Prado," Pamela recalled of the night's shoot:

> The company left at three o'clock in the morning with footage of some of the most beautiful paintings in the world, in some cases centuries old. "Las Meninas," the technical triumph of Velázquez, was featured as I toured the museum, unaware that I am being followed by Tony Franciosa.
>
> Since Jean Negulesco preferred El Greco to Goya, the former's works are seen in great number, including the vertical treatments of "The Crucifixion," "The Baptism," and "The Annunciation." There was a certain magic to the night. The usual noise of a movie group in action

was hushed to whispers, with work being done as quietly as possible. Everyone just stood for a moment or two as the arc lights illuminated paintings.

The colors jumped out from what appeared to be complicated, dull canvasses, and glowed with a life of their own. Seen in such ideal light, one could truly understand why they were considered masterpieces.

Every precautionary fire and safety measure was taken, obviously. The concern was over the endless feet of cable weaving from room to room. The smoke that panicked some turned out to be the usual smoke from scrims over the arc lights. However, the human element was present. After finishing my emotional scene, Tony and I tripped over a cable and nearly fell through an El Greco. Life was never the same after that. No damage, luckily.[10]

All seem to go smoothly working with Franciosa in the Prado. He and Pamela even had spirited conversations about Goya since the actor had played the artist opposite Ava Gardner in *The Naked Maja* (1958). Pamela revealed that things got heated at other times between the actor and Negulesco. Franciosa got so miffed during a car scene that he sped off with the actress sitting beside him. He drove for over two hours at breakneck speed out of Toledo with his terrified passenger thinking he was going to kill them both. Pamela reported another time that Negulesco wanted the actor to change his tie and the hothead put his hands around the director's throat and threatened him.

Other sites where filming took place included the gardens at the Royal Palace of Madrid; the Quixote Statues in the Plaza de Espana; the Buen Retiro Park, one of Madrid's largest public parks; and the city's busiest traffic area, Cibeles Circle. Scenes shot there opened and closed the movie.

Sometime later, the crew, Ann-Margret and Andre Lawrence headed to Segovia where they were to film a picnic scene overlooking the ancient town and the castle Alcazar. Pamela and Carol Lynley accompanied them because they wanted to visit the city. They reportedly toured the neighboring Escorial Palace of the seventeenth century rulers and also visited the Valley of the Dead, which was a monument that Franco built for the Civil War dead. Their last stop was the majestic Raphael tapestry of The Fishermen [The Miraculous Drought of Fishes], a crypt built deep into the very mountainside. Pamela wrote, "To stand before the structure and to look out over the rugged terrain, so much like our American West, it was hard to believe that such an inhuman war was fought there."[11]

Most of the cast and crew were interested in seeing a bullfight. Pamela was not, even though her character attends one in the movie. Everyone scrambled to get tickets to see Spain's most popular matador El Cordobés in his first Madrid bullfight. Most did not and saw it on television. According to Pamela, she watched the great matador El Cordobés in action and, with the thousands of hushed Spaniards, was horrified when he was badly gored.

The Pleasure Seekers wrapped filming on location at Malaga on the Costa del Sol where choreography Bob Sidney hired gypsies to populate the background beach scene where Ann-Margret and Andre Lawrence perform the song "Everything Makes Music When You're in Love." Problems arose when, after every rehearsal, a number of gypsies would wander off. Some would eventually return while others were never seen again.

The location shoot ended in dramatic fashion. The entire cast was shaken after an explosion rocked the Castallana Hilton Hotel in Madrid where they were staying. Terrorists planted a bomb inside a car parked in front of the hotel and it went off at 10:30 p.m. while most of the actors were settled in for the night. The explosive was a concussion rather than

Pamela Tiffin, Ann-Margret, and Carol Lynley in Spain.

a fragmentation type so it was most likely designed to frighten and not harm innocent civilians. Soon after, the cast and crew returned to Hollywood.

The one obviously missing detail from Pamela's musings about the film shoot in Spain was spending any significant time with Ann-Margret. Pamela's relationship with the sexy redhead seemed to be nonexistent. Though they both starred previously in *State Fair*, they only had one scene together so it is not known if they really got to know one another beyond just meeting. In March 1964, both actresses were on the Universal Pictures lot simultaneously. Pamela had just completed *The Lively Set* for the studio and Ann-Margret did *Kitten with a Whip*. It was reported in the press that Pamela was posing for photos in a gallery next door to where Ann-Margret was being photographed. Since both hailed from Chicago, a studio rep thought it would be a nice idea to photograph them together. Pamela agreed and went to join Ann-Margret, who turned the actress away because she felt this should have been arranged and approved by her first. Hedda Hopper chastised Ann-Margret for her conduct and remarked, "She should remember the late Gene Fowler's great line: 'Success is a toy balloon among children armed with sharp pins.'"[12]

After working so pleasurably with Dolores Hart and Lois Nettleton on *Come Fly with Me*, Tiffin perhaps went into *The Pleasure Seekers* thinking she would bond with her co-stars here as well. Unfortunately, it was the complete opposite as competitiveness seemed to rule the day though they all got along very well professionally per Pamela. She admitted that she tried to befriend Ann-Margret, who was not interested. This is perhaps because Ann-Margret felt Tiffin was a rival? Years later when Ann-Margret revealed all in her auto-biography, she offered just two meager paragraphs about *The Pleasure Seekers*. She didn't even mention Lynley and Pamela. She then goes on to opine that the movie's failure was because "audiences simply did not want to envision me as a sophisticated woman of the world."[13] The actress comes across self-centered considering that she was not the sole star of the movie.

Though Pamela wrote that she spent a day sightseeing with Carol Lynley, her relation-ship with the pretty blond also did not develop into a friendship of any kind due to Carol's aloofness. But Pamela conceded that Lynley had just had a baby and was entitled to her privacy. Carol's two-year-old daughter, who accompanied her to Spain, did seem to keep her occupied. The actress admitted that she was worried about kidnappers, but government officials tried to allay her fears that kidnappings were rare in Spain. Despite their assurances, the actress hired a bodyguard to play it safe.

As for Gardner McKay, he totally snubbed Tiffin. She didn't know what his problem was but he never spoke to her off-camera. Diane McBain had the same experience with the actor on his next and last movie *I Sailed to Tahiti with an All Girl Crew*. In her memoir she described him as being "extremely tall, extremely handsome, and extremely boring" and that he "seemed most content when he was alone in his cabin."[14]

Tiffin described Andre Lawrence as "a younger, thinner Omar Sharif" and as "the 'lone wolf' of the company [who] quietly appeared and disappeared after each day's work."[15] More recently she indicated that the ambitious actor would have done *anything* to help fur-ther his career. He was solely focused on becoming a movie star, which did not come to be.

Production delays in Spain pushed back the start date of filming interiors in Holly-wood, causing Dina Merrill to drop out of the picture. She had warned the producer and Fox that she needed to be released by a certain date because she had a family commitment in Europe (the twenty-first birthday of her nephew) and could not miss it. The studio now was scrambling again to recast the role. It was offered to actress Gene Tierney, who still owed Fox one picture from her long-ago contract, though she was now semi-retired and living in Houston, Texas with her husband, oil man Howard Lee. The actress was best known for her title role in Otto Preminger's classic mystery film *Laura* (1944) though it was her sensational performance as an insanely jealous femme fatale in *Leave Her to Heaven* (1945) for which she received her lone Academy Award nomination. She had recently played small roles in Otto Preminger's political drama *Advise and Consent* (1962) and the movie version of Tennessee Williams' *Toys in the Attic* (1963).

When Tierney returned to the Fox lot, she was shadowed by reporters. Asked what she thought of the newest crop of Fox starlets that she was working with, she replied, "They are sweet, but I think Ann-Margret especially is loaded with sex appeal. Of course she is a different sort of girl from those of my time. At the end of the day, she gets on her motorcycle and drives home."[16] As for Tiffin's relationship with Gene Tierney, there wasn't any. Tiffin sheepishly admits that she was so awed by Tierney that they never spoke. Pamela did how-ever develop a nice friendly rapport with Brian Keith, who played Tierney's husband. They would go on to work together again right after this in the western *The Hallelujah Trail*.

Ann-Margret has a wonderful Flamenco dance sequence in the movie so the studio wanted to partner her with Spain's foremost dancer Antonio Gades. Trouble was, he was appearing at the New York World's Fair and the studio had to make a special appeal to the Spanish government to get him sprung. They intervened, and Gades was released for ten days. He flew to Hollywood to rehearse with Ann-Margret, filmed the scene, and returned to New York.

Fox hired the talented team of Sammy Cahn and James Van Heusen to write the film's songs. The duo won Academy Awards for "All the Way" from *The Joker Is Wild* (1957) and "Call Me Irresponsible" from *Papa's Delicate Condition* (1963). For *The Pleasure Seekers* they penned four excellent songs: the flashy title tune; the love song "Something to Think About"; the feel good "Everything Makes Music When You're in Love"; and the torch ballad "Next Time." The film's score was by one of Fox's most esteemed composers, Lionel Newman, a multiple Academy Award nominee.

The shoot came to an end in mid-summer and the actors all went their separate ways. However, the competitiveness between them reared its ugly head well after the film was completed. Hedda Hopper reported that though Ann-Margret was cooperative and took publicity photos with Carol Lynley and Pamela Tiffin early on, things changed and she refused to be photographed with her co-stars any longer. A billing war then erupted between the "stars" just as columnist Sheilah Graham predicted. After reporting about the making of the movie in Spain, Graham asked, "I'm wondering who will get top billing. Each girl is beautiful, talented—and temperamental."[17]

Tiffin's billing troubles began with *Come Fly with Me*. After being billed third for *State Fair*, she fell to fourth with *Come Fly with Me* after Dolores Hart, Hugh O'Brian, and Karl Boehm. When Tiffin's husband learned that she was dropping to fifth place in the credits here (after Ann-Margret, Franciosa, Lynley, and McKay), he wanted to fight the studio, but Pamela talked him out of it. She just wanted to put this experience behind her. At the time, she didn't understand that billing represented your current status and why it was such a contentious issue.

It is reasonable to accept Tiffin being billed third after Ann-Margret and Carol Lynley, both of who were coming off big box office hits (Ann-Margret with *Bye Bye Birdie* and *Viva Las Vegas*, and Lynley with *Under the Yum Yum Tree* and *The Cardinal*). However, no way did Franciosa, who played her romantic partner, and Gardner McKay, who had no movie career to speak of at this point (or ever), deserve top billing over her. This was probably a fight worth having with the studio. However, considering Pamela's feelings about working with her co-stars and how it turned out, it is understandable why she just wanted to let it go.

The one thing that Pamela enjoyed about making *The Pleasure Seekers* that her co-stars could not ruin for her was Spain itself. "I loved Madrid, especially for its museums, its theater, and opera," she exclaimed. "Because I knew I was going there, I had a chance to study up on the art treasures of the Prado Museum."[18]

Unfortunately for Pamela, her involvement with *The Pleasure Seekers* did not end once filming wrapped. 20th Century–Fox coaxed her to shoot a fashion layout with Carol Lynley at the Spanish Pavilion at the World's Fair that had just closed in Flushing Meadows, New York. Ann-Margret was noticeably AWOL.

20th Century–Fox planned to release *The Pleasure Seekers* in mid–January 1965 with a big launch premiere. However, problems arose at the studio. Notre Dame filed an injunction against Fox, charging the studio "had illegally misappropriated the name, symbols, and prestige of the university" in the movie *John Goldfarb, Please Come Home*. It was a confusing, unfunny comedy about Notre Dame's football team going to Fawzia, a fictitious Middle Eastern country, to play an exhibition game—but ordered to lose by the CIA. Starring were Shirley MacLaine as a reporter undercover in a harem; Peter Ustinov as the king of Fawzia; and Richard Crenna as a downed pilot ordered to coach Fawzia's football team. The movie was supposed to open in over 200 theaters across the nation. Fox had to pull it and offered *The Pleasure Seekers* as a replacement. Most theaters accepted, so *The Pleasure Seekers* snuck into theaters without fanfare or promotion. In fact, *John Goldfarb* ads were still running because it was too late to pull them. This move severely hurt the box office chances of *The Pleasure Seekers*, an innocent victim of the lawsuit between Fox and Notre Dame.

The Pleasure Seekers opens with Maggie Williams (Carol Lynley) racing to the airport in a taxi cab to meet her former college roommate Susie Higgins (Pamela Tiffin). Susie emerges from her taxi when she spots Maggie on the side of the road after her taxi was involved in a minor accident. The gals greet each other in the middle of the street. Not to take anything away from the lovely Lynley, but Pamela's stunning beauty shines through on the big screen even with her just standing while being catcalled by some local men as Maggie goes to talk to the policeman. They decide to take Susie's cab back to Maggie's apartment considering the many suitcases strapped to the roof. ("You know me. I'm a just-in-case packer," Susie remarks.) As they pass some of Madrid's most famous landmarks, Susie eagerly identifies them. Maggie remarks that Susie has been reading again, to which she replies, "For weeks—I know everything about Spain, except Spanish."

At Maggie's apartment, Susie jumps out of the cab and, looking at the building, gasps, "Oh, it's so creepy—but I love it!" As Maggie pays the driver, a group of young men ogles the pretty girls. Maggie tries to get her landlord to carry up Susie's luggage but it is too much for him; his wife will do it later. Once inside, Maggie introduces Susie to her roommate Fran Hobson (Ann-Margret) who "sings, dances, a little modeling, a little bit of everything." The gals share a huge three-bedroom apartment across from an amorous neighbor (Vito Scotti) who, in the film's running joke, is forever trying to catch a glimpse of them as they parade around the apartment in baby doll pajamas or even less.

As the ladies breakfast on the terrace, Susie asks the big question: "Okay, you've told me everything about Spain but you haven't mentioned the men. Didn't you hear me? *What about the men*?" When Fran tells her that there aren't any, a shocked Susie replies, "What—the place is crawling with men," as she points to a man across the way. They go on to explain that the rich, attractive ones are already married and the poor ones are too proud to take on a rich American girl. They suggest she just have an affair. When Susie demurs, Fran delicately asks if she ever "you know" and she replies, "No, but don't spread it around. Have you?" Instead of answering, Fran hands Susie a sardine sandwich and, as she is about to bite into it, she gulps and says, "They got their heads on!" Fran replies with a wry smile, "That's the best part."

Maggie rushes off to the office to deal with a minor crisis caused by playboy reporter Pete (Gardner McKay). He angered the landlord because he is unhappy with the bureau chief Paul Barton (Brian Keith) whom Maggie is smitten with despite the fact that he has a wife Jane (Gene Tierney). Pete trashes Paul to Maggie about how Barton edited his story to shreds and Maggie defends their boss. She then needs to help Barton plan a party for a New York bigwig and gets Fran the job as entertainment.

After accepting Maggie's offer, Fran sets off for rehearsal. While running in the street, she is hit by a man on a scooter and knocked to the ground. As she turns to tell him off, she softens when she sees it is a gorgeous dark-haired Spaniard (Andre Lawrence). He's a doctor named Andres but departs before Fran can learn more.

Susie visits the Prado where she is spied on by Emilio Lacayo (Tony Franciosa) and his friend Juan. They try to guess her situation as she views the artwork; Emilio thinks she is lonesome when she begins to cry. Following her outside, he opens the passenger door of his sports car and she automatically gets in. After regaining her bearings, she asks, "Who are you?" Emilio introduces himself and asks, "Who are you?"

He then takes Susie to lunch at a fancy restaurant. She admits that she thought he was a gigolo because he was at a museum in the middle of the day. He assures her that he is just out of work. Emilio is taken aback when Susie mentions her good friend Maggie Williams. Emilio insists she will not have good things to say about him, but Susie assures him that she won't listen. When he can't find his wallet to pay the tab, she puts her purse near him to pick up. He becomes indignant and scolds her for hurting a man's pride. She begins to cry again due to homesickness, and he apologizes.

Susie is excited to attend her first Spanish party, but Maggie tells her not to expect much. She is right. Susie sighs, "What a dog," as the men are all with their wives and do not pay any attention to the beautiful single ladies. Emilio arrives with a handsome brunette on his arm. Susie points him out to Maggie as the man she met at the Prado. Maggie immediately tells her friend to start running because Emilio is "the most heartless, corrupt, inhuman man that ever lived." Susie replies, "Is that all? I was afraid that he was a gigolo." Emilio catches the ladies' eyes and, as he makes his way over alone, Susie recites, "He's a creep. He's a creep. He's a creep." Emilio pays her no attention and instead greets Maggie, who "introduces" him to Susie. He then asks Maggie out for lunch and departs without a word other than "hello" to Susie. Even still, she sighs, "Isn't he wonderful?"

Maggie, from experience, explains to her friend how Emilio will end the full court rush on her with a marriage proposal to get her to tumble into bed with him. Instead of turning her off to him, Susie is intrigued and anticipates his upcoming courtship. She does agree he is a creep, but then asks, while eyeing Emilio with his date, "If I am next on his list, why is he spending so much time with her?"

The party entertainment begins as the guests are treated to a solo performance by Flamenco dancer Antonio Gades, accompanied by Emilio Diego on guitar. Fran dances with Gades for a bit before she belts out "The Pleasure Seekers" wearing a skintight baby pink evening gown. Ann-Margret is a knockout and uses all her patented exaggerated arm moments and hair-tossing to deliver the number with gusto. She is able to steal back the movie from Tiffin … for a moment. Susie finds a man to dance with so Maggie asks her lap dog Pete to drive her home after her dance with Paul is interrupted by his wife.

The next day an assured Emilio, packing an overnight bag, calls to invite Susie to spend the day in Toledo. Fran is sitting nearby and quips, "Toledo—that's a new one. Tell him no!" Susie has another idea and accepts, to Fran's surprise. However, Emilio gets the bigger surprise as Susie gets into the car with Fran already sitting in back. As they speed through the plaza, Fran yells for Emilio to stop as she spots Andres speaking to the owner

Publicity photograph of Pamela Tiffin in *The Pleasure Seekers* **(20th Century–Fox, 1964).**

of the café where he brought her after the accident. She runs over to Andres talking to the café owner. Fran invites herself to spend the day fishing with him in Segovia and goes back to Emilio's car. Before Fran can finish asking why she won't be going with them, Emilio sarcastically quips, "What a terrible shame!" and drives off, leaving the singer in the street yelling to Susie, "Remember, the Spanish word for no is no!"

Fran and Andres realize they are falling in love as she sings the maudlin ballad "Something to Think About" while they picnic. Andres tries to stay aloof, but can't resist Fran's charms. In Toledo, Emilio takes Susie to see artworks by El Greco and other attractions. While at a hotel restaurant overlooking the city, Susie apologizes to Emilio for not trusting him and thanks him for being such a gentleman. Unbeknownst to her, the slick guy has already booked a suite for that night. Because he feels the need to be truthful with her, Emilio admits that every bad thing she has heard about him is true. When she defends him, he proposes marriage and Susie realizes that he is just playing her as Maggie predicted. However, she decides to teach him a lesson and accepts his proposal. She then pushes to meet his family and to set a date. Emilio says they need to see if they are "compatible" first. Susie states that is out of the question now that they are engaged and says they need to see if they are "compatible" in other ways. She says, "We both like art galleries. What about sports? Nothing that is stimulating or physical—no touching." He suggests a bullfight, but a nervous Susie says first it is time to take her home.

Later that week Emilio takes Susie as promised to a bullring where she watches most of it with her eyes closed behind dark sunglasses; almost insults the matador by throwing back his hat given to her in honor of the killing of the bull; and faints when it is over. In front of her building, Susie releases Emilio from their engagement. She says Maggie was right about him all along and sheepishly admits that she thought it would be different with her. Shocked that he is being dumped, Emilio sweet-talks his way back into Susie's arms and she falls for it, later gushing to Maggie that Emilio proposed for real this time.

Fran flies off with Andres to the Costa del Sol to visit his home. At a beach party, a bikini-clad Fran and Andres, looking very sexy in tight jeans and an open shirt, sing "Everything Make Music When You're in Love," while the locals join in and dance. Afterward, Fran asks what time her plane is and Andres quickly replies, "There's another one tomorrow morning," as they kiss. At the airport the next day, a lovelorn Fran begs Andres to return with her or let her stay to help him with his clinic, but he can't agree to either.

Meanwhile, Susie is preparing to meet her future mother-in-law—or so she thinks. Not wanting her skirt to wrinkle, she prances around her house in her panties and blouse waiting for Emilio to take her to meet his mother. When the doorbell rings, she is disappointed to see it is only Fran back from the Costa del Sol. She tells Susie it is over between her and Andres because "he can't afford me." In one of the movie's silliest moments, Susie, wearing five pounds of eye makeup, puts her head back because she begins to cry for her friend and doesn't want her mascara to run. Fran, with what looks like ten pounds of eye makeup, does the same. She then ridiculously says, "Wait a minute. What I am doing? I don't have any mascara on." Realizing that Emilio is one hour late, Susie rushes to his family's estate thinking she misinterpreted Emilio's instructions.

The ludicrousness of that prior scene leads to Tiffin's most dramatic scene and the movie's best thanks to the sympathetic playing of the elegant Isobel Elsom and the poignant performance from Pamela. Susie goes to meet Emilio's mother at her house. She is in the study with her secretary. Susie is surprised that not only was she not expected, but that Emilio never mentioned it. When Susie tells them that Emilio proposed to her, the looks on their faces makes Susie realize something is not right. The secretary exits and Mrs. Lacayo asks Susie how well she knows her son. Susie assures her that she is well aware of his techniques with women, but goes on and on about how different it was with her than with the prior girls. Pamela is touching as she really is trying to convince herself of it rather than Emilio's mother. Finally, dejected, she asks if he has done this before, to which Mrs. Lacayo responds, "Probably." Now knowing that she was the only one gullible enough to fall for his lies, Susie tearfully asks why he would do something like that as Emilio drives up with a beautiful raven-haired French girl in his sports car. Mrs. Lacayo tells Susie, who stands up to leave, they both will find out why.

As he sprints up the stairs to his room, his mother calls Emilio into her library. Before he notices Susie, he tells his mother in Spanish that he is driving to Toledo with his new friend; his mother repeats it in English so Susie can understand. A hurt Susie slinks back down into her chair. Emilio thinks his mother was responsible for Susie being there, but she assures him it was entirely his fault. As Susie sits there mortified, Emilio's mother says she does not know why her son would do something so despicable. She expounds on his charm, but also admits her son is also "selfish, spoiled, and a cad." She then apologizes profusely to Susie for any pain her family has brought her. A tearful Susie rushes out without a word, and Emilio tells his mother she forgot one thing when describing him. She knows exactly what he means and says he was also a coward in his behavior to the girl. Shamefully, Emilio agrees.

Maggie comes home to find both Susie and Fran packing for home. In an amateurishly acted scene, Ann-Margret as Fran breaks down into tears (never seen as she quickly covers her face with her hands, continuing her streak of some of the worst fake crying ever captured on film by any major actress) while explaining all to Maggie. Susie rails to Maggie that she is mad at herself for being such a fool for falling for Emilio's lies, but tearfully admits she still loves him. Before Maggie can wallow in their sadness, she is invited to a party by Paul. They are caught by his wife Jane, who confronts Maggie in the ladies room and calls her "a little tramp."

Jane rushes out of the party with Paul trailing after her. Pete comes to Maggie's rescue and leaves his "little lotus blossom" (Irene Tsu) in the hands of other willing men. On the steps where a statue of Don Quixote is displayed, a drunken Maggie rehashes the night and says, "She called me a little tramp." She admits she fell in love, but wiped the man's wife right out of her mind. Drunk and depressed, Maggie clutches Pete and wants his advice on what to do next. Pete drives her home. As they pull up in front of her house, she finishes the sad tale of Fran and Andres and Susie and Emilio. "Nice girls," she says. "Really rather nice—what happens to us? We all crash into flames." She then bemoans that even the man across the alley is not interested in them any longer. "We're too old for him," she explains before collapsing into Pete's arms. Maggie asks Pete to kiss her and as he makes his move, she passes out cold.

The secretary then decides she too has had it with Spain and decides to join her friends on a flight back to the States. Before they leave, they all reluctantly agree to attend a farewell party thrown by the Bartons. As Fran performs a torch song, she is elated to see Andres, who was prodded to come by Paul. They have a tearful reconciliation, as do Susie and Emilio, who shows up with his mother. Paul then announces that the party is actually for him and his wife; they are returning to New York, leaving a surprised Pete as the new bureau chief. Pete asks what he has to do about everything, and Paul replies, "Ask Maggie." The movie ends with all three couples reunited as they converge in separate vehicles on a police officer in one of many of Madrid's traffic circles while a chorus sings a reprise of the movie's title tune.

Reviews for *The Pleasure Seekers* were mixed. All had praise for Daniel L. Fapp's colorful cinematography of Spain and the Prado's art masterpieces that looked glorious in CinemaScope; Lionel Newman's lively musical score; and the Flamenco dancing by the renowned Antonio Gades. What transpired in front of the beautiful Spanish scenery was not as well received. Reviewers who did enjoy the movie used words like "diverting," "pleasant," "frothy," "enjoyable," "a feast for the eye," and "appealing" to describe it. An equal amount of negative reviews (for instance, Moira Walsh called it "pathetic") were received in sometimes a cruel but witty manner:

> "Film is aimed at the cliché seekers."—Mike McGrady, *Newsday*

> "What *Three Coins in the Fountain* did for Rome, this tries to do for Madrid. Or shall we say *to* Madrid? Three more insipid girls involved in more insipid romances could hardly be imagined."—William Wolf, *Cue*

Arguably, the funniest pan came from the *New York Morning Telegraph* critic who remarked, "Maybe John Goldfarb should come home after all. The picture that was thrown on the screen ... to fill the void left by his banishment under edict of law may stir no wrath in any institution of higher education, but it does leave a sodden, soggy feeling in the pit of the stomach that comes as near to colic as any ailment I can think of."

Pamela outclassed her two female co-stars and, as with *Come Fly with Me*, received the most consistently positive reviews, which was no surprise considering her comedic ability. The *Variety* reviewer found her "pert and appealing." A.H. Weiler of the *New York Times* described Tiffin as "cute ... [she] easily handles a role calling for wide-eyed naïveté." James Powers of *The Hollywood Reporter* called Pamela "attractive," but added that her "gift for comedy might have been better exploited."

Kevin Thomas in the *Los Angeles Times* had the most praise for the brunette pleasure seeker: "[Acting] honors go to the radiant Pamela Tiffin, whose delicate beauty and exquisite coloring are highlighted against a series of famous paintings.... She also has the best scene, a painful confrontation with the elegant Isabel Elsom, who portrays Franciosa's compassionate mother...."

The cast received a backhanded compliment from Helen Anne Aspbury of *The Sun*: "Carol Lynley, Pamela Tiffin, Ann-Margret and Gardner McKay are not walking studies of the art of acting, but they do their jobs inoffensively." Richard Roud of *The Guardian* found that all three roles, as played by the actresses, were "delightfully characterized" and Nadine M. Edwards of the *Hollywood Citizen-News* found the movie to contain "exemplary acting by a bevy of beauties."

All three actresses are made up and styled gorgeously in *The Pleasure Seekers*. Ann-Margret shakes her wild mane, sings, and dances extremely well, especially in the wonderfully staged number on the beach with throngs of locals and children dancing along. Her dramatic scenes, however, particularly when she cries (or makes the attempt), are laughable. Carol Lynley pouts prettily as a secretary whose only visible job duties seem to be making coffee and dusting off her boss's desk—so much for that college education. If Negulesco wanted to be more with-it, she should have been a reporter. Carol does fare better acting-wise than Ann-Margret due to her ladies room confrontation with Gene Tierney and her drunken scene near the end.

Pamela Tiffin, however, still steals the movie from both of them. She has the most rounded part and juggles the dramatic, comedic, and romantic scenes quite well. She also gets the best exterior scenes in Spain; the viewer does not mind looking at a vision as lovely as she in front of some gorgeous Madrid and Barcelona scenery. One of her most amusing scenes is when Susie attends her first Spanish party and Maggie schools her friend on the caddish ways of Emilio. Looking beautiful with her hair in a French Twist and wearing an elegant black dress with a sparkling black-and-white patterned wrap around her arms, Tiffin elicits laughs with just the quizzical look on her face or a quick quip as the conflicted Susie knows she should not care about Emilio, but cannot help being attracted to the no-good playboy. Lynley is lovely to look at here as well in her powder blue sparkly dress and is quite amusing too as she issues her warning, but Tiffin steals the scenes with her ability to play naïve humorously.

Another reason Pamela comes off best is that the screenwriter reversed her character's motivation from *Three Coins in the Fountain*. In that movie, Maggie MacNamara's new-comer to Rome is calculating and puts a plan in motion to trick Louis Jourdan's womanizing prince into falling for her. He gets the audience's sympathy as she lies and coos her way into his heart. Meeting his mother forces the guilt-ridden girl to confess to the prince after-wards. She comes off childish and not very sympathetic. While she lies in her bed pining for the prince, you feel she got what she deserved. In *The Pleasure Seekers*, Tiffin's Susie is the innocent throughout while Tony Franciosa's womanizing Emilio is the true cad with getting Susie into bed his main goal. Susie plays her own game in trying to checkmate Emilio's technique with the ladies, but he is just too experienced and slick for her. This makes the meeting between a duped Susie and his mother much more dramatic and heart-rending.

Tiffin also lucked out because her leading man is the most talented of the young roman-tic actors cast. Gardner McKay comes across like a poor man's Troy Donahue and is not as appealing as he should be. He admitted in *TV Guide* that he wasn't a good actor and put partial blame on the directors he worked with on his television program *Adventures in Par-adise*. "Nobody had given me help to improve. I had a long line of directors who were con-cerned with keeping the front office happy than working with the actors. When I suggested acting lessons, I was told to forget it because it would make me more introspective."[19] McKay should have taken his own advice.

Andre Lawrence with his smoldering dark looks is quite striking, but also quite wooden. One wonders why the producer cast him opposite arguably their biggest star. Only Franciosa makes an acting impression. He and Pamela make a handsome couple and play off each other very well. The actor is able to juggle Emilio's sleaziness with women with the true feelings he is having for Susie but trying to suppress. The scene with Isobel Elsom, after Tiffin rushes out, and he admits to being a coward as well as a cad, is well-played and quite tender for a movie of this ilk.

Just prior to *The Pleasure Seekers'* release, Negulesco predicted that his movie would be a hit because it was reaching an audience underserved by Hollywood. "Films these days are made by men," remarked the director, "and nearly all of them, seemingly, for men. They even have trouble finding five serious nominees in feminine categories of the Academy Awards. And yet, it has been an axiom of the film industry that women determine the audi-ence. We propose to change all this with *The Pleasure Seekers*."[20] Pamela was not so confi-dent. When asked at the time what she thought of *The Pleasure Seekers*, she replied, "There are good, bad and mediocre commercial movies. I suspect this will be a bad one."[21] For her personally it was that and more, though her fans just love this movie. Tiffin, however, admitted that she was so humiliated when watching it in a theater, she sat there with her hand over her face so no one would recognize her.

What should have embarrassed Pamela was the poster art rather than the actual movie. Front and center is Ann-Margret shimmying in the long tight gown she wears when performing the title song. A smaller image of Carol Lynley in a slip and an even smaller shot of Pamela in a blouse and panties surround the redhead under the titillating tagline "Where do good little girls go when they want to be bad?" It is quite ironic that Negulesco hyped his movie as being a film women would want to see and then exploits his leading ladies in the print ads.

Despite Pamela's feelings for the movie, it was reported that the actress agreed to Fox's request to go on a European publicity tour to promote it. However, she backed out due to her husband's wishes. He felt that they had spent the better part of their marriage apart due to Tiffin's shooting movies in Hollywood or on location, and they needed some time together.

The Pleasure Seekers missed out on awards season for pictures released in 1964 because it hadn't opened in Los Angeles. The following year it surprisingly picked up an Academy

Emilio (Tony Franciosa) and Susie (Pamela Tiffin) get the news that Fran (Ann-Margret) won't be accompanying them to Toledo in a scene from *The Pleasure Seekers* (20th Century–Fox, 1964).

Award nomination for Best Scoring: Adaption or Treatment. Not surprisingly, it lost to that year's Best Motion Picture winner, *The Sound of Music*.

Pamela's prediction that *The Pleasure Seekers* was going to be a "bad" movie proved to be right and wrong. Though most critics considered it an inferior remake of *Three Coins in the Fountain*, it has remained one of Pamela's most popular movies to this day. It is a bad-movie-we-love and remains a very entertaining camp romance in the "three girls" genre. Negulesco promised that this version would be more modern than his original, but all three gals act as staid and marriage-minded as their fifties counterparts though they do throw around "having affairs" a lot. Ann-Margret's Fran hits the sheets with Andre Lawrence's Andres (who could blame the girl with that broodingly handsome Latin lover hovering around her), but she keeps moaning about not being able to marry him due to the stupid reason that he is too poor and proud to take on a "rich" American wife. Well, Fran is poor too and scrapes by taking singing and dancing gigs. Lynley's Maggie, despite being called a tramp, never once acts on her sexual feelings for her boss and they are as chaste with each other as two Mormons on a blind date. All she does is talk and talk about her attraction. At least Tiffin's Susie starts as virgin and says up front she will remain one until her wedding day, archaic as they sounds today. Predictable yes, but so prettily done and it even can cause a tear or two from even the most hardened of viewers who love a happy ending.

Despite the cast and expense laid out to shoot on location, *The Pleasure Seekers* performed modestly, grossing an estimated $2 million (barely breaking even). An additional $1.2 million worldwide gross helped it generate a small profit. Sneaking it into theaters without promotion was a major factor in hurting its box office chances, but even when it officially opened in January 1965 in some major cities, it still disappointed when compared to *Three Coins in the Fountain*. That reaped $5 million in the U.S. alone, and was one of the Top Ten highest grossing films for 1954.

The Pleasure Seekers has grown in stature over the years, but not for being a great movie. Gay men have embraced the campiness of it; a lot were introduced to it from the myriad times it has aired on broadcast television. After its initial network primetime debut, *The Pleasure Seekers* became a staple of syndication.

It is not surprising that *The Pleasure Seekers* remains popular and is one of the movies propelled Pamela to cult icon status. When released on DVD-on-Demand in 2014, Jaime S. Rich of the website *DVD Talk* described Tiffin as "the girl-next-door version of Claudia Cardinale." Though nowhere near the iconic camp status of *What Ever Happened to Baby Jane?* or *Faster, Pussycat! Kill! Kill!*, it is ripe for discovery by gay millennials. For today's audience, it reeks of campiness from its trio of leading ladies at their 1960s starlet beauty and fashion pinnacle and the male mannequins who play opposite them, to the dated dialogue, to the entertaining musical numbers, to the gorgeous scenery. Most amusingly is that these gals think they are independent-minded and want to live their own lives by 1964 standards with even Ann-Margret and Carol Lynley's characters copping to not being virgins, but deep down all they want to do is trap husbands just like their *Three Coins in the Fountain* sisters in 1954. Despite what Negulesco claimed at the time, women in the movies had not come a long way, baby.

10

Where's Pamela?

The Hallelujah Trail

Pamela Tiffin was determined to progress to adult roles and not appear in any more teenage movies. Deciding to get serious with her career, she opted to take acting lessons, bucking the advice of Hal Wallis, Billy Wilder, and Ray Milland, who told her that she did not need them due to her beauty. This only frustrated her even more because she was not getting the roles she truly desired and everybody wanted to re-imagine her. "The publicity people wanted to make me into another Grace Kelly," Pamela stated at the time:

> Some thought I should be another Audrey Hepburn. Mr. Wallis wanted me to be another Greta Garbo. The trouble comes when you don't fit the image, then they try to superimpose the image over you. I don't want to cut my hair. I don't want to bleach my hair. I don't want to wear Sandra Dee and Doris Day clothes."[1]

Pamela began studying in New York with the esteemed Stella Adler, whose discoveries included Marlon Brando. Initially apprehensive, Tiffin was surprised how much she enjoyed the experience. "I used to think acting school was for showoffs, misfits, ostentatious Bohemians, but ours isn't at all like that," she remarked.[2] She was learning a lot from her acting coach. She thought Adler would teach her the basics like how to laugh and how to cry. Instead, Tiffin learned how to be more observant wherever she was and how to interpret plays.

Vowing to make no more surfing or teenage movies, Tiffin stated, "I'm waiting for a story about a believable girl. A believable girl and the pertinent things that happen to her."[3] Perhaps the closest she was offered to this ideal character was the role of Burt Lancaster's daughter in United Artists' western comedy *The Hallelujah Trail* (1965), about the temperance movement in the Old West. Most likely, she had to do this to fulfill her contract with the Mirisch Brothers. It turned out to be a thankless role, though it was a new genre for her and she had the opportunity to work with a wonderful veteran cast that also included Lee Remick, Jim Hutton, Donald Pleasence, and Brian Keith.

Pamela began making *The Hallelujah Trail* in the late summer of 1964. It was a big-budget epic satire about a whiskey dealer trying to get a shipment of his product to the mining town of Denver before winter. Indians want to hijack it; temperance ladies want to stop it; Denver's militia wants to protect it; and the cavalry is caught in the middle trying to maintain law and order. The movie was directed by John Sturges. The screenplay by John Gay (who won an Academy Award for his contribution to the screenplay for 1963's *How the West Was Won*) was based on a novel by Bill Gulick. For this lampoon on the Old

West, Gay told Sturges' biographer Glen Lovell that he and Sturges tried to do "the opposite of the stereotype and exaggerate the stereotype at the same time."[4] For instance, they had the temperance leader take a swig of alcohol after all her preaching.

Sturges wanted James Garner for the lead of the cavalry officer and father of Pamela. Garner passed because he found the script not very good and also a bit insulting to Native Americans. Other roles were offered to Lee Marvin and Art Carney, who also turned the movie down. Stepping in for them were Burt Lancaster, Brian Keith, and Donald Pleasence. Lee Remick played the temperance leader who strays and Jim Hutton a young cavalry officer smitten with Tiffin.

Pamela accepted the role of cavalry officer Lancaster's temperance movement daughter because she really liked the script and that her wardrobe was going to be designed by Edith Head, who created the costumes for her first movie, *Summer and Smoke*. She mused at the time, "I love the quiet of the Old West after the hurly-burly of Europe. I find the people kinder, more gracious and—well, the kind of people I really love."[5]

Another reason Pamela took the role was because her part would wrap in six weeks. However, after she received the final screenplay, she found out that she was needed from beginning to end, keeping her away from her husband for a few months.

Due to her past success in comedy, Pamela was not a surprise casting choice, but Lancaster was. The brawny star of such classic movies as *The Killers, From Here to Eternity, Come Back, Little Sheba, The Rose Tattoo, Trapeze, Sweet Smell of Success, Elmer Gantry, Judgment at Nuremberg* and *Birdman of Alcatraz* had never done a movie comedy before because (he claimed) nobody ever asked him. After this was released, nobody would ever again.

The Mirisch Brothers entrusted John Sturges with a hefty $7 million budget to deliver a super-sized motion picture to be shot in the Cinerama process of Ultra Panavision 70. According to Glen Lovell, from its inception the movie was destined to be "promoted as a road show attraction that would play the latest domed theaters … with over-

Pamela Tiffin, ca. 1964.

ture, intermission, reserved seating, and exit music."[6] The director had helmed a number of impressive westerns prior to this including *Gunfight at the O.K. Corral*, *Last Train from Gun Hill* and *The Magnificent Seven*, plus his biggest hit, the World War II adventure *The Great Escape*, so he was a good bet to deliver a first-rate movie. Sturges also had a brief history with Pamela Tiffin when she almost played a Japanese woman in *A Girl Named Tamiko* for him.

Filming *The Hallelujah Trail* on location proved to be a major adventure for cast and crew. Shooting was to take place between July to September when the New Mexico weather is normally beautiful and dry. However, Gallup was hit with the heaviest summer rains it had seen in over forty-seven years. Continuous downpours forced the production to close down for a month and return to Los Angeles.

When filming re-commenced in Gallup, a number of other problems arose. A Native American from the Navajo tribe drove his bright blue pickup truck into a scene while the cameras were rolling and disrupted the shoot, claiming the movie company was trespassing on private property. The crew produced papers proving that they were paying a fee to his Tribal Council, but he still refused to move his vehicle out of camera range. The production team had to disguise it as a covered wagon.

Tim Zinnemann worked as one of the many assistant directors on the movie. The son of Academy Award–winning director Fred Zinnemann, he started his career in the movie industry as an assistant film editor in Rome. When he returned to Hollywood, he began working as a second assistant director. *The Hallelujah Trail* was one of his first movies. He would go on to work as first assistant director and production manager on such films as *The Happening*, *Bullitt*, *The Reivers*, *The Great White Hope*, *Carnal Knowledge*, *The Cowboys*, *Day of the Locust*, and *Smile*. In 1975 he began producing movies including *Straight Time*, *The Long Riders*, *Fandango*, *The Running Man*, *Pet Semetary*, and *The Island of Dr. Moreau*.

As a novice assistant director on this major studio production, Zinnemann was assigned to make sure the cast, particularly leading ladies Remick and Tiffin, were taken care of. "My work day started between four and five in the morning and we worked until ten and eleven each night," he recalled:

> We filmed six days a week and had to work part of Sunday as well. There was no such thing as overtime, meal breaks, or the like. I was the "key second" AD, which meant I was in charge of three or four other guys. In turn, I reported to the first AD, who in turn took orders from the director. I was not allowed to talk to the director directly, but if he addressed me I was always to call him Mr. Sturges or sir. I would make sure the cast got their calls, got in and out of makeup, and were put in the right car to take them to the set.
>   On the set my main job, apart from getting the cast from their trailers to the set, was setting the background action per the instructions of the first AD. This meant that I was usually on a horse in wardrobe lining up wagons, cavalry, Indians, etc. None of this was intimidating because I was carrying out someone else's orders and I was far too tired to think about how big the whole affair was, which it was.[7]

With such a huge production being filmed on location, it is not surprising that there were a number of mishaps. More seriously, most of the cast and crew suffered from a painful stomach ailment nicknamed "Geronimo's Revenge," sidelining them for a day or two. The biggest problem, however, was just plain boredom. The town of Gallup did not have much to entertain the cast and crew when they were not filming. Lee Remick took to needlepoint. Burt Lancaster would escape to Los Angeles if he had a day off. The crew would gather at a local bar every night and pass the time drinking and counting freight cars that chugged by the window. Donald Pleasence and Tom Stern frequented a Chinese restaurant. Pamela Tiffin learned to play football and later to fly an airplane. Fly an airplane?!

The day's film had to be flown to Hollywood each night. A plane would make a short flight from Gallup to Albuquerque. The pilot would allow Pamela to sit in the cockpit to observe. Once on the ground, the film would be transferred to another plane for the longer flight to Los Angeles.

Boredom struck the actors even while working. Making movies involves a lot of down time waiting for the shot to be set up with lights, cameras in place, etc. According to Pamela, she and Lancaster would play jokes on each other to maker their fellow actors laugh. She recalled one particular incident when she and Lancaster started eating watermelon and couldn't stop until they both got sick. Lancaster began vomiting and Tiffin passed out due to the heat. Sturges was called over to see what was going on with two of his leading players. Despite his macho reputation, Sturges did not berate his stars and, per Tiffin, kept the shooting atmosphere relaxed and peaceful, which resulted in the actress having a wonderful time making this movie.

Though Sturges seemed to be more relaxed with Pamela and her co-stars, Tim Zinnemann remarks that his impression was that the director "was rather formal and uptight. I don't remember him spending too much time with the actors, but he must have. He definitely was the man in charge and seemed to thrive in the middle of this vast operation."[8]

While Pamela and the rest of the production team were slogging through, the Navajo tribesmen hired to work on *The Hallelujah Trail* were having a grand time. One hundred of them worked as extras, playing Sioux Indians. When the shoot shut down due to the rains, some of them were flown to Los Angeles (their first plane ride) for their first visit to Disneyland.

Working on *The Hallelujah Trail* turned out to be a joy for Pamela, especially after making *The Pleasure Seekers*. The natural setting of Gallup, New Mexico, and the Native Americans had a profound effect on the actress. "Gallup may not be the living end for a lot of people, but I love it," she remarked after completing the movie:

> It was exquisitely beautiful, with the buttes and bluffs changing their magnificent hues and shades with each new angle of sun. More important was the friendliness of the Indians and their lovely, simple way of life. Ted Markland, one of the actors in the picture, is an authority on Indians and spends his vacations and free time as their guest. Ted took me to a lot of his Navajo friends, lying in their simple hogans, and I got to know and love their uncomplicated existence.[9]

Zinnemann still feels that shooting in Gallup really made it a wonderful filmmaking experience. "I loved the area we were shooting in and the fact that we were outdoors all the time," he said. "Also I got to spend a great deal of time each day on a horse."[10] It also helped the newcomer hone his craft. "I was part of a huge production and learned how to be at ease working on a very large scale without being intimidated. It gave me a lot of confidence as I moved on to other productions. After this experience, nothing was ever too big or too complicated for me to handle."[11]

Another reason Pamela enjoyed making this movie was because of the cast (something she could not say about *The Pleasure Seekers*). She liked Jim Hutton, who played her love interest, and adored Burt Lancaster who she truly liked acting opposite and hanging around with on the set. Tiffin also found Lee Remick to be friendly and nice to work with.

Pamela was pleasurable to work with as well per Zinnemann. Luckily for the young AD she was nothing like Carroll Baker, with whom he worked on *Harlow*. He described Baker as "a *diva* of the worst kind—completely out of control most of the time. Neither man nor beast seemed able to tame her."[12] As for Tiffin, Zinnemann remembers her "with great fondness" and remarked that she "was very sweet and approachable. She was nothing at all like Carroll Baker. I did spend time with Pamela occasionally when we had some time. I remember her as being just part of the crew."[13] In fact he interacted with all the actors except Burt Lancaster. "He was very professional, but I had very little to do with him. When not working, he stuck to himself."[14]

According to Zinnemann the gunfight scene in the sand storm was "a real bitch"[15] to shoot, which is not surprising considering the scale in coordinating the actors and hundreds of extras. "We shot it with giant wind machines using fuller's earth," recalled Zinnemann.

Publicity photograph of Pamela Tiffin and Lee Remick in *The Hallelujah Trail* (United Artists, 1965).

"While doing it we were pretty much blinded and unable to breathe. When we saw the dailies it didn't even look like a dust storm, you could see everything quite clearly. We had to shoot the scene all over again, this time using debris and other things that would show up on camera."[16]

The Hallelujah Trail was marred by a tragedy: One of the stuntmen was killed in a stunt gone wrong. Two men dressed as cowboys were on a covered wagon being pulled by a truck into a ravine. One jumped clear, but the other's costume may have got snagged on the wagon and he was catapulted into the air with the wagon. He landed on the ground only to have the wagon crash down upon him. To make matters worse, his wife and young children were on the location that day to watch the filming. Reportedly, Sturges was devastated over the accident and tried to have it cut from the final print, but the producers said no and it remained in the movie.

The Hallelujah Trail was Pamela's eighth movie and the fifth that sent her on location. Despite the time separated from her husband, the actress appreciated the opportunities the movies gave her shooting away from the confines of Hollywood soundstages. It seemed she was always packing her bags to travel from one country or location to another: Germany for *One, Two, Three*; England, France, and Austria for *Come Fly with Me*; and Spain for *The Pleasure Seekers*. She mused back then, "Someday I'm going back to those places, definitely including Gallup, as a tourist, not a worker, in order that I may wander around at my own sweet leisure meeting the people and studying the customs."[17]

The Hallelujah Trail opened in early September 1965 with a huge premiere in New York. Afterwards, 1,000 invited guests attended a sumptuous western barbeque behind the Capitol Theatre. Pamela was in attendance along with Sturges, Elmer Bernstein, Lee Remick, Jim Hutton, and Martin Landau. Hopefully the catered affair made up for the very long, not-so-funny slog of a movie that the audience had to sit through.

In *The Hallelujah Trail*, Thaddeus Gearhart (Burt Lancaster), a colonel in the U.S. cavalry, has to contend with his men and a feisty daughter named Louise (Pamela Tiffin). Returning from the field, he finds her in a romantic clinch with one of his officers, Capt. Paul Slater (Jim Hutton), in his quarters. She admits to only distracting him so he wouldn't break up the women's march, led by suffragette and temperance leader Cora Massingale (Lee Remick). Worse, Louise has agreed to go with Cora to Denver to stop a whiskey supply from being delivered to the city's miners. Louise and Cora's actions cause the colonel to get drunk and wake the next morning with an extreme hangover as his daughter hovers over him. She is trying to persuade him to have the cavalry accompany them to Denver for protection from marauding Indians.

Gearhart relents and the cavalry and the temperance women begin their journey. Pamela is for the most part lost from view from this point straight through the intermission. Another cavalry unit is escorting the liquor with the owner Frank Wallingham (Brian Keith) and his team of unhappy Irish teamsters led by Kevin O'Flaherty (Tom Stern) to meet up with the Denver militia to retrieve it. Meanwhile, a band of Sioux plan to steal it. They all meet up just as a sandstorm hits. They fire on each other blindly in a long, drawn-out shootout that leads to an intermission.

When the movie restarts, the sky is blue and the air clear as Gearhart assembles all the parties to hear them out. Louise is seen sitting there silently as all the factions state their case on what to do with the whiskey. The Sioux pretend they were innocent victims on a Buffalo hunt when they got caught up in the gun battle and want a present before they'll return home peacefully: the whiskey. Meanwhile O'Flaherty, who has been flirting with Louise, gets the teamsters to strike. Louise is on-screen and not heard yet again when the temperance ladies form a barrier to protect the striking teamsters from their angered boss and the militia. Though she doesn't utter a word, Pamela bursts off the screen due to her Edith Head–designed outfit consisting of a brown skirt and bright red blouse with matching hat. Wearing such a robust color, you can't but help not look at her hoping she will have something to do other than just stand there and look pretty. Alas, she doesn't utter a line.

Pamela's screen time doesn't get any better as the movie enters its last phase. Louise turns up briefly to take over for Remick's Cora during a meeting. After saying one line she is almost immediately whisked away by the Indians who, impatient for the whiskey, kidnap the ladies to hold for ransom. Knowing it will ruin his career, Gearhart agrees to exchange the booze for the hostages. Louise once again is on screen during this, but remains mute. Cora is guilt-ridden for the trouble she has caused and takes a few slugs of whiskey to calm her nerves to the surprise of the colonel. Pie-eyed, she agrees to be at the exchange, which goes haywire due to Cora's interference and the discovery that the whiskey is actually pink champagne. The abrupt finale features a double wedding as both father and daughter get hitched.

The Hallelujah Trail is one of those movies that are either loved or hated and has a cult following to this day. Fans and critics all agreed that the film is expertly photographed by Robert Surtees in Ultra Panavision and Technicolor. The scenery is beautiful and Surtees captured some gorgeous vista shots of men on horseback and wagon trains making their way over the plains. The picture also featured a rousing title tune and musical score by Bernstein almost equal to his Oscar-nominated score from The Magnificent Seven. For Pamela Tiffin fans, these are all the movie has to offer.

Col. Gearhart (Burt Lancaster) and Capt. Slater (Jim Hutton) learn of Louise Gearhart's (Pamela Tiffin) involvement with the temperance movement in *The Hallelujah Trail* (United Artists, 1965).

Among the favorable notices, the spoof was hailed as "a lusty, gusty western comedy" (Whit., *Variety*); "a wild and way-out western" (Frank Leyendecker, *Boxoffice*); "a delightful time" (Frederick H. Guidry, *Christian Science Monitor*); "an eye-filling, wagon-wheeling situation comedy of the old West" (Edgar J. Driscoll, Jr., *Boston Globe*); and "one of the very few funny westerns ever made, and possibly the funniest" (Philip K. Scheuer, *Los Angeles Times*).

People who disliked the movie felt it was a convoluted, unfunny, and overlong mess of a western—a typical, bloated, overblown epic that the sixties were infamous for. In a number of negative reviews, blame was put on director Sturges for delivering a humorless motion picture. For example, the *Films and Filming* reviewer wrote, "[I]t is to be hoped that Sturges purged himself of any notions of his talent as a farceur with *The Hallelujah Trail*, … a long, *long* labored comedy, built around a number of cheap running gags, which are repeated so often that they end up in a crawl." Bosley Crowther of the *New York Times* felt the director was so intent on trying to deliver a feature combing the fast-paced slapstick of a Keystone Cops feature and an outdoor epic that he lost control and made the film "seem one long drawn, formless blur."

As for the actors, Burt Lancaster proves his forte is not comedy. Martin Gottfried in *Women's Wear Daily* quipped, "The notes for Burt Lancaster say that he 'will refuse to let them type him as a comedian as a result of his role.' Mr. Lancaster does not have a hell of a lot to worry about." He would return to drama for the remainder of his career. Lee Remick is quite spirited as his foil. Jim Hutton has been funnier and Pamela is almost a non-entity. Looking as pretty and fresh as she did in *State Fair* with a wavier hairdo, she is given little to do and Sturges does not take advantage of her comedic abilities in the least. The early scenes with Hutton and Lancaster are Pamela's best and most amusing. After this, Pamela takes a big back seat to Lee Remick—so much so that she is practically in the trunk.

Pamela received less screen time than some of the featured actors. It is shocking considering how long she spent making it. Critics took notice as well. Frank Leyendecker in *Boxoffice* remarked, "Miss Tiffin is charming but has almost nothing to do except add some pulchritude to an outdoors scene." Martin Gottfried of *Women's Wear Daily* noticed that she "disappeared from chunks of the film at a time, during which she probably had no more to do than when she was there." Leo Miskin of the *New York Morning Telegraph* commented that Pamela had a "minor role" and only played it "adequately."

Watching the movie, you have to hope that Pamela took this role because the script had her character more involved in the action. It seems there may have been a more fleshed-out subplot with Tom Stern's character trying to steal Tiffin's Louise away from Hutton's cavalry officer. Photo stills of Stern with Tiffin exist, but these scenes do not show up in the final print. It leads one to speculate these scenes were excised, most likely due to the excessive running time. The movie at two hours, 38 minutes is overlong as it is. Sturges may have cut Pamela's scenes, among others, to par it down somewhat.

Though filming *The Hallelujah Trail* was a wonderful experience for the actress, watching the movie is such a big disappointment to her fans. It is a shame Pamela wound up playing such a dispensable character in a not-so-memorable movie. Obviously she felt the role as written was better than what appeared on screen. And it was different from the parts she had been previously offered.

If Pamela really wanted to do a western, she should have campaigned for the female lead in *Cat Ballou* where her comedic talents (superior to Jane Fonda's) would have been put to much better use. However, by her own admission she was not career-driven and probably did not even know of that comedy western that won Lee Marvin an Academy Award for Best Actor.

The public seemed to side with the critics who panned the movie. The original 165-minute cut failed to draw the audiences into theaters for two daily showings as a road show attraction. United Artists then had the film cut to 145 minutes and gave it a regular release to try to attract more moviegoers. It didn't work. *The Hallelujah Trail* grossed an estimated $4 million, way short of its $7 million budget.

Tim Zinnemann weighed in with his review and concurred with the pans: "I saw the movie many years ago and didn't think that much of it. I don't think comedy was John Sturges' strong suit."[18] Most people would agree but not John Sturges, who thought that he delivered a hilarious hit and was shocked that most people did not find it funny. A true professional, he took full blame for its failure to generate the laughs and fill movie theaters' seats.

11

Jiggling the Diving Board

Harper

Pamela Tiffin was happily reunited with her husband back in New York after a long shoot on location in New Mexico for *The Hallelujah Trail*. Fully free from her contractual obligations, the actress could accept any role offered to her. She resumed studying with Stella Adler and began taking art classes at New York's Columbia University; she was enrolled as Pamela Felker and hid her profession from the teachers and students. She even disguised her looks by wearing her hair shaggy beatnik-style and wore clothes from Greenwich Village hoping her classmates would not recognize her. She wanted to fit in as Pamela Felker, fellow student, rather than Pamela Tiffin the movie actress. This way, if classmates agreed to have lunch with her, she'd know it was because they liked her and not because she was a celebrity.

Though she was able to remain anonymous with her classmates, school officials knew who she was and were perplexed by her enrollment. She commented, "Columbia doesn't know what to make of me. It just seems that an actress is not supposed to be in that academic world."[1] Pamela was a sort of trailblazer, as it was highly unusual in the sixties for starlets to juggle an acting career and school. Today it is common for movie stars to go to college. Jodie Foster, Brooke Shields, and James Franco are just a few examples of actors who returned to school with much fanfare.

Tiffin's screen career needed a change: She really had to make that all-important jump to more mature roles. Trying to help their client change her image and progress from the ingénue, Pamela's agents reportedly were vigorously trying to get her the lead role in *Candy*, thinking it was a role that guaranteed her stardom. Frank Perry was slated to direct from a script by Terry Southern based on his scandalous, bawdy novel about an innocent, sweet, wide-eyed girl and her sexual adventures with a host of oddball characters including a hunchback, a doctor, and a mystic. At that time nobody could play sexy and naïve as well as Pamela so she would have been perfect for this part.

The writer liked Tiffin according to his longtime companion, actress Gail Gerber. In her memoir *Trippin' with Terry Southern*, she wrote that she, Terry, and director Tony Richardson were having lunch in the MGM studio commissary one day during the making of *The Loved One*. Richardson spotted the sultry actress there and said that he wished that he would have signed her to play the female lead of offbeat cosmetician Aimee Thanatogenos in his movie rather than Anjanette Comer. Terry agreed and would have also welcomed Pamela as Candy. The role would have been Pamela's first adult sexy one, which she needed to progress. It was all for naught as *Candy* could not get financing and was shelved at that time. In 1968, actor-turned-director Christian Marquand picked up the option and the project went into production without Tiffin or the use of Terry Southern's screenplay.

During this period, Pamela was also up for some lead roles in major films. *The Great Race* was a big-budget comedy epic about a wacky car race across three continents during the early 20th century. Producer Martin Jurow and director Blake Edwards were "thrilled" with Pamela Tiffin's reading for the role of the contest's only female driver, who spouts women's rights throughout, but the part went to Natalie Wood. As with *Take Her, She's Mine*; Pamela lost a desired role to an actress with a bigger name at the box office but far less comedic ability.

Pamela was considered for the role of Honey, the ditzy, mousy wife of a young biology professor, in *Who's Afraid of Virginia Woolf?* She auditioned with Robert Redford. It was a part craved by all young actresses of the time including a delusional Connie Stevens who was behind an embarrassing, desperate media blitz to get the part, or at least an audition, but to no avail. Sandy Dennis won out and copped an Academy Award for Best Supporting Actress to boot.

Two other movies that Tiffin really wanted to make were *The Collector* and *The Group*. The former had what Tiffin described as Pamela's desired "believable girl" role, that of Miranda Grey, an art student kidnapped by a sociopath bank clerk and butterfly collector who decides to add her to his collection hoping she will fall in love with him. It becomes a psychological struggle of who can get the upper hand. Pamela recalled, "I flew out [from New York] to meet the producer … to test along with everybody else. I flew back the same day and the stress and strain affected my kidneys. The doctor said I had to take pills for a while."[2] Pamela knew that the competition was going to be tough for this part, but even still she was disappointed in not being cast. The producers and director William Wyler went instead with Samantha Eggar, who copped an Oscar nomination for her performance.

The Group had one of Tiffin's most desired roles, that of the gossipy sophisticate Libby. The movie was based on the popular novel by Mary McCarthy about eight female Vassar College graduates and their soap opera lives. Tiffin auditioned for director Sidney Lumet. Jessica Walter (whose only prior movie credit was *Lilith* starring Warren Beatty and Jean Seberg) got the part that Pamela wanted. Tiffin was devastatingly disappointed. Ever the gentleman, Lumet did write her a kind note, but he found her too funny for the part. This seemed to be a pattern in Pamela's movie career: losing dramatic roles due to producers considering her more of a comedienne and losing comedic roles to less deserving but more famous actresses

Pamela's name also came up, along with Carol Lynley, as a possible hostess on ABC-TV's proposed daytime talk show *The Young Set*. Leonard Goldberg, a network executive, thought either actress would be a wonderful choice to headline their new series featuring "bright, glamorous young people"[3] who would discuss their views on the current scene. It was proposed that all guests would be under the age of thirty-five. The series did go into production but with thirty-nine-year-old actress Phyllis Kirk as hostess. The series was not a hit, and was cancelled after only four months on the air.

Though Pamela suffered these career disappointments, as most actors do, it did not destroy her. She was living happily in New York and continuing her studies. Remember this was the actress who, when being fawned over after making her first two movies in 1961, remarked that her greatest ambition was "to be is a well-educated person."[4]

Hollywood *finally* beckoned again and she got a chance to act sexy, droll, and sophisticated in her biggest hit: *Harper* (1966) starring Paul Newman (reportedly first choice Frank Sinatra turned it down) as a down-and-out private gumshoe investigating the disappearance of an industrialist. Pamela played the missing millionaire's spoiled daughter who despises her paralyzed, icy stepmother. It was based on Ross MacDonald's novel *The Moving Target*, the first in a very popular series about tough-as-nails private detective Lew Archer. Pamela was joined by Lauren Bacall, Julie Harris, Arthur Hill, Robert Wagner, Robert Webber, and Shelley Winters in the eccentric cast of characters the private eye comes across in his investigation.

There were a number of supposed reasons given why the lead character's name was changed from Archer to Harper. One that may or may not be true was that since Newman had a run of very success-ful movies beginning with the letter "H"—*The Hustler* and *Hud*—he asked if his character's last name could be changed and then if it could be used as the movie's title. Hence, Lew Archer became Lew Harper and *The Moving Target* became *Harper* in the U.S. and Canada. As a huge box office draw and respected actor, Newman had the clout to get his way.

Harper was a throw-back to those hard-hitting private eye movies of the forties, usually starring Humphrey Bogart (the film was even nicknamed "Son of Sam Spade"). Bogart's wife and occasional co-star Lauren Bacall was cast in a supporting role. The movie, budgeted at $3.5 million, was directed and written by two relative newcomers to motion pictures. Jack Smight was a prolific TV director since

Cover of the Japanese press book for *Harper* (Warner Bros., 1966).

the early fifties, but had made only a handful of movies including the Sandra Dee comedy *I'd Rather Be Rich* and the suspense drama *The Third Day* with George Peppard. This was screenwriter William Goldman's first produced screenplay and he had one prior film credit, *Masquerade*, but he would go on to win Academy Awards for writing *Butch Cassidy and the Sundance Kid* and *All the President's Men*.

After playing a number of ingénue roles, Pamela had the chance to break free from them and to act sexy playing socialite Miranda Sampson. The actress described her character as "very sophisticated…. I have to smoke and as I don't smoke I had to learn how. I'm a coquette, have flirtations."[5] This was her first chance to play a bad girl on the silver screen. Miranda was spoiled, privileged, and insensitive. Her mouth seemed to have no filter. Even so, compared to the other vile characters Harper meets in his investigation, the brazen Miranda comes off the most likable due to Pamela's ability to get the audience to feel some empathy towards her due to the circumstances of the disappearance of her father and how shabbily she is treated by his wife and his private pilot.

When asked how she was able to jump from the "Miss Purity parts" to such a sexy vamp, she replied, "I really don't know how I bridged the gap…. I liked playing innocents. After attending Columbia, and then getting married, I simply did not feel that they were appropriate any longer."[6] This may explain the almost one-year gap between when Tiffin completed *The Hallelujah Trail* and making *Harper*. The choosy actress held fast to her goal to make the leap to more mature roles. It was an issue her contemporaries also were dealing with. Some, like Carol Lynley, went to extremes like posing semi-nude in *Playboy* and starring in *Harlow* to prove she was an adult. Tuesday Weld, on the other hand, embraced her young looks and successfully kept playing the teenager (in *Lord Love a Duck*, *Pretty Poison* and *I Walk the Line*) well into her twenties. Still others like Sandra Dee and Connie Stevens were just so typecast as the eternal ingénue they saw their big screen careers slip away before the sixties had ended.

Screenwriter Goldman made two changes with the character of Miranda. In the novel she actually kisses the detective, but in the movie Goldman has Harper keep Miranda at arm's length. Goldman also made stepmother Elaine and Miranda adversarial characters with bitchy dialogue exchanged between them. Their antagonism runs throughout the movie, giving the characters an edge.

Before shooting began, the main cast gathered around a long table to read through the script for a week or so. Per Pamela, this was due to Paul Newman, who liked to rehearse. Handsome blonde actor Martin West (whose prior movies included *Freckles*, *The Man from Galveston*, *The Girls on the Beach*, and *Lord Love a Duck*) played the young deputy who is always a few steps behind Harper. West did not attend the table read, but remarked, "I'm not surprised at hearing about Paul's need to rehearse. He wasn't an instinctual actor like so many are—he always had to work at it. I know that with my scenes with him we ran over lines many times, as much as I had with any actor."[7]

Filming began in July 1965 and lasted until September. With super-spies like James Bond and Matt Helm dominating the silver screen, Newman wanted to bring moviegoers back down to Earth with Lew Harper. He described his character as "an average person, intelligent and hard-working. His successes are based on brainwork, not trickery. His deductions are logical. He's a man—not Superman. Believe me, the plot's tricky enough to supply lots of excitement."[8]

Pamela thought Newman's reserve around her was due to his being a natural introvert, but added, "He won't permit himself to be shy. Paul is a very 'normal' man who happens to act. There's a core of masculinity, a *tough* quality—it's very attractive in a man—when you're around them, you feel protected in some way. Paul put up with a lot of nonsense during the filming … but he was very methodical and careful in fashioning his performance."[9] The actress also admired Newman's easy relationship with the crew and how she respected them and their craft. She said, "He sees everyone as vital on the movie set—doesn't take it too seriously. He knows the electrician's as important as he."[10]

Shooting their scenes on the streets of California was quite amusing to the actress due to Newman's many admirers. She recalled at the time, "When I was working with Paul in Bel Air, women with babies in their arms came to sigh over him."[11] The enthusiastic public almost caused an accident during one of the scenes with Newman and Tiffin in the car. Nobody was hurt, but Tiffin revealed that Newman told her, "They don't see you as a person but as an icon or object."[12]

Martin West also had the highest respect for Newman. "Paul was an actor's actor. He worked hard at every role he ever had and was a consummate actor to work with—professional and a gentleman. He was sometimes aloof, but I thought he was because he had to get back to memorizing the script."[13] West worked with Newman along with his wife Joanne Woodward years later, doing a production of *Our Town* in Westport, Connecticut, where they all lived. He remarked, "As Paul became older, it became increasingly difficult for him to learn lines. Joanne used to tell me that he would ask anyone around to run lines—Joanne, their daughters, even their dog."[14]

Pamela was also impressed with Lauren Bacall though the tense and standoffish actress would never attend rehearsals. Bacall played the diva despite the fact that the film's star Newman requested that his co-stars participate. Bacall was the only no-show. Even with her spoiled movie star behavior, Tiffin still found the actress fascinating and was honored to work with her.

Bacall was called out by Earl Wilson when she stood up Pamela and the other actresses for a publicity photo shoot. When the columnist asked if she was feuding with her co-stars, Bacall, who was appearing in *Cactus Flower* on Broadway at the time, roared, "Oh, come on, Earl, you can ask more libelous questions than that! I was too tired doing two shows. You know me. I don't feud. I got along with everybody."[15]

Miranda Sampson was one of Pamela's favorite roles and she enjoyed playing her immensely. It helped that the *Harper* shoot went quite smoothly for Tiffin except for one embarrassing incident: She walked on the set, tripped and fell flat on her face. "The photographer began turning the camera trying to find me, yelling, 'Where is she? Where did she go?' He found me on the floor."[16]

The floor is likely where Pamela wished she remained when Newman's wife Joanne Woodward visited the set one day. It was reported that the missus intimidated Pamela and that the interaction between the two actresses was minimal. Tiffin found Woodward "sober" and said, "She doesn't have a great sense of humor."[17]

Pamela's scenes at Miranda's family mansion were shot at the estate of the late silent film star Marion Davies. The house dazzled the actress as she roamed the vast dining room; peered into endless clothes closets scented with imported camphor wood; rode the private elevator; and sat in the enormous projection room. However, what she found most fascinating was that there were four black bank-sized safes scattered around the house including one in the kitchen. This prompted Tiffin to quip, "Those pre-tax days in Hollywood must have been wonderful! Even the cook needed a safe."[18]

During filming, Pamela was invited to attend the Moscow Film Festival. Though she had the available time, the film's producers made her decline because they did not want her to fly until the picture was completed.

After production wrapped, Warner Bros. asked the actress to do a series of publicity pin-up shots to help promote the movie. Some photos were taken in the polka-dot bikini she wears on the diving board, but many more were taken of her in a one-piece black swimsuit she briefly wears in the scene where Newman's Harper snoops around the guest house. Being a model, Pamela was used to having her picture taken, but for this particular shoot she felt especially exploited while clad in a bathing suit and high heels. She was instructed to turn her head one way and her body another, and felt like a puppet for the photographer's fantasies.

Harper opened in the U.S. beginning in late February of 1966. Prior, an extended trailer was released with new segments featuring the five lead actresses in character commenting on Lew Harper. Pamela is in the blue dress she wore when flirting with Harper in her father's bedroom at his L.A. bungalow. She says to the screen audience while sitting seductively on a round bed, "I'm not a child any more—so if Lew Harper won't come to me—then I'll go to him." She lies back on the bed, as a clip from that scene in the movie is shown.

In *Harper* the credit scroll begins as cool private eye Lew Harper (Paul Newman) awakes in bed. No actor in the sixties looked as sexy as the unshaven Newman wearing a white T-shirt and boxers staring at the bathroom mirror. He dresses and then finding he is out of coffee, reuses a discarded coffee filter. Per William Goldman, this sequence was added after the producers called him to write one and was not part of the original screenplay. Harper is hired by paralyzed ex-equestrienne Elaine Sampson (Lauren Bacall) to find her missing husband Ralph, a wealthy businessman. Harper was recommended to Elaine by Sampson's attorney Albert Graves (Arthur Hill), a friend of the detective's. This case helps distract the down-on-his-luck private eye from the divorce proceedings initiated by his wife Susan (Janet Leigh). Harper meets with Elaine at the palatial Sampson estate in St. Theresa, California, and realizes that the unfeeling wife couldn't care less about her husband's well-being. She suggests he go outside to talk with Sampson's young pilot Alan Taggert (Robert Wagner), the last to see him before he vanished after disembarking from his private jet in Los Angeles. Alan is poolside with Elaine's nubile stepdaughter Miranda (Pamela Tiffin). The heiress is seen dancing on the diving board in a white polka-dot bikini and gives a nonchalant wave over her head when Alan introduces her as she keeps shimmying to the music. On the *Harper* DVD released in 2006, the commentary featured screenwriter William Goldman who exclaimed the first second Pamela appears on screen, "Isn't she gorgeous!" He also remarked that when writing dialogue for Miranda he imagined that the words were going to be spoken by Marilyn Monroe.

Harper turns off Miranda's radio to talk. Realizing a private investigator has been hired, she sarcastically remarks, "My stepmother, Lady Macbeth, is always going to extremes.... Everything she does is extreme. Other women fall off horses without getting paralyzed—not Elaine. I think it is psychological, don't you?" As Harper questions Alan, Miranda sits caressing the pilot but he ignores her. When Alan reveals that Sampson did

The acid-tongued, hot-to-trot Miranda (Pamela Tiffin) dances on a diving board oblivious to all that is around her in a scene from *Harper* (Warner Bros., 1966).

not take any luggage, Miranda gets up and walks toward Harper, saying, "That doesn't mean anything. Daddy keeps a lot of clothes at the bungalow. He likes to be able to pick up fast—*so do I*." She then takes the sandwich Harper has been eating from him and finishes it while hungrily eyeing the private eye.

Taggert offers to fly Harper down to L.A. to check out Sampson's private bungalow at the Bel Air Hotel. Miranda entices Alan to stay with her instead and he quips, "I'll fly—it will keep me from getting bored." Harper makes a pit stop at Albert Graves' office where he learns, among other things, that the older attorney foolishly pines for Sampson's daughter, who doesn't return his affections. Miranda then decides to come along with the detective and Alan to the Bel Air. As Harper searches the bedroom, Miranda lies seductively on the round bed and entices him to relax with her as she puts a pillow underneath her lower back. Knowing what she is up to, he says, "For what? So that Beauty in the next room is going to get all hot and bothered. If you can't get him hot and bothered by yourself, I sure ain't going to do it for you." She continues to entice him so, fed up with her game-playing, he turns the lights off and makes his move. As he expected, she quickly rolls off the bed. On the nightstand Harper finds an autographed photo from a former movie starlet named Fay Estabrook (Shelley Winters). Asking Alan what happened to her, he laughs and says, "She got fat." He knows where the former actress hangs out and Harper leaves the pair to find her.

Harper keeps plying Fay with food and booze to get information out of her. They wind up at the Bel Air Hotel cocktail lounge where Miranda and Alan find them. A stunned Miranda reveals that Elaine received a letter from her father demanding that she withdraw $500,000 in exchange for Sampson's return. Harper instructs Miranda to do as the note says, but they are going to demand proof that her father is still alive before they hand the money over. Taking an inebriated Fay back to her home, Harper finds wads of cash hidden in her drawer and a connection to a singer, and former junkie, named Betty Frawley (Julie Harris) who works at the Piano. Before he can depart, Fay's gun-toting husband Dwight Troy (Robert Webber) shows up, but lets Harper leave thinking he is only a fan from Texas who gave his blowsy drunken wife a lift home.

At the Piano, Harper confronts Betty about Sampson. She denies knowing him and has the private eye thrown out. As he is being beaten up in the alley, Taggert fires a gun scaring off the bouncers. The next day Harper tries to convince Elaine to call in the Feds since her husband has most likely been kidnapped, but she refuses. Miranda interrupts and immediately she and Elaine begin trading catty barbs. Elaine taunts Miranda, or "Pussycat" as she calls her, about Alan giving her the brush-off once again while Miranda counters with insults about Elaine being frigid and her fear of aging. Harper rolls his eyes and exits. Left alone, Elaine remarks to Miranda, "I should think you'd be accustomed to not being loved by now." Miranda responds, "I love your *wrinkles*. I revel in them." To which Elaine retorts, "Puss, puss, puss."

In the drawing room Harper runs into Graves, who is putting the $500,000 into Sampson's safe. An irate Miranda comes storming down the staircase after her confrontation with Elaine ("I'm suicidal," she responds after Graves asks about her well-being) and offers to go with Harper to a mountaintop house that her father drunkenly gave away to strange religious cult leader Claude (Strother Martin).

On the drive up, spoiled Miranda and Harper keep sparring as well. When Miranda asks if he is speeding to impress her and then why his wife is divorcing him, both times Harper responds with, "You've got a way of starting conversations that ends conversations." She then calls his line of work "crummy," angering the private eye even more, and wants to know what Harper thinks her big deficiency is, as she snuggles up to him. Miranda gets really agitated when he replies, "Just that. Stop acting like a bitch in heat every time anything pretty in pants wanders by." She calls him "an old man" and sneers, "Just as stuffy as Albert— the same Victorian hang-up. You probably still think a woman's place is in the *home*." He retorts, "Not *my home*."

Miranda introduces Harper to Claude, who resides at the Temple of the Clouds, which is being constructed on the property. After looking around the grounds, Harper notices truck tracks that match the ones found outside of Fay Estabrook's house. As Harper drives Miranda back home, he spots a letter sticking out of the mailbox. Inside Harper goes to call Graves, as Miranda heads upstairs (and disappears from most of the second half of the movie). The letter is instructions regarding the money drop. Graves calls the sheriff and it is agreed that the lawyer and Alan will make the drop-off at an oil field. Harper stakes out the scene and sees the same truck that was at Fay's house, followed by a white convertible. By the time he appears on the scene, Eddie, the driver of the truck, is dead and the money gone. A discarded matchbook leads Harper to a dive bar and then back up to Claude's mountaintop abode where the private eye learns he and Troy are smuggling in illegal immigrant workers from Mexico. Harper informs Troy that his driver Eddie was the fall guy in the kidnapping of Sampson and whoever owns a white convertible took off with the ransom. A surprised Troy responds, "Oh, Mr. Harper, I am surrounded by very devious people." Harper then learns that Betty is the owner of the car, while Troy orders his goons to finish off Harper in the storage room at the Piano nightclub. During the melee, Harper gets away and ends up at his wife's house. She allows him to stay the night.

The next day Harper heads to the Sampson estate. When Graves informs him that Eddie is Betty's brother, a suspicious Harper wants to know where Alan lives. He and Miranda are at poolside as Harper heads to the pilot's guest house quarters. Shortly after, Taggert finds the detective snooping in his home and two play cat and mouse with Alan, denying any involvement with Sampson's disappearance. Harper believes him but when he starts saying ugly, vile things about Betty, Alan loses it and pulls a gun on Harper. He tells him that Betty and he concocted the kidnapping plot so they can have enough money to be together. As he is about to pull the trigger, Graves enters and shoots Alan dead. As a favor to the lawyer, Harper tells Miranda of Beauty's death and when he makes a crack of her being fooled by appearances, she lashes out at him. "Why don't you shut up?" she yells. "'Fooled by appearances?' I'm the grieving daughter, right? Not right. I don't give a damn about my father—never did. He is a terrible man and whatever he gets, he deserves." She then goes on to tearfully explain that once the second ransom note was received, she realized that she didn't care about anything. This made her feel no better than her horrid stepmother, so she hid. Miranda asks Graves if he thinks she is horrid and when he says of course not, she runs into his arms for comfort as an eye-rolling Harper exits.

Harper heads to Castle Beach where Alan told him he and Betty were going to stay hidden in plain sight. He arrives just as Troy, Claude, and Fay are torturing the singer to find out where she hid the money. Harper bursts in and shoots Troy. After pistol whipping Claude and locking hapless Fay in a closet, he helps Betty to his car. As they drive, she tries to barter for her happiness with Alan only to learn he is dead. She then reveals to Harper where Sampson is being held. He stops to call Graves to meet him at an abandoned barge. As Harper searches for the millionaire, Betty hotwires his car and drives off. Harper gets clobbered on the head and awakes to find Graves there. They then find Sampson murdered. The two chase after Betty, who loses control of Harper's car and careens off a ravine. She doesn't survive. Harper makes a call to Elaine to give her the news about Sampson. When Stepmommie Dearest learns that her husband is dead, she feigns sorrow and can't believe someone would hurt her kind husband. After putting the phone down, she maliciously calls out in a sing-song voice, "Miranda, dear—*Mommy has something to tell you!*" Miranda approaches the down staircase and swings the gate open.

After stopping at the locker to retrieve the ransom money, Harper realizes that Graves' theory about a fourth man working with Betty, Alan, and Eddie is bogus. A fourth man would have searched his pockets for the locker key. Harper realizes that Graves found Sampson first and killed him. His friend confesses that Sampson was such a vile man that the world would be better off without him. It ends without the audience knowing if Harper will turn Graves over to the police.

To promote the movie in New York City when it opened, Warner Bros. held a "premiere-a-thon" at three theaters (the Forum, RKO 58th Street, and RKO 23rd Street) with personal appearances by Pamela, whom the studio dubbed "Harper's Private Eyeful." Between noon and 4:30 p.m. the busy actress raced through the city to attend autograph and interview sessions at all three theaters.

In its first week, *Harper* grossed over $1 million in the New York metro area alone. For an old-fashioned private eye tale released during the height of the sixties spy boom

Miranda (Pamela Tiffin) and Harper (Paul Newman) exit the hilltop domain of religious cult leader Claude in an excised scene from *Harper* (Warner Bros., 1966). Billy Rose Theatre Division, The New York Public Library for the Performing Arts, Astor, Lenox and Tilden Foundations.

with cool secret agents like James Bond, Derek Flint, and Matt Helm dominating the silver screen, it was a triumph despite the mixed notices from the critics. Reviews ranged from "a slam-bang mystery yarn" (*New York Times*), to "consistently entertaining" (*Cosmopolitan*), to "the classiest private eye movie in years" (*Newsday*), to "more messy than tough" (*Newsweek*), to "terrible" (*The New Yorker*).

For critics unhappy with the movie, most of the blame went to director Jack Smight. The *New Yorker* critic was especially lethal with his comments, calling him the movie's "friendly funeral director." On the other hand, most reviewers showered praise on William Goldman's suspenseful script with its biting dialogue, sardonic wit, and surprise ending. Here too Goldman made a change from the novel, which ended with the detective entering the Sampson house with news of Ralph Sampson's death at the hands of Graves. Harper (Archer in the book) and Miranda then go to the authorities where they discover that Graves has already confessed. For his screenplay, Goldman received an Edgar Allan Poe Award for Best Written Motion Picture and a Writers Guild nomination for Best Written American Drama.

Despite the accolades Goldman received, his script left some of the cast perplexed. Pamela admitted that though she loved the opportunity to play Miranda she "never understood the script of *Harper*—I did the whole movie without understanding what it was about."[19] Martin West agreed with her: "Goldman's original script was confusing and hard to follow."[20] West did go on to defend director Smight: "Paul and Jack had a great relationship. In fact, after working with Smight, Paul thought it would be a much better film. The script was the main problem from the outset."[21]

Pamela received some of her finest notices for playing Miranda. *New York Times* critic Bosley Crowther described her as "a gorgeous scratching kitten." Bert Prelutsky of the *Los Angeles Magazine* found Pamela "convincing" and thought her Frug on the diving board was done "very nicely and with style." More praise came from *The Hollywood Reporter*'s James Powers, who had raved about Tiffin's talent in previous reviews, most recently for *The Lively Set*. Now he remarked, "Miss Tiffin continues to make a fine impression as one of the best character ingénues." One ambiguous review came from Richard L. Coe of *The Washington Post* who commented that Tiffin played Miranda "*à la* Ann-Margret." Compliment or pan?

In this one movie, Pamela completely erased her innocent ingénue image. She was quite a vision of loveliness and elegance, especially in her sexy dance on the diving board where moviegoers are first introduced to Miranda. It has become one of sixties cinema's most iconic images, so much so that a clip of it was prominently used in director Barry Levinson's hit film *Sleepers* (1996) starring Robert DeNiro, Kevin Bacon, Dustin Hoffman, and Brad Pitt. The actress played off Paul Newman quite well during the entire movie with her rude insights delivered in a droll manner. His private eye sees right through her man-hungry ways to the unloved little girl deep inside, making him able to resist her desperate come-ons. She also is good with Robert Wagner, looking extremely handsome and fit, especially in his tight white boxer swim trunks. He delivers an amusingly winning performance. When the spoiled heiress doesn't get her way, the wildcat emerges. Pamela's best scenes are when Miranda is insulting both Harper and Elaine, such as during the car ride up to her father's mountaintop sanctuary, when she and Newman bicker the entire time. Tiffin's scene in Elaine's bedroom is another standout as the catty insults between Tiffin and Lauren

Bacall come fast and biting. Pamela proved she had the acting chops to go toe to toe with these acting legends and more than held her own with them on screen.

In terms of screen time, Pamela dominates the first half of the movie along with Newman, only to disappear during the latter half. Her absence is obvious and she is greatly missed. This hurts the film, especially since she and Newman had such great chemistry. She has only one major scene in the last hour plus two scenes where she is seen but not heard. The first is when she is glimpsed lounging by the pool with Alan as Harper becomes suspicious of the pilot; the other is when Elaine maliciously calls for Miranda to inform her about her father's death. Pamela's big scene in this part of the movie is when a hardened Miranda reveals herself, admitting she despised her father and is more like her stepmother than she cares to admit. Pamela plays the scene with conviction. When she sees Albert approaching, she quickly switches gears and plays the victim ("You don't think I am horrid," she sympathetically asks) before running into his arms. With Alan dead and daddy still missing, Miranda needs any man in her life.

Film historian Dean Brierly, who has written for *Cinema Retro* and *Filmfax* magazines, agrees that Pamela was a standout and felt that she made her biggest impact in *Harper*. In particular he praised the scene where "she tries to seduce Newman's character by slipping a pillow under her derriere and purring, 'Say, Harper, don't you want to relax?' This scene probably did more to corrupt and inspire the youth of America than illicit copies of *Playboy*. Tiffin balanced such scorching moments with some emotionally dark scenes with Lauren Bacall in the same film, exhibiting a depth that was largely overlooked in light of her obvious charms."[22]

Pamela's new screen persona probably cost her a role when she was next rejected by director Norman Jewison to play the teenage babysitter in the hit comedy *The Russians Are Coming, the Russians Are Coming*. The Mirisch Brothers were pushing Pamela for the part because they felt she had proven she could do comedy well. Despite their backing, Pamela was not cast. Perhaps Jewison was not convinced that she was physically right for the part? At age twenty-three, she *was* a bit too-mature looking and sexy to play an adolescent. The director gave the role to newcomer and former model Andrea Dromm.

Harper became Pamela Tiffin's biggest box office hit. It grossed $6 million and was the fifteenth highest grossing movie of 1966. Unbeknownst to Pamela, it would also turn out to be her last film made for a major Hollywood studio. She should have followed up with another, but a call from Italy and then Broadway deterred her.

Blondes Do Have More Fun

Oggi, domani, dopodomani
Delitto quasi perfecto
(*The Imperfect Murder*)

Pamela's next film offer came not from Hollywood, but Rome, and would change her life and career forever. She was chosen to play opposite Italian mega-star Marcello Mastroianni in the three-part comedy *Oggi, domani, dopodomani* (1966). The movie was being produced by Carlo Ponti and was to be distributed with the title *Paranoia* in the U.S. through Joseph E. Levine's Embassy Pictures. Both producers felt a Hollywood name would boost the box office in the States. After being cast, Pamela was hailed as Italian film star Mastroianni's first American leading lady. However, she was not the original choice for the part.

With much fanfare, Sue Lyon was originally announced for the movie. She was personally recommended by Mastroianni: He had seen the blonde nymphet in *Lolita* and *The Night of the Iguana* and thought she would be perfect for the part of his sexy, vapid wife in the segment originally entitled "Moglie in vendita" ("Wife for Sale") before being changed to "La moglie bionda" ("The Blonde Wife"). Lyon and her agent met with Ponti and Levine in New York. The smitten Italian producer was not only ready to sign her for this movie, but also for a second film with Mastroianni, the futuristic *The 10th Victim*. However, there was one problem: producer Ray Stark. He had the blonde under contract to his Seven Arts production company and refused to let her do the movie because of a possible picture he was mulling over. A furious Lyon thought he was just being spiteful for the trouble he had with her while shooting *The Night of the Iguana*. As Lyon suspected, there was no movie for her and the actress wound up enrolling in Santa Monica City College to keep busy.

With Lyon out, Ponti needed a replacement and took a chance on Pamela. It would be interesting to know what made him think of Tiffin in the first place. Usually if Sue Lyon was not available for a part, it went to Carol Lynley or Yvette Mimieux, and vice versa, as producers and even moviegoers found these ethereal blondes interchangeable. Not only was Pamela a brunette, but she had never played such a hyper sexual woman before on screen. This part specifically called for someone that exuded overt sex appeal but was also naïve and a bit innocent to the machinations of her husband. Pamela proved expert playing the latter and Ponti must have saw the untapped potential in the actress to go full throttle as the sexpot. She was kittenish in *Harper*, but the role in *Oggi, domani, dopodomani* was beyond anything that Pamela had played on screen. This was probably one of the reasons she said yes to the part without seeing the script. As the twenty-three-year-old beauty commented, "I was getting tired of playing the fleeing virgin and the professional daughter. I played so many teenage parts, I felt like I was regressing."[1]

The other reason was that her spouse encouraged her to accept the offer. After completing *Harper*, Pamela said, "I was anticipating a long, lovely summer with Clay and having fun redecorating our apartment when I got the offer ... to go to Rome in September and make [this] picture with Marcello Mastroianni. Clay helped me make the decision. He advised me to accept; it was an entrée into foreign films."[2] Little did Clay Felker know what the future had in store.

Ponti had one stipulation before cementing the deal: She had to go blonde, which was a dilemma for the actress.

Publicity photograph of the new sexy blonde Pamela Tiffin in *Oggi, domani, dopodomani* (Compagnia Cinematografica Champion, 1966).

Hollywood was always trying to change her appearance, always wanting to bleach her hair or cut it. She liked her long, wild mane, and refused to go blonde because in her mind that wasn't something nice Midwestern girls did. However, wanting to work with Mastroianni, Pamela countered with wearing a blonde wig. That seemed agreeable, but it didn't work out. The producers decided that they wanted her natural hair, so she talked them into only bleaching the front and top layer of it, so she could hold on to her natural look with the back and underneath staying brunette.

To prepare for her role, Pamela took a crash course in Italian at Berlitz. She spent two weeks studying all day. She was determined to dub her own voice into Italian and not let them use another actress who sounded nothing like her. Unfortunately, when the two weeks were up, she had struggled with the language and not learned enough to reach her goal. Ponti was not too worried about her Italian. He wanted her visual impact to wow the audience. Pamela also took the language course because she wanted to at least try to communicate with Mastroianni, who was notorious for not speaking English. She felt extremely lucky to be sharing the screen with him. A number of her contemporaries were no doubt envious of the actress' great opportunity.

Not picking up enough of the language to hold a conversation, Pamela knew that it would be difficult shooting her scenes with Mastroianni. Worried, she asked Ponti how she was going to know when to start talking and was told that one end of the thinnest thread would be tied around her wrist; a gentle jerk from someone at the other end would be her cue. More worrisome was that she still had not seen the script and would have to learn her dialogue in Rome. Taking it in stride, she remarked, "But you have heard how the Italians work, without a story and invent lines as they go along. I hope I can keep up with them."[3]

Actually, Tiffin did not head to Rome but to Granada in the Southern part of Spain to shoot most of her scenes. This was typical with European productions in the sixties: a movie would be financed by one country, but filmed in another with actors speaking different languages. Once in Europe, Pamela told the producers she needed to diet, but was told not to. She was delighted and remarked, "That was fine with me. I love to eat bread and pasta, all the fattening things."[4]

Just before she left for Europe, the day of reckoning came for Pamela when she had to go from brunette to blonde. She dreaded it, but quickly came to like her new look. Back in the States shortly afterward, she recalled that day and said, "The first day I dyed I was very upset. I kept looking in the mirror to find myself. But I now feel like I was when I was ten years old."[5]

Before shooting began, a blonde, more voluptuous Pamela Tiffin paid a visit to Spain. It was a whirlwind tour where she visited the Prado, trailed incessantly by the paparazzi. This was her first time back in the country since filming *The Pleasure Seekers* two years earlier. While there, Pamela ran into actor and future co-star George Hamilton, whom she had met a few times at Hollywood soirées. However, the debonair actor did not recognize the new Pamela Tiffin. He kept smiling at her and she returned the smile thinking he knew it was her. He didn't and when they finally spoke the actor admitted to being embarrassed because he thought she was just a friendly Swedish gal—no doubt the next on the playboy actor's list to try to romance.

The filming of some of Pamela's scenes took place in the Moorish capital's centuries-old palace, the Alhambra. The production crew turned the gold-and-ivory Mirador of Linda Raja into the office of a sheik. For another scene, a huge dining table was constructed around the center fountain in the Court of the Lions. Harem girls, Bedouin guards with saber swords, and belly dancers populated the background. To avoid the tourists, filming began at midnight and went into the early morning hours. Pamela learned that her dressing room where she kept practicing her dance routine was where sultan Mulay Abul Hassan deserted his wife.

After returning to New York, Pamela was questioned about her experience making a movie in Italy ("Hollywood is so comfortable, but Rome is exciting...."[6]). Most of the questions focused on Mastroianni and what was it like to act with the Italian icon. She considered him to be "very special" and "the world's best actor.... He looks so casual, but he's really working on his material all the time. Always smoothing the edges and trying new ideas."[7] Despite the communication gap, Pamela felt there was a connection between the two.

When asked about if Mastroianni's appeal to women around the world held true to her as well, Tiffin excitedly agreed and exclaimed, "He's totally a hunk of man. He's romantic, he's elegant, he's sensual, he's a Latin lover and yet he's a Teddy bear, too. There's something cuddly about him. And that voice of his! It makes your bones vibrate."[8] Her affection for Mastroianni never waned. A few years later she still named him her favorite leading man because "he works with quiet intensity and is not an exhibitionist."[9]

Each segment of *Oggi, domain, dopodomani* featured Mastroianni with a different leading lady. The opening segment was the only one in black and white, as it was filmed prior as a standalone movie but deemed unreleasable. It was titled *L'uomo dai cinque palloni*

("The Man with the Five Balloons"), featured Catherine Spaak and was directed by Marco Ferreri. Mastroianni played a man so obsessed with balloon-blowing that he loses his lover, friends, and job. It was trimmed down to be a single segment. The others were filmed in color specifically for this release. The second segment was "L'ora di punta" ("The Peak Time") with Virna Lisi and directed by Eduardo De Filippo. Here he plays a visiting jittery physics professor who gets caught between a gun-toting husband and his sexy wife. Tiffin's "La moglie bionda" ("The Blonde Wife"), the final segment, was directed by Luciano Salce, who played Lisi's spouse in the other segment. The majority of the movies he directed, however, never made it over to U.S. shores.

"La moglie bionda" featured Pamela as Pepita the fair-haired wife of money-loving bank clerk Michele (Marcello Mastroianni). The film opens with a dream sequence with Michele and Pepita driving in his convertible. They get into an accident in an alleyway. Pepita, wearing a flowing white dress similar to what Marilyn Monroe wore in *The Seven Year Itch*, begins to dance on top of the car, drawing the attention of many men who begin to ravage her. Michele awakens suddenly to find his wife safely sleeping by his side. When he leaves for work, she is still asleep.

Though beautiful and sexy, Pepita is lazy (she lounges in bed all day as the housekeeper cleans up around her); sloppy (she later serves Michele spaghetti from a can on paper plates and then nonchalantly throws the garbage off the balcony); and much too amorous (she tries to entice her husband standing on their bed chewing her hair seductively while dancing to pop music). Fed up with her, Michele decides she must go. He gets the idea to sell her on the international wife market after being impressed by a wealthy sheik on a buying trip to add more blondes to his harem. Michele decides that he will sell Pepita and make a fortune.

The next day he takes her to a photographer where she poses provocatively wearing a harem girl outfit; then a hula skirt; and then nothing but a big straw hat strategically covering her naked body. When the shoot is completed, Pepita turns to Michele and innocently asks, "All this just to get a driver's license?" With portfolio in place, Michele approaches a sheik who is accompanied by a bevy of beautiful blondes clad in Pucci print dresses. One of them has too much of a resemblance to Pepita. The sheik passes on her, but recommends some friends in Africa who he knows will be interested in "such high-quality merchandise."

Next we see Michele and Pepita riding camels in the desert (he got her there on the pretext of a bank business meeting with an emir). At his palace, Michele waits on line to present the portfolio when a blonde woman is rejected because the emir accuses her of not being natural. When Michele shows the photos of Pepita, the harem girls gasp at her beauty and he agrees to the sale.

The emir arranges a sumptuous celebratory feast in tribute to Pepita complete with belly dancers as entertainment. Michele fidgets when the guest of honor is late. The wait is worth it as his sexy young wife, unaware of what her husband is up to, makes a spectacular entrance in a tight-fitting white gown with a feather headdress, impressing all. When the emir asks to see her blonde tresses, Michele removes her headdress and he is shocked to see her sporting short dark hair. Everyone gasps, as the outraged host orders Michele to be taken away. Pepita reveals it is only a wig and Michele pulls it off to reveal her beautiful flowing blonde mane.

To seal the deal, Michele convinces Pepita to dance for the emir. As she shakes and shimmies while doing the Swim to the music, Michele begins negotiations, asking for $4 million. The emir counters with an offer of $2 million and they settle on $3 million. When Michele goes to be paid, he is given promissory notes. Outraged, he rips up the contract, grabs an oblivious Pepita, and makes a run for it with the palace guards in hot pursuit. The pair makes their escape and wind up on a bus heading out onto the desert. When it makes a stop for the passengers' daily prayers, Pepita entices a hesitant Michele to make love in the sand dunes. While most red-blooded men in the audience would have jumped at the chance, Michele reluctantly appeases his wife as if it was a chore like raking leaves or shoveling snow.

He then drags her to Sheik Mohammed Hakim's desert playground. As he begins showing the photos of Pepita to the sheik, the man's disinterest is written all over his face. One of his harem girls removes her veil, revealing that she is a he complete with mustache. The entire harem is made up of men and they begin to paw at the handsome Michele, who flees in a panic. He runs into a local who sells him information about the gay sheik's even richer brother Salim. Pepita, meanwhile, lounging at the pool, learns from another blonde woman about these harems and falls into the pool. Michele saves her and she begs him not to sell her off. He assures her that in a few years he will buy her back after investing the money.

Pepita is not as dumb and flighty as she seems: She turns the tables and sells Michele to Akim, terminating Michele's deal for her with Salim. As the now wealthy Pepita is driven off in a chauffeured car, Michele, in his harem girl garb, chases after her begging for forgiveness. She just pooh-poohs him away, as the sheik's guards catch up and drag him back to the harem.

Joseph E. Levine was contracteded to release *Oggi, domani, dopodomani* in the U.S. as *Paranoia* through his company, Embassy Pictures. He had a very successful distribution deal with Carlo Ponti going back to 1961 with *Two Women* that won its star Sophia Loren an Academy Award for Best Actress. Embassy also released *Boccaccio '70*; *Contempt*; and the 1964 Academy Award winner for Best Foreign-Language Film *Yesterday, Today and Tomorrow*, among others. However, the movie received disappointing reviews in Italy and the first two segments were considered bombs. Guido Fin of *Cinema Nuovo* thought it was just "scandalous" that Ponti would try to pad out his original movie *L'uomo dai cinque palloni* with two "tasteless" comedies.

Critic Hawk, writing for *Variety*, called it "disappointing" and liked the second featurette a bit better than other reviewers did. As for "La moglie bionda," he remarked that it "suffers from over-extension, and although intermittently amusing and with Miss Tiffin lovely to look at, it winds up in ho-hum tedium." The *Segnalazioni cinematografiche* reviewer found the movie to be "a humorous comedy in three episodes [more] farcical than satirical, heterogeneous throughout, except in vulgarity." Most did agree that all technical aspects of the film were good especially "La moglie bionda's" musical score by Argentine Luis Enriquez Bacalov, who went on to win an Academy Award for *Il Postino* (1994).

In their book *Le Straniere del nostro Cinema*, Enrico Lancia and Fabio Melelli wrote in their profile on Tiffin that she was well paired with Mastroianni. Ponti stated that he cast the actress for the visual effect she would project and boy, does she deliver. There is no doubt that as a brunette, Pamela was one of the most beautiful starlets of the day. She had a cool, sultry persona about her even while playing comedy. However, as a blonde she

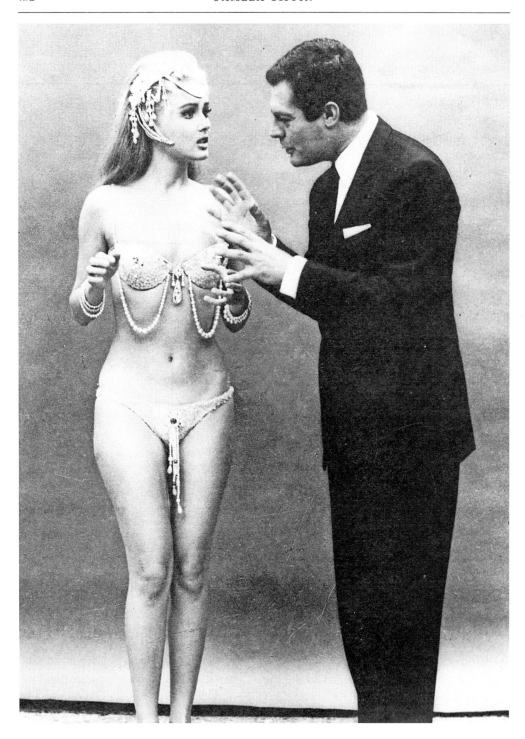

A confused Pepita (Pamela Tiffin) listens while her husband Michele (Marcello Mastroianni) explains why she has to wear a harem girl costume for her driver's license photograph in a scene from *Oggi, domani, dopodomani* (Compagnia Cinematografica Champion, 1966). Billy Rose Theatre Division, The New York Public Library for the Performing Arts, Astor, Lenox and Tilden Foundations.

just blossomed. Not only was she stunning, with her flaxen hair, but her personality seemed to change. A more jovial and sexy on-screen personality seemed to have overtaken the more staid, proper one she developed in Hollywood. Though her lines are dubbed in *Oggi, domani, dopodomani*, Pamela's facial expressions are not and with just an askance look or a glance or eye roll, she was able to elicit a laugh. Pamela thought she "looks like a fat cat"[10] in the picture, but didn't care. What Pamela describes as heavy is in comparison to her paper-thin weight when she modeled. Looking at her in the movie, voluptuousness comes to mind.

Arguably, the best part of the movie, other than the new Pamela Tiffin, was its lively trailer. It was brilliantly edited, bringing together the best clips from all three segments bridged with the infectious theme song "La notte è chiara" that keeps you enthralled.

In March 1966 it was reported that Joseph E. Levine refused to distribute *Oggi, domani, dopodomani* as *Paranoia* in the U.S. despite having already devised a marketing campaign complete with press releases ready to be sent to all the major newspapers. Early speculation was that he was not happy that Ponti reneged on delivering a Sophia Loren picture, but the Italian superstar was working for more money at MGM. Eventually, Embassy Pictures filed a $2.6 million lawsuit in Federal Court against Ponti and his production company for breach of contract. The suit claimed they did not fulfill the requirements of the contract to produce and deliver a first-class motion picture. Levine demanded reimbursement of his investment. Ponti countersued. As usually happens with these cases, it was settled out of court with the terms never revealed, but it created a permanent rift between the once friendly filmmakers. Whatever was agreed upon, *Oggi, domani, dopodomani* never reached U.S. theaters as *Paranoia*.

Mastroianni sided with Levine and disliked the movie as well. He commented, "In the last two years, I made some unpleasant, vulgar films."[11] His displeasure may have come through on screen as the Time-Life bureau chief in Rome, Israel Shenker, commented, "Mastroianni moves through the film's three episodes with the disdain for plot that the material demands."[12]

Pamela at least enjoyed making the movie immensely and enjoyed playing her second sexy role. All the newfound attention she was getting as a blonde surprised her, so she decided to keep the hair color. The actress' attitude had changed in five years. Early in her career, teenage Tiffin was considered prim and proper and even had her mother accompany her on film shoots before she married. She also once politely asked Earl Wilson not to label her a sexpot. He agreed and she explained, "To me a sexpot is somebody like Jayne Mansfield—not somebody I'd like to be."[13] Now into her twenties, the demure actress and woman was being seen in a different light as a sexpot and loving every minute of it, giving credence to that old saying, "Blondes do have more fun."

Ponti was so impressed with the new sexy Pamela in *Oggi, domani, dopodomani* that he voiced a wish to work with her again. An item ran in *The Hollywood Reporter* that he was teaming her with Vittorio Gassman for a film whose title translated into *Very Softly*. It never came to be though she did work with the Italian actor in another movie. It is too bad Ponti didn't offer Tiffin *The 10th Victim* as he originally did with Sue Lyon. Seeing her wearing a killer brassiere would have been some sight in this sci-fi cult classic about a futuristic Europe where the most popular TV game show has victims being hunted by sharpshooting hunters.

With the movie shelved for the time being, the press was now only talking about Pamela's new look. Being blonde seemed to give her a new vitality. You can even see the difference in still photos of the actress. Whatever the color of her hair, Pamela Tiffin is a stunning beauty but as a blonde there is more overt sexiness to her. She seems more confident in her womanhood and it leaps from the photos. You can tell she is enjoying posing scantily clad whereas in some of her cheesecake shots as a brunette she looks a bit uncomfortable. This new sexy persona comes through on screen as well.

Pamela claimed that being blonde gave her a new freedom and compared her feelings about it with the surfers' philosophy she learned about when living in Malibu, California for a short time: "Just to be out in the sun makes you sort of lazy—and offers contentment. The impression is often given that surfers are stupid. They're not. They're just having a good time. That's what I am doing now and its heaven!"[14]

The new Pamela made a favorable impression on everybody but her husband Clay Felker, who wanted his dark-haired wife back. Pamela revealed, "He prefers me as a brunette but I'm going to stay blonde unless my next picture calls for me to darken my hair and I'll see that it doesn't. I have one life to live and I want to live it as a blonde. It has changed my personality. I feel better."[15]

Hair color was not the only thing that the actress would alter after doing her first Italian motion picture. She also junked her passion for multi-colored contact lenses because they were a nuisance and her aversion to food due to weight gain. "I'm awfully changeable," she went on to say:

> I've changed many things about myself since my modeling days. I've began to relax and mature and have developed more self-confidence and assurance. When I was modeling I had to watch my weight, and the fluctuation of as much as an ounce was a worry. I lived on skimmed milk and tasteless salads. Ughhh. It seems to me I was always nervous, high-strung, and dreaming of food. Even when I started my film career, the old habits persisted.
> Then I went to Italy and I learned to enjoy eating. How I ate and what a pleasure it was. I gained fifteen pounds. What surprised me was instead of the angular, coltish lines of a young girl, I became fuller, rounder, and softer. I feel so much more feminine, more womanly, [and] happy."[16]

The Italians were so impressed with Pamela that she barely had time to unpack once in New York when another offer came from Rome and back she went. Fortunately, *Delitto quasi perfecto* (translation: *The Almost Perfect Crime*), from prolific award-winning director Mario Camerini, did not wind up in a lawsuit. Unfortunately, the film is almost impossible to find nowadays on DVD in a dubbed English or subtitled version.

In this thriller with comedic overtones, Pamela went the damsel-in-distress route (or did she?) as a kidnapped heiress. Her co-star was the strikingly handsome French actor Philippe Leroy, who was popular in Italy but not a box office draw in the U.S. His notable films for American audiences included producer Samuel Bronston's epic *55 Days at Peking* and the horror movie *Castle of the Living Dead* with Christopher Lee. He played supporting roles in both.

Once again, Pamela had to contend with a screenplay in Italian. "When I did the Mastroianni film, I found it hard to memorize the lines," she recalled. "Afterwards, I realized it was because the English wasn't translated very well. It seemed that some Englishman who had been living in Rome too long translated it. Beginning with this movie, whenever

I had permission, I would translate the script into English with the appropriate slang or phrases for the dubbed version."[17]

In *Delitto quasi perfecto* Pamela played heiress Annie Robson, who meets journalist Paolo Respinghi on a flight from Rome to Beirut. There she is to meet her uncle Col. Robson and to collect a five million dollar inheritance. Smitten with the beautiful blonde, Paolo follows her when she is met at the airport by an elderly house-

Reporter Paolo Respighi (Philippe Leroy) becomes intrigued with heiress Annie Robson (Pamela Tiffin), whom he has just met on a flight to Beirut, in a scene from *Delitto quasi perfecto* (Rizzoli Film, 1966).

keeper and two suspicious-looking men who take her to a secluded villa. The next morning he reads about a past murder in the same villa. Hurrying back there, he sneaks into the abode only to find the housekeeper dead and Annie in hiding. Paolo whisks the frightened girl away, but they run right into the two thugs, who snatch her.

Paolo then contacts Col. Robson for help just as another woman comes forth claiming to be Annie Robson. Paulo tracks down the two thugs and kills them in a gun battle while rescuing Annie in the process. On a ship to meet the colonel, Paolo is shocked to discover that the two men are alive and that Annie is a fraud in cahoots with them to steal the fortune. Meanwhile her uncle is plotting to kill the real Annie to get the money, which he has been embezzling for years. The movie ends with the deaths of the colonel and the two men, the fake Annie arrested, and Paolo and the real Annie left with a depleted fortune.

Delitto quasi perfecto opened in Italy in April 1966. Francesco Dorigo of *Cineforum* found the movie to be "not completely undeserving of attention, Camerini, as a good craftsman, always manages to keep alive the interest in the story." He then goes on to say how the plot becomes tangled and a bit muddled but insisting it was entertaining nevertheless.

Roberto Curti is an Italian film critic and a contributor to several film magazines as well as an author of many books about Italian cinema including *Italian Crime Filmography, 1968–1980* (McFarland, 2013). He commented that *Delitto quasi perfecto* was "a not-so-good, light-hearted mystery-comedy, but rather important since Camerini was one of Italy's most important directors during the 1930s. He directed a number of "telefoni bianchi" ("white telephones") comedies, roughly the Italian equivalent to American screwball comedies. This film was rather popular in its day."[18]

Though the film was a commercial hit in Italy and other parts of continental Europe, it did not get a release in the United Kingdom until late 1970 where it was titled *The Imperfect Murder.* It may have been the producers' way to try to cash in on the popularity of the giallo film though it was not part of this genre at all. Nevertheless, it intrigued moviegoers despite the very mixed reviews. Graham Clarke, writing in *Kinematograph Weekly,* said,

"This is a fairly trite story, but the recurred mayhem and murder is decorated lavishly with red herrings and misleading mystery, so that improbabilities are generally glossed over and the simple convenience with which all the baddies are suddenly disposed of at the end is made acceptable." He praised Philippe Leroy for his convincing performance in a tough role as an experienced international journalist caught up in a situation out of his element. He remarked that Tiffin "looks very pretty and does a bit of acting as the spurious Annie."

Richard Combs of *Monthly Film Bulletin* called it an "undistinguished comedy thriller with charmless characters and a plot whose various interweaving double-crosses suggest less an inventive complexity than sheer witless absurdity." He went on to say that "the editing occasionally has a bemusing elliptical air which if anything only adds to the general pointlessness of the proceedings. There is some glossy photography to watch at a sufficiently insulating distance."

Despite its release in the United Kingdom, *Delitto quasi perfecto* never made it to the U.S. It was unfortunately the start of a pattern where Pamela's Italian films did not get distributed in the States even in dubbed versions. However, this was the beginning of the actress becoming a major star in Italy for the next few years due to the box office returns of her movies.

The truth about Annie Robson (Pamela Tiffin) is revealed in a scene from *Delitto quasi perfecto* (Rizzoli Film, 1966).

Broadway Baby

Dinner at Eight (stage play)

Pamela Tiffin had a quiet 1966 after returning from Italy. It was hoped *Oggi, domani, dopodomani* would have catapulted her into super stardom, but it remained unreleased in America. This truly was a disappointing blow to her career. The movie had all the signs of being a hit, especially when the distributor is Joseph Levine, a master of film promotion. It also was a perfect follow-up to *Harper*, expounding on the new sexy adult image Tiffin was now projecting and a return to her comedy roots, reminding Hollywood that she was one of the prettiest comediennes around. Though the new Pamela Tiffin impressed movie-goers in Italy, in the U.S. her fans were kept waiting for her next big screen offering. We know Pamela's blonde sexpot image, light years away from the *State Fair* ingénue, cost her a role in *The Russians Are Coming, the Russians Are Coming*, but it is unknown what other movie proposals came from Hollywood. Per Pamela, one major film shown interest and it was surprisingly *Bonnie and Clyde*. The film was from Warner Bros., so considering how well she performed in their *Harper* it is very plausible they pushed her for Bonnie. Natalie Wood, Jane Fonda, and Tuesday Weld are always mentioned for turning down the part. Reportedly, Warren Beatty considered Carol Lynley and perhaps was going to offer the role to Sue Lyon before Faye Dunaway was brought to his attention. Per Pamela, she was in talks to play Bonnie but Beatty's womanizing reputation scared her off and she dropped out of the running to her regret.

Perhaps Pamela's lack of drive to get a follow-up to *Oggi* had to do with her personal life. The actress seemed content living in New York and being a wife. She may have enjoyed the break from filmmaking and spending time with her husband.

Pamela kept busy with her modeling gigs including the International Fabrics Fashion Show where she walked the runway in new designs by the renowned Donald Brooks who not only created fashions for the public but also for television and motion pictures. He had just received an Academy Award nomination for Best Costume Design—Color for *The Cardinal*. Pamela next turned up briefly as herself in a black-and-white documentary short titled *The Responsive Eye* (1966), directed by Brian De Palma. *The Responsive Eye* was the name of a Museum of Modern Art (MoMA) exhibition that was open from February through April 1965. Created by William F. Seitz, it focused on op art, which is visual art that uses optical illusion (usually abstract) with the more well-known pieces in black-and-white. Among the artists featured were Frank Stella, Ellsworth Kelly, and Alexander Lieberman.

This short featured the curator and other experts talking about the art and some artists on how they achieved their works juxtaposed with the reactions of some of New York City's social elite, including Pamela Tiffin, to the artwork at the black tie exhibition opening. A beautifully gowned Pamela, looking stunning with her dark hair worn up, is glimpsed entering the Museum of Modern Art on the arm of Clay Felker. She appears again toward the end of the film and is asked by the interviewer what she thought of the exhibition pieces. Pamela, the art history major, replied, "I find them a little dizzy. And my eyes feel very stimulated after looking at it. A lot of paintings you look at and think, what's the form? What's the structure? And this just affects you immediately. You don't even have to think about it."

The documentary was well-received and De Palma boasted, "It is very good and very successful. It's distributed by Pathe Contemporary and makes lots of money. I shot it in four hours, with synched sound."[1]

Pamela then surprised her admirers when she was cast as gold-digging, two-timing Kitty Packard in the 1966 Broadway revival of *Dinner at Eight*. This was the part made famous by Jean Harlow in the 1933 movie version. When her agent told her the play's producers wanted her to read for a role, she assumed it was the debutante daughter and it had no appeal. When she learned it was for Kitty, the former hat check girl, she became intrigued at the chance to play a tough-as-nails type of broad. However, she approached it with mixed emotions, as it would be her stage debut. After working mostly in cinema, Pamela was not sure she had the confidence to tackle a Broadway role (she had previously turned down three plays). She felt her voice was not yet trained and that was one of the reasons she began studying with Stella Adler. But it was her fondness for the thirties that utterly influenced her decision to audition for Kitty.

After Pamela decided to go for the part, her first inclination was to call her former acting coach for guidance. However, she decided not to depend on Stella Adler or others and to approach the role herself. Her intuition to read her own way proved correct and she won the role.

Shortly after, it was reported that producer Charles Feldman wanted Pamela to make a cameo appearance in the James Bond movie spoof *Casino Royale* filming in London. This was the renegade production and not considered an "official" Bond movie. The role was not named in the announcement, but one wonders if it was not that of the seductive assassin Giovanna Goodthighs played by Jacqueline Bisset? Goodthighs is sent by the head of SMERSH to terminate bungling agent Evelyn Tremble (Peter Sellers), one of many spies masquerading as James Bond. Waiting for him in his hotel room clad only in a man's shirt, she tries to kill him as they roll around the bed. The new, sexy Pamela would have been perfect for the part, as she definitely had the gorgeous legs and looks to pull it off, not to mention comedic skills which would have been put to good use opposite Sellers.

Alas, the producer could not guarantee that her part, whatever it may have been, would wrap by August 27 when she had to report for *Dinner at Eight* rehearsals and she had to turn it down.

This was a major missed opportunity for Pamela. Though *Casino Royale* was a bloated mess, this spy spoof was a big hit at the box office and remains a cult favorite. Had she been able to accept the role offered to her, it would have once again showcased her comedic chops to the public as well as introducing her new sexy blonde look. It would have been a wonderful follow up to *Harper*. Her stock in Hollywood surely would have risen and given her lots of publicity as it did for its female leads Ursula Andress, Joanna Pettet, Dahlia Lavi, and Jacqueline Bisset. One could only imagine what a memorable quasi–Bond Girl Pamela Tiffin would have made. Alas the timing was off and as they say "timing is everything" especially in the movie business.

Written by George S. Kaufman and Edna Ferber, *Dinner at Eight* was first produced on Broadway in 1932. It was a comic look at the society set during the Depression. Kitty Packard is the adulterous social-climbing wife of brusque businessman Oliver Packard. The couple is forever battling and he refuses to accept an invitation to the Jordans' party until he hears that an even richer couple from England will be in attendance. Kitty delivers one of the play's most famous lines, "Politics? You couldn't get in anywhere…. You couldn't get into the men's room at the Astor." The roles were made famous by the aforementioned Jean Harlow and Wallace Beery in the very successful 1933 film version. In the revival, Tiffin acted opposite Robert Burr (substituting for Darren McGavin who switched to the role of the fading film star) as her husband.

Dinner at Eight's cast also included June Havoc and Walter Pidgeon as the hosting couple plus Arlene Francis, Blanche Yurka, and future soap opera stars Judith Barcroft (*All My Children*), Joseph Mascolo (*Days of Our Lives*), and Niki Flacks (*One Life to Live*). A one-time critic of American acting, Britisher Tyrone Guthrie accepted the offer to direct because he found the play to be marvelously written. His prior Broadway shows included *Six Characters in Search of an Author*, *Tamburlaine the Great*, *The Matchmaker* (for which he won a Tony Award for Best Director), and *Gideon*.

Stepping into Harlow's shoes was a big risky undertaking for Pamela. Just one year prior, actresses Carroll Baker and Carol Lynley played the blonde bombshell in two different biographical films, both titled *Harlow*, to mostly negative reviews. It was surprising to hear from Pamela Tiffin that she tackled the part differently than Harlow and did not try to ape the movie actress; instead she made Kitty softer and gentler. Pamela said, "I didn't see Jean Harlow in the role of Kitty Packard on purpose. I didn't think it would help my performance…. As I see Kitty Packard, she is an intellectually limited child, who marries a rich man, is confused by all his business activities and that is what leads her to infidelity."[2] Considering her whispery, sing-song voice, it is hard not to visualize Pamela playing the role any other way.

Today Niki Flacks is a well-respected director, acting teacher, and author of the books *PowerTalk* and *Acting with Passion*. By 1966, she had earned a B.S. from Northwestern University and worked with Tyrone Guthrie at the Guthrie Theater in Minnesota. She wrote the director a letter asking permission to audition for a part in *Dinner at Eight* after learning that a revival was headed for Broadway. According to the actress, she received back a script and a note saying, "What nonsense, child. You don't have to audition. The part is yours."[3] Having great confidence in her, Guthrie gave Flacks the role of Tina, Kitty's blackmailing maid. In the movie, the part of Tina was portrayed by a much older actress (Hilda Vaughn) in a sinister fashion, as compared to the humorous interpretation in this stage version. When asked if she was familiar with Tiffin's work, Flacks admitted, "I knew Pamela Tiffin was a movie star, but I had no idea what she looked like or anything. I was so busy doing serious theater at Northwestern and the Guthrie that I really never watched light-hearted teenage movies."[4]

Flacks felt Pamela's admitted trepidation about playing Kitty showed during rehearsals

Pamela Tiffin in 1966. Photograph by Friedman-Abeles/©Billy Rose Theatre Division, The New York Public Library for the Performing Arts, Astor, Lenox and Tilden Foundations.

and on stage. "Pamela Tiffin was a lovely creature—just staggeringly lovely," gushed Flacks:

> But because she had so little stage experience, I think she was nervous about it. Pamela just seemed so fragile and insecure. Since I had already worked for Tyrone Guthrie, whom I think was just a genius and the greatest director of the 20th century, I wasn't intimidated at all and

so rehearsals were a very different experience for me. However, observing Pamela, I knew that it was scary. Stage energy is very different from film energy. I know that Guthrie pushed her and pushed her to up the energy level. That just wasn't something that Pamela could do. She was very languid and soft. I think she may have been aware of his frustration though she never discussed it with me. I know that was an issue.[5]

As for Robert Burr who played Kitty's husband, Flacks exclaimed, "He was not a movie name, but a big respected stage actor who had done major roles on Broadway for years. He had amazing stage energy and when he was doing a scene it crackled."[6]

Despite her decision not to watch Jean Harlow in the film version, Tiffin was asked what she thought about the eventual comparison from the critics. It wasn't weighing on her mind, but she mused, "In the movies, you make a film, five or six months

Robert Burr and Pamela Tiffin in rehearsal for the stage production *Dinner at Eight*. Photograph by Friedman-Abeles/© Billy Rose Theatre Division, The New York Public Library for the Performing Arts.

go by and quite often movie people don't look at their reviews. You've made the picture and it is over. But in the theater it is hard to get used to the fact that your work will be judged so directly hours after the curtain goes down and they've seen your work."[7]

The producers spared no expense in recreating New York's high society of the thirties. Robert Houseman, brought in to design the sets, gave special attention to the abode of Tiffin's Kitty Packard. He took a 1966 approach to make the set feel homey to Pamela despite its thirties trappings. As described in *The News-Palladium*, "Glitter and chrome, silver and feather boas, 1930 overblown Cabbage Roses in 1966 coloration, evoke a sense of past and present—all to catch the elusive personality of Pamela whose platinum vamp is at once offset by the real Pamela Tiffin, perhaps a shy little girl with a strong sense of taste and sophistication."[8]

Despite the huge cast, all worked together professionally and got along backstage. The one actor who stood out personally for Flacks was June Havoc, sister of Gypsy Rose Lee and daughter of Mama Rose. "June was a phenomenal experience to know," Flacks said, laughing:

She was absolutely cuckoo, but wonderful. She had fabulous stage energy. She had performed in burlesque and knew her way around the stage. She was in her fifties and I was the arrogance of youth. She would talk baby talk when she wanted something from the stage manager like, "Junie needs a new light in her dressing room." It was hysterical. June was such a character and she was often a dinner companion between shows. She was great fun and had great stories.[9]

The play opened on September 27, 1966, at the Alvin Theatre to decidedly mixed reviews. Pamela did not receive unanimous praise, but most of her New York notices were positive and her softer approach to the part was deemed a success. She received the most print from critic Norman Nadel of the *World Journal Tribune* who called her "a phenomenal eyeballer. It is not so much her acting … but the combination of that alternatingly babyish and bitchy voice, the whining petulance, the innate vulgarity, and especially the body. Miss Tiffin's legs are stunning, and when she … is hurling herself about that draped and quilted white boudoir, it's enough to take a man's mind off his work."

Critics from outside of New York also weighed in. Richard L. Coe of the *Los Angeles Times* found her to be "touchingly amusing." *Variety* called her "impressive." Edward Sothern Hipp of the *Newark Evening News* said she "offers much more than an exceptionally shapely form…." Across the pond, the *London Times* critic raved, "Pamela Tiffin reveals unsuspect talents for vulgarity as the nouveau riche wife."

On the negative side, the Associated Press drama critic William Glover commented, "Pamela Tiffin looks acceptable but proceeds on the regrettable assumption that screeching is acting." George Oppenheimer in *Newsday* called Pamela a "luscious lady who looks somewhat like Jean Harlow," but found her performance to be "far too obvious" and "unreal."

John Gassner, writing his annual "Broadway in Review" for the *Educational Theatre Journal*, was disappointed with most of the performances in *Dinner at Eight*. Pamela was an exception: "[Her] doll-like but flannel-mouthed impersonation of the lavishly kept but two-timing wife of the business marauder was a sheer delight."

Pamela was proud of her performances as Kitty. She claimed it was stimulating to play such a character and felt she brought newfound vigor to the part. "This is the very first time I have been on stage and believe me, it took guts to try. Tyrone Guthrie is such a giant, six feet five, that he found a place for my energy. You know, the way I spit out 'Nerts,' in the play. I give off energy."[10]

Since Pamela was playing the blonde bombshell in *Dinner at Eight*, columnist Whitney Bolton of the *New York Morning Telegraph* naively expected her to be of the Jean Harlow and Marilyn Monroe kind. He was pleasantly surprised to find she was not and described the actress as being "an extremely pleasant young woman, less than overwhelmed with her stature in show business, avid to learn all there is to learn and possessed of a natural enough and not over-exhibited yearning to reach higher levels of competence and importance."[11]

Pamela shared some of her stage mishaps with Bolton. Her character is supposed to eat candy in one scene and she was ever fearful a caramel would slip in. Sure enough one night it did and despite it gumming up her teeth, she was able to say her lines audibly while trying to chew the candy down. The candy was eventually replaced with squares of black bread (the audience could not distinguish them from candy) which enabled Pamela to speak clearly while nibbling on the edges. Another time an over-zealous Robert Burr, as her husband, threw her handbag across the stage and it landed near the flood lights instead of near her feet. Pamela had to ad lib as she went to retrieve it and handled the mishap like a pro.

As if appearing on Broadway at night didn't keep Tiffin busy enough, the forever student was taking acting classes with Harold Clurman during the day, playing Yelena in *Uncle Vanya*. Being three different people in one day was challenging for the actress, who revealed, "It's hard to change from both and it's hard to live with me."[12]

Niki Flacks and Tiffin became friendly and would socialize off-set. Flacks briefly witnessed the relationship between Pamela and her husband. "I would dine frequently with Pamela and Clay Felker between shows on the days when we had a matinee and evening performance," Niki said. "He was considerably older and treated her like a child. I just found it incredible. She would say in her whispery voice, 'I don't know what I should eat.' He'd say, 'You'll have the lamp chops and baked potato.' And she obeyed."[13] Pamela would soon leave Felker; his attitude towards her may have been one of the reasons why she ran off.

Pamela did her part to bring attention to *Dinner at Eight* with her appearances on TV talk and game shows of the time including *The Mike Douglas Show*, *Girl Talk*, and *What's My Line?* Moderated by John Charles Daly, *What's My Line?* was the longest running television primetime game show. The premise was very simple: A celebrity panel of four would try to identify the occupation of various guests who would win money for every wrong

Pamela Tiffin and Niki Flacks in a scene from *Dinner at Eight*. Photograph by Friedman-Abeles/© Billy Rose Theatre Division, The New York Public Library for the Performing Arts.

guess. During the show's Mystery Guest segment, the panel would put on blindfolds and try to identify the celebrity who would try to disguise their voices in various ways to fool them.

Pamela Tiffin joined a number of her Broadway co-stars from *Dinner at Eight* including Robert Burr, June Havoc, Darren McGavin and Walter Pidgeon as Mystery Guests trying

Pamela Tiffin in the role of Kitty Packard in a scene from the 1966 Broadway stage revival of *Dinner at Eight*. Photograph by Friedman-Abeles/©Billy Rose Theatre Division, The New York Public Library for the Performing Arts, Astor, Lenox and Tilden Foundations.

to stump the panel of Arlene Francis (also a cast member in the play), Jayne Meadows, Steve Allen, and publisher Bennett Cerf, who identified the entire cast of *Dinner at Eight* as the Mystery Guests. Daly had Arlene Francis come center stage to introduce each cast member and announced, "And Pamela Tiffin, who is the witch," a line that got a big laugh from the studio audience.

Due to her glowing reviews for *Dinner at Eight*, Tiffin received a Theatre World Award for her New York stage debut. Other winners that year for their Broadway or Off-Broadway bows included Richard Benjamin and Connie Stevens for *Star-Spangled Girl*; Leslie Uggams for *Hallelujah, Baby!*; Dustin Hoffman for *Eh?*; Jon Voight for *That Summer—That Fall*; and Christopher Walken for *The Rose Tattoo*.

Dinner at Eight closed on January 14, 1967, after 127 performances despite a last-ditch effort to save the show by offering two tickets for the price of one. The show lost an estimated $100,000 per Lester Osterman, one of the producers and owner of the theater. It was a financial disappointment considering the all-star cast assembled for it. Come Tony Award time, the play was snubbed: It did not receive a single nomination.

There was talk that Pamela would return to the stage playing Marilyn Monroe. Poet-playwright Norman Rosten was a very good friend of the late actress and had written a play about her. He thought Pamela would be perfect to bring the glamorous platinum blonde movie star to life on the stage based on seeing her in *Dinner at Eight*. Pamela confessed trepidation about being compared to the film icon after having just been compared to Jean Harlow. She never had to make the decision as the play never came to be. At least Pamela now had the satisfaction of knowing that people were no longer looking at her as the demure ingénue but as a sexy adult woman.

Pamela continued modeling while doing *Dinner at Eight* and appeared in a layout of very sensual photographs by the renowned Timothy Galfas. Galfas was known for his magazine cover shots of some of the world's most beautiful motion picture stars such as Elizabeth Taylor, Audrey Hepburn, Natalie Wood, Suzy Parker, Tina Louise, and Stella Stevens. Regarding his photography technique, Galfas stated, "I can take a portrait of a woman and do as much as *Playboy* can with a nude. Take ... Pamela's eyes. They say romance, sex, that particular something. They say more than a nude."[14]

One assignment that she did turn down was the chance to be photographed by Andy Warhol for the cover of *Esquire* magazine. He wanted the young beauty to pose in a garbage can; Pamela passed on the opportunity, as did actress Jessica Walter. Warhol then got fashion model Edie Sedgwick, who was hanging around his art studio (dubbed The Factory) to be his model.

In March, after *Dinner at Eight* closed, Pamela made a return appearance to *What's My Line?*, this time as a panelist along with Arlene Francis, Martin Gabel, and Bennett Cerf. The first Mystery Guests that evening were the sons of Francis and Cerf. The second was actor Robert Morse, who used a cowboy-type drawl to disguise his voice. Host John Charles Daly started the questioning with Pamela, who seemed a bit nervous and awkward, asking, "Are you in the entertainment world?" When Morse responded yes, Tiffin began to ask a second question when Daly cut her off, going to Bennett Cerf.

When the questioning came back around to Pamela she softly queried, "Did you receive a lot of your training in New York?" to which Morse drolly replied, "Ah, in which respect, Miss Tiffin?" It drew loads of laughter from the audience, as well as from Pamela, who clarified by asking, "Did you go to the Strasberg school of acting?" Tiffin's final question to Morse was if he worked in movie westerns. After his reply of no, Cerf was able to identify the actor. Unfortunately for Tiffin fans, after the panelists removed their blindfolds, she was left out of the banter between the actor and the rest of the panel. However, as he was departing, Morse did steal a kiss from the beauty. The lost look on Pamela's face throughout this episode did not go unnoticed: Fans on TV.com commented on her lack of attention and confusion regarding the rules. It would be her lone appearance on the panel.

Coincidentally, she and Robert Morse almost became on-screen co-stars in a 1964 comedy to be called *The Unusual Life of Willy Wildy*. Morse was scheduled to play an embezzler and Pamela his ditzy, cat-loving wife. At the time Pamela was very enthusiastic about doing this movie and gushed, "It would be shot in New York. Bobby's wife is in New York and my husband is there so it would be just right for all of us!"[15] It never came to be.

Movie-wise, Pamela may have not known it, but she was on producer Larry Turman's short list to play Mrs. Robinson's nubile daughter Elaine, engaged to another man but attracted to recent college graduate Benjamin Braddock, in 1967's *The Graduate*. Others on the list, after Patty Duke and Sally Field turned it down, included Natalie Wood, Lee Remick, Tuesday Weld, Suzanne Pleshette, Sue Lyon, Yvette Mimieux, and Carol Lynley. Katharine Ross got the role and an Academy Award nomination.

There was one other movie at this time Pamela should have been a contender for. She had worked for producer David Weisbart on *The Pleasure Seekers* and it would be interesting to know if she was even considered for his 1967 hit *Valley of the Dolls*, based on Jacqueline Susann's steamy bestseller. Tiffin, with her wild blonde hair and new sexy persona, would have been perfect for the role of the ill-fated Jennifer (played by Sharon Tate), the showgirl-turned-nudie film star who offs herself by taking the blue pills when she has to undergo a mastectomy. Actually, one could easily see all three gals from *The Pleasure Seekers* slipping into the movie with Ann-Margret as the musical mess Neely and Carol Lynley as icy model Anne joining Pamela. Though Ann-Margret reportedly turned the role down, Lynley and Tiffin's names never came up in the trades as being considered for any role.

14

Marcello Mastroianni: Take Two

Kiss the Other Sheik

In the summer of 1967, Tiffin was coaxed back to Italy by producer Carlo Ponti, who was trying to salvage his investment in *Oggi, domani, dopodomani*. It was the film that would not die. Despite the critical barbs and Embassy Pictures' refusal to distribute it in 1966, Ponti was determined to recoup his losses and salvage the movie for U.S. audiences by focusing on "La moglie bionda." It was to be extended by combining it with the other color segment "L'ora di punta" with Virna Lisi to pad the running time for a feature-length movie.

Ponti asked Pamela and Marcello Mastroianni to film additional scenes with director Luciano Salce, who played Lisi's husband in the other segment. Pamela agreed to film a few new scenes and flew in from New York, but Mastroianni agreed to only one and the production had to wait until he was available during the summer of 1967. Virna Lisi refused to participate, but also asked that her name be removed from the credits. The director of her segment Eduard De Filippo and screenwriter Isabella Quarantotti also refused screen credit due to their objections to this refurbished film.

This version begins with a crazed naked man found on the Spanish Steps in Rome. He is long-lost Mario Gasparri (Marcello Mastroianni) and he is brought to the police station where his wife Pepita (Tiffin) goes to claim him in the new footage. She has not seen him in almost two years and explains to the police inspector what happened. Mario's friend Arturo (Luciano Salce) is there to help fill in the gaps.

The movie then flashes back to the beginning of "La moglie bionda." However, where that ended with Pepita selling Mario to a homosexual sheik, this new version continues incorporating the other segment with Mario eventually escaping and winding up with gun-toting friend Arturo and his wife Dorotea (Virna Lisi). However, their sick, childish love games (he shoots at her with his gun every time he is upset and then they make up afterwards as if nothing has happened) drive him mad. That is how he ended up in the nude on the Spanish Steps. Pepita takes her husband home, with the police inspector suspecting that she intends to return him to the pursuing sheik. He thinks his assumption is correct when he spots her delivering a body in a trunk to the sheik. However, it is Arturo, not Mario, who is heading to Africa. Pepita and her husband happily reunite.

MGM picked up the distribution rights to the new movie in 1968. Ponti originally titled this new version *Lo Smemorato* (*Scatterbrain*). MGM first changed it to *The Man*

Who Lost His Memory but then released it under the catchier name *Kiss the Other Sheik* during the late summer. The screen credits were also changeable as Luciano Salce was listed as sole director and as one of the screenwriters, but was not credited for his performance as Lisi's husband. Most of the crew from "L'ora di punta" was also uncredited.

Playing up the promised debut of Tiffin as a blonde sex goddess, some press material asked, "Is Stanley Wonso prepared to see his daughter oiled in a Sultan's bath, stripped of all but her tassels and veils, wandering around in the lord-awful nearly altogether with a price tied to her slave bracelet?" In some more staid places, the film did not get released until early 1969 under the title *The Man, the Woman and the Money* with the sex played down.

Virna Lisi also did not escape the exploitation. Though Ponti agreed to keep her name from being used in promoting the picture or in the credits, her image was prominently displayed in two different print ads. One had the tagline "Love's oldest game—the double-cross … is double the fun when the Italians are doing the crossing.… Harem-style!" The other read, "A naughty, new switch on those amorous Arabian nights!" The wittiest tagline came with a cartoon print ad that declared, "His vice was selling his wife … until the vice went versa!"

Reviews were mixed. *New York Times* critic Renata Adler called it "one of those sodden, gross off-color comedies that the Italians do so badly." She found that Pamela "has been misphotographed, or mis-directed, or mis-made-up, so that she looks simultaneously inflated and floury, like some kind of Betty Crocker water toy."

The *Variety* critic called the new police station footage "stagey and awkward." The reviewer for *Cue* said Tiffin was "a good-looker," but carped that the film itself was "as thin as Marcello's veil." Ray

Promotional poster art for *Kiss the Other Sheik* (MGM, 1968).

Loynd of *The Hollywood Reporter* described it as "a particularly chaotic and mindless sexual farce as mystifying in form and content as in its bewildering production notes and screen credits.... [It] features Miss Tiffin in poses ranging from center spread kitten to fashion plate hauteur." Marjory Adams, writing in the *Boston Globe*, was shocked that so many writers were needed "to put together such a sorry story of sex" and quipped that this "new romp ends with a joke, but audience was in mourning." *Box Office* skewered the movie, calling it "a vulgar, one-joke, Italian language attempt at comedy that is only sporadically interesting." It also mentioned the inept dubbing, especially for the "Barbie Doll"—looking Pamela Tiffin.

The United States Conference of Catholic Bishops condemned the movie, giving it an "O" rating for morally offensive.

Pepita (Pamela Tiffin) poses for her "driver's license" photograph in a scene from *Kiss the Other Sheik* (MGM, 1968).

Its critic remarked, "Luciano Salce's heavy-handed treatment is flat and extremely vulgar." This review may have indirectly helped its box office chances, perking the interests of the prurient. By this time, a number of movies were breaking free of the crippling Motion Picture Code.

On the positive side, Bob Micklin of *Newsday* described *Kiss the Other Sheik* as "a sprightly sex comedy" and ended his review with, "[I]t's not the best comedy we've seen, but its foolish fun is frequently entertaining." The reviewer from *The Independent Film Journal* said, "Some funny moments, all of them provided by Pamela Tiffin.... [L]ush production values also help, but film is a mild art house entry." PFC Rick Goetz, reviewing in *Pacific Stars & Stripes*, said the movie provides "some fun and laughter." The critic for *The Post-Standard Syracuse* wittily wrote, "In this silly-farce comedy, about the only two real things appear to be the sand and Pamela Tiffin's curves.... Her costumes are too abbreviated or cut-out to conceal anything or reveal anyone put Pamela ... [who] would be a prize in any harem."

Another impressed by Pamela's beauty and talent was reviewer Tom Gray (*Motion Picture Herald*): "The most tangible asset this Italian-made comedy farce has in its favor is young, vivacious and glamorous Pamela Tiffin, displaying a great knack for comedy as she leads Marcello Mastroianni on a laugh-filled chase from Rome to Morocco and back again." But despite the sexy shots of Pamela, provocative dialogue, and funny sight gags, Gray felt that, "due to the uneven pacing and the occasional use of flashbacks.... *Sheik* tends to lack the smooth flow and velocity essential to good comedy."

One of the problems with *Kiss the Other Sheik*, and Italian cinema in general during the sixties, is the directors' disregard with synchronization of dialogue. This was usually

Michele (Marcello Mastroianni) coaxes his wife Pepita (Pamela Tiffin) to dance for the sheik in a scene from *Kiss the Other Sheik* (MGM, 1968). Billy Rose Theatre Division, The New York Public Library for the Performing Arts, Astor, Lenox and Tilden Foundations.

left for the looping and dubbing stages afterwards. For picky American movie audiences, nothing is more annoying than seeing mouths move with nothing coming out. Even more frustrating, when Italian movies were dubbed into English, rarely did they let the American actors do their own looping. "The Italian industry has always insisted on dubbing … for many reasons," explains Roberto Curti:

> The dubbing industry was—and still is—a very powerful one. When America started flooding the market with Hollywood films after World War II, it was unthinkable to show subtitled films, given the fact that a huge part of the population was illiterate. Italian films were shot on noisy sets, with actors speaking in their own language and later re-dubbed (and with dialogues sometimes re-written in post-production). Moreover, Italian audiences would not accept a foreign actor dubbing himself—even many popular Italian actors were dubbed by someone else, examples being Giuliano Gemma, Bud Spencer and Terence Hill, Maurizio Merli, etc.
>
> Even nowadays, it's a rare occurrence to find subtitled foreign films in Italian theaters. For instance, Tarantino's *Inglorious Basterds*, where different languages are an essential part in the plot, was dubbed, with the result that the scene in which Brad Pitt does a laughably bad Italian impression and Christopher Waltz mocks him became a scene where he speaks in Sicilian dialect (!) while everyone else speaks Italian—thus completely losing the point of the scene itself.[1]

But why the continuance in the sixties and seventies of the practice of not using the American stars of Italian movies to do their own dubbing into English? Perhaps because they were not part of the Italian dubbing industry and they required only English-speaking Italian actors to do the dubbing? Curti thinks that may be so and added that it was also a way to cut costs, "as foreign actors were hired for a limited number of days (and with tight schedules in order to shoot as much as possible) whereas dubbing their own lines would require them to get back to Italy for post-production. Moreover, since many films were aimed primarily at the Italian market, the English dubbing was not a priority."[2]

In *Kiss the Other Sheik* Tiffin in particular is atrociously dubbed. The movie itself, with the new footage and old footage stitched together in a slapdash matter, is not as good as when it was a standalone in *Oggi, domani dopodomani* as "La moglie bionda."

On the plus side, American moviegoers finally got to see the "new" Pamela Tiffin who does not disappoint. She looks stunning as the naïve playful wife and kept the movie from bombing at the box office in the U.S. though in New York City it played the bottom of a double bill with a reissue of *Blow Up* and only grossed a meager $22,000 in seven days of release. It does take some time to get used to seeing Tiffin as a blonde, but she is not "misphotographed" as stated by critic Renata Adler. During the photo session sequence she matches the sex kitten persona of Ann-Margret. The sweet dark-haired ingénue of *State Fair* only a scant three years prior is long gone. Watching her pose with nothing but a straw hat or seductively trying to entice her husband into the boudoir or dancing in a tight gown for a sheik, Pamela is a stunner. Pamela holds her own with Mastroianni. Her knack for comedy comes through even with just her facial expressions, be it surprise running from sword-wielding guards or satisfaction in her revenge on her louse of a husband. After seeing her in this movie, her decision to remain blonde makes perfect sense.

15

Arrivederci, Hollywood!

When Pamela returned home to New York after *Kiss the Other Sheik*, she almost immediately packed her bags and relocated to Rome for good, as reported by Earl Wilson in October 1967. Her reason was to escape her unhappy marriage. Despite what she told the press previously, she didn't want to act any more after her marriage to Felker, and wanted to raise a family. But to her disillusionment, her husband, very modern for the time, liked having a working wife. This caused Pamela to believe she was unloved. Feeling alone and rejected, she ran away to Italy.

The prim and proper Tiffin, who had lived by the code of conduct for formal young women, proved she could be just as free-spirited and impetuous as other young people now that the Age of Aquarius was dawning. In 1967, twentysomethings were tuning in, turning on, and dropping out. They were rebelling against the establishment in many ways, from practicing free love, to smoking marijuana and dropping acid, to protesting an unjust war. Abandoning her husband and her Hollywood film career was twenty-four-year-old Pamela's final rebellion that began bubbling up with the bleaching of her hair and her new-found enjoyment of eating whatever she wanted without the guilt of calorie counting.

On a personal level, Pamela's decision was impetuous, but understandable. On a professional level it was not. Where were her agents at the time and why did they not try to dissuade her from making such a career-changing decision? You would think they would have tried to protect their investment and their commission and at least try to talk her out of it. Or why didn't they try to get her cast in English-language productions shot throughout Europe? She surely had the marquee value and did not have to appear only in Italian-language films even if she did reside in Rome. Not shifting the blame to her agents, Pamela did feel that their interest in her was not as devoted and supportive as they professed and none of them ever acted as long-term planners. There seemed to be no one in her life equivalent to a Svengali such as Patrick Curtis who guided Raquel Welch to fame or a Roger Smith who got Ann-Margret's career back on track.

One person who was not surprised about Tiffin's decision to head to Italy rather than Hollywood was her friend and co-star from *The Lively Set*, Carole Wells. "Pamela was very esoteric and had this kind of mysterious veil around her," commented Carole:

> She didn't talk to people and didn't let everybody know who she was. I think that kind of worked for her in many ways because people stayed interested in her. She didn't seem like an actress and I always thought to myself, "I don't think she is going to have a long career because she just isn't interested in it." I don't know why, but I always felt like that when I was with her. Pamela really wasn't happy in Hollywood.[1]

It should not be too much of a surprise that Pamela chose not to relocate west and instead gave the finger to all as she headed to Roma considering the time period and that she was never a typical Hollywood starlet. While her contemporaries were attending premieres and parties and going on studio-arranged dates in Hollywood, the forever intellectual was attending college classes in New York where she resided. Pamela was definitely not a Raquel Welch–type determined to become a superstar no matter what she had to do. She really had no strong loyalties or connection to Hollywood (seven of the eleven motion pictures she made up to this point were shot partly on location outside of California) and they totally misused her talents, never offering her a project equal to *One, Two, Three* to spotlight her comedic abilities.

Alas, Pamela's choice to head to Rome proved the musing of *Show Business Illustrated* correct in 1962. Despite the predictions that Tiffin would be Hollywood's next Audrey Hepburn, the magazine declared that odds were she would go the way of other promising newcomers such as Debra Paget, Faith Domergue, and Millie Perkins. These ladies flashed brightly for a little while before drifting back into semi-obscurity. Pamela did have the talent and the backing of impressing important producers and directors. However, she did not have the power to prevent the studios from putting her in movies that she was contractually bound to do but she did not want to make. Though they made her extremely popular, the world of teenage movies was not where she saw herself. This did weaken her resolve in Hollywood, and with her move to Italy, it all but killed any chance of top stardom. As with Faith Domergue, Tiffin too would become more of a cult pop icon.

The unfortunate part of this was that with *Harper* and then *Oggi, domani, dopodomani/Kiss the Other Sheik* Pamela achieved her goal of breaking free of the ingénue roles. She proved she could play sexy adult parts and not just the marriage-minded naïve virgin. A number of other actresses trapped with this persona in the sixties such as Sandra Dee, Annette Funicello, Hayley Mills, and Connie Stevens never could break the mold on the big screen though they did play more varied parts on television. By running off to Italy, she never gave Hollywood the chance to see what roles they would offer the new Pamela Tiffin.

If Pamela had remained in the U.S. or gone to London, it is fun to speculate what movie roles she may have been considered for or landed. Undoubtedly the spy genre would have used her light comedic flair and one can see her playfully sparring with Dean Martin in any of the Matt Helm adventures or perhaps in the British Bulldog Drummond series with Richard Johnson. She would have been perfect for the role of flighty Alice in *Bob & Carol & Ted & Alice*; her soft voice and more subtle comedic playing would have been a great contrast to the more hardened Dyan Cannon who got the role.

Pamela was not the only Hollywood actress who had the idea to relocate to Rome in the sixties. Tina Louise had come and gone. Ann-Margret had just arrived, and Carroll Baker, Barbara Bouchet, and Mimsy Farmer, among others, soon followed. All came due to their disenchantment with the roles being offered (or not being offered) to them in Hollywood.

Tina Louise set the movie screens ablaze in her film debut as the sexy farm nymph Griselda in *God's Little Acre* (1958), based on the bestselling Erskine Caldwell novel. She won a Golden Globe and followed up with dramatic roles in three above-par movies in 1959, *The Trap* with Richard Widmark; *The Hangman* with Robert Taylor; and *Day of the Outlaw* with Robert Ryan. Unhappy with the roles being offered to her in Hollywood,

Pamela Tiffin on the cover of the March 1966 issue of *Photoplay Film Monthly*.

Louise moved to Rome. Though she did work with the esteemed director Roberto Rossellini, playing a small role in *Viva l'Italia*, she was relegated to sword-and-sandal films such as *Warrior Empress* and *Siege of Syracuse*. When she returned to the U.S. in 1963 she settled in New York and still ignored her movie career.

Ann-Margret was unhappy with her image in America as a wild-haired, booty-shaking sex kitten. With Hollywood laughing at her and thinking she had become a joke due to less than stellar performances in bad movies, she went to Italy to find better parts. Carroll Baker's lawsuit with Paramount Pictures regarding the disappointing film bio *Harlow* (they claimed she did not fulfill her contractual duties in promoting the movie and got her blackballed by all the major studios). With almost two years of no film offers, Baker accepted a chance to star in *L'harem* in Italy to pay the bills in 1967. She loved it there so much, she packed up her children and relocated. Pretty blonde Barbara Bouchet, in movies since 1964, most notably as naval officer Kirk Douglas' adulterous, ill-fated wife in *In Harm's Way* (1965), was receiving a lot of press due to her high-profile role in Bob Fosse's *Sweet Charity* (1969), attracting the attention of some Italian producers. This coincided with a personal problem she was having with an older gentleman infatuated with her. When she was offered a movie in Rome, she wanted to get away and leaped at the chance to work abroad. She never returned.

As for Mimsy Farmer, she decided to stay in Europe after completing *The Wild Racers* in 1968, her third exploitation movie for American International Pictures. She didn't think she would act again, but *Racers'* associate producer brought her to the attention of director Barbet Schroeder. He gave her the female lead in *More* about a free-spirited American girl who, into all sorts of drug-taking, leads an infatuated German grad student to Ibiza, where they meet a bad end. Farmer became the hit of the Continent and moved to Rome. Explaining why she preferred to make movies in Europe rather than Hollywood, Mimsy remarked, "In Europe, actors were not shuffled off to their trailers between shots and were invited to participate and collaborate with the director and other crew members. It was so different. Nobody was anxious about my 'bottom' (admittedly much diminished) and nobody was redesigning my eyebrows and curling my hair. I just had the feeling that nobody wanted me to act or look like anyone but myself—such a relief!"[2]

While those other actresses starred in various genres, Pamela Tiffin was mostly confined to *commedia all'Italiana*—not really a genre, but more a description of comedies about Italian middle-class situations and manners tinged with a touch of sadness. They were produced from about 1958 to 1980. Most of these movies never made it to America, as they were geared to Italian audiences. Considering she was told in Hollywood that she was best suited for light comedy, it shouldn't be a surprise that Pamela found most film work there.

Though Pamela played a sexpot in her first Italian movie, she steered away from that type of role in her future movies. She yearned to become a character actress and, hidden under different wigs, played roles ranging from a simple country girl and New York City housewife to a conniving gold digger, a Danish porn star, a western whore, and an adulteress.

Despite her varied roles, moviegoers worldwide always imagined her as a sex goddess due to the provocative photos of her that appeared in or on the covers (in some cases more than once) of the international movie and men's magazines of the day including *Io* (Italy), *Tempo* (Italy), *Playmen* (Italy), *Kent* (Italy), *TV Illustrazione* (Italy), *TV Sorrisi e canzoni* (Italy), *Bolero Film* (Italy), *L'Europeo* (Italy), *Cine Monde* (France), *Cine Revue* (France), *Topless* (France), *Pomanteo* (Greece), *Demongeo* (Japan), *Plateia* (Portugal), *Hayat* (Turkey), *Parade* (UK), *Photoplay Film Monthly* (UK), and *EXYU* (Yugoslavia), among others. She landed on more covers as a blonde in Europe than she did while as a demure brunette in Hollywood. Posing skimpily clad with her wild mane of flaxen hair ("Lady Pamela" was long gone), she projected a sex symbol image that was not indicative of her film career.

Inadvertently, Tiffin's sexy photos got one newspaper in trouble in India. Running a photo where she was barely clothed, a leftist political weekly got convicted of obscenity. The conviction was later overturned, but not before its editor spent fifteen days in jail.

Pamela created a duality of herself in print and on screen. The wild-haired, scantily clad blonde sexpot seen in photos was nowhere to be found in the cinema. She avoided most roles that played up her sexiness. Even when playing a coed who moonlights as a porn actress in *Il vichingo venuto dal Sud* she maintains a mature independence rather than going the purring sex kitten route. The closest she came was in *L'arcangelo* where she is gorgeously made up and draped in high fashion as a scheming gold digger out to dupe a schlep into committing murder for her. The two Pamela Tiffins no doubt frustrated her fans, especially males who may have wanted to see their sex goddess emerge from the pages of their magazines and burst onto the screen. Unlike Carroll Baker and Barbara Bouchet, Pamela stuck to her determination to remain clothed on screen. However, her natural sex appeal could not help but exude no matter what roles she played.

16

Pamela, Italian Style

I Protagonisti (*The Protagonists*)
Straziami, ma di baci saziami (*Kill Me with Kisses*)
L'archangelo (*The Archangel*)

Pamela's first movie after her permanent move to Rome was *I Protagonisti* (*The Protagonists*), directed and co-written by Marcello Fondato. This was the screenwriter's directorial debut and considered one of his best efforts in Italian circles. It was one of the very few movies at the time shot on the island of Sardinia, just off the Italian peninsula. It was also Pamela's first non-western adventure movie where she had running and shootout scenes. Fans were not used to seeing Pamela in this type of movie, and neither was she used to the physicality the part required. It would be her sole appearance in this genre.

I Protagonisti went into production at a time when lawlessness on the Mediterranean island had become a problem for the Italian government. A prominent radiologist had recently been kidnapped, bringing the number of abductions on Sardinia to an all-time high that year. The movie itself addresses the rampant crime wave vexing the island. Director Fondato remarked in *Variety*, "Sardinia banditry is not just a local phenomenon, but it is also strongly indicative of an inert national conscience."[1] But he felt that Italians loved this kind of spectacle, as do his main characters who get an emotional charge being part of the action when the police conduct a surprise manhunt for the bandits they've become enamored with.

Roberto Curti describes Paolo Mereghetti as "one of Italy's leading film critics and historians. He is a regular contributor to the daily newspaper *Il Corriere della Sera* and since 1993 he is the editor of *Il Mereghetti*, Italy's best selling movie guide." He can be considered the equivalent to America's Leonard Maltin. Mereghetti described Tiffin's character Gabriela as "a cynical bourgeoisie … looking for kicks with a Sardinian bandit on the run but eventually revealing all her conformism and inadequacy in the moment of danger."[2]

I Protagonisti featured an interesting Euro-cast headed by Sylva Koscina, from the former Yugoslavia, who had just co-starred in the popular spy film *Deadlier Than the Male* with Richard Johnson and the comedy *Three Bites of the Apple* with David McCallum. Handsome French actor Jean Sorel (best known to American audiences for the previous year's *Belle de Jour* opposite Catherine Deneuve) and Lou Castel had the male leading roles. Born in Colombia, Castel was a relative newcomer and had just scored with an impressive

While on the island of Sardinia, worried tourists Gabriella (Pamela Tiffin) and Nancy (Sylva Koscina) contemplate what to do next in a scene from *I Protagonisti* (Ital-Noleggio Cinematografico, 1968).

performance as epileptic young man who murders some of his family members in Marco Bellocchio's *Fists in the Pocket* (1965).

In the movie, sportsman Roberto (Sorel) puts together a group of adventurers including Nancy (Koscina), Tassoni (Luigi Pistilli), Nino (Maurizio Bonuglia), and a blonde secretary named Gabriella (Tiffin), each of whom pays half a million lire to meet and photograph egocentric outlaw Giovanni Taddeu (Castel) in his Sardinia mountain hideout. The trek to his locale is treacherous. The group is patted down to make sure they are not carrying weapons with viewers getting close-ups of Pamela's cleavage. They then are blindfolded and led up the mountainside. Once they arrive, the audacious Taddeu gives the thrill-seeking vacationers the emotional jolt they crave: He poses with his weapons as they photograph and film him. Things go awry when police helicopters move in, and the tourists go on the run with the outlaws. Tiffin's Gabriella, wearing a mini-dress and heels, has a hard time and stumbles her way down the mountainside. The situation worsens when the thrill-seekers get caught between a shootout with the police and the bandits and are forced to choose sides.

I Protagonisti was one of three movies from Italy invited to screen at the 1968 Cannes Film Festival. However, it was not Italy's official entrant; that honor went to another motion picture. Then choice of *I Protagonisti* surprised the Italian film industry because it was not a hit and received mixed reviews. For instance, the reviewer in *Variety* thought the film "original" and said that it "stirs curiosity, but not conviction." Speculation had it that the state-owned company that produced *I Protagonisti* made a deal for this and another movie with the Cannes Film Festival organizer though it was never proven. Guessing was all for naught though, as the competition was halted when some directors withdrew their movies and others staged a protest during a screening expressing their solidarity with striking students and laborers in France.

Roberto Curti said *I Protagonisti* was "an ambitious film which flopped at its release. It's a drama with ambitions of social commentary, with a strong cast, but rather disappointing overall."[3]

With its failure in its native Italy, it is no surprise that it did not get a U.S. release despite the presence of the popular Sylva Koscina and Tiffin, who seemed to be overshadowed by her co-stars in flashier roles. Pamela just played the frightened girl part though it was a first for her and she looks bewildered in scenes that have materialized online. It is a shame American audiences did not get an option to see it because the movie had an interesting original premise; was intensely acted by a handsome cast; was nicely photographed; and made for a truly edgy outdoor adventure. Perhaps with spaghetti westerns and spy spoofs being imported by the droves, distributors may have felt *I Protagonisti*'s soul-searching wannabe adventurers may not have had the same drawing power as no-name gunslingers and suave secret agents.

Next the actress appeared in a string of comedies beginning with her biggest and most beloved Italian movie *Straziami, ma di baci saziami* (aka *Torture Me, But Kill Me with Kisses* or just simply *Kill Me with Kisses*). It was directed by the prolific Dino Risi, one of the masters of the commedia all'Italiana, and released in 1968. Despite being a fine comedic director, most of Risi's movies were never released in the U.S. except for his previous comedy-drama *The Tiger and the Pussycat* with Ann-Margret. In *Straziami* he cast the brunette "Pleasure Seeker" Pamela Tiffin as a country girl who finds herself engulfed in a romantic triangle.

"I did this movie because I was playing an Italian from the Ciociara region," she remarked. "I love to do those character parts."[4]

In 1983, Pamela appeared as herself in the documentary *Dolce Cinema* where she and other actors spoke of their time working in the Italian film industry. Regarding *Straziami*, Tiffin remarked about how grateful she was that Dino Risi cast her in this role. She called Risi, "a very elegant man" and compared him to any of the top directors in Hollywood. Growing up in the Midwest, she identified with her character because she too came from a "simple life." She was thankful to be cast because she always wanted a sexy role that was not cliché. It is too her credit that she made the simple village girl so desirable that it is totally believable that her ex-fiancé would go to such extremes. including plotting murder, to get her back.

Co-starring opposite Tiffin were Nino Manfredi as the young lover and Ugo Tognazzi as her mute tailor husband. Though extremely handsome and similar in looks to Pamela's future co-star Franco Nero, Manfredi was not well-known in the U.S. unlike Nero who just starred in the big American musical *Camelot* (1967). However, he was extremely popular in his homeland where he began acting in films during the fifties. Tognazzi was considered one of Italy's top comedic actors, but he too never caught on with American audiences though he was being recognized for his role in *Barbarella*. The supporting cast included Canadian bodybuilder Samson Burke, who came to Italy to star in a series of sword-and-sandal pictures, but here plays a small role as Tiffin's ex-boyfriend.

Straziami, ma di baci saziami, written by Age (Agenore Incrocci) and Scarpelli (Furio Scarpelli), was a parody of fumetti or photo novels that were popular in parts of Europe at the time. These were basically comic books illustrated with photographs rather than drawings. American audiences were not familiar with this; not until the seventies did they catch on a bit here, beginning with *National Lampoon*'s "photo funnies."

Also featured was a handsome young American actor named Jed Curtis, cast as a monk. A composer, he had come to Italy in the early sixties to be with friends and to pursue his music career. To help support himself, he began working as a movie extra and then graduated to small acting roles. One of his first was as a monk in Otto Preminger's *The Cardinal* (1963). "My scenes were with John Huston. I was such a moron. I hadn't heard of John Huston or Otto Preminger. I was just this dumb pretty boy who would get hired because they liked me and I did what I was supposed to do."[5] Curtis followed with small roles in a number of other Italian movies, which led to *Straziami*. "My music experience had nothing to do with me being cast in this movie," he said. "They liked that I was blonde and had experience on movie sets."[6]

What Curtis didn't know was that making *Straziami* held a huge surprise for him. "I was absolutely in love with Pamela Tiffin in my teens back in my hick town in Indiana, just from watching her on screen," he recalled:

> I thought she was the ideal sex object and fall-in-love object, far, far above any other actress! Then to my amazement, there she was on the set on one of the days I was shooting *Straziami*. Nobody told me that she was the star of the movie. I almost fainted, no shit! I was totally starstruck and went up to her and said, "Pamela, I am your biggest fan!" I worked with a lot of big stars and don't get star-struck with anybody. She was the only one. I went to every movie of hers and sometimes went back four, five, six, or seven times. I was never that obsessed with an actress before. She was the only pretty "starlet" of the time who had this effect on me. I was

Mexican promotional lobby card for *Straziami, ma di baci saziami* (FIDA Cinematografica, 1968).

seriously in love with her. I think one of the reasons I felt this way about Pamela was because I could tell just by looking at her eyes that she was very smart. There was intellect there along with her beauty.

Somehow, I managed to hide my star-struck frog-in-the-throat symptoms, and soon she and I were chatting glibly. Pamela was so nice, sweet, and charming. She was impressed that I, being American, had quickly mastered fluent Italian. And we shared a passion for classical Indian music. I am very chatty and she was too. She told me about her experiences in New York and that she still had an apartment there. She wasn't sure if she was going to go back or stay on in Rome for awhile. Of course for me, my greatest desire in life was to make love with Pamela Tiffin! And she even mentioned, in passing, the possibility of my popping by her flat there in Rome! Probably the biggest mistake of my life was that … *I chickened out.* What a worthless coward I was. Looking back, I was a bit shy at the time and she was too glorious to me.[7]

In the movie, Curtis turns up at the film's end after Umberto has regained his voice and joined a monastery. Curtis is seen walking with him outside the monastery when Marisa and Marino come to visit and is at Umberto's side in a chapel as they sing at the couple's wedding ceremony. Curtis remembered, "I saw an earlier version of the movie that had not been cut down so much, and there were a lot more scenes with me. Ugo Tognazzi was so much shorter than me that they had to put him up on *two* apple boxes! We didn't actually sing and the voices were dubbed in afterwards. Ugo was a bit of an egomaniac but that wasn't a problem. Everybody respected that I had worked in a lot of movies and was very nice to me."[8]

Asked if he noticed much interaction between Pamela and her male co-stars, Curtis laughed and said, "I had the impression she was trying to avoid them and that is why she was hanging out with me. I was always the gentleman. We were also the only Americans on the set. Italian actors, actually Italian men in general, had a reputation of coming on strong with women. Of the actors, I heard a lot of stories about Lando Buzzanca."[9] Pamela would have her own unpleasant experience working with Buzzanca soon enough.

Curtis was honored to be working with Dino Risi. "[He was] one of the greatest Italian directors and I totally respected him. He seemed not to give much acting direction to Pamela and her co-stars and let them do what they wanted. I do remember that Pamela spoke her dialogue in English, while Tognazzi and Manfredi spoke theirs in Italian. In Italy, they take their scripts very seriously. Age and Scarpelli were very good writers."[10]

When asked what an Italian movie shoot was like, Curtis explained, "I worked on many sets in different countries. The Americans and Germans are much disciplined; the most disciplined are the Japanese. In Italy, you get to a movie set and think you have landed in the middle of an LSD party. Everybody is nuts. Everybody is screaming and people are doing things they are not supposed to. You think, 'How is this going to be a movie?' and then when you see the final product you think it is a miracle how good it turned out."[11] Despite Risi's reputation, shooting *Straziami* seemed to be no different than a typical Italian shoot.

Years later, Risi almost cast Jed Curtis in his comedy *Tolgo il disturbo* (1990). "I went in and gave a very funny audition. Risi absolutely wanted me, but the producers insisted that he hire Elliott Gould. He wasn't right for Italian comedy and the movie was a flop."[12] Though Jed missed out working with Risi a second time, he did get to work with his director son Marco Risi in *Il muro di gomma* (1992), which received the David di Donatello Award for Best Film. Almost fifty years after he worked on *Straziami*, Curtis' feelings toward Pamela have not changed and he confessed, "Yes, after all this time, I am still in love with Pamela Tiffin!"[13]

Straziami, ma di baci saziami opens at a folklore festival in a stadium in Rome. People from different parts of Italy are dressed in native costumes as they do their region's folk dance. Pamela's American fans will be taken aback as she is first glimpsed with auburn-looking wavy hair under a white scarf, folk dancing with Italians. This is not the Pamela of *For Those Who Think Young*, for sure. She plays Marisa Di Giovanni, a working factory girl from the Ciociara region of Italy who experiences love at first sight when she makes eye contact with Marino (Nino Manfredi) from across the field. The two stare wordlessly at each other until they are both shaken back into reality and continue their dancing with their villagers. After the program ends, Marino searches her out, but the tongue-tied girl doesn't have much to say to him. Her friend does most of the talking for her. When he leaves, Marisa's friend comments, "You mean you call him good-looking?! He's old already!"

Marino tracks down Marisa in her snow-covered village. He takes a job as a barber to stay close to her. By the time spring rolls around, the pair are planning their marriage as they frolic around the green mountainside. Marisa's father disapproves of Marino marrying his daughter so the lovers decide to commit suicide together rather than be apart. The couple lies on railroad tracks to wait. In a funny moment, Marino says "'Scuse!" as he reaches under his back and nonchalantly tosses a huge rock to the side. The train engineer is able to stop the locomotive inches from Marino and pleads with them to get off the tracks but they refuse. A melee breaks out as the engineer begins to forcefully remove them. Back at his flat, Marino has to put up with Adeleaide (Moira Orfei), his amorous, busty landlady, who won't take no for an answer. She spies on him through a keyhole and then hides in the bathroom where she pounces on him as he readies his bath. Being true to Marisa, he rejects her advances. To spite him, she tells him that there is another man in Marisa's life named Guido (Samson Burke).

After going to meet Guido, Marino believes the rumor that Marisa spent the night in a hotel with him while on vacation. He confronts her as she is leaving work during a rainstorm. He calls her insincere and receives a slap across the face before the hurt girl runs off. After his fight with Marisa, Marino has a dream where he is Dr. Zhivago and Guido as Komarovsky has run off with Marisa as Lara. As he chases his love on horseback, he is shot by Komarovsky. Waking up in a sweat, he finds Guido and some other men in his bedroom and they tell him that Adelaide lied about Marisa. Realizing he made a terrible mistake, Marino runs to find his love only to discover that she has decided to leave town by train and move to Rome. At the railway station, Marino makes a mad dash for the departing train and hops on out of breath, only to discover it is the wrong one as the conductor points to another going in the opposite direction.

Marino makes it to Rome, but has no idea where to find Marisa. All the naïve villager has is a photograph of her that he shows police officers and even the consulate in hopes that someone has spotted her (not taking into account the millions of people who come and go in such a vast city). Marisa meanwhile winds up at a shelter run by nuns where she learns of a job opening as a seamstress. She rushes over to meet with the owner, a mute, eccentric tailor named Umberto (Ugo Tognazzi channeling Harpo Marx). During her interview she breaks down into tears and tells Umberto that she had no choice but to leave her home town. Her fiancé "accused me of all sorts of things. It was horrible." Taking pity on the girl, Umberto gives her a job and eventually falls in love with her.

Marino has taken a job as a sort of butler to a very rich woman, but after an altercation with one of her guests at a party he quits. Umberto takes Marisa to a swinging nightclub where the out-of-place country girl is a bit stiff and uncomfortable trying to dance to modern music. Meanwhile, a now homeless, unshaven Marino wanders the streets of Rome. He meets a volunteer dressed as Santa Claus collecting money for the Red Cross. Feeling badly for Marino, the man reaches into his bowl and gives him some lira. Still despondent, the lovelorn lad throws himself into the Tiber, but is rescued and taken to the hospital. Marisa reads about his attempted suicide in the newspaper and runs to his bedside. He thinks he is dreaming and that she is a vision. When he realizes it is really his love, he tells Marisa that he grew a beard because he was too upset to shave with his hand trembling after losing her and he gave up his barbershop business. He now thinks they can be reunited, but she delivers the bad news that it is too late: She is married to another—a good man named Umberto.

After being released from the hospital, Marino discovers that he won the lottery. He immediately heads over to Umberto's to purchase all new tailored clothes. Marisa is aghast to see him in their home ("Leave us in peace," she exclaims) and later tells a smug Marino as Umberto takes his measurements, "You think you are being funny, don't you?" but she is not laughing. Umberto invites Marino to stay for dinner and he accepts. While the two ex-lovers quarrel, an oblivious Umberto prepares their meal in the kitchen. Marino then forces himself on Marisa, who at first resists, but then gives in. They almost make love on the floor when they remember about Umberto and jump up into their seats around the table before he returns with their spaghetti dinner.

The next day Marino and Marisa meet at a restaurant and he then takes her to his hotel room for a romantic tryst. Marino begins kissing her and a robotic Marisa just stands there. He says, "You're acting funny." She replies, "Funny? How should I act?" Feeling guilty, Marisa then lets her body go limp as he undresses her and tells him, "I knew you just wanted my body. My soul will be all mine." He turns out the lights and Marisa passes out on the floor. After she comes to, Marino realizes he is hurting Marisa and is willing to give her up. Touched, Marisa's longing for Marino gets the better of her and they tumble into bed.

Some time after, Umberto, Marisa, and Marino attend a costume party. Marino, in drag, cuts in on Umberto dressed as an American Indian to dance with Marisa, looking simply lovely in a princess costume complete with a long silver-bluish wig. As Umberto returns to his table, the lovers bemoan their separation. A determined Marisa then states, "We don't have any choice. Death is our answer." Marino says an immediate no and Marisa replies, "Don't get me wrong. Not us," and nods her head toward Umberto. Marino is taken aback since Marisa has told him that he is a kind and gentle man. But she fabricates a lie

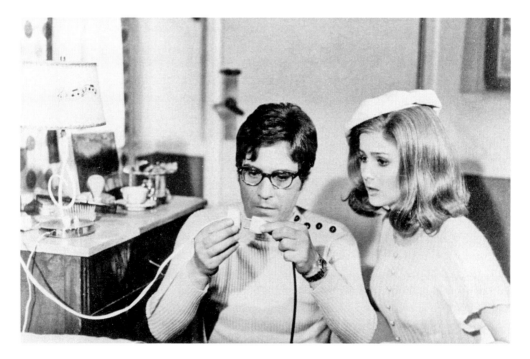

Scheming lovers Marino (Nino Manfredi) and Marisa (Pamela Tiffin) test an explosive that they plan to use to kill Marisa's husband in a scene from *Straziami, ma di baci saziami* (FIDA Cinematografica, 1968).

that in their "intimate privacy" Umberto is a "monster" and "he beats me and I cannot stand him any longer." Marisa gets Marino to believe that Umberto is a pervert and must be dealt with.

The scheming pair test putting a bomb in a kerosene heater. Marino assures Marisa that Umberto won't suffer and will be killed instantly. When the bomb explodes without a hitch, they then attach one to Umberto's iron. They have a change of heart, but it is too late. The bomb goes off, but instead of killing Umberto it restores his hearing and speech, which he lost fighting during the war. Thinking his recovery is a miracle, he joins a monastery, as he promised his mother he would if he ever regained his senses, and gives his blessing for his would-be killers to reunite. The movie ends with Umberto leading a choir of chanting monks as Marisa and Marino wed.

Straziami, ma di baci saziami received its Italian release in October 1968. When it was praised by the country's critics, it was usually for taking a simple Romeo and Juliet plot and creating a sentimental parody of Italian pop culture including soap operas and the population's love of *Doctor Zhivago*. The reenactment fantasy sequence with Manfredi as Zhivago in pursuit of Pamela (looking ravishing with her long blonde hair and clad in a fur coat as Lara, thrashing around as she is being taken away) is quite amusing. One rave came from Giovanni Grazini, writing for *Corriere della Sera*. He found the movie to be "lively and colorful" and "among the best of Dino Risi." He praised it for successfully mixing irony and tenderness, and praised the performances of Nino Manfredi and the "irresistible" Tognazzi.

However, most reviews were mixed. *Variety* found *Straziami* to be a "semi-satirical, semi-serious, sentimental comedy … several notches above usual Fida product." Nino Manfredi received the most praise for his believable performance as a country boy who quickly picks up city slicker ways. *Variety* thought Tiffin's role was "subordinate and restrictive." Zaria Zanelli of *Il Resto del Carlino* praised Manfredi's wit and thought Pamela was equally as good.

In the book *Nino Manfredi*, the actor told the author he found the film's screenplay just beautiful and really liked how the songs were used. He was very pleased that the public took to the movie and gave a lot of credit for its success to director Risi. Pamela's opinion: "It is a sweet, innocent movie, but it escapes me why people like it so much."[14]

Roberto Curti says the movie is steeped in Italian pop culture and geared for Italian audiences who loved it despite some critical barbs thrown its way. He explains why:

> Age and Scarpelli were two of Italy's best scriptwriters. Risi's satirical intent was to comment on the conflict between a traditional and ignorant mentality based on traditional values (virginity, pure love, etc.) and the sudden change of customs by 1968 in a culturally underdeveloped country such as Italy. The basic idea was to tell a story from the point of view of two very simple (or rather obtuse) country people. The film is very much rooted in Italian popular culture. Most of the dialogue—and even the title itself—is made of quotes from Italian pop songs, often very banal, syrupy ones (the sort that could be heard at the Sanremo Music Festival, Italy's most important musical contest), which the characters recite as if they were reciting very profound sonnets.
>
> In one scene, for instance, Nino Manfredi's Marino and Pamela Tiffin's Marisa are reciting the lyrics of a song called "L'immensità" (by Don Backy, real name Aldo Caponi), which was that year's best selling hit, and commenting on them as if they were reading one of Giacomo Leopardi's poems. They really believe reality is like it's told in love songs, and act accordingly.
>
> The plot is filled with unlikely reversals of fortune and ironically dramatic and passionate twists and turns. In one scene, after watching *Doctor Zhivago*, Marisa and Marino decide to

commit suicide and lay on the tracks waiting for a train with hilarious results. After being dumped by Marisa, Marino goes to the big city, where he becomes a bum and tries to commit suicide again when he suddenly becomes wealthy after winning a lottery, and returns with a vengeance, like some sort of third-rate Count of Monte Cristo. And so on....

    What's more, *Straziami, ma di baci saziami* is told as if it was some kind of dumb feuilleton [a section of European newspapers devoted to general entertainment articles], but in an ironic way and through the point of view of two simpletons—something which Italian critics at the time didn't fully get. Risi was often harshly reviewed in comparison to his previous classics such as *Il sorpasso* (*The Easy Life*, 1962).[15]

Pamela looks radiant in Technicolor and seems picture perfect for the role of naïve Marisa. Most Italian historians agree that this is the one film that moviegoers in Italy remember the American actress most. Lancia and Melelli in *Le Straniere del nostro Cinema* found the movie to be "the best interpretation of Tiffin in our country."[16] Curti remarked, "Tiffin is incredibly sexy in this film, and totally believable as the ravishing but naive country girl, sort of a female version of Voltaire's Candide."[17]

    Paolo Mereghetti called *Straziami, ma di baci saziami* "one of the true swan songs of the 'Commedia all'italiana' and one of the more intelligent and funniest scripts written by Age and Scarpelli. Thanks also to the perfect voice dubbing on the part of Flaminia Jandolo, Pamela gave the viewers one of those characters that stay in the memory: a perfect mixture of naive ingenuity and popular subculture, photonovel-like sentimentalism and instinctive working-class romanticism. The work of a great actress, which Tiffin was (and had showed in her Hollywood days, keeping up with such thespians as James Cagney and Paul Newman), and a role unfortunately Italian cinema was no longer able to offer her."[18]

    Though Pamela was mastering the Italian language at this point, she had to be dubbed. Per Curti, "Pamela couldn't have possibly done her own dubbing, as her character has a strong regional accent (and quite funny, indeed)."[19] There was no way she could have replicated it believably with her American-accented Italian. Luckily, Tiffin was able to dub her own voice for an English-language version that unfortunately never made it to the U.S.

    FIDA Cinematografica produced *Straziami, ma di baci saziami* and attempted to find an American distributor. They took out trade ads in early 1969 for the movie, now with the title and tagline "Kill Me with Kisses ... will kill you with laughter." Despite setting a box office record for its opening weekend in Rome per *Variety* and earning over $2 million in Italy alone, they could not find any takers.

    An English-language version did surface in a few countries. Pamela, using her own voice, gives a wonderfully amusing performance. You cannot help but feel sympathetic to her character Marisa's plight, torn between two men before giving in to her sexual desires for handsome Marino. The scene with the secret lovers making out while an oblivious Umberto cooks a pasta dinner is extremely funny. Even when she joins Marino to off Umberto, Tiffin projects such sweetness and vulnerability that you feel empathy for her even though she is plotting a murder. The only minor disappointment is that the part did not take full advantage of her comedic skills and she was more the straight man to the over-the-top antics of Manfredi and Tognazzi. Even so, seeing Pamela in this English version is a rare treat indeed, though the dialogue synchronization is off and mouths move with no words emanating.

    In February 1973 an *Independent Film Journal* item announced that Paragon Pictures acquired the distribution rights to *Straziami, ma di baci saziami* and planned to release it in its original Italian language with subtitles in the U.S. However, there is no evidence that this ever came to be. The dubbed English version never made it to the U.S. either.

The *Variety* reviewer was prophetic when he opined that the movie would be a hit in Italy and parts of Europe but not in more sophisticated areas where "its regional comedy will not project the entertainment values it holds for Latins." Actor Jed Curtis felt that the movie "would not play well in other cultures."[20] Roberto Curti also was not surprised that the film never found much popularity outside of Italy. "I think Risi's *Straziami, ma di baci saziami* is impossible to understand if you are not into Italian popular culture. It's very heavy on dialogue, and—as often in Italian comedies—the dialogue is very sophisticated on many levels. It's not just a matter of funny lines, but in the way Age and Scarpelli build a totally convincing 'popular' language, which is witty and sharply satirical in intent."[21]

Due to the major success of this movie in Italy, Pamela was now much sought-after in the Italian film industry. This should have carried over to the States, but because the movie never was released there, nobody knew about it. Though the movie's success further solidified her as a top-notch comedienne, it may have also hindered her chances of working in the thriller and horror genres that were soon to become quite popular in Italy and worldwide.

Pamela followed up the hit *Straziami, ma di baci saziami* with yet another black comedy, *L'arcangelo* (aka *The Archangel*) from Mario Cecchi Gori's Fair Films. Seeing how much money Italian movies raked in at the box office, 20th Century–Fox entered into a preproduction deal with Fair Films to distribute *L'Arcangelo* and another yet to be announced movie worldwide.

Per Roberto Curti, "*L'arcangelo* was initially to be directed by Luigi Comencini and tell the story of an archangel who comes down to Earth, but the project was dropped and the title, which had already been sold as a finished project to Fox and had to be shot in English, was recycled for a new script by [Giorgio] Capitani, Renato Castellani, Adriano Baracco and Steno. A pretext opening line duly informs us, 'The attorney is for his client like justice's archangel, with a flaming sword in the hand.'"

In the film, Pamela plays a woman whose motives are not as innocent as they first seem to be. Authors Lancia and Melelli in their book *Le Straniere del nostro Cinema*, were not surprised that Pamela was cast. Per the historians, "These are roles that usually most Italian cinema offers beautiful actresses, roles in which the angelic purity of the features is in conflict with the ambiguity of the characters…."[22] This was perfectly true in Tiffin's case and it is too bad that directors of gialli did not take advantage of her talent.

L'arcangelo was directed by Giorgio Capitani. Like a lot of directors in Italian cinema, only his peplums and spaghetti westerns were known to American audiences. In Capitani's case it was *Samson and His Mighty Challenge* and *The Ruthless Four*. Pamela's leading man was Vittorio Gassman. "He was wonderful to work with,"[23] exclaimed Pamela, who thought of the actor as a helpful big brother. Gassman was paired with a number of American leading ladies at this time, including Ann-Margret, Tina Aumont, Martha Hyer, and Sharon Tate (in her last movie), before he worked with Pamela.

The supporting cast included Irina Demick (whose English-language films include *The Longest Day* and *Those Magnificent Men in Their Flying Machines*) and Adolfo Celi (best remembered as villainous Emilio Largo in the James Bond adventure *Thunderball*). It also features an early appearance by actress Laura Antonelli, who hit it big a few years later by disrobing in a string of popular seventies sex comedies and dramas.

Duplicitous Gloria (Pamela Tiffin) dines with an infatuated Fulvio (Vittorio Gassman) in
L'archangelo **(Fair Film, 1969).**

In the documentary *Dolce Cinema*, behind-the-scenes footage from *L'archangelo* is shown—specifically a scene where they are shooting Pamela and Vittorio Gassman dining at a restaurant. Pamela talked about the chaos on a movie set just before the director yells, "action." She explained that in Hollywood, everything goes silent but in Italy nobody keeps quiet because they loop a lot of the dialog in post-production. As an actor, she revealed how she had to get used to and adjust to acting with all the commotion going on behind the camera.

She then went on to expound on the working conditions in Rome and how they would be asked to work "beyond human hours. By the time you went home, slept, and were back on the set, you really didn't have much time to eat." She said how exhausted she'd be for the next day's shoot. Though she was always fighting the physical and mental aspects of working such hours, she said "it never became a crisis" due to the Italian crew whom she felt, as compared to Hollywood's, "were friendlier and looser and had a great sense of humor." They were never happy though with the catering on the set and there were always complaints. As an example she stated that on one movie "they served the actors fried and breaded veal cutlets, warm mineral water, and cold wine at 5 a.m.!"

L'archangelo has a very convoluted plot which seemed to be the norm with Pamela's Italian comedies. Here she is beautifully made-up and stylishly clad in mod clothes playing fashion model Gloria Bianchi, who goes to down-on-his-luck lawyer Fulvio Bertuccia (Gassman) for help. Fulvio has tried nine cases and lost ten. He is so broke that he is living in his office. Descending on him in the middle of the night, Gloria confesses that she killed her lover Prof. Crescenzi. Fulvio is reluctant to help her, but is persuaded by her beauty and money. It turns out that she hasn't killed Crescenzi; instead she cops to murdering millionaire businessman Marco Roda (Celi) from Milan. But that turns out to be a lie, too. Gloria is only planning on killing Roda and wants Fulvio's help. Roda's wife (Demick) thinks she is the intended victim, complicating matters. Fulvio blunders on in their scheme, as he is enticed by Gloria's promises of sex and riches. He joins her at Roda's villa pretending to be her lover, but realizes too late that he is being used. He is arrested and charged with the murder while Gloria and Signora Roda go off together to enjoy the late millionaire's vast fortune.

L'arcangelo received mediocre notices. *Segnalazioni Cinematografiche* described it as a "cumbersome comedy." This may have hurt its box office chances. Though the movie was a hit in Italy, it was not as big a moneymaker as expected for a Vittorio Gassman movie. It earned 640,950,000 liri ($449,065) and ranked 44th at the box office for the year.

Reviewing the film, Roberto Curti opined, "Obviously conceived as a vehicle for Vittorio Gassman, Giorgio Capitani's film uneasily injects satiric elements from the 'commedia all'italiana' within a black comedy plot which sometimes borders on farce. Saddled with a hardly irresistible script, director Giorgio Capitani shows little flair for slapstick comedy, and the visual tricks he often employs (such as speeded up shots or fish-eye lenses) are more distracting than funny. Tiffin is simply ravishing, and is provided by the costume designer with an array of fashionable mises, including a breathtaking swimming suit and a scarlet red wig which replaces her long blonde hair in a scene. However, her character is a lazy variation on the typical play-dumb blonde, with more than a hint of misogyny, while Gassman overacts frantically, turning his character into nothing more than a rather insufferable buffoon. Celi fares much better as the despicable industrialist who gets an amusing comeuppance in the end. Overall, the picture looks gorgeous, thanks to Stelvio Massi's cinematography, Dario Micheli's pop sets, plus a delicious score by Piero Umiliani."

Tiffin agreed with the negative reviews and opined, "This could have been a very funny film, but Giorgio Capitani had no idea how to direct a comedy. It was too dark. During the shoot I kept thinking how good this could have been if someone like Billy Wilder was directing."[24]

Though Pamela may not have liked the film, she looks stunning throughout. Her character wears the latest mod late sixties high society fashions and sports some outrageous hairdos. PETA supporters beware: she is also swathed in furs from a white lynx with hood, to a gray fox coat she wears to greet Adolfo Celi at the airport, to matching red fox coats and hats she and Irina Demick sport at the end of the movie.

Fox released this comedy-thriller throughout Europe and other parts of the world. *The Times of India* called it an "over-involved, sumptuously mounted but far from funny murder comedy" and "a sick farce at its unfunniest." In 1971 Fox gave it a very limited U.S. release as *The Archangel*. The comedy, with the tagline "A murderously funny film," slipped into American theaters in smaller cities, but seemed to be ignored by the critics. It is yet another of Tiffin's films that has never been given a proper release on DVD.

Some time in 1969, Tiffin lent her voice to the roughly eleven-minute short film *L'isola degli uccelli* (*The Island of Birds*), directed by Vittorio Armentano. He studied medicine before working as a journalist, which led him to directing commercials and then documentaries. Beautiful shots of the beaks, eyes, and feathers of various types of birds are intercut with photos of women made-up to resemble birds in an avant-garde fashion to dramatize the meaning of the poetic verse.

While the male narrator speaks mostly in Italian, Tiffin delivers her lines in English at the beginning of the film. She is heard calling the narrator a cannibal and protesting his carrying her off to Cannibal Island where she will be the victimized missionary. A number of the poetic verses recited are by T.S. Eliot. It is a strange film, though colorful and pretty to look at. It recently surfaced on YouTube.

In This Corner ...
Lana Turner

The Survivors (TV)

Shortly after filming *L'archangelo*, Tiffin found herself on the French Riviera in late 1968 filming episodes of the new American TV show *Harold Robbins' The Survivors* (as it was then titled), scheduled for broadcast in the fall of 1969. Lana Turner and George Hamilton headlined an all-star cast. It was Tiffin's first foray back into episodic television since her 1963 appearance on *The Fugitive*.

According to TV historian Les Brown, "*The Survivors* began on bravado. It was one of those announcements for the future—when ABC was at a particularly low point in the standings—that seemed to say; don't lose heart in ABC, great things are ahead, the network is on the move with a spectacular sure-fire idea for the season after next."[1] ABC corporate president Leonard Goldenson had made a deal with bestselling author Harold Robbins (movies based on his novels were always moneymakers) to create a ratings hit for the network. The show, a forerunner to such later extravagant primetime soaps as *Dallas* and *Dynasty*, was about the fabulously wealthy, jet-setting Carlyle family. Robbins wrote the pilot episode and created an outline for each remaining chapter, which was assigned to a writer to turn into a teleplay that was partially self-contained but also had a storyline that continued to the next episode.

One of the creators of *The Survivors* was Emmy Award–nominated producer John Wilder. He started his career as an actor during the mid-fifties appearing in *The Unguarded Moment*, *Rock, Pretty Baby*, *Until They Sail* and *Summer Love* and making numerous guest appearances on top TV shows of the time. He began writing for TV in 1966 beginning with the western series *Branded*, then joined the staff of *Peyton Place*, which led to him becoming one of the creators of *The Survivors*. He wrote, "I believe ABC felt they could build on the huge ratings success of *Peyton Place*, the first prime-time serialized drama, by mounting a glitzy production with a couple of high-profile movie stars in a series created by a bestselling author of racy stories, Harold Robbins. It was a good commercial idea that ran off the rails, an example of how too many chefs in the kitchen can spoil the broth. In the short span of a dozen or so episodes, there were three executive producers, each trying to deal with the dictates of network and studio executives."[2]

Another *Survivors* co-creator was writer Richard DeRoy. He was a playwright who broke into television in the early fifties writing for live anthology series. By the end of the decade and into the sixties, he was contributing teleplays to such episodic TV shows as

Surfside 6, Checkmate, 77 Sunset Strip, and *Mr. Novak*, the latter starring James Franciscus as a high school teacher. DeRoy's success with that show (especially where he was able to create realistic dialog for both adults and adolescents) led to writing for *Peyton Place* where he rose from contributing writer to producer. His experience made him a very good choice to be script supervisor on *The Survivors* working in conjunction with Harold Robbins. However, DeRoy admitted to writer–TV historian Stephen Bowie that he was reluctant to accept the job. He agreed after being prodded by Universal executive Grant Tinker.

Hired to produce was William Frye, who had began his career in TV, but recently was working for Columbia Pictures where he produced the hit movie comedy *The Trouble with Angels* starring Hayley Mills and its sequel, *Where Angels Go, Trouble Follows*. He moved over to Universal hoping to continue in motion pictures, but the studio honchos "prevailed on him"[3] to work on *The Survivors* as its executive producer. DeRoy told Bowie that Frye was only hired because he was an escort for such Hollywood legends as Irene Dunne and Loretta Young and the studio thought he would get along well with Lana Turner. But, per DeRoy, "he was used to … all these very fine Christian ladies. Lana was not that. They never hit it off."[4] Co-star George Hamilton noticed that too and commented at the time, "They were circling each other from the start. It was a matter of temperament."[5]

Per John Wilder, "The story originally began with the plug being pulled on the life-support system of a wealthy patriarch lying in an ICU. It was a story that dealt with the struggle for control of their dead father's empire between the heirs—The Survivors—a glamorous middle-aged woman [Lana Turner] and her younger playboy brother [George Hamilton], both deeply flawed by the privilege of too much money and lack of moral scruples. As conceived by Harold Robbins, it was to chronicle the excessive lifestyles and scandals in the world of the rich-and-infamous."[6]

Tiffin was cast as Rosemary Price, who is involved with Hamilton's Duncan Carlyle. She was persuaded to accept the role by Frye. She enjoyed his elegance and thought he was just marvelous. Alas, Lana Turner did not and that was the crux of the trouble to come. The one issue that caused Tiffin pause was that she would have to work with George Hamilton. Per Pamela, "I had known George casually from parties in New York and Hollywood. I thought that he was a superficial playboy and decided to keep my distance from him. Well, George is delightful and fun! He has a Christian generosity and wants harmony so much that he brings it wherever he goes. He's rather special and never got the recognition he deserved."[7]

The Survivors was now set to begin filming on location in Europe, making it the most expensive television series at the time with a budget of $300,000 an episode. It would also turn out to be one of the most troubled productions in television history. On a Saturday, two days before shooting was to begin, some of the cast and production crew members were invited by the heiress to Firestone and her husband to afternoon brunch at their estate, which DeRoy said "hangs over the Mediterranean with two yachts floating in front, and it is just so moneyed you can't stand it."[8] Lana Turner and William Frye both got drunk, per DeRoy. Frye and costume designer Luis Estevez accompanied Turner to her waiting limo to leave. DeRoy kept waiting for Frye to return and when he did, the producer admitted he had slapped the star. It was the slap heard around the world.

According to columnist Norma Lee Browning, Frye was having an argument with Estevez, Lana stepped in to calm Frye down and he used some choice words telling her to mind her own business. Stunned by his insults, she hauled off and belted him. He then slapped her back. Frye came back and told DeRoy what had just transpired. "That's what you need to hear 48 hours before you're supposed to go before the cameras! He slapped your star? Well, he was out of the show before Sunday morning. Grant had to take it over [temporarily]. He really was not an experienced producer...."[9]

Later that night there was another party at a yacht club and Lana Turner was well enough to attend. Per DeRoy, she said to him, "Dick, nobody touches this face!" DeRoy continued, "That's a line I've never forgotten. She knew what her fortune was, you know. The bones!"[10] Shooting began on Monday and everybody knew the story except Pamela. Almost a week went by before she found out why she hadn't seen Frye for awhile.

Publicity photograph of Pamela Tiffin in *The Survivors* (Universal Television, 1969).

Though Frye was out and Lana Turner (whom Pamela described as being "an old-time movie star—spoiled and very tough"[11]) was happy again, the problems did not stop there. Frye's permanent replacement Gordon Oliver immediately began having "creative differences" with the studio. Harold Robbins filled his story with lots of sex and, per Universal's directive, violence. However, ABC was much too nervous about it since all three networks were recently chastised by the public and government for the amount of brutality in their TV shows.

By June of 1969, Oliver was replaced by Walter Doniger, the long-time director of the hit TV show *Peyton Place*, and Robbins dropped out of the project. This was most likely because the new team felt that most of the footage shot in the French Riviera, (costing approximately $1.5 million and where all of Pamela Tiffin's scenes were shot) was unusable because the character motivations were hazy. They also felt that the three lead characters were unlikable and that the audience would not care what happens to them. The new producer and writers wanted the audience to see what made the Carlyle family tick and to clear up the relationships. "As ultimately designed by the third executive producer, Walter Doniger, following the dictates of network and studio execs, the patriarch doesn't die, he lives," wrote John Wilder. "And the series became a dark version of *One Man's Family*; a dysfunctional family melodrama in fancy settings and wardrobe. But by that time, the money was gone [each episode was now budgeted at $50,000] and the production became another back lot Universal series; one that lacked focus and any reason for existing other than that a deal had been made."[12]

The new story had Turner's Tracy Carlyle Hastings unhappily married to a snake of a businessman named Philip (Kevin McCarthy). Her father (Ralph Bellamy) has just discovered that his son-in-law has swindled the family bank of over $600,000. Tracy also holds a deep dark secret: Their twenty-year-old-son Jeffrey (Jan-Michael Vincent) was sired by another man. The other major plot featured George Hamilton as Tracy's playboy brother Duncan Carlyle. Fresh from winning the Grand Prix, his private jet is hijacked to South America where a Che Guevara–type buddy wants him to back his revolution with the money from daddy's fortune.

With such major changes, it is no wonder the press was questioning if ABC would stick with *The Survivors* and air it at all. Surprisingly, when the network officially announced their new fall season in the spring of 1969, *The Survivors* had survived and was set to air on Monday nights at 9:00 p.m. in the timeslot once held by *Peyton Place.*

Though most of the French Riviera footage was scrapped, Pamela's scenes seemed to have been salvaged and she is spotted in ABC-TV's promotional ads for it, looking quite glamorous in an evening gown as she watches George Hamilton playing roulette at a casino.

Duncan Carlyle (George Hamilton) and his paramour Rosemary Price (Pamela Tiffin) go for a drive in *The Survivors* (Universal Television, 1969).

Tiffin appears only in the last episode aired. John Wilder confirmed that Pamela was hired only to guest star on the series. "I remember Pamela Tiffin, a stunningly beautiful woman," he wrote. "She was not a regular on the short-lived series. Wish she had been—would have made for some pleasant-to-look-at dailies, at least. Miss Tiffin certainly did work on much better shows. Fortunately, so did I."[13]

Trying to distance itself from nighttime's *Peyton Place* and daytime soap operas, ABC-TV hailed *The Survivors* as television's first novel with a chapter a week. The critics weren't buying that for a second. Cecil Smith in the *Los Angeles Times* called it "a soap opera served up with Chanel No. 5 soap in a platinum dish ... produced in a saga of incredible ineptitude." The *New York Times'* Jack Gould found it to be "cheesy hokum ... with pathetic dialogue and hapless acting."

Clarence Petersen of the *Chicago Tribune* concisely pointed out why *The Survivors* was unsuccessful. With its lavish trappings and super-rich Carlyle family at the core, it should have been fun escapist entertainment. But instead, all the main characters are unhappy, from Lana Turner's Tracy hiding the paternity of her grown son; to Ralph Bellamy as her father, stuck with an embezzling son-in-law his daughter won't let him fire; to George Hamilton as her brother, chagrined that his father won't finance his college buddy's South American revolution. As Petersen remarked, "As the hour wore on the plot thickened and thickened until it had the consistency of Elmer's Glue and was about as colorful."

Weekly viewers wanted to be entertained and *The Survivors* was not delivering. It was consistently trounced in the ratings by *Mayberry R.F.D.* and *The Doris Day Show* on CBS and *The NBC Sunday Night Movie* on NBC. After fifteen episodes, *The Survivors* expired. It was one of the most expensive flops in TV history.

The last episode, "Chapter 15," which featured Pamela as Rosemary Price, aired on January 12, 1970. It was received more favorably than all the episodes that ran prior. Percy Shain remarked in the *Boston Globe*, "Even with the awkward device of interpolation and frequent cutbacks from present to past and return—this was a rounded story with bite to it that not only brought all antagonisms into focus but provided a resolvement of the issues and a true sense of finality." He added, "The usual cast ... was enhanced by such lovelies as Diana Muldaur and Pamela Tiffin."

In hindsight, perhaps *The Survivors* should have stuck with the original story in the French Riviera. The beautiful location scenery alone would have provided the escapist entertainment TV viewers longed for. The final episode got a Nielsen rating of 11.5 and 18 share, a hair off the season average. Today, the show would have been a huge hit, but in the days of only three major networks it was a flop. It finished the 1969–70 TV season ranked 89th. Because George Hamilton had a firm contract with Universal Television for a twenty-five–week series, he immediately went into ABC's *Paris 7000*, a foreign intrigue series. This too was cancelled after only half a season.

Summing up his experience on *The Survivors*, John Wilder stated, "A dying horse that had once held so much promise staggered to an inglorious finish after half a season. I was young and learning. What I learned on that show was how not to do things if I were ever in charge. I saw that while collaboration is a given, a producer must have convictions about concept and material and be firm in those convictions. Be strong. I learned, too, to never take a job, or stay on one just for a payday. Love it, or leave it. Those lessons proved invaluable to me, and in retrospect it was a very worthwhile experience. But at the time it was just plain hell."[14]

Following the pattern it set with a few of its previous series such as *Pistols 'n' Petticoats*, *Tammy*, and many more, Universal Studios edited a few of the episodes together to produce a feature entitled *The Last of the Powerseekers*. Commenting on this practice, historian Stephen Bowie wrote on his Classic TV Blog:

> In the seventies, Universal began to cannibalize these write-offs, sewing together two or more episodes of forgotten series, giving them a generic new title, and dropping them into syndication packages along with authentic telefilms. With few reference books and no internet to consult, unsuspecting viewers would recognize these hybrids as recycled television episodes only if they'd been among the few to watch the failed show when it was on the air. That these telefilm Frankensteins were incoherent and unsatisfying—instead of telling a single story, they put the characters through several abrupt, unconnected plots—didn't matter. They added to Universal's profits, without any obvious negative consequences.

The Last of the Powerseekers was set loose on the unsuspecting TV viewer in 1971. It continued to be broadcast throughout the decade and into the early eighties before disappearing. It is unknown if any of Pamela Tiffin's scenes made it into the telemovie.

The Survivors was Pamela Tiffin's last episodic TV appearance. It is too bad that she didn't do any more. A number of light-hearted British television shows from the ITC Entertainment were being filmed throughout Europe between 1970 and 1973 and she would have made a wonderfully glamorous guest star. One could easily see her cavorting with the likes of Tony Curtis and Roger Moore in *The Persuaders*, Gene Barry in *The Adventurer*, or Robert Vaughn in *The Protectors*.

Pamela almost did another TV show. In 1971 Gold Key Entertainment announced it was producing a British anthology series to be titled *Zodiac*. Each episode was to feature a sign of the zodiac in its title such as "The Aries Computer," "The Left Hand of Gemini," and "Vengeance of Virgo." Some big names were touted as guest stars including Vincent Price, Christopher Lee, Stephanie Beacham, Ian McShane—and Pamela.

She was scheduled to appear in "Prelude to Taurus" with Michael Crawford and Robert Walker, the story of a scientist who discovers three frozen corpses in the Arctic who have the potential to change all modern perceptions about the origins and age of civilization. But *Zodiac* seems to have been scrapped for unknown reasons. Too bad; it would have been quite interesting to see how Pamela would have handled herself in the sci-fi genre.

Back in the U.S.A.

Viva Max
Uncle Vanya (stage play)

Tiffin was back in the United States in 1969, starring opposite Peter Ustinov in the political satire *Viva Max*. It was her lone American movie since relocating to Italy. In this film version of newspaperman Jim Lehrer's 1966 comic novel, a modern Mexican general, and his ragtag bunch of soldiers from Nuevo Laredo, retake the Alamo, causing U.S. embarrassment. The book was a bestseller despite some less than stellar reviews such as in the *New York Times* where critic Martin Levin said it "begins with the impossible and descends to anticlimactic foolishness."

Lehrer sold the rights to the book for about $45,000. It was to come from the amount of money the producer would raise for the film's entire production budget rather than from Hollywood's elusive "net profits." Reportedly, Lehrer used the money to quit his newspaper job and head to Washington, D.C., to try to land a TV anchor gig. He succeeded with public television's *The MacNeil/Lehrer News Hour*, which morphed into *The News Hour with Jim Lehrer* and then *The PBS News Hour*.

In September 1967, it was announced that *Viva Max* was to begin filming the following month in San Antonio, Texas. Mark Carliner Productions was producing for MGM. Thirty-year-old Carliner was a former CBS television executive and this was his first motion picture project after leaving the network. Arthur Hiller was attached to direct. An experienced comedy director, his recent credits included *The Wheeler Dealers*, *The Americanization of Emily*, *Penelope*, and *The Tiger Makes Out*. The novel was adapted by Elliott Baker, whose prior credits included *A Fine Madness* and *Luv*.

The movie was postponed. Almost a year later, Carliner announced that the movie was again set to commence. However, it was now a Commonwealth United production in association with CBS. Under a new plan of providing new movies to be shown on television, the TV network put up an estimated $800,000 towards the $2.7 million budget with a guaranteed broadcast date in January 1973. Exteriors would be filmed on location at the Alamo and interiors at Cinecittà Studios in Rome.

Carliner lost his director, Arthur Hiller, when the project moved from MGM to Commonwealth United. He was replaced by Emmy-winning TV comedy director Jerry Paris. He worked on such hit TV series *as The Joey Bishop Show*, *The Dick Van Dyke Show*, *The Farmer's Daughter*, *The Munsters* and *Here's Lucy* and had in release two 1968 movie comedies, *Don't Raise the Bridge, Lower the River* with Jerry Lewis and *How Sweet It Is!* with Debbie Reynolds.

Peter Ustinov would be starring as the Mexican general with filming to begin in the spring of 1969. The actor accepted the part because he liked the premise that though the U.S. is technologically equipped enough to track the flight of birds, they could not detect a small group of men crossing the border to take over the Alamo with indirect help from the local police. Jim Lehrer, happy with the casting of Ustinov, said, "When they showed me a picture of Ustinov in his uniform on a great white horse, I nearly dropped. He *was* Max!"[1]

Speculation was running rampant on who would play the lone major female role, that of the pretty blonde gift shop cashier (and radical college student) taken hostage along with two others. The top contender was Amy Thomson, an actress being hailed as the "New Garbo."[2] Well, at least her managers were calling her that. She had just made an impressive film debut in the Richard Widmark western *Death of a Gunfighter*. She did not get the role and the producer somehow decided on Pamela Tiffin.

Commenting on her character, Pamela said, "It's a marvelously funny role. I play this girl who could have been yesterday's cheerleader or baton twirler, but today she is a go-go political science major, an activist who loves to use big words like 'absolutism' or 'totalitarian.' She might never have been out of San Antonio yet you know that she cares for the world."[3]

To keep the comedy quotient high, the producer surrounded Ustinov with a number of talented comedic actors including Jonathan Winters, John Astin, Keenan Wynn, Harry Morgan, Kenneth Mars, and Gino Conforti. Among the young actors chosen to play Mexican soldiers was Larry Hankin. Tall and lanky, he did comedy improv and began working in Hollywood in 1966 with a guest spot on the TV sitcom *That Girl*. He worked twice prior with Paris, on the unsold TV pilot *Sheriff Who* and the film *How Sweet It Is!*

Peter Gonzales Falcon was also cast as a soldier. A senior majoring in Drama/Speech at Southwest Texas State College, he accompanied a female friend to an open casting call for the movie. While waiting in an outer room, he heard someone yell, "That face!" That someone was Jerry Paris and it was Mexican-American Gonzales Falcon's handsome features and bone structure that got Paris excited. After reading for the director, he got the role. Knowing it was going to be at least a twelve-week shoot including time in Italy, the excited young man decided to drop out of school to pursue his dream of acting. When asked if he was familiar with Pamela Tiffin, Gonzales exclaimed, "Oh yeah! Pamela was a big movie star. I first saw her in *State Fair* and then in another film. I thought she was just wonderful and very beautiful."[4]

Another young actor, cast in the role of a government representative, was handsome, sandy-blonde haired Eldon Quick, who started his acting career at the American Shakespeare Festival in Stratford, Connecticut. He had a number of TV sitcom appearances under his belt including *Occasional Wife*, *Gomer Pyle, U.S.M.C.*, *The Monkees*, and *Bewitched*, and was adept at comedy, usually cast as the nerdy brain. *Viva Max* was his second movie after a supporting role in the Academy Award–winning *In the Heat of the Night*.

Location shooting began in the spring of 1969, but a battle quickly erupted between the film's producers and the Daughters of the Republic of Texas who were the gate keepers to the Alamo, holding custody to it and the grounds within its walls. The organization originally gave permission to shoot inside and outside the Alamo. A few scenes, including the guided tour of the Alamo, were shot within, but the Daughters withdrew their support

Spanish DVD cover art for *Viva Max*.

when they realized *Viva Max* was going to be a satire. They did not want the movie to be filmed anywhere near their sacred mission where Jim Bowie, Davy Crockett, and 185 soldiers battled General Santa Anna and his army in 1836. They found the movie to be blasphemous, especially the part where the Mexican flag is hoisted over the Alamo.

The producers then found out that the Daughters had no jurisdiction over the plaza outside the Alamo, which was city-owned property. They went to the San Antonio City Council to get a permit. However, the Daughters were not giving up. The City Council had to make a decision and heard testimony from both sides.

The DRT president, Mrs. William Lawrence Scarborough, told the council, "I come before you to plead with you and ask you not to permit this movie on the premises owned by you. We feel this movie is a mockery and a desecration of our heroes who died for our liberty there."[5] A representative of the movie countered and declared, "There is nothing in this movie that could possible be offensive."[6]

The war of words continued in the press. Mrs. Scarborough bemoaned to anyone who would listen, "This is not a movie we could be proud of. Why couldn't they make a beautiful movie like John Wayne did?"[7] Producer Carliner issued a statement that said, "The movie does not desecrate, defame, deface, damage or compromise either the structure or heritage of the Alamo."[8]

The city council declared it a draw. By a vote of six to two, it gave permission to shoot on city-held property leading up to the doors of the mission. However, there was to be no filming inside or on the grounds of the Alamo, nor could they touch the outside walls. The people of San Antonio were not against the movie being filmed in their city and actually signed up to work as extras. Eighty-seven Mexican men were cast as soldiers in Max's army and about forty Caucasians were cast as members of the city's right-wing militia. A native Texan, Peter Gonzales added, "The whole movie was a big deal to San Antonio. It was a big city, but was becoming a player with other big cities at the time. The long awaited Hemisfair [the 1968 World's Fair] was in full gear. Everyone was an extra, even the city's richest people who were there in the heat all day. Millionaire fathers would introduce their beauty queen daughters to Jerry Paris hoping to get them in the movie."[9]

Despite the ruling and the welcome mat the people of San Antonio put out for the movie people, the Daughters of the Republic—like the outnumbered Alamo defenders— would not give up the fight. The movie's attorney reported to the Council that the ladies were disrupting filming on city property: They stood in front of the Alamo in black costumes and draped the shrine in black paper. The latter action was a protest against the raising of the Mexican flag over the Alamo. The attorney said the Daughters were miffed by the decision and were doing this for personal vengeance. Mrs. Scarborough pooh-poohed the attorney's accusation and remarked, "I can't think of anything lower than the idea of making a comedy about a shrine where heroes died. It's like making a comedy on the fallen heroes of Vietnam."[10]

Scarborough then filed a petition for a restraining order against the moviemakers, claiming harassment and threatening actions. The court action also stated that already completed filming and more scheduled "will do irreparable damage and harm to the Alamo and to the continued efforts of its custodians to make it a symbol of Texas independence and freedom."[11] The filmmakers countered that they were the ones being harassed by Mrs. Scarborough and her organization.

While his producer battled the meddling Daughters of the Revolution, Paris kept plodding on. Eldon Quick was not impressed with his directing style: "We gathered in the city of San Antonio perhaps the greatest collection of comedic talent assembled since *It's a Mad Mad Mad Mad World,*" he commented, continuing:

Unfortunately we didn't have Stanley Kramer to direct us. We had Jerry Paris. It's hard to imagine a more typical Hollywood-type director. Since we were in Texas one could say he was all belt buckle and no cattle. As I watched the filming, I saw scene after scene fizzle away.

A typical scene preparation went this way: Jerry would urge the actors in the scene to go for the real human values. His approach seemed to be very "Method." The actors would read through the scene being very legitimate. Jerry would then ask them to do it again—again a very legitimate rehearsal. Jerry would ask for another go-through, but by now the talent of the caliber we were working with are bored out of their minds and someone would do something wild or nutty just to relieve the boredom. Then Jerry would say, "Oh, that's good, keep that." The other actors would say to themselves, "If that's in the scene, no one in the audience will even know I am in it." So next rehearsal some comedic take by someone would be added, and Jerry would say, "Oh, that's good, keep that in." Scene after scene faded away into shtick acting.

This may have affected Jonathan Winters most of all. His ad libs and improvisations were truly hilarious. The cast and crew would fall down laughing in rehearsals. When the camera was rolling, Jonathan would try to repeat what he had done in rehearsal and because it was no longer spontaneous it just fell flat. Jerry should have filmed the rehearsals and let the camera run empty for the take. If only the humor that was in the script had made it to the screen.[12]

Larry Hankin agrees with Quick's opinion of Paris. "Though Jerry liked my acting a lot, we had a very huge 'disagreement' while we were shooting in front of the Alamo one day in front of the entire cast (including 50 extras) and again at a screening at Cinecittá in Italy (where we did some interiors of the Alamo which they replicated perfectly)," he wrote:

In general, he was a perfect, "smile, you're on camera" TV director, but not a good film director is the best I can say. He had no idea how to work with actors—particularly talented ones, which he had in *Viva Max*. All Jerry wanted was to be liked—toxically so. He wasn't a storyteller. He was an excellent traffic manager, which is perfect for sitcom directing and he was obviously great at that.[13]

Writer Michael Etchison was on location the day when Paris was shooting the scene where Ustinov's Max takes Pamela's character to a gardener's shed to seduce her, but it turns into a political conversation. It was shot on what was the Japanese pavilion at the 1968 HemisFair. He reported that Tiffin spent most of the day in her hotel room rehearsing, paying special attention to her costume (white blouse and miniskirt) and makeup. Pamela commented to him, "It has to be right. The way you look changes the character you play."[14] To prove her point, she recited some of her dialogue while pretending to chew gum.

Describing the actual shooting of the scene, Etchison reported, "Ustinov does not need to imagine nervous sweat; he stalks and paces, circling Miss Tiffin like a dog preparing to lie down. No one can forget he is Ustinov, but no one could be unmoved by his awkward explanation of his plan."[15]

Though Pamela mingled with Ustinov and Jonathan Winters, she and the other bigger stars did not hang out with the actors playing soldiers or other small roles. Peter Gonzales explained, "There were tiers of actors on this shoot, but that is a Hollywood thing. This was my first film so I was not acquainted on how things worked on a shoot. The main stars hung out separately from the featured players who stuck together. It was very clannish—sort of like a pyramid."[16]

Hankin, Gonzales and Quick had minimal interaction with Pamela Tiffin. Despite his improvisation talents, Hankin admitted to being quiet and shy. Suffice it to say, he did not make much contact with Pamela on the set and never off it, but found her to be "cool

Coed Paula Whitland (Pamela Tiffin) and tourist Hattie (Alice Ghostley) are taken captive at the Alamo by Mexican soldier Contreras (Gino Conforti) and General DeSantos (Peter Ustinov) in a scene from *Viva Max* (Commonwealth United, 1969).

and pretty."[17] Gonzales said, "I only interacted with Pamela a little bit on the shoot. When I did, she was always very nice. She seemed to get along beautifully with everyone."[18] Quick also had very little contact with the actress. "As I was a bit player in the movie, I was not in her social circle," he remarked, adding:

> I don't remember her socializing much with the cast, we were almost all male and our sense of humor was really pretty crude. It was rumored that she and Peter Ustinov were sharing dinners in his hotel room and perhaps Peter was the only cast member she was friendly other than cordial with.
>
> I do have two memories of Pamela. One was of her table manners. They were impeccable. It was obvious she had spent considerable dining among the elite of Europe. For instance, Americans will butter a slice of bread, then take a bite out of it. Pamela would break off a small piece of bread, butter it, and then most daintily put it in her mouth. She reeked of "class."
>
> My other memory is that during filming outside of the Alamo, cast members who were waiting for their scene or, like me, who wanted to watch the filming, would sit on the grass in front. Pamela wandered onto the lawn in her horseback riding clothes carrying her purse and a bag with a riding crop in it. She placed the bag on the lawn, then turned to spread out a blanket to sit on. As she bent over to spread out the blanket, she goosed herself with the riding crop.

She sprang up, spun around, and cocked her arm to deliver a killing slap to whoever had assaulted her. As I was the nearest one, she glared at me, ready to let me have it. I blinked at her trying to look innocent, and trying not to laugh, pointed at the riding crop. She relaxed, but never spoke to me again.[19]

With shootings delays occurring frequently due to the legal challenges, it stretched out the time spent in Texas to the chagrin of a cadre of Italian crew members who despised the Texas cuisine. Co-star John Astin noticed they were only eating cold meats and cheese in their room and invited ten of them out to dinner. He took them to a grand restaurant called La Louisianne where they enjoyed a wonderful meal with a huge tab to match. The liquor bill alone was $190. Afterwards, Astin quipped to writer Bob Rose, "The next time I see an Italian eating alone in his room, I am going to ask *him* for a bite."[20]

Pamela had not spent such an extended time in the U.S. since almost two years prior, before she relocated to Rome. When asked if she felt anything had changed, she replied, "Of course, I did find America different. It seemed that the old were more starchy, more diffident, and the young more daring, more rebellious. Having been away, I had the outsider's point of view with the insider's understanding."[21]

Despite the shooting obstacles and barriers, the filmmakers were able to shoot the on-location scenes that they intended though the Daughter of the Republic made one last effort, posting a covering so film could not be shot through the fence outside the Alamo. The movie company then packed up and headed to Rome to film interiors at Cinecittà Studios where a $250,000 replica of the Alamo was constructed. Paris thought this affected the performances of his actors and was a problem because any character walking into the Alamo didn't get to complete his entrance until eight weeks later when the production moved to Rome. Though Paris was annoyed with this, his actors (including Larry Hankin and Eldon Quick) weren't because they were getting a free trip to Italy.

Hankin's most vivid memory was "forcing my way onto Federico Fellini's set watching him direct and into his editing room. He was filming *Satyricon* while we were at Cinecittà filming *Viva Max*."[22] Quick recalled, "I cashed in my first class airplane fare, bought coach class for my wife and 18-month-old son and we all went to Rome. In Rome the one day of work I had to do was scheduled as the emergency shoot. That is if for any reason the scheduled shooting could not be done, my scene would be shot. So for four weeks in Rome all I had to do was check in with the company to see if my scene was up, then go out and explore the city. And get paid for it to boot."[23]

Filming wrapped in Italy on schedule with the movie coming in at $3 million, a few hundred thousand dollars over budget due to shooting delays in Texas.

A few months later, at a special preview screening of the completed *Viva Max* at UCLA, Jerry Paris was asked by some film students about shooting on location. He replied, "People are nice to you if you are nice to them. If you don't pop up at a few civic things, they'll be unfriendly. The people of San Antonio—except for the ladies at the Alamo—were marvelous."[24]

He continued, "I'll tell you all something: If you ever get to do a picture, I hope it will be one like this. I've never been happier with a group of actors. We did it ourselves, we remained friends throughout and everyone worked very hard."[25]

Pamela concurred with her director, commenting, "I especially enjoyed working with Jonathan Winters. He's a national treasure, in his way. We would clown around in the swimming pool of this motel. The whole cast would hang out together all of the time."[26] Peter Gonzales remembers one instance in particular: "One time they all got dressed up to watch the Oscars on TV at Peter Ustinov's apartment. It was kind of strange to me that people would do that, but they did. Pamela got all done up in this beautiful silver lamé dress that looked like the one Marilyn Monroe wore when she sang 'Happy Birthday' to President Kennedy. However, Pamela's was a mini-dress. She had hair piled up with lots of curls and looked like a Barbie Doll come to life."[27]

As for her leading man (and party host), Tiffin fondly remembers Peter Ustinov for courtliness, grace, and wit. Gonzales described Ustinov as being "very nice and very friendly, but he made a lot of faces all the time. I guess that happens when you are in the business that long. John Astin was kind and very elegant—always dressed to the tees off-camera. But it wasn't like I was hanging out with them—it wasn't until we got to Italy where I socialized with them more. In Texas, they were just so surrounded with people."[28]

Eldon Quick only had wonderful memories of Winters and Ustinov. "Jonathan was the most brilliantly funny human I have ever had the pleasure of being around," he wrote:

> One did not have a conversation with Jonathan, one just fed him straight lines and let him run away with juxtaposing concepts that one would never think would work together to hilarious effect. For instance, when the cast and crew gathered on wooden benches to watch dailies, Jonathan became a Japanese soldier who had snuck into a movie night on a Pacific island and wanted to know if Mickey Mouse was going to be on. He carried that improvisation on for a good five minutes.
>
> As Jonathan was the funniest, Peter was the most versatile, talented human I have ever met. Actors use a tool called "sense memory" to recall emotions or reactions to a moment so they may use it in a scene. Peter had the most incredible sense memory I have ever seen. Peter could not only recall emotional experiences, he could recall sounds and reproduce them. He could recall what he had seen and draw it. He could recall conversations he had had years ago and reproduce them in the voice of the person he had talked to. He had a very low threshold for boredom. One had to be very interesting to engage his attention. If he got bored he would entertain himself by singing an opera—all the parts, male and female, and sound effects for the orchestra. To make it a little bit more interesting, he would sing an Italian opera as performed by a Norwegian Opera company singing Italian with a Norwegian accent.[29]

While doing promotion for the movie, Pamela was asked what about the differences between making movies in America versus Italy. "Europeans are more organized, strange as it may sound," she replied:

> They have to because they don't have the kind of money the Americans have. Italians productions work much harder at it since there are no stringent union rules and everybody seems to do more than is expected from a Hollywood crew. Of course, this is not necessarily easy on someone like me, who is used to working a five-day week, eight-hour-a-day schedule. Here it is most of the time a six-day week, ten to fourteen hours a day. At times I feel I shall collapse from exhaustion. Yet it is exhilarating to work with Italians. They are great improvisers, great artisans, and artists on all levels.[30]

The producers decided to debut *Viva Max* in three theaters in San Antonio on December 18, 1969, perhaps to stick it to the Daughters of the Republic. It was organized by the city's top theater manager Tommy Powers, who had a knack for getting movie studios to premiere their films in his city. A number of the stars, including Pamela, were in attendance.

The movie opens with Mexican General Maximilian Rodrigues De Santos (Ustinov), mounted on a proud white horse, leading his trustworthy sergeant Valdez (John Astin) and a motley band of 87 soldiers across the Texas border disguised as a military band to march in the annual Washington's Birthday parade in Laredo. However, they detour to San Antonio to reclaim the Alamo. Disguised as tourists, Max and one of his bungling soldiers, Romero (Larry Hankin), stake the place out as they tour the grounds. At the gift shop, they accidentally knock over a postcard stand. They are helped by the souvenir clerk (Tiffin), a pretty blonde with big horn-rimmed glasses, long straight blonde hair tied with a black bow into a pigtail, and clad in a very short maroon miniskirt with a long-sleeved white blouse. When she notices that Romero is wearing a Baylor sweatshirt, she tells him that she attends school there too and wonders if he was part of her group that took over the administration building. Max then rushes him out of before he can blow their cover.

Max and his men march to the Alamo and enter it seconds before it closes. They quickly take over, raising the Mexican flag in celebration. Max also takes three hostages: the gatekeeper (Charles Barnett); the souvenir clerk who recognizes Max from earlier in the day and introduces herself (between sneezing fits) as "Paula Whitland, vice-president for the Student Action for a New Society" and her rightwing customer Hattie Longstreet (Alice Ghostley, a last-minute replacement for actress Ruth White who broke her arm just before filming began). Hattie immediately thinks the general is working for the Chinese Communists.

Police Chief Sylvester (Harry Morgan) descends on the Alamo and tries to convince Max to retreat. He politely refuses and will only speak to a member of the Pentagon despite the chief's threats. Max seems more worried about Paula's hayfever. He offers to free her, but she insists on staying, so he agrees to have her prescription filled. When a high-strung Hattie asks Paula why she didn't take his offer, the coed says with a wry smile, "He's kind of cute."

The chief finds the only army man in town to go speak with Max, a retired general named Hallson (Jonathan Winters) who heads up the local National Guard. The Mexican general realizes immediately that Hallson has no power in the Pentagon and sends him away with only a request for Paula's pills, which the chief orders one of his men to pick up and to deliver to the Alamo.

While Hattie still insists the invasion has been orchestrated by Chinese Communists, Paula is fascinated from a political science angle. Max takes her to a tool shed (his men think he is going to "conquer" her due to Valdez's innuendos) and reveals his reason for taking the Alamo. Paula feels that Max is another Che Guevera and plans to do her graduate thesis on him as the new 20th Century revolutionary hero. Her idolization soon turns to disappointment as Max explains that his actions are to impress his woman back in Mexico: She ridiculed him and said that his men wouldn't even follow him into a whorehouse (though his sergeant assured him that his men *would* most definitely follow him into a whorehouse). All Max wants from the U.S. is a letter proving what he achieved and that his men followed him so he can make his girlfriend eat her words. Paula insists that Max put aside his personal reasons and use the taking of the Alamo to represent mistreatment of the Mexicans by the U.S. as an example of the anti-establishment movement happening all over the world.

Hattie escapes from her cell and telephones her nephew Sam Gillison (Kenneth Mars), the leader of a secret paramilitary group called the Sentries. They make their way to the Alamo, as does a junior rep from the State Department named Quincy (Eldon Quick). All

Max wants is his acknowledgment letter but Quincy, acting on behalf of the government, refuses. They then bring in the military led by General Lacomber (Keenan Wynn), who orders his men and the National Guard not to use live ammo because the government wants no casualties.

After a series of bungles and mishaps by the U.S. army, Max captures the platoon. He goes to gloat to Paula, who surprisingly tells him he has to give up. She learned from one of his soldiers that they are being forced to obey him by Sergeant Valdez, who has threatened to shoot any who desert. She tells Max a true revolution needs to be voluntary or else it is just totalitarianism. Refusing to listen and chalking up her baffling behavior to being a woman, he storms out.

Questioning Valdez, Max realizes what Paula said is true and decides to surrender. The company departs the Alamo with their hostages, waving a white flag, only to be confronted by the Sentries, the only group with live ammo. Goaded by his Aunt Hattie, Gillison shoots an unarmed Max. The outraged general and his men advance on the militia, who break and run. Paula comes to her hero's aid and tells him that his soldiers followed him without being pressured. Gillison is arrested. Max, wanting to go home, bids Paula adieu and triumphantly walks out of the Alamo followed by his men with shouts of "Viva Max!" as they march through the streets.

Viva Max premiered in Texas in December 1969. It did not open nationally until January 1970 with its tagline proclaiming, "February 27, 1969—the world's funniest general recaptures the Alamo, and the world's mightiest army can't get him out!" The film was received warmly. Charles Champlin of the *Los Angeles Times* called it "a light, bright comedy and a further testament to the comical genius of Ustinov." Vincent Canby of the *New York Times* remarked, "The general surprise of *Viva Max* is that a lot of it is funny." Marjory Adams of the *Boston Globe* said, "Most of the story is highly hilarious, although the jokes begin to wear thin after an hour." The reviewer for *Film Daily* called it "a full-blooded comedy caper capable of delighting everyone up and down the age scale." Judith Crist of *The Today Show* found it "quite irresistible." According to *Variety*, it had a "captivatingly original idea, well produced but questionably cast with Peter Ustinov in the lead." *Variety* also thought it had something to offend everyone from John Wayne to Texans to right-wing militias. The movie was well-received enough for the National Screen Council members to award it the February Blue Ribbon Award for outstanding merit and suitability for family entertainment.

But it was not all praise for *Viva Max*. A few pans did sneak in, such as Gene Siskel's witty quip in the *Chicago Tribune*, "Remember the Alamo! Forget *Viva Max!*"

Pamela was usually left out come review time, though Champlin in the *Los Angeles Times* did describe her as a "captive beauty"; John Goff of *The Hollywood Reporter* remarked that she was "attractive as the souvenir clerk"; and Bridget Byrne in the *Los Angeles Herald-Examiner* found her "pert enough." Perhaps her worst review came from Harry Clein of *Entertainment World*: "Pamela Tiffin is completely miscast as a Baylor coed.... Her pseudo-southern accent ... adds a ludicrous quality to an already silly character."

This is one of Pamela's sexiest roles as her pretty activist coed can't seem to stop herself from being attracted to General Max and she plays it quite well. It is also appropriate that she would end the sixties just like she began it, co-starring in a political satire. However, her Paula Whitland is no Scarlett Hazeltine of *One, Two, Three*. The differences between the two truly represented the dichotomy of the turbulent decade. While Scarlett was a spoiled apolitical brat who spent her college days seeing how many students could be stuffed into a phone booth, Paula was idealistic and studious, spending her days on campus taking over administration buildings to protest the Vietnam War and other wrongs happening around the world. What they do have in common, though, is that both fall for revolutionaries. Paula turns hers into one, while Scarlett does the reverse. Paula helps General Max see that his taking back the Alamo is much bigger than his first desire to impress a woman back in Mexico. She feels that it represents the struggles of all people who strike back against their oppressors—in this case, the United States that took land from the Mexicans. Scarlett begins to shed her shallowness, spending time with her Communist lover Otto and is even willing to give up her privileged lifestyle to be with him. However, after being barred from East Germany, Otto has to given up his Communist ideology and be transformed into a debonair capitalist by Scarlett and James Cagney's MacNamara to impress his new in-laws.

Viva Max was also the first time U.S. moviegoers got to both see and hear Pamela on the big screen without dubbing since *Harper* (1966). It would be another four years until they had the opportunity again with *Deaf Smith & Johnny Ears* in 1973.

A jet-setting Pamela returned to the U.S. after *Viva Max* wrapped in Italy. A friend, director Harold Clurman, offered her the chance to do *Uncle Vanya* (by Russian playwright

General DeSantos (Peter Ustinov) reveals to hostage Paula Whitland (Pamela Tiffin) the real reason he has retaken the Alamo in a scene from *Viva Max* (Commonwealth United, 1969).

Anton Chekhov) on stage at the Mark Taper Forum in Los Angeles with a cast that included Richard Basehart, Joseph Wiseman, Lois Smith, and Gale Sondergaard. She wrote a thesis on Chekhov for one of her college courses ("How provocative he is and how modern he is with his concern about the changing world around him"[31]) and jumped at the chance to play Yelena with such a distinguished cast though she was a bit apprehensive. She admitted at the time, "I am terribly excited about it and at the same time a bit frightened because I very much want to be good at it."[32]

Pamela had already played the role of the beautiful Yelena for the director in a workshop production a few years prior in New York while she was doing *Dinner at Eight* on Broadway. The character is the beautiful, discontented second wife of an elderly professor whose urban lifestyle is supported by his late first wife's rural estate. While visiting for a short period, Yelena captivates a local doctor named Astrov and the estate's manager Vanya, who lives there with the professor's homely daughter Sonya. Romantic entanglements arise and then the professor announces he has decided to sell the estate to use the money for a higher standard of living for himself and Yelena despite the repercussions to Vanya and Sonya. While in California doing *Uncle Vanya*, Pamela resided at the then shabby Chateau Marmont just off Sunset Boulevard.

The play received rave reviews for presenting Chekhov "played slowly and juicily, with lots of nuance and rubato—a tone-poem evoking a society where people had time to savor their private disasters," as reviewer Dan Sullivan wrote in the *Los Angeles Times*. Curiously, both he and the *New York Times* critic used the same adjective, "exquisite," when praising Pamela's performance as the petulant wife. It was perhaps her finest hour on stage.

Despite the few months she spent in Los Angeles, Pamela limited her work to the *Uncle Vanya* stage production though she guested on the talk programs *The David Frost Show* and *The Tonight Show Starring Johnny Carson* to promote the play and the upcoming *Viva Max*. She did not pursue or was not offered any film or television work With Pamela it is hard to say which. It would be not be surprising if she just sat back, wanting to concentrate on the play. It would have been a treat to see her show up as a lead guest star in a segment of *Love, American Style*, a series perfectly suited to her comedic talents and looks.

On the other hand, she may have gone after some film roles without success. She hadn't made a movie in Hollywood in over four years. Actresses who came after her (Faye Dunaway, Katharine Ross, Mia Farrow, Candice Bergen, Ali MacGraw, Leigh Taylor-Young, and Jacqueline Bisset) were the newest "It" girls. They beat out Pamela's earlier contemporaries for some very high-profile roles in the later half of the sixties, forcing them to take ensemble or drive-in movies or to retreat to the small screen. For example, Ann-Margret was paired with Joe Namath in a biker movie; Carol Lynley was co-starring in films with the likes of Rowan & Martin and Glen Campbell; Susan Strasberg, Diane McBain, and Sandra Dee were working for American International Pictures, the leader in exploitation films; Yvette Mimieux was the last-minute replacement for Inger Stevens in the forgettable TV series *The Most Wanted Game*; and Sue Lyon was in Spain making a spaghetti western. With the studio system collapsing and the rise of the independent filmmaker, new faces were in. If the Lynleys and Mimieuxs who remained in the Hollywood spotlight could not land high profile roles, it is not surprising Pamela may have had trouble too.

Pamela was still in Hollywood in early 1970 when *The Survivors* was cancelled after only half a season and when *Viva Max* was released. She then got blindsided when *Playboy* magazine got hold of a few topless photos of her and ran them in a pictorial called "A Toast to Tiffin" in the February 1970 issue. Those pictures were test shots. Pamela was offered the lead role in *The Libertine*, an erotic drama about a recently widowed young woman who learns her deceased husband had a secret apartment that he used for romantic trysts. She decides to keep it to explore her sexual desires. The part required nudity. Pamela asked a female photographer to take photos of her to see if she felt comfortable *au naturel* in front of the camera (and also because she thought she might not look good naked). She photographed spectacularly, no surprise there, but she did feel uneasy about baring her body, so she passed on the part. A more uninhibited Catherine Spaak stepped in for her.

Once she decided not to make the movie, Pamela thought that was the end of the photos. She was horrified when they showed up in *Playboy*, which she had turned down previously even when they offered her $100,000. The piece falsely implied that Pamela posed specially for the magazine with the opening line "Jet-set cinema star Pamela Tiffin pauses between overseas movies for an exclusive—and revealing—*Playboy* pictorial." The photos of the topless actress are not up to par with some of *Playboy*'s past photo shoots of other movie stars such as Ursula Andress and Elke Sommer. At least the pictures were tastefully shot, with a few set outdoors. Some featured Pamela with her long flowing straight blonde hair while others had her with wild hair styles. In some she is cradling a doll and in others flowers. A few have her with sheer linen draped over her. The most stunning shot is of a topless profile of her face looking down while sitting on the ground with her back to the camera and a furry boa draped across her lap. None of the photos shows full frontal nudity. At the time, she thought of filing a lawsuit, but then decided not to bring added attention to it. She let it go though she strongly felt that it did not represent her or her career.

Her *Playboy* issue was a sensation in the U.S. and proved that the gorgeous actress was not forgotten by American men. The photos also ran in the Italian edition of *Playboy* with the article title translated to "Un brindisi a Tiffin." Due to her status in Italy at the time, it was one of *Playboy*'s most popular issues of the day.

Back in 1969 when talking about her frustration with *Playboy*, Pamela did admit to the press that as for nude scenes in movies, if Federico Fellini or Stanley Kramer asked, that would give her pause. They never did, but two lesser directors did ask a few years later. Pamela by then had loosened up about film nudity and glimpses of her bosom and shapely derriere would be exposed in two films to come.

About the same time that Pamela was bashing *Playboy*, which was founded in Chicago, she was praising the Blank Panther Party, the radical African American revolutionary socialist organization. Members were recently involved in a shootout with the Chicago police that left their leader dead, which caused quite a stir. When asked if she was in favor of violence, Tiffin responded, "Who's been violent? It's the police. I grew up in Chicago. Everybody can have a gun except the Black Panthers."[33] Nowadays, celebrities insinuate themselves into political and social situations regularly, but back in the late sixties it was still new, especially if the celebrity had a more liberal point of view. The more conservative establishment took them to task, especially with such a controversial organization as the Black Panthers. Tiffin's comments raised quite a few eyebrows, but at least she did not wind up on the FBI's watch list as did actress Jean Seberg for her defense of and financial contribution to the organization.

It is too bad Pamela did not make the decision to stay in California at this point. She had a hit film in release, and TV viewers got to see her on the last episode of *The Survivors*. Her sexy *Playboy* pictorial along with her comments about the Black Panthers brought her notoriety that she hadn't seen in the U.S. since she went blonde in 1965. She may have been able to capitalize on the attention and no doubt could have landed some lead movie roles— perhaps even a breakout role *à la* Ann-Margret with *Carnal Knowledge*. Alas, Pamela high-tailed it back to Rome, squashing her last chance to attain superstardom. Years later she lamented, "I did any stupid movie in Italy just to stay there."[34]

The Godfather It Ain't

Cosi di Cosa Nostra (*The Godson*)

Tiffin left Hollywood for good in 1970 and Italy once again welcomed her with open arms. *La Stampa* was one of the country's most popular daily newspapers and was published in Turin. Pamela was a favorite of the editors and many photos of her were published, keeping the Italian public up to date on her exploits professionally and personally. In October 1970 they ran an infamous photo of Pamela looking like a Haight-Asbury hippie while in attendance at a Rolling Stones rock concert.

In Rome, Pamela ran into actor Peter Gonzales, whom she worked with on *Viva Max*. When asked if the actress remembered him, Gonzales quipped with a laugh, "Of course, I was pretty striking back then. Why would she have forgotten me?" After *Viva Max* completed filming, Gonzales moved to London where he modeled for a year. He was back in Italy to try to ignite his acting career and boy, did he—landing the lead role in Federico Fellini's opulent *Roma* while simultaneously shooting *L'ospite/The Guest* for director Liliana Cavani. During this busy time, he would see Tiffin out socially. "I would run into Pamela at Via Aquino and Piazza del Popolo. We'd chat for awhile, but we didn't hang out."[1] This is not surprising, since Gonzales was immersed in Fellini's world—a world Pamela no doubt wished she was a part of.

Pamela didn't have much leisure time either, making four movies in quick succession with two in the comedia all'Italiana vein. The unreleased *Roma '70*, directed by Franceso Maselli (who had made the crime comedy *A Fine Pair* with Rock Hudson and Claudia Cardinale), was about the college student movement in Italy. It was probably going to be somewhat similar to Hollywood student protest movies such as *The Strawberry Statement* and *Getting Straight*. Pamela most likely played a coed. Filming was completed, but reportedly they ran out of money in post-production and the movie was never finished.

Cosi di Cosa Nostra (1971), an Italian-French co-production, was a labored comedy-drama from prolific Italian director Steno (real name: Stefano Vanzini). He had been working in the Italian cinema since the late 1930s, first as a screenwriter and eventually a director. Most of his movies are known only in his native country

This film (also known as *The Godson, Godfather of Crime*, and *Gang War*) gave Pamela another well-desired character role. She played an Italian living in America whose husband is forced to return to Italy to assassinate his Mafia uncle's rival. While her reluctant spouse tries to think of ways to avoid doing the deadly deed, Tiffin's character is pursued by a former lover who won't take no for answer. Carlo Giuffrè (a prolific Italian actor who was working in films since 1950) played her husband and the handsome, openly gay French actor Jean-Claude Brialy (best known up to this point for his roles in Claude Chabrol's *Le beau Serge* and *Les cousins* and for *La ronde* with Jane Fonda) played her pursuer. Both were well known in their respective countries but their names had little box office appeal internationally, especially in the U.S.

It is interesting to note that Giuffrè was Pamela's fifth leading man (after Marcello Mastroianni, Ugo Tognazzi, Nino Manfredi, and Vittorio Gassman) over the age of forty. *Variety* ran an interesting piece about the dearth of upcoming young Italian actors during the sixties in Italy and how younger foreign actors such as Clint Eastwood, Tomas Milian, Lou Castel, John Phillip Law, Brett Halsey, and Jean Sorel, among others, were coming into the country to fill the void.

The film featured in small roles the esteemed director Vittorio De Sica and Agnes Spaak, older sister of actress Catherine Spaak and daughter of screenwriter Charles Spaak. Also in the cast was rotund, bug-eyed comic actor Aldo Fabrizi (who co-wrote the script) as a police inspector who bumbles his way through the movie one step behind everyone else. Much beloved in his native Italy, Fabrizi never caught on with American audiences and made sporadic Hollywood movies including *The Angel Wore Red* (1960) with Ava Gardner and *Three Bites of the Apple* (1967) with David McCallum.

Cosi di Cosa Nostra opens with aerial views and then street scenes of New York City. The camera pans its way to the downtown neighborhood of Little Italy and then into the drab, nondescript apartment of Salvatore Lococo, a parking lot attendant who immigrated to America from Italy, and his wife Carmela. Hidden under a black wavy wig, lots of heavy dark eye makeup, and ratty house dress, Pamela is light years away from the blonde sex goddess persona she projected in magazine photos. Salvatore is proud that he saved $5 this week from his paycheck and when he goes to put it into the hidden piggy bank for a family trip to Italy, he finds the piggy bank is missing. Carmela realizes that their son Peter and daughter Maria found the stash and, after giving chase, Salvatore retrieves the bank from them. He explains to his children that even though they were born in America and are Italian-Americans, they are more Italian and he wants them to see their home country. Peter replies, "They're a bunch of Fascists in Italy."

While at work, Salvatore is paid a visit by two goons who strongly suggest he be at the pier at 5 that afternoon. The nervous immigrant is picked up in a car and learns that he is the godson of a Mafia don. He is forced to accept $30,000 and a trip to Italy to assassinate his uncle's rival Don Manzano. The mob feels that using an innocent would keep the focus off of them. If Salvatore doesn't follow through, he and his family will be eliminated

Telling his wife he won big at the horse races, the Lococos jet off to Rome. Salvatore emerges from the plane with a toothache. The fat Inspector Panzarani's drug-sniffing dog Pepino picks out Salvatore's suitcase, so he and Carmela are pulled into customs. While the couple is strip searched, Pepino gets a hashish doggie treat. The outraged Carmela rants and raves about the ill treatment to a real Italian family and how they are being profiled just because they are coming from America. Once the misunderstanding is cleared up, the family tours the Coliseum in Rome trailed by Panzarani and Pepino. Recognizing the fat man, Salvatore thinks he is a mob member making sure he goes ahead with the hit. Worried and distracted, he later ignores his amorous wife in her sexy lingerie, to her frustration. Instead of making love, they watch an old movie on television. It gives Salvatore the idea to hire someone to take his place as the killer.

Going to one of the seediest parts of Rome, Salvatore talks to a bunch of locals about the type of man he needs to hire. Misunderstanding Salvatore's vagaries, they set him up with Nandini, a homosexual. Taking him to a secluded spot, he calls Salvatore a "closet queen." The outrage husband flees the area, but bumps into Panzarini. Salvatore confides in him, using the metaphor "peeling an orange" as code for what he has to do, and the inspector, thinking it is a drug deal, offers a friend as a driver to help Salvatore out. He drives them first to Naples so Carmela can see her family. Salvatore is too nervous to enjoy himself, and Carmela is angered by his rudeness to her relations, who even hired musicians to perform for them. The driver has determined that Salvatore has to kill someone and telephones the inspector with this information.

While on her parents' balcony, Carmela is spotted by her former paramour Mimi whose girlfriend Bridget has just broken up with him due to his penchant for gambling. While Salvatore follows his driver to a soccer match where he will be the only one rooting for Roma against Napoli, Mimi gets Carmela away from her family under the pretense that his mother now lives in a beautiful villa and wishes to see her. He tries to woo her by playing "their song" and sharing his never-ending dreams of being with her. When he moves in for the kiss, the miffed Carmela tells him to keep his hands off her and to take her home. Meanwhile, the soccer excitement is too much for the driver, who succumbs to a heart attack when Roma scores the winning goal, ruining Salvatore's plan.

A forlorn Salvatore spots an older gentleman about to jump off a cliff and he stops him. The old man Don Michele, laments how he went from a rich and powerful attorney to nothing due to his gambling addiction. Salvatore takes him to a restaurant where he confesses to the Don his travails. Meanwhile Carmela

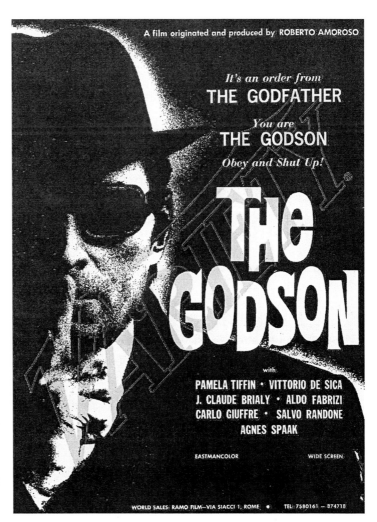

Trade ad created for *Cosi di Cosa Nostra*, renamed *The Godson*, to attract a U.S. film distributor.

confides in her aunt that Salvatore has not touched her once since they have been in Italy. Her aunt thinks he has been "shooting his bullets" at another woman. Reading the tarot cards, the meddling aunt convinces Carmela that Salvatore has been cheating on her with someone he met in Rome.

When Mimi hears through Don Michele that Salvatore is looking to off someone, he pretends to be a hired killer. He calls Salvatore to meet just as he is about to make love to an amorous Carmela. Deserting his frustrated wife yet again, Salvatore rushes out under the pretext of having to go to the morgue to identify the dead driver's body. Mimi lets on that he knows the entire situation and instructs Salvatore to leave his children in Naples but to take Carmela with them to avoid arousing suspicion. After hearing from Salvatore that they will act like newlyweds on their drive to Sicily, Carmela's happiness quickly turns to outrage when she sees Mimi is their driver. She accuses her former boyfriend of trying to break up their marriage and he admits it since he is still madly in love with her.

Arriving in the town of the intended victim, Salvatore and Mimi disappear at night. Meanwhile, Inspector Panzarini is getting frustrated since he can't reach his man posing as Salvatore's driver, not knowing he has died. The next morning Carmela corners Mimi and demands to know where Salvatore went. He continues making his passes at her ("You are getting very boring," she exclaims), but does let the distrustful wife know that they are going out again later that night. Mimi pretends that he will assassinate the Don if Salvatore can get him in front of the window at the pool hall, but his real intent is to have some alone time with Carmela. He barges into her room where she is clad in sexy black lingerie. Mimi grabs her passionately only to receive a slap across the face in return. Mimi says that she has to choose between him and Salvatore and pushes Carmela onto the bed. Screaming that there is no decision to make, she clobbers him over the head with a hair brush and demands he leave at once.

The Don inadvertently puts into Salvatore's head the idea that his driver is having an affair with Carmela. Enraged, the miffed husband pulls a knife on Mimi back at the hotel and, seeing him panic, realizes that he is no killer. He then threatens that Mimi will end up in a body bag if he doesn't off Manzano. The fat Inspector shows up and is immediately whisked off to the Don by his thugs.

Mimi tries to get out of the job by feigning illness, but Salvatore is determined that he will shoot the Don to save his family. He sneaks off when Salvatore is distracted by an upset Carmela, who is packing her bags to return to Naples. Mimi hides in a van to avoid Salvatore, but ends up at Manzano's home. The Don instructs his men to pick up Salvatore. Carmela spots him getting into a car with Manzano's girlfriend. She then flags down a cab to follow them.

Everyone ends up in the Don's villa where the convoluted truth is slowly "peeled like an orange" to all. Manzano gets his deadly revenge on the rival gang in New York, while Mimi and Salvatore get into a fight over Carmela and wind up falling over the villa's balcony. Luckily for them, the inspector was sneaking away and they land on the fat man, who breaks their fall. All sustain broken bones and are confined to wheelchairs. Salvatore finally wants to make love to his sexy wife despite his being in a cast. She quips, "All you have is a stiff leg." He then reaches over and pulls her into bed as the end credits roll.

Cosi di Cosa Nostra received mediocre reviews in Italy. Most critics found it to be an unoriginal farce though enlivened by some zesty characterizations. Moviegoers were not impressed and it was only the 66th highest grossing Italian film that year with a take of 553,442,000 liri ($387,755).

The dubbing is above-average and the voices a good match for the actors, which is surprising since its leading players spoke different languages: Italian by Giuffrè, French by Brialy, and of course English by Tiffin. The movie itself shifts awkwardly from comedy to drama, but it does keep you curious and mildly entertained due to the appealing cast. The colorful cinematography (featuring spectacular shots of Rome and Naples) and a lively musical score help too.

The movie has an array of misunderstandings as usually found in Italian comedies. However here they extend to the hero being mistaken for a homosexual three times. Besides the incident with the gay guy in Rome, Don Michele asks Salvatore if he is gay and later a black woman at a cocktail lounge asks the same question when Salvatore completely ignores her. The irony is that his wife thinks he is the complete opposite and is two-timing her with another woman.

Pamela is almost unrecognizable in this movie, as she is saddled with a less-than-flattering wig and way too much eye makeup to make her look more Southern Italian. All she really gets to do is to pine for Salvatore when he is not to be found and then show only anger and frustration when they are together due to his secret preoccupation with killing the Don. She releases that same anger with her predatory ex-boyfriend, whom she wants no part of. The role was not written with any nuance and never takes advantage of Tiffin's comedic abilities, which is surprising since this is more farce than drama.

The movie's original Italian poster art featured a rendering of Carlo Giuffrè in bed with a broken leg and Pamela beside him in black lingerie. To choose the last scene of the movie as its representation was an odd choice, and may have made moviegoers think it was more a bedroom sex farce than a parody about the Mafia.

Ads for the movie, with the title *The Godson*, ran in the trades in 1971 with Tiffin top-billed with the tagline, "It's an order from the Godfather. You are the Godson. *Obey and shut up!*" It doesn't seem the producers were able to find a U.S. distributor at that point. Then the hugely successful *The Godfather* was released in 1972 followed by its even better sequel in 1974. To cash in, Independent-International Pictures Corp. picked up the distribution rights in 1975 and gave it a very limited release in America using the title *Godfather of Crime* to make ticket buyers think it was a violent gangster picture rather than a comedy. In some quarters it was re-titled *Gang War*. No matter what the title, the movie did not get any traction in the States and went almost unnoticed.

Pamela Bares Some Skin

Il vichingo venuto dal Sud
(*The Blonde in the Blue Movie*)

Tiffin was once again in the hands of director Steno in another comedy, *Il vichingo venuto dal Sud* (*The Viking Who Came from the South*), but this time with no wigs or heavy eye makeup. This comedy was not well-received by the critics, but it was hugely popular with ticket buyers and remains one of Tiffin's biggest European hits. That's not surprising since she played a Dutch coed who moonlights as a porn star and falls in love with an old-fashioned Sicilian. He is newly arrived in Denmark and not used to the more liberal Scandinavian ways.

Steno paired his leading lady with one of Italy's top comedic actors, ruggedly handsome Lando Buzzanca. He appeared opposite some of the sexiest actresses of the day including Ann-Margret, Ursula Andress, Sylva Koscina, and Virna Lisi. His lone English-language film up to this point was the comedy *Those Daring Young Men in Their Jaunty Jalopies* (1969) starring Tony Curtis. In his native Italy he was known for playing secret agent James Tont in two James Bond spy spoofs and for playing macho working class types too entrenched in tradition to accept changes in the world. Roberto Curti confirms that Buzzanca was one of Italy's most popular stars at the time, but went on to describe him as only a "mediocre actor" who "specialized in oversexed, overzealous"[1] caricature-types. The role he played in *Il vichingo venuto dal Sud* is a perfect example.

Despite his popularity with Italian moviegoers, Buzzanca was not one of Tiffin's favorite leading men. She mentioned that a few of her Italian co-stars were not gentlemanly and singled out Buzzanca as the worst. He bet the crew that he could bed the actress within a week. She had to complain to the producers, who forced the determined, lascivious actor to leave her alone.

Besides trying to fend off an amorous leading man, Pamela also had to contend with cold, damp weather during the many outdoor scenes. "This movie was filmed during the winter, but we were pretending it was summer," said Pamela. "I would be wearing lightweight cotton dresses in thirty-degree weather and was always freezing. Between takes, the crew would wrap me in blankets. I remember filming a picnic scene with Lando where we were supposed to roll around on the soft ground—except the ground was frozen and hard as a rock!"[2]

Pamela also had a problem with the screen nudity. Per the actress, due to her being uncomfortable, a body double was used for the nude scenes in the completed porn movie screened for the Italians, but there is no doubt that it is her right bosom that is exposed during the filming of the second porn movie.

It is ironic to learn that despite Buzzanca's boorish behavior towards her; the cold, gloomy weather; and the nudity issues, that this light comedy is one of Pamela's favorite working experiences. Credit goes to the well-respected director, Steno, and the free-spirited character she played.

In the story, Buzzanca plays Rosario Trapanese a Sicilian businessman who, trying to prove that he is not old-fashioned, asks to run his shoe company's Copenhagen division in the more sexually liberated Denmark. Departing the plane, he is hit with "Garibaldi's Revenge" when he bends over to kiss the ground and throws his back out. Gustav Larsen (Renzo Marignano) sets Rosario up in his new office complete with a homely secretary (to the Italian's dismay). An outdoor photo shoot with nude models wearing only the company's new high fashion boots cheers Rosario up quickly though he thinks nobody is going to be looking at the products. Larsen disagrees and tells him that in Denmark, nudity doesn't attract much attention. When Larsen brags that the shoot came in under budget, he asks Rosario what it would cost in Italy and he drolly replies, "Two years in jail."

At a mall to visit a store selling his company's shoes, Rosario bumps into a beautiful blonde shopper (Pamela Tiffin) wearing a fur hat and a red maxi coat over a very short miniskirt. He knocks a package out of her hand and apologizes in Italian. She responds in Italian, catching him off-guard, before moving on. While meeting with the store's director, he spots the blonde on a security camera and arranges to meet her using market research as an excuse. Karin is a psychology student at a local university. She doesn't have the time to participate, so Rosario accompanies her as she heads to school while "interviewing" her. Karin suspects he is using this as a ruse to try to get her into bed, but he strongly insists he only has a professional interest. Liking that, she surprises the Italian and invites him to dinner at her place as long as he doesn't mention shoes. Late for class, she jumps onto a tram as he looks for a taxi. Rosario can't get on and she departs without him knowing where to find her.

At a swingers' party, Rosario keeps striking out since his date arrives drunk. She belches before passing out. He leaves frustrated, but his spirits are immediately lifted when he finds a note from Karin at his hotel. He goes to her place and, after her two friends depart, they begin to make love when "Garibaldi's Revenge" strikes the unlucky Italian. He heads back to his hotel, leaving the amorous Karin unsatisfied.

As their romance commences, there are lots of scenes as the happy couple bicycle around the city and countryside. Karin even brings him to meet her parents. He is surprised when her mother allows the couple to share a bedroom. But Rosario is stunned when Karin won't let him make love to her in the family home. She explains that at first she was just sexually attracted to him but now it has turned into love. If they have sex, she feels she will lose her freedom and will just want to be with him all the time. With that said, she breaks it off with him. Her attitude totally confuses the Sicilian, who is used to the man calling the shots.

Rosario is so obsessed with Karin, he can't think of anything else while at work or play. But the obstinate girl refuses to speak to him or see him. Desperate, he stalks her at the university, and then chases after her when she spots him and takes off on her bicycle. While in hot pursuit, he professes his love but the girl won't listen. He even proposes, but she still refuses. The next scene, however, finds the couple at the altar being wed. At their

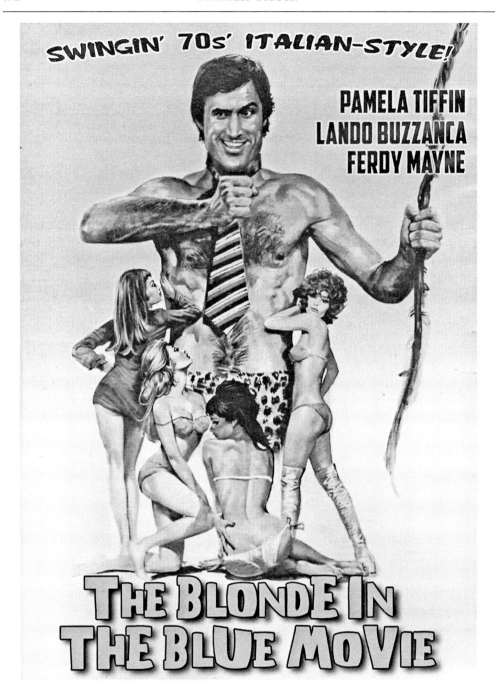

Cover art for the 2013 American DVD release of *Il vichingo venuto dal Sud*, re-titled *The Blonde in the Blue Movie*.

honeymoon cottage, Rosario attempts to carry Karin over the threshold. However, taking no chances on him hurting his back, the bride carries him over it instead.

After meeting her professor (Ferdy Mayne, best known to American audiences as the count in Roman Polanski's *The Fearless Vampire Killers*) at a party, Rosario returns to Italy on business and brings his boss Silvio Borelon (Gigi Ballista) some requested Danish porn. Borelon seems oblivious to his wife Luisa's slutty manner right under his nose. At the soiree, the party guests become anxious to see their first adult movie. Rosario chides them for behaving so immaturely and tells them that nudity is no big thing to him. He sits at the bar behind the movie screen as a beautiful masked blonde named Miss Aphrodite, dressed in black, enters an all-white bedroom with a handsome man, clad in white. She removes her top and they began to kiss passionately. She pulls her mask off as they fall onto the bed and the dominatrix is revealed to be Karin. Seeing the audience transfixed, Rosario walks around to take a peek and faints when he sees his wife making love on camera.

An outraged Rosario returns to Copenhagen. While on the plane, he fantasizes about the outrageous ways he is going to torture and kill his new bride. When he finally arrives home, he pulls the covers off of his sleeping wife and says, "You whore!" As he goes to slap the startled Karin, Garibaldi's Revenge strikes again. While he screams insults at her despite his pain, Karin races to get Rosario his medication. She pulls down his pants to reveal his butt (the first bit of male nudity in the film but more to come) and injects him to ease his suffering. Not wanting to argue with the outraged Rosario, she agrees to a divorce and promises never to see him again. Heartbroken, she then rushes from the apartment. As she closes the door behind her, we get a close-up of Pamela, whose face shows sorrow and embarrassment. This is just another example of how wonderful a talent she was and how she could convey feelings without saying a word.

While Rosario is packing to move out, Karin's Danish-speaking father shows up to retrieve her things. The hot-headed Italian hurls insults at the man and his daughter despite the language barrier in this quite amusing scene. At his hotel, Rosario imagines his reflection in the mirror calling him a savage and telling him to reflect on the different moral standards of sex in Denmark versus Italy. And to remember that one of the reasons he moved there was the more liberal attitudes toward life. Rosario then goes to Karin's professor for some guidance. He takes him to a psychology course where two students have sex in front of the entire class to help them lose their inhibitions. Rosario is shocked but watches and observes the students' indifference, including the couple performing it. With prodding from the professor, he realizes that Karin must have been feeling the same and decides to go back to her.

Arriving at her parents' home, he peers into the window and sees the bottom half of Karin suspended in air. Thinking she is committing suicide, he races into the house only to find her exercising on parallel bars. She continues her physical routine, ignoring him, and one point accidentally slaps him in the face, as he tries to apologize for his brutish behavior. They make up, but Karin reveals that in her anger she agreed to do another porn movie for the same director and now is contractually bound to it.

The next day at the producer's office, he agrees to let Karin out of the contract but only if she pays the penalty fee of 40 million lira. The couple doesn't have the money, so they need to find a solution. Rosario's boss refuses to loan him any money. Rosario convinces himself to let her make the movie.

While Karin rehearses with her partner on the movie set, a perturbed Rosario sits on the sidelines helping the wife of the actor with her knitting. The director reveals to Rosario that the leading man lacks expression. When Rosario suggests he be replaced, the director says, "He has *other* qualities." Rosario is perplexed by that statement. The next scene finds all three men naked in the steam room. The director complains again about the actor, but this time Rosario realizes what the actor's "other" quality is. Rosario tries to keep an open mind while on the set the next day but loses it and takes Karin away, with the producer yelling for his penalty fee if she does not come back.

Rosario's boss shows up unexpectedly in Copenhagen and the happy Sicilian thinks he has changed his mind about the loan. While meeting at a hotel, Borelon spots Karin (Pamela a vision of loveliness wearing a full-length white fur coat) waving to Rosario and recognizes her as Miss Aphrodite. He insists that the reluctant Rosario introduce them and he will think about the loan. After explaining the situation to Karin, she agrees to go along with Rosario's ruse of her only speaking Danish. But at lunch the insulting comments from Borelon, followed by a pass, become unbearable for Karin, who explodes and tells him off. Furious, she also slaps her husband for not coming to her defense and reveals that she is Rosario's wife before storming off. When Rosario confirms that Karin is his spouse, Borelon calls her a whore and insists that Rosario give her up to keep his job. Rosario almost goes through with it but at the airport realizes what a hypocrite Borelon and Italians in general are. He tells Borelon the real whore is his wife Luisa who sleeps around behind Borelon's back while he turns a blind eye to it. After a shouting match, Borelon fires him and Rosario vows to do his own thing. That turns out to be becoming Karin's leading man playing Tarzan to her waiting Jane!

When *Il Vichingo venuto dal Sud* was released in Italy, it was reviewed by *Variety* critic Werb., who remarked, "Steno has co-authored and directed his slickest film to date" and found that his comedy about the contrasting attitudes about sex in Italy and Denmark had "satirical piquancy and a lot more sex farce.... [T]his confrontation lifts timeworn comedy situations to the level of raw but relevant entertainment...." Werb. commented that Pamela "plays her emancipation with easy-going unrestraint and the sincerity of a sex evangelist." The film's impressive production values were extolled ("Polished mounting with its Holly-wood look..."), in particular the color cinematography, the art direction, and costuming. It was predicted that the movie would be an international success and it was.

Paolo Mereghetti called *Il Vichingo venuto dal Sud* "quite a forgettable film, were it not for Tiffin's grace and stunning looks."[3] Pamela concurred with Mereghetti about the movie and freely admitted, "Its aim was to be a farcical comedy contrasting Nordic and Mediterranean attitudes about men and women and life and love. I found it to be silly and dumb."[4]

Il Vichingo venuto dal Sud was a box office hit in Italy and earned 1,751,000,000 lire ($1.2 million), making it the 17th highest grossing movie of the year. No doubt the film's enticing subject manner and nudity lured audiences into theaters. It was reported in *Variety* that 20th Century–Fox signed an exclusive agreement with the film's production company IFC to distribute this and other motion pictures outside of Italy. The movie was released with the title *The Blonde in the Blue Movie* in some English-speaking countries, but not the United States. In Israel, the *Jerusalem Post* critic said, "[T]he movie starts off very well, with several amusing episodes ... later it drags somewhat." Steno was praised for "making the most of its Copenhagen location" and for consistently delighting "the eye with his glimpses of the old city's charming palaces, canals and green spaces."

United Kingdom reviewers did not take to the comedy at all, calling it "dumb." Malcolm Derek of *The Guardian* called it "unspeakable," adding, "The film is supposed to be both

Karen (Pamela Tiffin) and Rosario (Lando Buzzanca) stroll the streets of Copenhagen in *Il vichingo venuto dal Sud* (International Film Company, 1971). Billy Rose Theatre Division, The New York Public Library for the Performing Arts, Astor, Lenox and Tilden Foundations.

funny and daring but it's as hypocritical as the Italian morality it attacks." *The Observer*'s George Melly echoed Derek's criticism and described the movie as "shabby," going on to say, "The amount of cynical manipulation and moral cheating that goes into a film like this is amazing." Philip French of the *New Statesman* called it "a repellent Italian comedy.... [T]his tedious mixture of prudery and puriance [is] aimed at an audience of uninhibited peasants." He then went on to call out the producers for not fully knowing the country's geography and noted that the scene of an afternoon of biking by Buzzanca and Tiffin "would have taxed the endurance of a Tour de France champion."

Gareth Jones of the *Monthly Film Bulletin* was equally ferocious in his criticism: "The blonde is as promised, but the blue movie is a sham; and so is the rest of this complacent Italian sex farce, which manages to incorporate scenes of wife-swapping, fantasy flagellation, on-stage sex and a blue movie shooting session without once endangering its audience with any show of either genuine eroticism or humor.... Predictable, labored, embarrassingly dubbed, and misdirected in an unending trickle of flat dialogue scenes which are entirely dependent upon zooms and jokey ham-acting."

Cinema TV Today found it better than the other U.K. critics: "Lurking behind the titillation of the title and all the hysterical larking around there is a sharply edged satirical comedy about a Latin lecher who is as shocked as he is delighted by the free and easy morality of Denmark." However, she did predict that the film's faults (slow pacing, repetitious visual humor) would hamper its box office chances with British audiences.

Looking at *The Blonde in the Blue Movie* from a 2015 viewpoint, it is not as bad as the British critics insisted back then. Though a bit over long, it's quite funny and makes some interesting points in an amusing fashion about the differences in attitudes about sex between the different parts of Europe. Buzzanca and Tiffin are paired well and make a believable

couple. Tiffin's perform-
ance unfortunately cannot
be judged because she
was dubbed into both Italian and English by other
actresses though Pamela
has such a visually expressive face that you just
know she is giving it her
all. The film is highlighted
by Angelo Filippini's color
on-location lensing in and
around Copenhagen and
Armando Trovajoli's tune-
ful score, which includes a
number of light, bouncy
pop songs performed in
the tradition of late sixties
harmony groups such as
the Association or the
Buckinghams.

Whatever the critics
felt seem to have no bear-
ing on moviegoers who
were drawn to seeing the
movie due to the subject
manner and the titillation
promised. The exploitative
movie poster featured the
tagline, "Shocks and Sex-
sations! Her husband
thought she had a part-
time job until he discov-
ered her as…. *The Blonde
in the Blue Movie*." It had
sketches of scantily clad
Tiffin to lure the more
lecherous into the the-
aters. (The woman kissing
Buzzanca on a bear-skin
rug is not her.)

The cast, too, helped
draw moviegoers hoping

Pamela Tiffin, ca. 1971.

to see if Buzzanca or more probably Pamela revealed any skin. Both didn't disappoint. Lando sported a slim physique and nice round backside, while Pamela undoubtedly looks gorgeous throughout. She is at her sexiest here with her blonde hair worn naturally straight while clad in the micro mini-dresses or appearing semi-nude.

The movie was released on DVD in the U.S. in 2013 by Retromedia. The cover art includes the title *The Blonde in the Blue Movie*. However, the actual movie when played is titled *No One Will Notice You're Naked*. This name was taken from the ad campaign slogan used by Buzzanca's character to promote his company's new ladies boot line. It is indicated that the DVD was produced from the sole remaining 35mm print (found in a library sale) of the version that *may* have received very limited release in the States in 1981. Watching, you notice from the get-go that the transfer was from a very poor quality print with lots of wear and tear. Though Pamela receives top billing on the DVD cover, she is nowhere to be found in the artwork which features Buzzanca, clad in only a tie and leopard-print loin-cloth, being pawed by four nubile, scantily clad women. Incidentally, he is given much more chest hair here than he actually has in the movie. Perhaps they wanted him to appear manlier.

Pamela's fans will be disappointed that she did not dub her own voice. Making matters even worse, the actress who *did* is from International Recording and has a slight Italian accent though the character is Dutch. Pamela looks gorgeous running around Amsterdam in her stylish early seventies garb. Just savor her beauty and try to ignore the voice.

Despite its DVD release in 2013, the movie was not reviewed much as of this printing. Eric Cotenas of DVDdrive-in.com found the movie to be "a softcore-lite sex comedy meant to appeal to an older audience seeking harmless titillation." As for the two stars, he remarked, "Buzzanca seems to be a good lead, but the mugging and physical comedy wear thin. Tiffin fares better." She surely does. This remains one of her standout Italian movies.

Giallo Time

Giornata nera per l'Ariete
(*The Fifth Cord*)

Between her Italian movie roles, Pamela continued posing for European and Far Eastern magazines, and also began spending more time in New York with Clay Felker. Columnists were speculating that the couple would reconcile, but they did not and eventually divorced. Pamela commented at the time, "We still love each other, we have dinner together. But life it seems is not a Doris Day movie."[1]

A few years later, Felker weighed in publicly, blaming their breakup on the time they spent apart due to his wife having to be on location for her movies. He stated, "When we were not together, we were not married. And one day, the bonds of marriage weren't there."

In late 1971, Tiffin finally broke free from the commedia all'Italiana and ventured into the thriller and western genres with her most popular co-star: the extremely handsome Franco Nero, who was dubbed the Italian Steve McQueen. First up was arguably her best and slickest Italian movie, the stylish giallo *Giornata nera per l'Ariete* (English translation: *Black Day for Aries*), which received limited release in some English-speaking countries as *Evil Fingers*. Most U.S. fans know the movie as *The Fifth Cord*, the name of the D.M. Devine novel the movie was based on. This title was used when it was released on DVD in 2006. It was the third movie directed by former documentary filmmaker Luigi Bazzoni. He, Nero, and director of photography Vittorio Storaro were all good friends who had collaborated on projects previously.

Pamela admitted that she only did this movie for the hefty salary they paid her. It proved to be a win-win decision for her and the producers. She is once again part of an ensemble and, just like with *Harper*, she is a standout. Receiving "sort of" guest star billing, her name is listed last in the credits: "And Pamela Tiffin as Lu."

Nero had previously worked for producer Manolo Bolognini in the westerns *Django* and *Texas, Addio*. But it was director Luigi Bazzoni who was the main reason the actor agreed to do this movie. "I owe a lot to Bazzoni," Nero stated:

> When I was very young about twenty-two I was part of a group of friends with Bazzoni, his brother Camillo Bazzoni, Vittorio Storaro, and another friend Gian Franco. Luigi taught us everything about movies. The five us would go to the north of Italy near Parma to shoot short films. They were so fantastic. That is the reason when I had a contract with Warner Bros. to do other movies after *Camelot* I begged Jack Warner to let me go back to Italy because Bazzoni wanted to do a version of *Carmen*. Bazzoni said, "Franco now that you are a big name it will be easy for us to put together a movie." Jack Warner was extremely nice and said, "I think you

are crazy, but if you want to go back home that is fine by me. I am selling the studio anyway to Seven-Arts." I went back to Italy and we did the movie [*Carmen* as a spaghetti western *L'uomo, l'orgoglio, la vendetta*] and four of us who started together worked on it. We then all did *Giornata nera per l'Ariete*.[2]

Then Nero was offered a part in the epic British film *Pope Joan* whose shooting schedule overlapped with *Giornata Nera*. The *Pope Joan* producers wanted him so much that they agreed to shoot his scenes on weekends. For three straight weeks Nero hopped on a plane from Rome to London early Saturday morning and returned late Sunday night to be back on the *Giornata Nera* set by Monday morning.

When asked if he knew Pamela before they began working together, the Italian superstar replied, "Yes, Pamela and I belonged to the same talent agency. My agent was Paola Petri, and she was the wife of the great director Elio Petri, who won an Oscar for *Investigation of a Citizen Above Suspicion*. Sometimes I would go to their house and that is where I met Pamela, who was extremely friendly, and as we say in Italian "molto simpatica!"[3]

Pamela Tiffin had just come off working with leading man Lando Buzzanca whom she disliked and caused her some grief. Asked if she was a bit guarded about doing the movie or working with him especially in the scenes where she had to bare some skin, Nero replied, "From my point Pamela seemed to like doing this movie. We didn't talk much about what she did before. She was very professional and open to direction."[4]

In the movie, Nero had three leading ladies: Sylvia Monti, Ira von Fürstenberg, and Pamela, who only had scenes with Nero so she never met the other actresses on set. At the premiere, Tiffin tried to talk with von Fürstenberg. The competitive actress rudely ignored her, to Tiffin's bemusement. They would go on to appear in *Deaf Smith & Johnny Ears*; however, to Pamela's great relief she did not have to work with the unfriendly actress.

Pamela says *Giornata nera per l'Ariete* holds up to this day because of the "impressive cinematography by Vittorio Storaro who captured the real Europe and not the Europe of tourists."[5] The locations chosen for the movie are not your typical homes, office buildings, or apartments. Exterior scenes at a hospital were shot on a large stone spiral staircase and Helene's house is an ultra-modern, multi-level dwelling with floor-to-ceiling windows. As reviewer Stuart Galbraith IV wrote on the website *DVD Talk*, "Storaro obviously sought out architecturally interesting locations for both exteriors and interiors where he could shoot the film's characters against modernistic geometrical patterns and shapes."

"*The Fifth Cord* is the story of an unbalanced man," Storaro remarked in the DVD featurette *Giornata Nera*. He went on to explain why he used contrasting light and shadows in relationship to the plot:

> He lives an unbalanced life because of some psychological problems he had when he was young, which unfortunately have a negative effect on him. He hasn't resolved them. He can only find satisfaction by carrying out actions that unfortunately come from a dark subconscious from a past that is unresolved. The battle between these two internal forces in a human being I represented with light and shadow. I was telling the story with a visual conflict to reflect the narrative elements.

Pamela picked up on Storaro's technique: "During production, I noticed that Storaro lit our scenes the way Richard Avedon did during my modeling days. When I commented on this, he froze and then said, 'Tu sei molte intelligente!'"[6] No wonder Pamela is gorgeous in the movie. Storaro had the skill to shoot and light her to make sure she looked even more stunning than usual.

Giornata nera per l'Ariete was released in Italy in 1971 and shortly thereafter throughout Europe, including the United Kingdom and other English-speaking countries where it was titled either *Evil Fingers* or *The Fifth Cord*. Despite her on-screen guest star billing, Pamela is billed second on the poster art, which shows her in a man's shirt spread across a bed with her neck slashed.

In the movie, Nero played a self-loathing, disheveled reporter named Andrea Bild (an outsider who is the typical center of Italian gialli) who pines for his former lover Helene (Silvia Monti) even though he is now sleeping with gorgeous coed Lu Auer (Tiffin). His career is on the slide due to his drinking and what his editor calls his "crazy nonconformist ideas." An inebriated Andrea leaves a New Year's Eve party where one of the guests, John Lubbock (Maurizio Bonuglia), is attacked under a bridge. He is saved by race car driver Walter Auer (Luciano Baroli), Lu's brother, and his quasi-girlfriend Giulia (Agostina Belli), a hooker. At the party, a dejected Lubbock had watched forlornly as the beautiful Isabel (Ira von Fürstenberg) danced and kissed his older colleague Eduoard Vermont (Edmund Purdom).

The next day Andrea, assigned to the story by his editor, tries to visit Lubbock in the hospital but he is denied entry. Guilia refuses to talk to him about the attack. Andrea then goes to Helene, who was at the celebration that night, and she fills him in on John's character and his unrequited love for Isabel. The following week another party guest, the crippled, unpleasant wife (Rossella Falk) of Dr. Richard Bini (Renato Romano), is terrorized and brutally murdered in their home. It is learned that her husband was summoned from the house by a phony emergency called in by the killer. Andrea is surprised to hear that the good doctor is glad to be rid of her.

Soon all the New Year's Eve revelers are suspects, but the police inspector (Wolfgang Preiss) has his eye on Andrea as more evidence points to the reporter with each murder, plus the knifing of Andrea's editor in the park. The lone clue left at each crime scene is a single black glove. The fingers are cut out based on what number murder victim they are. Andrea realizes that the killer is framing him for the crimes. His investigation intensifies as he becomes desperate to prove his innocence. As he gets closer to the truth, he begins getting threatening phone calls from the killer. He suspicion shifts from one partier to the next, and even to Lu who is acting mysteriously and disappears for a time, only to resurface in a short black wig. After he learns from Walter that the first attack had nothing to do with the subsequent murders and was perpetrated by Guilia's perverted father, Andrea thinks the killer is Dr. Bini, who paid to watch Walter and Giulia have sex in front of strangers. The reporter threatens to publish the whole sordid story in another newspaper.

That night Andrea remembers that Walter mentioned that all the murders happened on a Tuesday and the attack on Lubbock was on a Monday. Andrea consults an astrology book and learns that Tuesday is a lucky day for people born under the sign of Aries. This leads him to the killer, who is about to strike against Helene. However, she is out of the country. A trick call sends her babysitter to the airport, leaving her vulnerable young son Tony alone. Helene learns this when calling and frantically instructs Tony to lock all the windows and doors. But the killer is already inside. This is the movie's most harrowing scene as the killer chases the boy around the house. The boy becomes trapped in a small hallway with only light from a window he can't reach. His blood-curdling screams and yelling for his mother are spine-tingling, as the madman reaches towards his neck. Will Andrea get there in time to save the boy and reveal the murderer?

In Pamela's first scene as Lu, she emerges from Andrea's bathroom in a robe on the morning of New Year's Day. She bemoans that a drunken Andrea took hours to come home and when he did, "he was in no shape to do anything." Lu acts comfortable with her casual relationship with the reporter, whose machismo does not let him feel the same for her exploits. She even calls herself his "part-time mistress and not the maid" when he tries to get her to make him breakfast. When she leaves town for a few days, the note she leaves gives him permission to get laid "as you know it doesn't bother me."

Lu pops up briefly as the passenger in a red sports car driven by a handsome young man; Andrea watches them drive off. It then quickly cuts to Andrea returning home, finding Lu lying naked on her stomach in his bed. Storaro shoots and lights Pamela exquisitely in this scene. It is arguably the best she ever looked on film as a blonde. Andrea smacks Lu across the face when she tells him she has been home study-ing for a history exam. He accuses her of being a liar and a whore who will jump into any sports car; an angered Lu returns the insults. She tells him that it belongs to her brother Walter and that Andrea hasn't gotten anything right since he started playing detective. Her attitude quickly softens when Andrea leaves. He returns contrite and to his horror finds Lu dangling off the bed with blood dripping down her neck. It turns out to be a prank. A relieved Andrea begins playfully chasing Lu around the apartment and then they fall onto the bed together.

Lu shows up one more time wearing a short black wig that is never quite explained. She says she is getting married to a man who wants children. Though she acted the liberated young woman, deep down she

Cover art for the American DVD release of *Giornata nera per l'Ariete*, renamed *The Fifth Cord*.

desired the typical family life with a husband and knew Andrea could not give that to her. When she doesn't get any type of reaction from Andrea, she tells him a woman named Isabel called and said that she needs to see him urgently in her hotel room. Lu drives Andrea there and he discovers her drowned in the bathtub. Lu provides Andrea an alibi the next day. Andrea asks her why she lied to the police inspector and Lu replies, matter-of-factly, "I wanted to give you a farewell present," as she drives off to start her new life without him.

David McGillivray of *Monthly Film Bulletin* commented when the movie was released in the United Kingdom, "Shoals of red herrings do little to make up for *Evil Fingers*' meager characterizations, the scrambled course of its plot, or its shamefully deceptive ending. Luigi Bazzoni's briskly paced direction (combined with the efforts of the British censor) contrives to sweep it all under the carpet as quickly as possible." Danny Shipka, author of *Perverse Titillation: The Exploitation Cinema of Italy, Spain and France, 1960–1980*, found the movie to be "engrossing" and "good."[7] However, he added, "Gialli are known for their convoluted plots, but this one seems to take it to the extreme."[8]

The movie is a stylish suspenseful thriller, but the real treat for Pamela Tiffin fans is that she and Franco Nero acted their roles speaking English. It was her second Italian movie where this was done and reminds moviegoers of what a light, lilting voice she possessed. Though this role is by no means an acting stretch for Pamela, it is wonderful to see her play a sexy, contemporary, vibrant role with a bit of mystery. You could feel the heat she and Nero project, and could tell they enjoyed working together. Her character brings out the playful side of Andrea (despite his mistreatment of her) rather than his gloominess seen throughout the rest of the movie. In fact, she is perhaps the only character who is happy and perky, as the other characters must deal with the deaths of friends. Considering her knack for comedy, it is no surprise she would be cast in the most lighthearted role in a violent giallo. Roberto Curti, however, felt that "perhaps Pamela's character is a bit sacrificed in the script."[9]

Although *Giornata nera per l'Ariete* is fast-moving, first-rate entertainment, it suffers from some bad dubbing (especially awful is the voice used for the little boy Tony), a muddled screenplay, and an ending that feels like a bit of a cheat as the motivation for the killer is barely hinted at, making it tough for viewers to guess whodunit. However, the wonderful cast, Storaro's exquisite photography, and an underrated score by Ennio Morricone more than compensate for its shortcomings, making this giallo well worth watching on any size screen.

Howard Hughes is a British film scholar and author specializing in European cinema. His many books include *Once Upon in the Italian West* and *Cinema Italiano*. He found Tiffin to be "good in the film as Lu Auer, Andrea's live-in lover who shares his untidy apartment. In one scene they play murder games, in the manner of Elio Petri's *Investigation of a Citizen Above Suspicion* (1970), as she pretends to be a victim of the murderer. When Tiffin lies naked on the bed her pose and flaxen blonde hair recalls Brigitte Bardot in Godard's *Contempt* (1963). Tiffin also seems to be channeling Bardot as Camille in Godard's film later when she switches her hair color and style to a black bob, by donning a wig."[10]

Storaro's impressive cinematography elevates this giallo despite its twisty plot and he received almost unanimous praise. At a certain point you just sit back and watch the sumptuous visuals as Nero trails the killer. Storaro was one of the first to show the killer's point of view using a fish-eye lens at different angles. When the movie came out on DVD in 2006 in the U.S., critics praised Storaro to the hilt. Judge Steve Evans (*DVD Verdict*) called it "gorgeous filmmaking" due to "the brilliant visualist Storaro." He continued, "This is Storaro's show all the way. His work here is easily the film's selling point; truly, Storaro's artistry with film and camera transcends the tawdry material." Glenn Erickson (*DVD Savant*) found the movie "always interesting from a visual standpoint, even when the storyline sags." According to *Cult Movies Review*, the real star of the movie was Storaro: "I don't think anyone has used shadows more effectively and more moodily in color than Storaro does in this film." His camerawork, even during the killing scenes such as the chase of the editor in the park and especially the doctor's wife being terrorized in her darkened bedroom where he uses shadows effectively, were steps above most movies of this ilk."

Roberto Curti calls *The Fifth Cord* "a good giallo, very stylish and with great cinematography by Vittorio Storaro."[11] Howard Hughes lauded Storaro's "stylish photography"[12] and heaped equal praise on the music: "Like so many gialli, it benefits greatly from an Ennio Morricone Euro-lounge score, which moves from breathy bubble-gum pop and full-blast organ fugues to his usual atmospherics: tinkling, ethereal or jagged."[13] In his book *La Dolce Morte*, Mikle J. Koven also praised the movie for its visual style, but criticized its contrivances and the surfeit of red herrings, which hampered many gialli of the time.

Franco Nero weighed in with his thoughts about the movie and commented, "The movie has a great cast and is very well photographed. Compared to the way movies are shot now, it may be a little bit slow for today's audiences. At that time, that is the pace Luigi [Bazzoni] set. I still think the movie has great qualities."[14]

Most everyone praised the work of Storaro and Morricone while director Luigi Bazzoni received blame for everything that did *not* work in the movie. When he did get positive notices, it was not for his direction, but for having the good sense to hire Morricone and Storaro (who turned down an offer to work with Michelangelo Antonioni because he had already given Bazzoni his word that he would do the movie). Howard Hughes observed, "With these personnel on board, *The Fifth Cord* very much has the texture of an imitation [Dario] Argento movie and Bazzoni is quite successful at staging the mystery and sustaining its tension."[15]

Though critics gave short shrift to Bazzoni's direction, his co-workers did not. Storaro opined in the DVD featurette *Giornata Nera*, "He is probably one of the directors I care for the most, I respect the most and I love the most. Maybe because [of] the way I worked with him, in harmony. There is never a sense of conflict with Luigi because his knowledge is so vast and his aesthetic vision is so harmonious and [he] has so much taste that [it] is like being with a master or a wise man."

Nero exclaimed in *Giornata Nera*, "I considered Luigi Bazzoni one of the greatest directors I've ever worked with. He's very sensitive as a director, very reserved. He never did any self-promotion. This is perhaps why he did not have a great career." As an example of how well-respected the director was among his peers, Nero remarked, "After Vittorio Storaro won his three Oscars [for *Apocalypse Now*, *Reds* and *The Last Emperor*] and was considered one of the world's best cinematographers he was offered to shoot *Roma Imago Urbis* [1994] an incredible long documentary about Roman history. They wanted to work with a different director for each episode. Vittorio said he'd do the film on one condition if they hire Luigi Bazzoni for the entire program. They did. That is how much we admired Luigi."[16]

Pamela too only had praise for Bazzoni, but also had one major disagreement with him: She did not want to wear that short black wig. "I remember constantly arguing with Bazzoni over it," said Pamela. "I have long blonde hair throughout the film and then suddenly, with no explanation, I'm wearing this wig. I couldn't understand it."[17] Neither does the audience. But Bazzoni was insistent. Being the professional that she was, Pamela begrudgingly followed her director's orders. The only thing one can guess about the wig is that Tiffin's character was leaving Nero's to marry a more conventional man she had been seeing simultaneously. Bazzoni may have been using the wig to symbolize the new direction her life was going and that she wanted to start fresh with a different look.

Despite the popularity of gialli at the time, *Giornata nera per l'Ariete* was not a big hit in Italy. Its box office take was 545,705,000 lire ($396,680). It grossed a bit less than the inferior *Cose di Cosa Nostra* and finished 67th at the box office for the year. Per Roberto Curti, this "was not so good for a giallo. Argento's *Cat O'Nine Tails* did 2,300,000,000 lire ($1.6 million) and *Four Flies on Grey Velvet* did almost the same."[18]

Despite its disappointing box office in Italy, it is still a mystery why the movie did not receive a wide release in the U.S., only sneaking in a very few theaters under the name *Evil Fingers* in 1975. Franco Nero was at his prime, Pamela's name still meant something at the box office, and the supporting cast included many actors well known in America. It is truly a shame that most U.S. audiences did not get the chance to see it on the big screen.

Howard Hughes weighed in on the movie's distribution problems, stating that is was "a B.R.C. Produzione, but B.R.C. didn't seem to have very good distribution links with the United Kingdom and U.S. *Django* [Franco Nero's classic spaghetti western] hadn't made it to the U.S. either, and most of the company's films weren't shown in the States. It was released in the U.K. with an X certificate."[19]

For a U.S. audience, *The Fifth Cord* is arguably Tiffin's best Italian movie. Despite her amusing performance, the giallo genre never came calling again. Perhaps Pamela was just so immersed in the comedia all'Italiana and thought of only as a comedienne that she was just never considered for them. Even in *The Fifth Cord*, she delivered the most playful performance and lightened the mood whenever she was on screen. It could be that she was so skilled at comedy that she wasn't considered versatile enough. If so, this was a mistaken assumption by directors because she certainly was as talented, perhaps even more so, than actresses Mimsy Farmer and Barbara Bouchet, both of whom seemed to have worked consistently in gialli. Tiffin's being uncomfortable with screen nudity also may have hindered her getting these roles as Farmer, Bouchet, and Carroll Baker disrobed quite frequently in their movies. Roberto Curti commented, "She probably became typecast after starring in a row of successful comedies. What's more, Baker and Bouchet had a more sexily aggressive image, while Pamela usually played the ingénue character."[20]

Howard Hughes wrote, "I'm not quite sure how Mimsy Farmer ended up working for Dario Argento and Lucio Fulci, as she's an okay actress but certainly no better (or better looking) than actresses of Tiffin's caliber. Perhaps directors thought Pamela's screen persona lacked the edge to play ambiguous characters, the multi-faceted dualism which was required to keep the audience guessing, especially in gialli mysteries. I find Farmer unconvincing in Argento's *Four Flies on Grey Velvet* and it's interesting to speculate what Tiffin would have made of the deceitful murderess."[21]

As most historians attest, Pamela's comedic expertise seemed to have pigeonholed her in the minds of Italian producers who only wanted her to be funny. Even when she ventured into more wide-reaching genres like westerns and gialli, she played light-hearted roles. However, she had the talent and was versatile enough to go dramatic if given the chance. It is too bad an Argento or a Fulci did not take notice.

22

Tiffin Makes Three

Los Amigos
(*Deaf Smith & Johnny Ears*)

In 1973, Pamela appeared in her second western *Los Amigos* (translation: *The Friends*), which was re-titled *Deaf Smith & Johnny Ears* for American and United Kingdom audiences, and reunited her with Franco Nero. Late in the cycle of spaghetti westerns, the gimmick here was to make one of the lead characters deaf and mute and have his younger sidekick act as his ears and voice.

Franco Nero was very excited to make this western, but he thought he would be playing Deaf Smith. "The producer was an Italian named Joseph Janni who used to work in England," he explained:

> He produced some great movies [such as *Billy Liar*; *Darling*; *Modesty Blaise*; *Far from the Madding Crowd*; and *Sunday, Bloody Sunday*.] One day he came to Italy to meet with me and said, "I would like to do something like *Midnight Cowboy* about two friends. One talks all the time and the other is mute." I replied, "I would love to play the one who doesn't talk." He then told me that Anthony Quinn had already read the script and wanted to play the deaf mute. I said, "But he is American and is more comfortable speaking English." We went back and forth for about a month. Getting nowhere, Janni then set up a meeting with him, me, and Tony. It was very funny. Tony kept insisting he play the part and I kept saying, "But you are the American!" At the end, we decided to flip a coin. Who ever wins plays Deaf Smith. We did and Tony won."[1]

With the two lead characters finally settled, Janni knew he would need a beautiful actress who could be funny for the role of Susie the whore who falls for Johnny. Franco Nero had only one actress in mind for the part. "Pamela was cast because of me," boasted Nero. "We were both very popular. I remember talking to Paola Petri and saying that I would love to have Pamela in the movie because she was born to play comedy."[2] The agent worked it out and Tiffin was Nero's leading lady for the second time.

Directed by Paolo Cavara, it was a co-production between companies in Rome and Milan with a $1.2 million budget. MGM picked up international distribution rights. Filming began in October 1972 on location in Southern Italy for four weeks before moving to Rome to shoot interiors. According to Howard Hughes, "The arid landscape footage, which looks like Almeria [in Spain where many westerns were shot], was actually filmed in Calabria. The town set and interiors were at Elios Studios, Rome."[3]

Right from the get-go, Cavara made pronouncements that he was not making a spaghetti western: "The day of those blood-and-guts oaters made over here is over."[4] He went on to call his movie a "psychological western,"[5] which he also infused with humor. Some film historians agree with the director and classify it as a Euro-western, but most critics at the time and fans considered it part of the popular spaghetti western genre.

One of the main reasons that the movie was almost automatically classified as a spaghetti western was because it co-starred Franco Nero. In 1966, he starred in one of the most popular and violent spaghetti westerns of all time, the aforementioned *Django*, directed by Sergio Corbucci. Nero played a vengeful drifter who dragged around a closed coffin meant for the man who killed his wife. *Django* launched a number of sequels and rip-offs between 1966 and 1972, none starring Nero. He continued in the spaghetti western genre with two more extremely popular and well-received films directed by Corbucci. *The Mercenary* (1968) featured Nero as, believe it or not, a Polish professional mercenary who is paid by a Mexican peasant to help his band of rebels fight his country's army; the even better *Compañeros* (1970) also had Nero playing a mercenary, this time a Swedish one, again aiding Mexican peasants. Nero also appeared in one of horror film director Lucio Fulci's rare spaghetti westerns, *Massacre Time* (1966), playing a prospector who takes on a powerful family that has taken control of his town.

Set during the time of upheaval in Texas, *Los Amigos* stars Anthony Quinn as mercenary Eratus "Deaf" Smith (who was a real-life hearing-impaired scout, though not mute, for Texas president Sam Houston). Nero is his woman-crazy partner Johnny Ears (a totally fictional character). When an ex-general attempts to install himself as dictator, Sam Houston calls in "Deaf" Smith for help. Pamela has one of her best roles as an angelic-faced whore with a heart of gold, who falls in love with Johnny.

Citing the reasons he used Quinn and Nero, Cavara explained, "With an older man and a younger man you have covered all of life. The older man has experience and knows about life; the younger man represents youth and its desire to change everything. Thus conflict."[6] He went on to say that he was hoping that Nero and Quinn would replicate the classic partnering of John Wayne and Montgomery Clift in the 1948 western *Red River*.

The story is credited to American writers Harry Essex and Oscar Paul, who wrote it a few years earlier. In fact, their screenplay was optioned by Sinatra Enterprises in 1968 as a starring feature for Frank Sinatra as Deaf Smith; this never came to be. Essex, a former newspaperman and playwright turned screenwriter, began scriptwriting in 1946 with *Boston Blackie and the Law*. He specialized in B-grade fifties monster and teenage exploitation movies such as *It Came from Outer Space*, *Creature from the Black Lagoon*, and *Teen-age Crime Wave*, as well as the well-received western *The Sons of Katie Elder* (1965). His last movie prior to this was the schlocky *Octaman* (1971), most notable as the last film appearance for Pier Angeli. Oscar Saul received a Writers Guild Award nomination for Best Screenplay Musical for *The Joker Is Wild* in 1957 and went on to script such big-screen westerns as *The Second Time Around* (1961), a comedy starring Debbie Reynolds; *Major Dundee* (1965) with Charlton Heston in the title role; and *Man and Boy* (1971) with Bill Cosby. On *Deaf Smith & Johnny Ears*, Essex and Saul also received screenplay credit but, as with most Italian movies, other writers who tinkered with the original scripts received credit as well, including the director.

The week before production was to commence, director Cavara took his actors to the desert area near Bari, on the Southern tip of the Italian peninsula; "I wanted them to bum around a bit and do nothing but absorb. By the time we started shooting I really didn't have to exert myself. I became almost an editor. A good cast is a director's best insurance outside of his script."[7]

When filming began, another thing that Cavara did which was outside of the norm for Italian filmmaking is that he recorded sound on location. For most Italian movies, all the dialogue was looped afterwards and added in post-production with sound effects. *Giornata nera per l'Ariete* was also shot with direct sound and that is why Franco and Pamela's real voices can be heard in the English-language versions of both movies. Italian films were slowly pulling away from looping entire movies in the dubbing booths. Nero remarked, "In Italy at the time the mentality was not to shoot direct sound because noise would be picked up and they would dub everything. I remember my character at the beginning in the script was an American. I said, 'I can't play an American. I have an accent.' They rewrote it to make an excuse for my accent. So my character states he is Spanish [and not Mexican in a very funny scene with Pamela's golden-haired harlot]. In westerns they can always find an excuse not to be pure American. At that time, at least 90 percent of the population spoke with accents."[8]

Cavara also used a portable lightweight 35mm Arriflex camera to shoot the picture. His cinematographer was the brilliant and prolific Tonio Delli Colli, whose prior credits included Sergio Leone's classic westerns *The Good, the Bad and the Ugly* and *Once Upon a Time in the West*. His work here makes this movie one of the very best photographed westerns of this period.

Anthony Quinn, who had appeared in numerous westerns prior to this, strongly desired the role of Eratus Smith because he felt it would be a challenge to play a deaf-mute. However, as shooting began, he knew he needed guidance. He commented, "When I started to play the part it was so tricky that I knew I was in danger of overdoing it. I went to Paolo Cavara and asked him to hold me down and keep me in line."[9] One of Quinn's favorite directors was Stanley Kramer, whom he called "an actor's director"[10]; they worked together on the Golden Globe–winning World War II comedy *The Secret of Santa Vittoria* (1969) and the less successful campus unrest drama *R.P.M.* (1970). Comparing Cavara to Kramer, Quinn

Publicity photograph of Pamela Tiffin in *Deaf Smith & Johnny Ears* (MGM, 1973).

said, "Cavara doesn't have Kramer's tough attitude, but operates his own way. He is a very sensitive man, a diplomat. He gets what *he* wants. A director must never be afraid of an actor no matter how big he is."[11] Perhaps it was this sensitivity that made Cavara determined *not* to make a western in the spaghetti genre style and instead to strive for something more. Unfortunately, the final result was not the success he was aiming for.

Though Franco Nero felt that the movie was an easy pleasant shoot, the actor was not as enarmored with his director as much as Quinn. "Paola Cavara was very professional," opined Nero. "They gave him the script and he did his job. I would not call him a very creative director. But we got lucky because we had the great cinematographer Tonino Delli Colli. He was fantastic and had worked with Fellini and Leone."[12]

Filming seemed to have progressed smoothly and everyone got along nicely. Pamela exclaimed, "I so enjoyed making this movie. I love westerns because I love nature and that kind of folklore. Anthony Quinn is larger than life and is attractive in a primordial kind of way. He was very easy to work with. Franco Nero is very tall, very handsome, and very decent. He had the impact in Europe that Paul Newman had in America."[13]

Franco Nero concurred with Pamela and remarked, "Tony, Pamela, and I got along greatly. We had such a fun time making this film." He then added with a mischevious laugh, "I admit if I was not already—how can I say engaged?—I would have loved to have—you know—with Pamela. But I never did."[14]

Quinn liked working on this movie and especially liked playing "Deaf" Smith, which he felt helped him grow as an actor since he had to listen to others, a trait he felt most actors lacked. He remarked, "If every actor could play a deaf-mute once it would be the best thing that could happen to him. I had to react to everything and everyone around me. It was a terrific experience."[15]

Pamela was especially fond of Franco Nero because he helped her out during a love scene where she didn't have a top on. "I said to Franco, 'I didn't want my bosom to show.' He understood and we thought how could we outsmart the director. We found a way to hold each other very tight or he'd have an elbow or an arm in the way. I can remember the frustrated director shouting in Italian, 'Do it again!' We'd respond, 'Well we just did it!' Sometimes actors band together in a wonderful way. I'll always be grateful to him."[16]

Franco Nero remembers this incident and takes no special bows for coming to the aid of a fellow actor. He says, "Pamela was feeling uncomfortable about doing the scene so I helped her. She said, 'Franco I don't want my bosom to show.' I didn't think the movie was the kind that had to show bosoms anyway. It wasn't called for in this western that was funny and very violent. It really wasn't about sex."[17]

Franco Nero seemed to have fun doing these scenes as well and commented at the time, "I just got through spending a week in bed with Pamela Tiffin…. My lips are so numb that I can't feel a thing. But if I have to do it, there's no one I'd rather match lips with than Pamela."[18]

While filming these scenes with Nero in Rome, Pamela admitted, "I'm terrified of spending my youth—or my life on a soundstage. I don't want to be one of those tragic ladies who go from pills to countless love affairs."[19] Pamela Tiffin was too smart a lady to descend into the Valley of the Dolls despite her trepidation. Only two years later, she would marry and retire from moviemaking.

Los Amigos was re-titled *Deaf Smith & Johnny Ears* when released in the U.S. in the spring of 1973 with the tagline "The Man who hears with his eyes and speaks with his gun…. He lives to kill. And he's gonna live it up tonight." It premiered in the U.K. in July 1973. It opens with Quinn and Nero roaming the prairie. Nero's voiceover informs the audience that Quinn's Eratus Smith is a deaf-mute who understands people by reading lips. He is described as "a hero" and President Houston's personal spy. Nero is his Spanish partner Juanito, nicknamed Johnny Ears. He gets "Deaf" Smith's attention by throwing stones at him. They have been sent by the president to help a general in Austin subvert a group of Texan rebels, backed by a "foreign power," trying to stop the Republic of Texas from becoming part of the United States. As the duo are making their way to Texas, rebels raid the general's house, slaughtering him, his family, and all who work there.

Smith and Johnny stop at a small lake with a waterfall to rest. Johnny spots a beautiful blonde bathing up near the falls. He follows the naked woman (who may be Pamela Tiffin or a double) up the rocky crag as she walks back to where she left her clothes. We see her shapely derriere with a mole on the right cheek as she puts on her undergarments and then her dress. As she turns to the camera, this is the audience's first look at Pamela, who looks stunningly beautiful with her blonde hair put up with light curls falling down the back to her shoulders. As she ties her bonnet on her head, she notices Johnny watching her from behind some bushes.

The mysterious woman quickly makes her way back to her wagon with him trailing right behind her. They don't say a word to each other, but Pamela's facial expressions and body language express her character's discomfort. However, as she rides off she gives Johnny a coquettish smile. Rejected, he is left standing there and walks back to Smith. He asks his friend, pointing in her direction, "Did you see that? She wanted to. But you know I didn't want to."

As the pair ride to the general's compound, they observe the rebels riding away from it and discover the carnage. Later, in town, they hear a preacher leading the rallying cry for independence and the rebels threatening anyone who disagrees. Smith learns that the rebels are led by General Morton (Franco Graziosi), who wants to be Texas' new president and brings his wife (Ira von Fürstenberg) to the murdered general's home to face the truth about Morton. She agrees to help Smith and sneaks him into her house to spy on Morton. Smith pretends to be a drunk at the saloon where the rebels are drinking. Johnny accompanies him, but is distracted when he recognizes the backside of his blonde beauty being drawn by an artist. Finding out that she is a whore, he heads right over to the brothel where she works.

After paying his ten dollar fee, Johnny spots his dream girl, Susie, ascending the main staircase with her client. He grabs her from behind and a struggle ensues. The feisty Susie tries to fight him off and states, "You're trying to get something for free again and I don't like it." However, he succeeds in getting her up the stairs. Pamela, beautifully clad in a green satin dress, is delightfully funny here trying to get away from him and demanding to know if he has paid for her services. As she is being pulled along by Nero, she amusingly delivers lines such as "We have order in this house! *Aaah*! Are you a Mexican or something?"

The laughs continue with Johnny trapped in a headlock by Susie as they barrel into her room. She bangs his head on the bedpost a few times and asks again if he is Mexican. He replies, "You are kind of choosy for your line of work, aren't you?" When she demands an answer after flinging him to the floor, he tells her that he is Spanish. She lets out a disbelieving laugh and quips, "They all say that!" Standing up, Johnny grabs her by the waist and states, "I am not here to discuss my pedigree. I am here for physical reasons." After calling him "Mustache" and telling him he stinks (he counters, "Hey lady, you're smelling a real man!"), she heads back downstairs to speak with Miss Porter, the brothel's madam. Susie refuses to service "a saddle tramp," but is ordered back to her room since Johnny paid for her.

Susie, in a huff, heads upstairs. She is bemused to find a half-naked Johnny listening to her music box while smoking a cigar. They make wordless love while a romantic song extolling how their love has just begun plays on the soundtrack. This is the scene where Nero kept a topless Pamela from exposing her bosom by purposely holding her body close to his, though her shapely bottom with the mole is briefly on display. After their lovemaking, Johnny confides in Susie that he and Smith bought a gold mine and will be rich one day. Susie laughs and quips, "I never met one saddle bum yet that didn't own a gold mine." She then confesses she has one too, the Susie Q. Johnny says they cannot dig for gold yet because Smith has something else to do first.

The next day, while Smith watches the rebels led by the reverend burn an effigy of President Houston in the town square, Johnny goes to visit Susie. He finds her with a client

Hooker Susie (Pamela Tiffin) and gunslinger Johnny (Franco Nero) frolic in bed in a scene from ***Deaf Smith & Johnny Ears*** **(MGM, 1973).**

and, dejected, slips away. The "client" is one of the rebel leaders, more interested in information about Johnny than in having relations with Susie. He forks over $50 in cash to get her to cooperate. Does she? The audience never knows for sure though in the next scene the rebels turn up at "Deaf" Smith's bedroom door.

The reverend orders his men to kill Smith, who is sleeping in his room. But the shrewd Smith has tied a string from the doorknob to his finger, so he is awakened after one of the rebels slowly pushes the door open. Smith gets the best of him.

Meanwhile, an excited Susie is trying to convince Johnny to run away with her and suggests they go to his mine. When he says they need money to start digging, she offers up her $200 in gold dollars and $1,000 she has in the bank to prove her sincerity. To her dismay, Johnny declines, saying he won't abandon his friend who needs him badly. The miffed hooker calls Smith "a dummy" and tells Johnny, "You need Eratus far more than Eratus needs you." A shreik disrupts their argument and they run to the room of a screaming hooker to find the body of the dead reverend strangled earlier by the avenging "Deaf" Smith. Johnny makes a joke and everyone breaks into laughter, angering Miss Porter.

Back in Susie's room, they find a waiting Smith. After introducing Susie to him, Smith pushes the reluctant Johnny out the door and toward the staircase. Johnny rails, "Look, "Deaf," I told you once before. One thing that you can't interfere with is my screwing." Smith ignores both Johnny and Susie's protestations ("You're kidnapping him!"). The duo departs with Johnny promising to be back and a worried-looking Susie going back to her room.

In these scenes, Pamela plays with great conviction, as they are less comical and more serious than her prior ones. Clad in long white lingerie accentuating her shapely derriere (her statements to the press about not starving herself were true), she is quite believable showing her character's willingness to leave her life as a whore, even offering money to a man she has just met and fallen in love with. She perfectly portrays Susie's excitement that quickly turns to anger when she realizes she is competing for Johnny with another man. Despite his protestations about how he cannot desert his deaf friend, Susie intuitively realizes that it is a weak Johnny who is dependent on Eratus and just uses his disability as an excuse not to leave him.

With Susie left at the brothel, Pamela disappears until the end of the movie. Her presence is sorely missed as the action sequences take over. "Deaf" Smith and Johnny roam the Texas plains and, due to Smith's expert tracking, come across the rebel-guarded outpost, teeming with gunmen. Smith wants the pair to infiltrate, but Johnny refuses. He tries to make Eratus understand that he is in love now and won't risk his life. He then accuses the determined Smith of wanting to play hero to make up for his lack of hearing. They have a brief scuffle, but Smith won't hit his friend back despite the goading from Johnny. Fed up, the young saddle tramp deserts Smith and heads back to town, choosing Susie over Smith.

Eratus sneaks into the fort and discovers covered wagons full of dynamite. After he steals a few sticks, he is spotted and chased by rebels on horseback. When his horse falls, Smith flees into a cave with three gunslingers in pursuit. He's rescued by Johnny, who had a change of heart and returned despite his love for Susie. They devise a plan to blow up General Morton's wagon trains, but have to abandon it at the last second because a band of children gets in the way.

Smith and Johnny return to the rebels' fort and get control of their machine-gun.

Eratus is able to operate it because from a distance he had read the lips of the rebel who was instructing his men how to use it. After a fierce gun battle that rages on and on and on, the rebels are wiped out. Afterwards, a radiant Susie joins Johnny and Eratus at their camp. The ex-hooker is so happy to be reunited with Johnny that she is more accommodating to Smith and even makes him a cup of coffee, which he secretly spits out. The next morning, Johnny awakens with a smile on his face and Susie sleeping by his side. However, he soon notices Smith's coveted gold pocket watch hanging from a branch; the gunslinger is nowhere to be found. The panicked Johnny runs toward it and screams, "No!" as the movie ends with a freeze frame of his pained face, proving Susie was right all along about Johnny needing "Deaf" Smith.

Despite Paolo Cavara's insistence that his movie was not a spaghetti western and the fact that Nero's character, more interested in loving than fighting, is atypical for a hero in this genre, reviewers seemed to disagree with him. Most critics opined back then that *Deaf Smith & Johnny Ears* was not a very good western no matter what type it was labeled. *New York Times* critic A.H. Weiler commented that it was "as limp an example of the so-called 'spaghetti Western' as has turned up in recent memory" and "an ersatz adventure that is neither as explosive or as funny as most movies in the genre." He also opined, "Pamela Tiffin is merely naive as a pouting, babyish blond prostitute." *Cue* called it "an exercise in dullness and ineptitude." Rex Reed (the *New York Daily News*) wrote, "There is nothing to commend this paella western." Even *Variety* had harsh words for it, calling the movie "a mostly dull, occasionally ludicrous oater sorely lacking in the excessive violence or marquee voltage that might earn it an action-loving audience." Tiffin was called "by now a bit ripe for her assignment as a prostie wooed by Nero."

The Hollywood Reporter also jumped on the bandwagon with critic Alan R. Howard slamming the movie as being "a pedestrian western, long on talk, awkwardly structured and neither as endearing nor comic as it's supposed to be." However, Howard also found that Pamela played her role of a whore "amusingly."

A reviewer for *The Independent Film Journal* found *Deaf Smith & Johnny Ears* "a slight cut above the spaghetti western." Pamela is mentioned with a "remember her?" (it was four years since American audiences last saw her on the silver screen in *Viva Max*). The critic went on to compliment her and remarked, "Pamela Tiffin bounces through her moments with a bit more pizzazz than she showed in Hollywood with the result that the sauce on this spaghetti is not that untasty."

The British critics also were not impressed. Derek Malcolm of *The Guardian* called it "a tepid spaghetti western directed with graceless stoicism." *Cinema TV Today* called it a "so-so bang-bang adventure," the reviewer adding, "Anthony Quinn looking inscrutable and conversing in sign language, and Franco Nero gabbing and giggling hysterically … make as unlikely and unlikable a team as ever rode this away and that away." Tony Rayns of the *Monthly Film Bulletin* described it as a "timid, undernourished contender in the post–Leone Western stakes.… [It] comes too late and stays too long." He was one of the few critics to address the homoerotic connection between the two male leads as the screenwriters pushed the political situation of Texas at the time to the background and "brought out the tragic-comic love/hate relationship of the heroes, so that the film emerges as a kind of sketch in sublimated homosexuality…."

Today, there is a revisionist view of the movie and it is considered much more memorable than when first released. Howard Hughes included the movie in his books *Spaghetti Westerns* (Oldcastle Books, 2010) and *Once Upon a Time in the Italian West: The Filmgoers' Guide to Spaghetti Westerns* (I.B. Tauris, 2006). "I'm very fond of this movie and it remains one of the unheralded gems of the Italian western genre," he wrote, adding:

> Tonino Delli Colli was the cinematographer and the film looks tremendous, while Daniele Patucchi provided a deft, atmospherically folksy score.
>
> This is my favorite performance by Tiffin and her role as prostitute Susie is intrinsic to the plot. The added dynamic of Susie to the "Deaf"-Johnny partnership creates a fine tension, as Johnny is torn between his friend and his lover. The scenes at the bordello … are well played by Tiffin and Nero and there's real onscreen chemistry between them. Her delivery of her summing up of Johnny's avoidance of commitment to her and loyalty to his friend "Deaf" is brilliantly delivered, "You need Eratus far more than Eratus needs you."
>
> The shock ending is well staged by Cavara, as Johnny and Susie are left together in the desert and Eratus departs. He doesn't like the taste of her coffee, but more importantly he realizes that three's a crowd. Johnny's realization and agonizing scream of "Deaf!" freeze-framed on the fade-out, when he sees Eratus has left his pocket watch, is very effective and emotional.[20]

Perhaps the pans the movie received at the time was due to the overload of European westerns flooding the U.S. and Great Britain. On its own, *Deaf Smith & Johnny Ears* is quite entertaining. The movie's premise, one of the leads being deaf and mute, is novel and intriguing. There are some nice touches, like seeing the action through "Deaf" Smith's eyes with no sound. Though quite amusing for the most part, the plot is a bit implausible, expecting moviegoers to believe that the fate of Texas is left in the hands of only two men. It is also full of plot holes. The audience is left guessing if Susie accepted a rebel's bribe to give him information on Smith and Johnny though in the next scene we see them breaking into Smith's room. Did she rat him out? Ira von Fürstenberg's Hester, the wife of the general, looks as if she is going to be an important one, but after sneaking Smith into her house to spy on her husband she disappears from the movie completely despite Fürstenberg's fourth billing. (Tony Rayns in *Monthly Film Bulletin* quipped, "Ira Fürstenberg walks on and off like a living name-drop.") Even ninth billed Francesca Benedetti, as Miss Porter the madam, has more scenes.

Deaf Smith & Johnny Ears is buoyed by the three lead actors. Pamela is a vision of loveliness from the moment she first appears on screen, bathing in a creek. Cavara and cinematographer Tonino Delli Colli frame her in a medium shot and she is lit to perfection, making it almost equal to the way Vittorio Storaro shot her in *Giornata nera per l'Ariete*. For the rest of the movie Colli swaths Pamela in lots of light, completely opposite from the way Storaro filmed her with his use of shadows and contrasting dark and light but with almost equal results.

Performance-wise, this is arguably Pamela's best performance after *One, Two, Three*. She is well-matched with Franco Nero and they play off each other expertly. She is wonderfully funny in their early scene at the whorehouse as she tries to fight him off as they climb and tumble up the stairs. You can tell Pamela was really into this scene by the exasperated faces she made as she tries to pull away from Nero's Johnny, who is determined to have sex with her and pulls the battling girl into her room. Still refusing to accommodate him, she marches out to speak to the madam of the house.

After being assured that she has been paid for, Susie reluctantly goes back to her room to find Johnny Ears raring to go. It is a treat to see Pamela emote in these scenes, which

Johnny (Franco Nero) wakes the sleeping Susie (Pamela Tiffin) the morning after defeating the Texas rebels in a scene from *Deaf Smith & Johnny Ears* (MGM, 1973).

really gave her a chance to show her range: funny in one scene complete with pratfalls, and tough and hardened in the next, as she pushes and flings Nero's Johnny away from her only to wind up in his bed where the two realize they are in love. Her character has many nuances and is reminiscent of Tiffin's excellent turn in *Harper* where her Miranda was a woman of many emotions ranging from spoiled and seductive with Paul Newman's private eye, to desperately flirty with Robert Wagner's pilot, to deliciously catty with Lauren Bacall as her stepmonster. Her lively Susie projects an array of feelings believably enacted by Pamela.

Anthony Quinn is quite expressive without saying a word. Franco Nero is ruggedly handsome and in fine comic form as Johnny Ears. He has good rapport with Quinn. He does his best to bridge the energetic, humorous scenes with Tiffin's hooker with the more somber and serious scenes with Quinn's deaf scout, determined to help Texas become part of the United States. The movie really rests on his shoulders and he succeeds in projecting Johnny's love for Susie and need to be wanted by "Deaf" Smith. However, it is like watching two different movies. Here is a western where the interplay between the characters is the most interesting aspect. Usually it is the reverse with the talky moments getting in the way of the action. But the finale with the duo taking over a fort with dozens of men is a bit over-the-top, even with the machine-gun in their control.

Critical pans at the time doomed the movie, as it was not a hit in the U.S. and disappeared from most theaters in a week or less. It couldn't even recoup its modest $1.2 million budget. It definitely was a victim of bad timing and despite director Cavara's emphatic statements that it was a conventional western, audiences in America automatically associated it with the spaghetti western genre, which had long peaked in the U.S. Perhaps if it was made a few years prior, it would have attracted a larger audience.

Box office–wise it fared no better in Italy, grossing 421,241,000 lira (roughly $285,364). Roberto Curti said that, compared to other spaghetti westerns released in Italy, this was "disappointing considering the cast. That year Tonino Valeri's *My Name Is Nobody* did 3,620,000 lire ($2.5 million) at the box office."[21] The movie did better business in the U.K. When it opened in London it was the highest grossing new film of that week, outperforming *Bad Company*, *The 14*, and *Voices*.

The real shame of *Deaf Smith & Johnny Ears'* failure in the United States is that most American moviegoers missed seeing Pamela Tiffin in one of her finest hours. Not only was it her sole venture into the Euro-western or spaghetti western genre, she played against type as a feisty whore. She is paired again time with Franco Nero, arguably her most handsome Italian leading man, with whom she showed true sparks with on screen. Their comic interplay is first-rate. She acted her lines in English and was not dubbed by another actress. Though this would be her swan song from the big screen for American audiences, at least she went out on a high note performance-wise.

Today, most film historians and aficionados (and Franco Nero as well) consider *Deaf Smith & Johnny Ears* as part of the spaghetti western genre despite Cavara's insistence it was not. Besides Howard Hughes' spaghetti western books, the film is also included in Bert Fridlund's *The Spaghetti Western: A Thematic Analysis* (McFarland, 2006) and Thomas Weisser's *Spaghetti Westerns: The Good, the Bad, and the Violent* (McFarland, 1992). Weisser remarked in his tome that Pamela "looks good but is mostly insignificant in the (onscreen) action."

Explaining why he included the movie in his books, Hughes wrote, "It bears all the hallmarks of the genre: the music, the desert, the showdowns, and the violence. The two heroes take on a renegade who is ruling a town with terror tactics and the finale sees them attacking the villain's stockade fortress, which was a popular ending to European westerns of the period, such as *El Condor* and *Massacre at Fort Holman/A Reason to Live, A Reason to Die*."[22]

The movie is also reviewed online on such spaghetti western websites as *The Spaghetti Western Database* (www.spaghetti-western.net), *Shobarry's Spaghetti Westerns* (www.spaghettiwesterns.1g.fi), and *Fistful of Pasta* (www.fistfulofpasta.com) where it was deemed merely watchable due to the unfunny antics of a "quite annoying Franco Nero." It is also considered a spaghetti western in *Leonard Maltin's 2015 Movie Guide* where it earned three stars and was hailed as "a well made buddy western."

The verdict seems to be that the movie is considered part of the spaghetti western genre (sorry, Paolo Cavara) though its gimmicks of one hero with a disability and the other hero who would rather love than fight, makes it a bit different than most in the genre.

23

Questo è tutto gente!

E se per caso una mattina...
Amore mio, uccidimi! (Kill Me, My Love!)
La signora è stata violentata!
(*The Lady Has Been Raped*)

Brigitte, Laura, Ursula, Monica, Raquel, Litz, Florinda, Barbara, Claudia, e Sofia le chiamo tutte ... anima mia

Pamela Tiffin's film career began to wind down in Italy in 1973. Considering that she entered the movie industry on such a high note with *Summer and Smoke* and *One, Two, Three*, it is disappointing that it ended with a whimper as she appeared in four undistinguished movies including the melodrama *Amore mio, uccidimi!* (aka *Kill Me, My Love!*); the black comedy *La signora è stata violentata* (aka *The Lady Has Been Raped*); and the mystery–sex comedy *Brigitte, Laura, Ursula, Monica, Raquel, Litz, Florinda, Barbara, Claudia, e Sofia le chiamo tutte ... anima mia*.

Sandwiched in between her two films with Franco Nero was the little seen *E se per caso una mattina ...* (English translation: *And If By Chance One Morning...*). It was one of the first movies for a new production company called Gruppo Cinema 66 formed by director Vittorio Sindoni. The English working title was *Period, New Paragraph*. It was one of a very few Italian movies that tried to explain the hippie movement of that period.

After strong leading men like Franco Nero and Vittorio Gassman, here she was paired with an almost-newcomer named Virgilio Gazzolo who was unknown then and still is today. Pamela admitted that she did this film for free as a favor to a friend of Sindoni to help him out and because she wanted to spend the month of August working.

Pamela played a free-spirited hippie girl who so enthralls a middle-aged man that he deserts his family to follow her. He hangs out with her friends, including her former lover, who have rejected the hypocrisy and false values of the bourgeois society to which the married man belongs. However, as much as he tries, he cannot suppress his middle class conventions in terms of accepting this new free-spirited world, and tragedy results.

The movie came along a few years after *Zabriskie Point* and *Easy Rider*; by now the hippie movement was waning so the movie felt dated. Even its one-sheet poster art felt

Pamela Tiffin strikes a provocative pose, ca. 1972.

more 1967 Haight-Ashbury Summer of Love than 1972. It was very colorful and psychedelic with renderings of yellow flowers, a headless man in a suit holding a briefcase in one hand and giving the peace sign with the other, and a topless Pamela Tiffin looking left from behind with her long blonde hair covering her breast and wearing very tight jeans. The film's daybill went in a different direction and played up Pamela's sexiness with a color photo of the actress lying on the sand in a leopard-patterned bikini next to a black-and-white rendering of a suit-clad Virgilio Gazzolo reaching out to her.

Roberto Curti called it "a disaster" and remarked, "Pamela's star was rapidly fading out."[1] Though she did make a strong comeback performance-wise with *Deaf Smith & Johnny Ears*, *E se per caso una mattina …* did not even get a national distribution deal in Italy and only played in certain regions. Hence its box office take was a measly 22,192,000 lire ($15,034), making it the lowest grossing Italian film of Pamela Tiffin's career.

Regarding the movie, Pamela conceded, "The film wasn't very good."[2] However, she had a wonderful time making it because she loved playing a hippie. "I liked it so much that I pretended to be one in real life," she revealed. "I would braid my hair and wear shabby clothes. Finally it occurred to me that I have a PR man, an accountant, a manager, and an agent. Stop it, I'm not a hippie! I'm a businesswoman, though I don't go about anything in a business-like way. Sometimes roles hang on after filming whether you like them or not."[3]

Pamela's first film released in 1973 after *Deaf Smith & Johnny Ears* was the melodrama *Amore mio, uccidimi!* (*Kill Me, My Love!*), shot on location in Manila. Its working titles were *Day of the Sun* and *Love Stroke*. Director-writer Franco Prosperi's previous credits ranged from the peplum *Hercules in the Haunted World* (1961) to the crime drama *Hired Killer* (1966). She co-starred with American film star Farley Granger (best known for his starring role in Alfred Hitchcock's *Rope* and *Strangers on a Train*) and the sexy, brooding Giancarlo Prete (who followed this with the popular vigilante film *Street Law* with Franco Nero).

"I agreed to do this because they offered me a lot of money and it was to be filmed in the Philippines," revealed Pamela. "I always wanted to visit the Orient. I hated doing this film for those reasons, but I thought, 'Everyone else is crass and commercial, why shouldn't I be?'"[4]

The arrival of movie star Pamela Tiffin in the Philippines was much heralded. One of the country's most popular print entertainment columnists Joe Quirino, from the *Philippine Star* newspaper, was sent to interview her during a press conference held at the Hyatt-Regency Hotel. In his book *Like Dew in April and Other Stories*, he described Pamela as

Laureen (Pamela Tiffin) lunching with Guido (Giancarlo Prete) at left and friends in a scene from *Amore mio, uccidimi!* **(Ciclone Cinematografica Internazionale, 1973). Billy Rose Theatre Division, The New York Public Library for the Performing Arts, Astor, Lenox and Tilden Foundations.**

"the feminine of Clint Eastwood, Steve Reeves, and Brad Harris"[5]—actors who fled Hollywood to find fame in Rome. Seeing her sitting with her co-stars, including Farley Granger, the director, and the producer, Quirino remarked, "She struck me as a little bird who has just fallen from the nest. She looked that helpless."[6] He was proved wrong when Pamela began fielding questions from the reporters in the room and voiced her views on more serious subjects than the movie she was there to make, including her anti–Vietnam War stance; her Democratic ideals: and her take on the Kennedy family.

Surprised by Pamela's poise and intelligence, Quirino wrote, "Pamela has kept her very clear blonde beauty and her cool style, very different from the usual torrid manner affected by sex queens. Pamela Tiffin is that rare combination—a sex kitten who is the girl next door."[7]

When Quirino asked the actress about Women's Liberation, Tiffin exclaimed, "Women need more freedom."[8] She went on to say that the whole world was changing, including herself. "Even my career involves change. I even change the color of my hair, the color of my skin, the color of my eyes."[9] The one thing Pamela would not change was her saying no to drugs; she had abstained from taking LSD and other narcotics. However, she fervently felt it was not right to condemn young people who do.

Quirino then invited Pamela and the movie's male leads to be guests on his popular TV talk show *Seeing Stars with Joe Quirino*. Other guests that night were the Pangkat Kawayan (a group of elementary school musicians) and sixteen beauty contestants vying to become Miss Republic of the Philippines. When asked by Quirino what she liked most about her time working in his country, Pamela replied, "I like birds, shells, Oriental art, sunsets—you've got the most fabulous sunsets—and people. I have fallen in love with the Philippines and the Filipinos."[10]

After the taping was completed, Pamela confided in the talk show host that her randy Italian co-stars were quite enamored with "those very lovely Filipino beauty candidates."[11] Pamela too was fascinated with their natural beauty and commented, "There are so many lovely girls in the Philippines."[12]

In the movie, Pamela played Lauren Baxter, the younger wife of Granger's rich Manny Baxter. Lauren is not happy with their superficial life of glamorous parties. All the money, jewels, and furs Manny lavishes on her can't keep her content. Unsure of her feelings toward her husband and their lifestyle, she is questioning it all when she meets the poor Guido (Giancarlo Prete) who works with cars. The two immediately fall in love. Manny suspects something is up with his wife and has her watched constantly. The two lovers do all they can to avoid the prying eyes. To throw Manny off, Lauren even cops to the affair and admits it was only a fleeting whim. The young couple, however, makes plans to get away to Bangkok. Manny is on to their scheme and is determined to stop them. Guido, however, is equally resolved to run off with the woman he loves.

Despite the marquee lure of veteran actors Tiffin and Granger and the up-and-coming Giancarlo Prete, the movie failed to get noticed and is even an obscurity in its native Italy. Pamela is top-billed and her image in a sexy pose is front and center on the poster art, her name misspelled Tyffin. Another film released only regionally in Italy, it fared a bit better than *E se per caso una Mattina …* but still only brought in 42,598,000 lire ($28,857).

"This was a bad movie," exclaimed Pamela. "I suspected it would be. I wasn't bad in it, but I wasn't good either."[13]

Farley Granger must have agreed with Pamela's distaste for *Amore mio, uccidimi!* and

Guido (Giancarlo Prete) and Laureen (Pamela Tiffin) make love on the sand in a scene from *Amore mio, uccidimi!* (Ciclone Cinematografica Internazionale, 1973). Billy Rose Theatre Division, The New York Public Library for the Performing Arts, Astor, Lenox and Tilden Foundations.

didn't even mention it in his memoir *Include Me Out*. In fact, he names only one of his many seventies Italian films. He commented, "In the four years we spent in Rome, I averaged two films a year, none of which were worth writing home about."[14]

The actress used this trip as a springboard to see other parts of the Far East. "Afterwards I spent six months tooling around ... on Air France tickets with about eighteen pieces of luggage," she exclaimed. "I got away with it because everyone loves you when you're young and in movies."[15]

After finally returning to Italy, Pamela began working on *La signora è stata violentata* (aka *The Lady Has Been Raped*), her second film directed by Vittorio Sindoni. Though *E se per Caso una Mattina ...* was a failure, Pamela enjoyed working with Sindoni so much that she agreed to appear in this for him. The director's fourth movie, it reunited Tiffin with Luciano Salce from *Kiss the Other Sheik* here playing a monsignor and Carlo Giuffrè, her co-star from *Cose di Cosa Nostra*. They once again played a married couple in this strange dark comedy. And again Pamela is hidden under a wig. This time it is reddish in color since she is playing an Irish lassie.

Also in the cast playing one of the partygoers and suspected rapists was handsome, curly-haired young actor Ninetto Davoli. He was not known to American audiences, but was popular in Italy due to his starring roles in two of director Pier Paolo Pasolini's controversial motion pictures, *Il Decameron* (1971) and *I racconti di Canterbury* (1972). Again being cast in a role that required semi-nude sex scenes, Pamela once again opted for a body double to the disappointment of her many male admirers.

At a drug-fueled party, neurotic Sandro Traversa's (Carlo Giuffrè) lovely Irish Catholic wife Pamela (Tiffin) is raped by a masked satyr after inadvertently taking drugs. Not knowing who the assailant is, she thinks it was the devil and refuses to have sex with her husband any more. A frustrated Sandro goes to a psychoanalyst who explains that his wife may have to relive the experience to overcome her fear of sex. Sandro then pushes his wife into the arms of the other men who attended the party (an industrialist, an upright priest, a homosexual Indian, and the soiree's young bartender) to see if one of them is the rapist, but it is useless. The couple then separates. A porn magazine photographer who was snapping photos at the party comes forward and reveals that the man who had sex with her was Sandro. The relieved couple then reunites.

Sindoni once again produced a movie that was not liked by the critics. The Italian journal *Segnalazioni Cinematografiche* called it "a tasteless comedy" and a "trivial satire of psychoanalysis." Roberto Curti said it is a "bad erotic comedy."[16] On the other hand, *The Film Library of Cain*, a film webzine, found the movie to be a "sexy comedy" and that "the sexy part of the film is entirely entrusted to her [Tiffin's] charms...."

Surprisingly, the film was a hit. Curti surmises perhaps it was due to the lurid title and the fact the film's rating geared it towards adults, attracting the more adventurous moviegoer. It brought in 894,659,000 lire ($606,074).

Despite the critical barbs his two movies with Pamela received, Sindoni has continued directing to the present though since the mid-eighties he has concentrated working in Italian television.

Pamela's final theatrical release, and third time working with Vittorio Sindoni (acting as co-producer here), was the inanely titled comedy *Brigitte, Laura, Ursula, Monica, Raquel, Litz, Florinda, Barbara, Claudia, e Sofia le chiamo tutte ... anima mia* (1974), which unfortunately followed the path of most of her other recent movies and was barely shown in Italy let alone in the U.S. It was the directorial debut of Mauro Ivaldi. Pamela's

Promotional poster art for *La signora è stata violentata* (Megavision FilmTV, 1973).

leading man was Orazio Orlando, who had a supporting role in *Amore mio, uccidimi!*

Orlando played a rich, handsome playboy named Marco who has romanced and deserted many beautiful women, hence all the names in the title. However, he falls head over heels with the stunning Carmen Villani. Pamela played a tabloid journalist who reports on their upcoming nuptials. Soon after, one of Marco's jilted conquests threatens to kill him if he goes through with the marriage. A police commissioner (Mario Adorf) begins to investigate. He gets a cheap thrill questioning and then consoling all of Marco's former lovers, now all suspects. The twist ending reveals that the culprit was not a former girlfriend but an envious friend.

This is another movie where it is difficult to find reviews. Roberti Curti called it a "very bad erotic comedy-mystery"[17] infamous for its "long and stupid title."[18] At least Tiffin's name was spelled correctly on the movie poster art. Though it received only a limited release in Italy, it did a bit better than Pamela's other regionally distributed movies, grossing 55,516,000 lire ($37,609).

Unfortunately, Tiffin did not go out on a high note with this movie in Italy and just faded away in the minds of Italian moviegoers. At least for American audiences, her last big screen appearance in

Publicity photograph of Pamela Tiffin in *La signora è stata violentata* (Megavision FilmTV, 1973).

Deaf Smith & Johnny Ears featured Pamela at her blonde loveliest and delivering one of her most spirited performances, leaving her many fans craving more.

In *Dolce Cinema*, Pamela revealed why she stopped working. She explained that as time went by films began to change. She remarked, "Italian films started to become increasing erotic. And though there is certainly a place for Eros, it got to the point when I would go meet with a producer or director about a role and the conversation would disintegrate into if I would be nude—or if I would expose my breast or if my bottom could be shown. Or in what kind of scene—would I take a nude shower or could the bedroom scene be a naked one and so on." Growing up in the forties and fifties in America, she felt uncomfortable exposing her body on screen. She was offered a very comedic character role opposite Giancarlo Gianni in *The Sensuous Sicilian* by director Marco Vicario. The actress in her really wanted to do it, but the nudity required prevented her from accepting. Tired of having to deal with this issue, she decided not to work in Italy any longer. Realizing she could still survive ("Like a squirrel, I saved my money") she left.

24

Life After Moviemaking

After wrapping up her last movie in Italy, Tiffin returned to New York in 1973. She told columnist Earl Wilson that she enrolled at Columbia University to study Japanese art. However, she still remained active amongst the cinema set. She attended Bette Davis and John Springer's *Legendary Ladies of the Movies* show at Town Hall and after-party at the Rainbow Room, among other functions.

Sometime after, she married Edmondo Danon, the son of film producer Marcello Danon of *La cage aux folles* fame, and retired from acting. However, for a short period of time she did attend film-related events. In April 1975, she was a guest at a formal fundraising tribute to Paul Newman and Joanne Woodward at the Film Society of Lincoln Center. Other attendees included Lauren Bacall, Tony Perkins, Myrna Loy, Joan Fontaine, Arthur Penn, Tony Randall, Pat Hingle, and Shirley Knight. That December, she trekked to the Fourth International Teheran Film Festival as part of an American contingent of movie stars that included William Holden, Ellen Burstyn, Deborah Raffin, Dyan Cannon, Shirley Jones, Craig Stevens, and Alexis Smith.

Pamela soon gave birth to two daughters, Echo and Aurora, and her number one priority was to raise her family. She was now very content being a housewife and mother. As the years went by, and gossip columnists stopped writing about her, Pamela faded from the public eye though her fans did not forget her. From New York to Rome, she was still being recognized well into the nineties. She admitted that she sometimes had to deal with insensitive people who could not believe that she walked away from a lucrative movie career. Sometimes their hurtful comments made her feel "quite foolish and dense."[1] Being an actor is not all glitz and glamor, as some people with stars in their eyes think it is. As Pamela opined, "There are primordial things in our lives, the moon, birds, swamp, and flower and honeysuckle. You can't always live in a world of paychecks—that's very important, of course—you have to stay close to nature and human nature, or get back to it often."[2]

Despite her exit from show business, Pamela did step in front of the cameras a few more times. Shortly after the birth of her second daughter, she appeared on PBS' *Live from Lincoln Center* in "The Film Society of Lincoln Center: A Tribute to Billy Wilder," held in Avery Fischer Hall. The program featured a number of actors and friends singing the praises of the esteemed director. Among the participants were Shirley MacLaine, Ginger Rogers, John Huston, and Austin Pendleton. Pamela appeared onstage with Horst Buchholz to talk about making their classic comedy *One, Two, Three*.

As he did when they worked together on the movie, Buchholz could not help but ad-lib. Pamela recalled, "We had a prepared script. I was nursing my newborn, so I didn't want my bosom to show on national television. I wore dark blue, but suddenly there was this mother's milk. I'm nervous it would show, Mr. Wilder's in the balcony, and Horst starts to goof off with the lines. I thought I'd die! But I couldn't really fault his enthusiasm."[3]

Shortly after, Pamela participated in an Italian documentary, *La Dolce Cinema*, by filmmakers Francesco Bortolini and Claudio Masenza, which received a very limited release in the U.S. It featured an array of interviews with American actors who worked in the Italian cinema during the fifties and sixties including Pamela, Carroll Baker, Steve Reeves, Stewart Granger, Sterling Hayden, and Ernest Borgnine. Pamela was interviewed in the living room of her Upper West Side Duplex. Her long blonde hair is pulled back into a side pony tail and she is wearing an elegant black dress. She appears in four segments talking about her experiences making pictures in Italy. *Filmex Reviews* said the movie "is much too long, but it's fun and could easily end up a cult classic. It does offer fascinating insight…."

Two years later, while vacationing in Italy, Pamela was coaxed out of retirement by nostalgia buff and director Tomaso Sherman to play the married friend of single forty-something businesswoman Valerie Perrine in *Rose*. Perrine's title character jilts an American man (Brett Halsey) close to her age in favor of a romance with a college-aged Italian boy. After an almost twelve-year absence from acting, Tiffin was given special billing, "e con la partecipazione di Pamela Tiffin," in the credits.

While Rose was a more modern-type career woman, Pamela's Meg was an old-fashioned, staid housewife with a husband (former heartthrob Nino Castelnuovo of *The Umbrellas of Cherbourg* fame) and a son, Giovanni, who's the same age as Perrine's lover. Pamela's first scene finds her Meg distraught in bed wearing a nightgown and her hair messed as she binges on chocolates to dull the pain caused by her husband whom she thinks is cheating on her. Rose tries to motivate her to get out of bed. Memories of Pamela at her comedic best in *One, Two, Three* and *Deaf Smith & Johnny Ears* are evoked as a manic Meg runs around her home trailed by a lecturing Rose. Mario convinces his wife that he is faithful and they make love while Meg chats with their son. Later scenes find a well-dressed and more put-together Meg having lunch with Rose at an outdoor café and later dining with her and her family at a ritzy restaurant. More voluptuous than moviegoers had last seen her, Tiffin resembles a blonde version of Delta Burke from her latter days on the TV sitcom *Designing Women* and that is a compliment.

"*Rose* was a pointless movie … with an incredible wasteful budget," said Pamela. "I was in Europe anyway so I did it. I had a lot of fun."[4] The film once again finds Tiffin dubbed into Italian by another actress. It is still a treat to watch her final acting role. It also begs the question why the director was so anxious to hire American actors for a movie that would be televised only in Italy and no doubt dubbed into Italian by others.

Pamela returned to New York and a life of domesticity, but in 1989 the acting bug bit her again and she wanted to return to work. She commented to columnist Liz Smith, "I don't mind playing a 46-year-old character part. That's what I am."[5] Alas, acting offers never materialized, which is not surprising. A lot of her contemporaries also saw their careers dry up after they hit their forties. Her former co-star Carol Lynley is a perfect example. She worked constantly up to that point in her life and then the acting offers just slowed down.

In 1997, Pamela participated in a public program series entitled *Lillian Gish Remembered* at the New York Public Library for the Performing Arts in celebration of their acquirement of the actress' papers. There was written correspondence between Gish and director

Peter Glenville and actress Una Merkel. Since Tiffin worked with both of them on *Summer and Smoke*, she was asked to read a few letters by them (as well as by Charles Laughton) during the April 26 program and she readily agreed. Other participants in the series included Hal Holbrook, Irene Worth, Julie Harris, Lauren Hutton, Teresa Wright, Robert Anderson, Barnard Hughes, Gloria Vanderbilt, Douglas Fairbanks, Jr., and James MacArthur. The Library's Program Manager at the time, Alan Pally, was very proud of the esteemed array of people participating. He presented the complete list to Gish's personal manager, who later telephoned him. To Alan's surprise, the manager was most excited about seeing Pamela Tiffin's name on the program. He wanted to know where Alan found her and what her life was like. He found out in person when Pamela attended the program's opening (with Irene Worth) and the reception afterwards, where she spent a lot of time chatting with Douglas Fairbanks, Jr.

For her program, Pamela arrived at the Performing Arts Library wearing a sharp blue skirt with matching jacket, white blouse and white gloves. A number of people stopped in the green room to wish her well and to get autographs. Appearing before a full house, Pamela was wonderful. Some of the letters were humorous and Pamela, with her sense of comedic delivery, got the laughs. After a hearty round of applause, fans were treated to two Lillian Gish movies, *One Romantic Night* and *The Night of the Hunter*.

Tiffin remained off the radar after that live event. Her last credit is the documentary *Abel Ferrara: Not Guilty* (2003) about the director of *Bad Lieutenant*, *King of New York*, *Body Snatchers*, and *The Funeral*. Iranian filmmaker Rafi Pitts originally made *Abel Ferrara: Not Guilty* for the French TV series *Cinema de notre temps*: For five days, he followed the outgoing and eccentric Ferrara around New York as he played piano, discussed how he filmed scenes from some of his movies; shot a music video; and rehearsed Tiffin and her daughter Echo Danon, who had appeared in Ferrara's *New Rose Hotel* (1998). They were reading from the script of Ferrara's upcoming project *Go Go Tales*, about the infighting between the owners of a strip club.

While Echo had the acting bug, she studied with esteemed coach Marcia Haufrecht of the Actors Studio and her mother took a few classes as well. Pamela though needed to be coaxed into participating in the Ferrara film, but being such a big fan of the director's movie *King of New York*, she relented. An idea to make a short film with mother and daughter was discussed, but it never came to be.

Pitts released *Abel Ferrara: Not Guilty* theatrically in 2003 and it won the Grand Prix Award for Best Feature Documentary at the Entrevues Film Festival. Critic Leslie Felperin of *Variety* found it "fascinating and frustrating in near equal measure.... [T]he focus, metaphorically and almost literally, gets slightly fuzzy." Ali Catterall of Film4.com remarked, "An intimate night-in-the-life portrait of Abel Ferrara ... as he wanders around New York City making mischief with his scabrous wit. Funny, sometimes melancholy 80 minutes spent in the company of a true original. This may tell you more about the filmmaker and his works than any conventional documentary could."

Go Go Tales did not go into production and release until 2007 with neither Pamela nor her daughter involved. Too bad—it would have been a treat for her cadre of fans to see Pamela on the big screen in one last acting role.

Recalling her decision to quit acting, Pamela years later remarked, "I cared about my career when I was working and I didn't care about it the minute it stopped. But looking back on it (from my Protestant work ethic), that was very wrong. I should have striven for more but I didn't."[6]

Pamela is mistaken if she thinks she didn't strive enough. She tried valiantly to land good roles in important pictures, but Hollywood politics hampered her and then seemed to have beaten her drive down. Accepting the offer to work with Marcello Mastroinanni was a great opportunity and should have catapulted her to even greater fame, but as fate had it the film remained unreleased in America for three years. Luckily, the Paul Newman film *Harper* gave her the career boost she needed, but her decision to move to Italy ceased the momentum of her career dejactory. Even so, Pamela Tiffin became one of the decade's most memorable young actresses. If she had the determination and a career plan of a Raquel Welch, she certainly would have become a superstar.

Pamela Tiffin leaves behind a body of work which still delights her fans years later. None are considered classics in the traditional sense, but are more cult films or camp fests. However, they elevated Pamela above most of her contemporaries due to her standout comedic performances, particularly as the scatterbrained Southern belle in *One, Two, Three*; as a flighty flight attendant in *Come Fly with Me*; as a surfing coed trying to keep playboy James Darren at arm's length in *For Those Who Think Young*; as a naïve tourist in Spain playing romantic games with master player Tony Franciosa in *The Pleasure Seekers*; as a sexy but insensitive heiress who irks detective Paul Newman in *Harper*; as a militant coed who cheers on Mexican general Peter Ustinov who has reclaimed the Alamo in *Viva Max*; and as a feisty whore who wins the heart of saddle tramp Franco Nero in *Deaf Smith & Johnny Ears*. All should be viewed to see what makes her an iconic sixties actress to this day.

Looking back at her Hollywood career, Dean Brierly opined, "It goes without saying that Pamela Tiffin was one of the most charismatic and stunning starlets of the sixties and seventies, but she was much more than just a pretty face and gorgeous body. She was a fine actress who could hold her own with some of Hollywood's biggest stars. Her scenes with James Cagney in Billy Wilder's *One, Two, Three* sparkle, thanks to her deft comic touch and timing."[7]

When asked about Pamela Tiffin's place in Italian film history, Roberto Curti wrote, "Pamela Tiffin is still remembered fondly by Italian moviegoers due to the success of her popular comedies and for her revealing spread in *Playboy*."[8]

"A strange destiny was that of Pamela Tiffin," Paolo Mereghetti opined (and hits the nail on the head regarding the actress' then frustrations with Italian cinema at that time):

> Despite the efforts of producers (and filmmakers) to exploit her attractiveness, she never became part of the legion of nude starlets who populated Italian cinema between the 1960s and the 1970s, and this ultimately influenced negatively [on] her popularity. She made the audience dream, without showing too much. Even the photo shoot she did in *Playboy* was of the "now-you-see-me-now-you-don't" kind. In those years, Italian cinema was losing the driving force of the best Commedia all'italiana, and the loosening of mores was encouraging stories that were closer to Boccaccio than to Rossellini—which wasn't the ideal for an actress who, like Pamela, wanted to *act*. Nevertheless Tiffin proved to be a remarkable screen presence.[9]

With more of Pamela's movies becoming available online or on DVD in English-language versions, it will only increase the interest in her Italian cinema career. Howard Hughes feels that most of Pamela's movies "are currently filed under 'still-to-discover' for English-speaking Italian cinema fans.... There's a receptive retro cult movie fanbase out

Publicity photograph of Pamela Tiffin doing her iconic sixties dance on the diving board in *Harper* (Warner Bros., 1966).

there for this type of cinema—I would say that through home video, TV and DVD, some of the films, directors, actors and actresses are more better known now than in their heydays. Tiffin may fall into that category."[10]

Her co-star Franco Nero also thought Pamela Tiffin did not fulfill her potential. He remarked enthusiastically, "I think Pamela Tiffin is a fantastic comedienne and deserved much more as a comedienne. She is a wonderful actress and could play everything, but her personality and even her voice made her born for comedy."[11]

James Cagney will have the last word on the career of Pamela Tiffin. In the eighties while reflecting on the movie business, the actor paid the highest compliment to the actress: "The movies keep looking for new talent but so frequently fail to utilize the talent they have. In *One, Two, Three* Pamela Tiffin showed a remarkable flair for comedy, and as far as I know that is the only opportunity she was given. It is so rare to find a beautiful girl who can play comedy well. Carole Lombard, Kay Kendall, Lucille Ball, and you've just about gone down the roster. Because of sheer neglect, talents like Pamela Tiffin never come to their majority."[12]

Credits

Film Credits

SUMMER AND SMOKE
U.S. Release Date: November 1961

CAST: Laurence Harvey (*Dr. John Buchanan, Jr.*), Geraldine Page (*Alma Winemiller*), Rita Moreno (*Rosa Zacharias*), Una Merkel (*Mrs. Winemiller*), John McIntire (*Dr. Buchanan*), Thomas Gomez (*Papa Zacharias*), Pamela Tiffin (*Nellie Ewell*), Malcolm Atterbury (*Rev. Winemiller*), Lee Patrick (*Mrs. Ewell*), Earl Holliman (*Archie Kramer*).

CREW: *Director:* Peter Glenville, *Producer:* Hal B. Wallis, *Executive Producer:* Paul Nathan, *Screenplay:* James Poe and Meade Roberts, based on the play by Tennessee Williams, *Music:* Elmer Bernstein, *Cinematography:* Charles Lang, *Editing:* Warren Low.

A Hal Wallis production released by Paramount Pictures

The film is set in the pre–World War I South. Pamela Tiffin debuts as Nellie Ewell, a sweet, sheltered seventeen-year-old, who immediately falls for callous doctor John Buchanan, Jr. A fast-driving drinker, gambler, and womanizer, he has been secretly loved by his childhood friend Alma Winemiller, the repressed, refined daughter of a preacher and a loony, malicious mother who mocks her daughter's desperate longings for the boy next door.

ONE, TWO, THREE
U.S. Release Date: December 1961

CAST: James Cagney (*C.R. MacNamara*), Horst Buchholz (*Otto Ludwig Piffl*), Pamela Tiffin (*Scarlett Hazeltine*), Arlene Francis (*Phyllis MacNamara*), Howard St. John (*Wendell P. Hazeltine*), Hanns Lothar (*Schlemmer*), Leon Askin (*Peripetchikoff*), Ralf Wolter (*Borodenko*), Karl Lieffen (*Fritz*), Lilo Pulver (*Ingeborg*).

CREW: *Producer-Director:* Billy Wilder, *Associate Producers:* I.A.L. Diamond and Doane Harrison, *Screenplay:* Billy Wilder and I.A.L. Diamond, based on the play by Ferenc Molnar, *Music:* André Previn, *Cinematography:* Daniel L. Fapp, *Editing:* Daniel Mandell.

A Mirisch Corporation production released by United Artists

Pamela Tiffin gives her most memorable performance as impetuous Southern belle Scarlett Hazeltine. While under the care of Coca-Cola's man in West Berlin C.R. MacNamara, she sneaks across the border into East Berlin and marries Communist Otto Ludwig Piffl, causing all sorts of comedic trouble.

STATE FAIR
U.S. Release Date: March 1962

CAST: Pat Boone (*Wayne Frake*), Bobby Darin (*Jerry Dundee*), Pamela Tiffin (*Margy Frake*), Ann-Margret (*Emily Porter*), Tom Ewell (*Abel Frake*), Alice Faye (*Melissa Frake*), Wally Cox (*Hipplewaite*), David Brandon (*Harry Ware*), Clem Harvey (*Doc Cramer*), Robert Woulk (*Mincemeat Judge*), Linda Heinrich (*Betty Jean*).

CREW: *Director:* José Ferrer, *Producer:* Charles Brackett, *Screenplay:* Richard L. Breen, *Music:* Alfred Newman, *Cinematography:* William C. Mellor, *Editing:* David Bretherton.

A 20th Century–Fox Film Corporation production and release

In this musical, Pamela Tiffin is sweet, restless farm gal Margy who accompanies her family to the Texas State Fair where she finds love with a brash TV announcer.

COME FLY WITH ME
U.S. Release Date: March 1963

CAST: Dolores Hart (*Donna Stuart*), Hugh O'Brian (*First Officer Ray Winsley*), Karl Boehm (*Baron Franz Von Elzingen*), Pamela Tiffin (*Carol Brewster*), Lois Nettleton (*Hilda "Bergie" Bergstrom*), Dawn Addams (*Katie Rinard*), Karl Malden (*Walter Lucas*), Richard Wattis (*Oliver Garson*), James Dobson (*Flight Engineer Teddy Shepard*), Lois Maxwell (*Gwen Sandley*).

CREW: *Director:* Henry Levin, *Producer:* Anatole de Grunwald, *Associate Producer:* Roy Parkinson, *Screenplay:* Williams Roberts, based on the novel *Girl on a Wing* by Bernard Glemser, *Music:* Lyn Murray, *Cinematography:* Oswald Morris, *Editing:* Frank Clarke.

A De Grunwald production released by Metro-Goldwyn-Mayer

Pamela Tiffin is a flight attendant who, on her first day on the job, falls for co-pilot Ray Winsley. Her fellow air hostesses Donna and Bergie find romance too as they fly the New York to Paris and Vienna routes.

FOR THOSE WHO THINK YOUNG
U.S. Release Date: June 1964

CAST: James Darren (*Gardner "Ding" Pruitt III*), Pamela Tiffin (*Sandy Palmer*), Paul Lynde (*Sid Hoyt*), Tina Louise (*Topaz McQueen*), Bob Denver (*Kelp*), Robert Middleton (*Burford Sanford Cronin*), Nancy Sinatra (*Karen Cross*), Claudia Martin (*Sue Lewis*), Ellen McRae [Ellen Burstyn] (*Dr. Pauline Swenson*), Woody Woodbury (*Woody Woodbury*).

CREW: *Director:* Leslie H. Martinson, *Producer:* Hugh Benson, *Executive Producer:* Howard W. Koch, *Screenplay:* James O'Hanlon, George O'Hanlon and Don Beaumont, *Music:* Jerry Fielding, *Cinematography:* Harold E. Stine, *Editing:* Frank P. Keller.

An Aubrey Schenck production released by United Artists

Pamela Tiffin as poor coed Sandy Palmer tries to resist dashing, rich playboy "Ding" Pruitt but succumbs to his charms and then has to contend with his disapproving grandfather, in between shooting the curl at Malibu and watching her uncles' nightclub performances.

THE LIVELY SET
U.S. Release Date: October 1964

CAST: James Darren (*Casey Owens*), Pamela Tiffin (*Eadie Manning*), Doug McClure (*Chuck Manning*), Joanie Sommers (*Doreen Grey*), Marilyn Maxwell (*Marge Owens*), Charles Drake (*Paul Manning*), Peter Mann (*Sanford Rogers*), Carole Wells (*Mona*), Frances Robinson (*Celeste Manning*), Greg Morris (*Highway Patrol Officer*).

CREW: *Director:* Jack Arnold, *Producer:* William Alland, *Story:* William Alland, *Screenplay:* Mel Goldberg and William Wood, *Music:* Bobby Darin, *Cinematography:* Carl E. Guthrie, *Editing:* Archie Marshek.

A Universal Pictures production and release

Pamela Tiffin's man-chasing coed sets her sights on returned G.I. Casey Owens, but he is fixated on tinkering with his turbine engine and racing his sports car.

THE PLEASURE SEEKERS
U.S. Release Date: December 1964

CAST: Ann-Margret (*Fran Hobson*), Tony Franciosa (*Emile Lacayo*), Carol Lynley (*Maggie Williams*), Gardner McKay (*Pete McCoy*), Pamela Tiffin (*Susie Higgins*), Andre Lawrence (*Dr. Andres Briones*), Gene Tierney (*Jane Barton*), Brian Keith (*Paul Barton*), Vito Scotti (*Neighborhood Man*), Isobel Elsom (*Dona Teresa Lacayo*).

CREW: *Director:* Jean Negulesco, *Producer:* David Weisbart, *Screenplay:* Edith R. Sommer, based on the novel by John H. Secondari, *Music:* Lionel Newman, *Cinematography:* Daniel L. Fapp, *Editing:* Louis R. Loeffler.

A 20th Century–Fox production and release

This is another three-girls-looking-for-romance travelogue for Pamela Tiffin. Here she is naïve Susie Higgins, newly arrived in Madrid, who falls for caddish playboy Emile Lacayo while college friend Maggie Williams pines for her married boss and singer-dancer Fran Hobson falls for a poor Spanish doctor.

THE HALLELUJAH TRAIL
U.S. Release Date: June 1965

CAST: Burt Lancaster (*Col. Thaddeus Gearhart*), Lee Remick (*Cora Templeton Massingale*), Jim Hutton (*Capt. Paul Slater*), Pamela Tiffin (*Louise Gearhart*), Donald Pleasence (*"Oracle" Jones*), Brian Keith (*Frank Wallingham*), Martin Landau (*Chief Walks-Stooped-Over*), John Anderson (*Sgt. Buell*), Tom Stern (*Kevin O'Flaherty*), Robert J. Wilke (*Chief Five Barrels*).

CREW: *Producer-Director:* John Sturges, *Associate Producer:* Robert E. Relyea, *Screenplay:* John Gay, based on the novel by William Gulick, *Music:* Elmer Bernstein, *Cinematography:* Robert Surtees, *Editing:* Ferris Webster.

A Mirisch Corporation production released by United Artists

In Pamela Tiffin's first western she's an army colonel's daughter who joins a temperance movement to stop a whiskey shipment from reaching a Colorado mining town.

HARPER
U.S. Release Date: February 1966

CAST: Paul Newman (*Lew Harper*), Lauren Bacall (*Elaine Sampson*), Julie Harris (*Betty Fraley*), Arthur Hill (*Albert Graves*), Janet Leigh (*Susan Harper*), Pamela Tiffin (*Miranda Sampson*), Robert Wagner (*Allan Taggert*), Robert Webber (*Dwight Troy*), Shelley Winters (*Fay Estabrook*), Harold Gould (*Sheriff*).

CREW: *Director:* Jack Smight, *Producers:* Jerry Gershwin and Elliot Kastner, *Screenplay:* William Goldman, based on the novel by Ross Macdonald, *Music:* Johnny Mandel, *Cinematography:* Conrad L. Hall, *Editing:* Stefan Arnsten.

A Warner Bros. production and release

Pamela Tiffin gets to put her sexiness to good use as a spoiled, hot-to-trot heiress who vamps private detective Lew Harper on the trail of her missing father.

OGGI, DOMANI, DOPODOMANI
"LA MOGLIE BIONDA"
Italy Release Date: March 1966
Not released in the U.S.

CAST: Marcello Mastroianni (*Michele Gaspari*), Pamela Tiffin (*Pepita*), Lelio Luttazzi (*Amico di Michele*), Raimondo Vianello (*Il commissario*). Not credited (in alphabetical order): Ennio Antonelli, Luciano Bonanni, Antonio Ciani, Enzo La Torre.

CREW: *Director:* Luciano Salce, *Producer:* Carlo Ponti, *Screenplay:* Franco Castellano, Giuseppe Moccia and Luciano Salce, *Music:* Luis Enrique Bacalov, *Cinematography:* Gianni Di Venanzo, *Editing:* Marcello Malvestito.

A Compagnia Cinematografica Champion production

Taking her new kittenish persona from *Harper* one step further, the newly blonde Pamela Tiffin debuted as a sexy, lazy housewife whose husband plots to sell her to a sheik for his harem. The husband discovers that his wife is shrewder than he thought.

DELITTO QUASI PERFECTO
THE ALMOST PERFECT MURDER
THE IMPERFECT MURDER
Italy Release Date: April 1966
Not released in the U.S.

CAST: Philippe Leroy (*Paolo Respighi*), Pamela Tiffin (*First Annie Robson*), Graziella Granata (*Second Annie Robson*), Bernard Blier (*Colonel Robson*), Massimo Serato (*Preston*), Fernando Sancho (*Omar*), Alan Collins (*Salah*), Giullo Donnini (*Foster*), Silla Bettini (*Commissario*), Ignazio Leone (*Mazzullo*).

CREW: *Director:* Mario Camerini, *Producer:* Luigi Rovere, *Story:* Mario Camerini and

Steno, *Screenplay:* Leo Benvenuti, Piero De Bernardi, Mario Camerini, Vittorio Gastaldi and Mario Gicca, *Music:* Carlo Rustichelli, *Cinematography:* Aldo Giordani, *Editing:* Tatiani Casini Morigi.

A Rizzoli Film and Franco London Film production released by Golden Era in the U.K.

In this comedy mystery, Pamela Tiffin is an heiress (or is she?) newly arrived in Beirut to claim her rightful inheritance. She is met with kidnapping and threats, and followed by an infatuated reporter.

Kiss the Other Sheik
U.S. Release Date: July 1968

CAST: Marcello Mastroianni (*Mario Gaspari*), Pamela Tiffin (*Pepita*), Virna Lisi (*Dorotea*), Luciano Salce (*Arturo*), Lelio Luttazzi (*Amico di Mario*), Raimondo Vianello (*Il commissario*). Not credited (in alphabetical order): Ennio Antonelli, Luciano Bonanni, Antonio Ciani, Enzo La Torre.

CREW: *Directors:* Luciano Salce and Eduardo De Filippo, *Producer:* Carlo Ponti, *Story and Screenplay:* Goffredo Parise, Renato Cassellano, Pipola, Luciano Salce, Eduardo De Filippo and Isabella Quarantotti, *Music:* Luis Enrique Bacalov and Nino Rota, *Cinematography:* Gianni Di Venanzo and Mario Montuori, *Editing:* Marcello Malvestito and Adriana Novelli.

A Compagnia Cinematografica Champion production released through Metro-Goldwyn-Mayer

A re-edited version of *Oggi, domani, dopodomani*, where the trying-to-sell-each-other-off-to-a-sheik married couple Mario and Pepita find happiness with each other at the end.

I Protagonisti
The Protagonists
Italy Release Date: May 1968
Not released in the U.S.

CAST: Sylva Koscina (*Nancy*), Jean Sorel (*Roberto*), Pamela Tiffin (*Gabriella*), Lou Castel (*Giovanni Taddeu*), Luigi Pistilli (*Tassoni*), Maurizio Bonuglia (*Nino*), Giovanni Petti (*Carlo*), Gabriele Ferzetti (*Il Commissario*).

CREW: *Director:* Marcello Fondato, *Producers:* Ugo Guerra and Elio Scardamaglia, *Story:* Marcello Fondato, *Screenplay:* Marcello Fondato and Ennio Flaiano, *Music:* Luis Bacalov, *Cinematography:* Marcello Gatti, *Editing:* Tatiana Casini Morigi.

A Ital-Noleggio Cinematografico production and release

In a change-of-pace role, Pamela Tiffin is part of a group of thrill seekers thinking it would be cool to hang out with some bandits in the hills of Sardinia until the police begin a major raid.

STRAZIAMI, MA DI BACI SAZIAMI
TORTURE ME, BUT KILL ME WITH KISSES
KILL ME WITH KISSES
Italy Release Date: October 1968
Not released in the U.S.

CAST: Nino Manfredi (*Marino Balestrini*), Ugo Tognazzi (*Umberto Ciceri*), Pamela Tiffin (*Marisa Di Giovanni*), Moira Orfei (*Adelaide*), Livio Lorenzon (*Artemio Di Giovanni*), Gigi Ballista (*Engineer*), Pietro Tordi (*Fra' Arduino*), Sam Burke (*Guido Scortichini*), Checco Durante (*Owner of Employment Agency*), Edda Ferronao (*Amica di Marissa*).

CREW: *Director:* Dino Risi, *Producers:* Edmondo Amati and Jacques Roitfeld, *Executive Producer:* Maurizio Amati, *Story:* Age-Scarpelli and Dino Risi, *Screenplay:* Age-Scarpelli, *Music:* Armando Trovajoli, *Cinematography:* Sandro D'Eva, *Editing:* Antonietta Zita.

A FIDA Cinematografica production and release

Pamela Tiffin's biggest Italian hit was this comedy where she is an auburn-haried country village girl living in Rome torn between her sweet mute older husband and the young lover who broke her heart but now wants her back.

L'ARCANGELO
THE ARCHANGEL
Italy Release Date: April 1969
Limited U.S. Release Date: 1971

CAST: Vittorio Gassman (*Fulvio Bertuccia*), Pamela Tiffin (*Gloria Bianchi*), Irina Demick (*Signora Tarocchi Roda*), Adolfo Celi (*Marco Tarocchi Roda*), Carlo Delle Piane (*Ninetto*), Corrado Olmi (*Prof. Crescenzi*), Carlo Pisacane (*Il barbone*), Tom Felleghy (*Fabris*), Pippo Starnazza (*L'uomo delle pulizie*).

CREW: *Director:* Giorgio Capitani, *Producer:* Mario Cecchi Gori, *Story and Screenplay:* Adriano Baracco, Giorgio Capitani, Renato Castellani and Steno, *Music:* Piero Umilani, *Cinematography:* Stelvio Massi, *Editing:* Sergio Montanari.

A Fair Film production released by 20th Century–Fox in the U.S.

Pamela Tiffin is a duplicitous beautiful blonde vixen who tempts a down-on-his-luck attorney to commit a murder with promises of them being together forever with the victim's money as their own.

VIVA MAX
U.S. Release Date: January 1970

CAST: Peter Ustinov (*General Maximilian Rodrigues De Santos*), Pamela Tiffin (*Paula Whitland*), Jonathan Winters (*General Billy Joe Hallson*), John Astin (*Sergeant Valdez*), Keenan Wynn (*General Lacomber*), Harry Morgan (*Chief of Police Sylvester*), Alice Ghostley (*Hattie*), Kenneth Mars (*Dr. Sam Gillison*), Ann Morgan Guilbert (*Edna Miller*), Larry Hankin (*Romero*), Eldon Quick (*Quincy*).

CREW: *Director:* Jerry Paris, *Producer:* Mark Carliner, *Associate Producer:* Wally Sampson, *Screenplay:* Elliot Baker, based on the novel by Jim Lehrer, *Music:* Hugo Montenegro, *Cinematography:* Henri Persin, *Editing:* David Berlatsky and Bud Molin.

A Commonwealth United Entertainment production and release

Pamela Tiffin returned to the States to play a mini-skirted activist coed taken hostage by a Mexican general and his army, who have retaken the Alamo.

Cosi di Cosa Nostra
The Godson
Gang War
Italy Release Date: January 1971
Limited U.S. Release Date: 1975

CAST: Carlo Giuffrè (*Salvatore Lococo*), Pamela Tiffin (*Carmela Lococo*), Jean-Claude Brialy (*Domenico "Mimi" Gargiulo*), Salvo Randone (*Nicola "Nicky' Manzano*), Agnes Spaak (*Bridget*), Mario Feliciani (*Calogero Bertuccione*), Vittorio De Sica (*Don Michele*), Aldo Fabrizi (*Il brigadiere Aldo Panzarani*), Mario Brega (*Bellacque*).

CREW: *Director:* Steno, *Producer:* Roberto Amoroso, *Story:* Roberto Amoroso, Giulio Scarnicci and Stefano Vanzina, *Screenplay:* Roberto Gianviti, Roberto Amoroso, Steno and Aldo Fabrizi, *Music:* Manuel De Sica, *Cinematography:* Carlo Carlini, *Editing:* Antonietta Zita.

A Ramofilm Roma and P.A.C. Film Parigi production released in Italy by Euro International Films

Pamela Tiffin is an Italian NYC housewife who thinks she and her family are on a simple vacation in Italy. She's unaware that a Mafia don has financed the trip so her unwilling husband can assassinate a rival mobster while she fights off the advances of an ex-lover.

Il vichingo venuto dal Sud
The Viking Who Came from the South
The Blonde in the Blue Movie
Italy Release Date: August 1971
Limited U.S. Release Date: 1981

CAST: Lando Buzzanca (*Rosario Trapanese*), Pamela Tiffin (*Karen*), Renzo Marignano (*Gustav Larsen*), Gigi Ballista (*Commendator Silvio Borelon*), Rita Forzano (*Ilse*), Steffen Zacharias (*Bosen*), Dominique Boschero (*Priscilla*), Victoria Zinni (*Luisa Borelon*), Donatella Della Nora (*Annelise*), Ferdy Mayne (*Professor Grutekoor*).

CREW: *Director:* Steno, *Producer:* Anis Nohra, *Story and Screenplay:* Giulio Scarnicci, Steno and Raimondo Vianello, *Music:* Armando Trovajoli, *Cinematography:* Angelo Filippini, *Editing:* Ruggero Mastroianni.

An International Film Company production, distributed by 20th Century–Fox

Looking especially stunning, Pamela Tiffin is a Danish coed who makes a porn movie to help pay for school. This comes back to haunt her when she falls for an old-fashioned Italian businessman newly arrived in Copenhagen who doesn't understand the more liberal Danish views on sex.

GIORNATA NERA PER L'ARIETE
EVIL FINGERS
THE FIFTH CORD
Italy Release Date: August 1971
Limited U.S. Release Date: 1975

CAST: Franco Nero (*Andrea Bild*), Silvia Monti (*Helene*), Wolfgang Preiss (*Police Inspector*), Ira von Fürstenberg (*Isabel Lancia*), Edmund Purdom (*Edouard Vermont*), Rossella Falk (*Sophia Bini*), Renato Romano (*Dr. Richard Bini*), Guido Alberti (*Traversi*), Luciano Baroli (*Walter Auer*), Pamela Tiffin (*Lu Auer*).

CREW: *Director:* Luigi Bazzoni, *Producer:* Manolo Bolognini, *Screenplay:* Luigi Bazzoni, Mario Fenelli and Mario di Nardi, based on a novel by D.M. Devine, *Music:* Ennio Morricone, *Cinematography:* Vittorio Storaro, *Editing:* Eugenio Alabiso.

A B.R.C. Produzione S.r.l.production released by Target International

In her one and only giallo, Pamela Tiffin is the free-spirited girlfriend of alcoholic reporter Andrea Bild who is investigating the murders of his acquaintances. Bild then becomes a police detective's number one suspect.

E SE PER CASO UNA MATTINA...
Italy Release Date: Summer 1972
Not released in the U.S.

CAST: Virgilio Gazzolo, Pamela Tiffin, Tony Mirando, Jr., Armando Furlai, Carlo Sabatini, Renato Lupi, Nino Musco.

CREW: *Director:* Vittorio Sandoni, *Producer:* Michele Macaluso, *Screenplay:* Rossana Faggiani, *Music:* Mario Bertoncini, *Cinematography:* Antonello Capponi, *Editing:* Marriano Faggiani.

A Gruppo Cinema 66 production

In this very psychedelic, "very seventies" movie, Pamela Tiffin portrays a beautiful hippie who so enthralls a middle-aged man that he deserts his family to follow her.

LOS AMIGOS
DEAF SMITH & JOHNNY EARS
Italy Release Date: March 1973
U.S. Release Date: July 1973

CAST: Franco Nero (*Johnny Ears*), Anthony Quinn (*Erastus "Deaf" Smith*), Pamela Tiffin (*Susie*), Ira von Fürstenberg (*Hester McDonald Morton*), Adolfo Lastretti (*Williams*),

Franco Graziosi (*Gen. Lucius Morton*), Antonino Faà di Bruno (*The Senator*), Renato Romano (*J.M. Hoffman*), Francesca Benedetti (*Mrs. Porter*), Cristina Airoldi (*Rosita McDonald*).

CREW: *Director:* Paolo Cavara, *Producers:* Joseph Janni and Luciano Perugia, *Story:* Harry Essex and Oscar Saul, *Screenplay:* Harry Essex, Oscar Saul, Paola Cavara, Lucia Drudi and Augusto Finocchi, *Music:* Daniele Patucchi, *Cinematography:* Tonino Delli Colli, *Editing:* Mario Morra.

A Compagnia Cinematografica production released by Metro-Goldwyn-Mayer

Pamela Tiffin gives a feisty performance as a whore with a heart and mine of gold. She falls for gunslinger Johnny Ears, the companion to the hearing-impaired "Deaf" Smith.

AMORE MIO, UCCIDIMI!
KILL ME, MY LOVE!
DAYS OF THE SUN
Italy Release Date: August 1973
Not released in the U.S.

CAST: Pamela Tiffin (*Laureen Baxter*), Giancarlo Prete (*Guido*), Farley Granger (*Manny Baxter*), Orazio Orlando (*Riccardo*).

CREW: *Director:* Franco Prosperi, *Producers:* Joseph Janni and Luciano Perugia, *Screenplay:* Luisa Montagnana and Franco Prosperi, *Music:* Carlos Pes, *Cinematography:* Franco Di Giacomo, *Editing:* Alberto Gallitti.

A Ciclone Cinematografica Internazionale production released by Regionale in Italy

In the Philippines, Pamela Tiffin's cheating wife wants to leave her wealthy husband to run off with her poor younger lover.

LA SIGNORA È STATA VIOLENTATA
THE LADY HAS BEEN RAPED
Italy Release Date: November 1973
Not released in the U.S.

CAST: Pamela Tiffin (*Pamela Traversa*), Carlo Giuffrè (*Sandro Traversa*), Enrico Montesano (*Padre O'Connor*), Ninetto Davoli (*Palla*), Gigi Ballista (*Carini*), Dominique Boschero (*Viviane Carini*), Leopoldo Trieste (*The Psychoanalyst*), Franco Fabrizi (*Il fotografo*), Luciano Salce (*Il monsignore*), Gino Pagnani (*Tommasino*).

CREW: *Director:* Vittorio Sindoni, Producers: Roel Bos and Vittorio Sindoni, *Executive Producer:* Enzo Giulioli, *Story:* Vittorio Sindoni, *Screenplay:* Ghigo De Chiara, *Music:* Peter Cook, *Cinematography:* Roel Vos, *Editing:* Marriano Faggiani.

A Megavision FilmTV production released by PAC

In a drug-induced state, Pamela Tiffin's religious wife thinks she was raped by Satan at a party and then refuses to have sex with her husband who sets out to catch the culprit.

BRIGITTE, LAURA, URSULA, MONICA, RAQUEL, LITZ, FLORINDA, BARBARA, CLAUDIA, E SOFIA LE CHIAMO TUTTE ... ANIMA MIA
Italy Release Date: January 1974
Not released in the U.S.

CAST: Orazio Orlando (*Marco Donati*), Pamela Tiffin (*Francesca*), Mario Adorf (*Il commissario Marzoli*), Gigi Ballista, Carmen Villani, Elena Veronese, Monica Monet, Alessandro Haber, Angela Covello, Edmonda Aldini.

CREW: *Director:* Mauro Ivaldi, *Producers:* Roel Bos and Vittorio Sindoni, *Executive Producer:* Enzo Giulioli, *Screenplay:* Francesco Castellano, Mauro Ivaldi and Pipolo, Music: Peter Cook, *Cinematography:* Aristide Massaccesi, *Editing:* Alessandro Lucidi.

A Tregar production released by Regionale in Italy

Pamela Tiffin plays a gossipy journalist whose story on the upcoming nuptials of a notorious womanizing playboy cause him to be stalked by a former paramour (or is he?).

TV Credits

THE FUGITIVE
"THE GIRL FROM LITTLE EGYPT"
Air date: December 24, 1963

CAST: David Janssen (*Dr. Richard Kimble*), Barry Morse (*Lt. Philip Gerard*). GUEST CAST: Pamela Tiffin (*Ruth Norton*), Ed Nelson (*Paul Clements*), Diane Brewster (*Helen Kimble*), June Dayton (*Doris Clements*), Bernard Kates (*Lester Rand*), Jerry Paris (*Jim Prestwick*).

CREW: *Director:* Vincent McEveety, *Teleplay:* Stanford Whitmore.

A Quinn Martin production in association with United Artists Television

Pamela Tiffin's lovelorn air hostess accidentally runs down Richard Kimble while fleeing from her paramour, who just revealed that he is married. She takes Kimble into her home to recuperate while he tries to help with her romantic problem.

THREE ON AN ISLAND
Unsold pilot
Air date: August 27, 1965

CAST: Pamela Tiffin (*Taffy Warren*), Julie Newmar (*Kris Meeker*), Monica Moran (*Andrea Franks*), Jody McCrea (*Julius "Bulldog" Sweetley*), Sheila Bromley (*Martha Sweetley*), Ned Glass (*Riley*), Ron Husmann (*Glenn*), Rhodes Reason (*Perry*).

CREW: *Director:* Vincent Sherman, *Teleplay:* Hal Kanter.

A 20th Century–Fox Television production

This was a failed TV pilot starring Pamela Tiffin as a sculptress who shares a brownstone with two roommates and who has just obtained half the contract to a mediocre boxer.

THE SURVIVORS
"CHAPTER 15"
Air date: January 12, 1970

CAST: Lana Turner (*Tracy Carlyle Hastings*), Ralph Bellamy (*Baylor Carlyle*), George Hamilton (*Duncan Carlyle*), Kevin McCarthy (*Philip Hastings*), Jan-Michael Vincent (*Jeffrey Hastings*).

GUEST CAST: Pamela Tiffin (*Rosemary Price*), Michael Bell (*Corbett*).

A Harold Robbins Company production in association with Universal Television

Pamela Tiffin played the glamorous girlfriend of rich Duncan Carlyle during the scenes shot in the French Riviera, most of which were excised by the time the series aired.

ROSE
ITALY—TV MOVIE
Air date: 1986

CAST: Valerie Perrine (*Rose*), Stefano Dionisi (*Stefano*), Nino Castelnuovo (*Mario*), Pamela Tiffin (*Meg*), Brett Halsey (*Max*), Teresa Ann Savoy (*Annie*), Luca Venantini (*Giovanni*).

CREW: *Director:* Tomaso Sherman, *Teleplay:* Ennio De Concini, *Music:* Fiorenzo Carpi, *Cinematography:* Luciano Tovoli, *Editing:* Sergio Montanari.

Pamela Tiffin played the disapproving married friend of a businesswoman named Rose who begins a love affair with a young man half her age.

Pamela Tiffin as Herself

PM East
Syndicated Late Night Talk Show
Air date: May 4, 1962

PM East was produced by Group W Productions and co-hosted by Mike Wallace and Joyce Davidson. It was filmed in New York City and was aired in direct competition with *The Tonight Show* on NBC. Pamela guested along with Henry Gibson, Jan Sterling, and Henry Mancini.

The show was notable for some of Barbra Streisand's earliest TV appearances. She so impressed Wallace that she was invited back over a dozen times. The series was cancelled after one year on the air (June 1961–June 1962) and a bonehead decision was made to erase and re-use the tapes, so no video remains of this series, only audio recordings of a handful of episodes.

HERE'S HOLLYWOOD
Daytime Program
Air date: October 5, 1962

Here's Hollywood was a half-hour celebrity daytime interview program broadcast by NBC-TV. Pamela was interviewed while in London by host Jack Linkletter. This episode's other guest was actor Harry Guardino.

"FILM EPIC OF THE WEST HAS NEW YORK PREMIERE"
British Pathe Newsreel
U.S. release date: Spring 1963

Pamela Tiffin, on the arm of Clay Felker, is seen attending the New York premiere of the MGM Cinerama production *How the West Was Won* at the Loew's Cinerama Theater. Also in attendance were the film's co-stars Carroll Baker and Thelma Ritter, plus Lois Nettleton and MGM president Robert H. O'Brien.

GIRL TALK
Syndicated Daytime TV Talk Show
Air date: April 21, 1964

Tiffin was a guest on this syndicated chat show hosted by Virginia Graham. This episode's other guests were actress Jennifer West and columnist Sheilah Graham. The show was extremely popular in its day, as three celebrity women, seated in a living room–type setting complete with tea service on the coffee table, would discuss everything from life, to their feelings about other celebrities, to current events. With the loud and sometimes overbearing Virginia Graham at the helm, the shows were never boring.

THE CELEBRITY GAME
Primetime TV Game Show
Air date: June 14, 1964

Carl Reiner hosted this primetime quiz show, a sort of precursor to *The Hollywood Squares*. Three contestants had to guess how the celebrity panel would answer moral-type questions. The celebrities playing this night were Tiffin, Howard Duff, Ida Lupino, Cliff Arquette (known to TV viewers as Charley Weaver), Jack E. Leonard, Anne Baxter, Macdonald Carey, Nancy Sinatra, and her husband Tommy Sands.

TO TELL THE TRUTH
Primetime TV Game Show
Air date: November 9, 1964

This popular primetime game show, hosted by Bud Collyer, featured a celebrity panel who would ask questions of three challengers, trying to identify which one was telling the truth and which were the imposters. On Pamela Tiffin's lone appearance, she joined Orson Bean, Kitty Carlisle, and Tom Poston. In one segment, the panel tried to guess which Marine was actually singer Anita Humes from the musical group The Essex, who had a big hit with "Easier Said Than Done."

Commenting on her appearance, the actress said, "I knew who the liars were on sheer instinct. But the show left me exhausted. Television is hard on you."[1]

THE HALLELUJAH TRAIL HOLLYWOOD PREMIERE
TV Special
Air date: June 11, 1965

Local Los Angeles station KTTV covered the Hollywood premiere of the epic western *The Hallelujah Trail*. It was hosted by Bill Welsh, the station's sports and special events director. Pamela was in attendance and interviewed along with co-stars Burt Lancaster, Lee Remick, Jim Hutton, and producer-director John Sturges, among others.

THE ED SULLIVAN SHOW
Primetime Variety Program
Air date: June 20, 1965

Pamela Tiffin appeared in a taped segment from the Hollywood premiere party of *The Hallelujah Trail* where she joined Burt Lancaster, Polly Bergen, Stephen Boyd, James Coburn, Bobby Darin, Glenn Ford, Brian Keith, Sal Mineo, Maureen O'Hara, Lee Remick, Edward G. Robinson, Rose Marie, Robert Stack, and Barry Sullivan to sing "Happy Anniversary" to Ed Sullivan, who was celebrating his 17th year hosting his variety show. The in-studio guests this night were the Dave Clark Five, Cab Calloway, Soupy Sales, Juliet Prowse, Totie Fields, British comedian Arthur Haynes, Swedish gymnasts The Malmo Girls, and knife throwers Elizabeth & Collins.

THIS PROUD LAND
"THE SUN COUNTRY"
TV Special
Air date: January 26, 1966

Pamela appeared with esteemed actress Greer Garson in the third installment of ABC-TV's *This Proud Land*, hosted by Robert Preston. Her segment focused on the wonders and the people of Texas, Oklahoma, Arizona, and New Mexico. Tiffin, an Oklahoma native, is oddly not seen in her state of birth, but at a Dallas fashion show. Though warmly received by critics (*Variety* called it "well-crafted and ambitious"), these specials were not very memorable.

THE MIKE DOUGLAS SHOW
Syndicated Daytime TV Talk Show
Air date: March 29, 1966

Affable Mike Douglas hosted one of the most popular (and longest running) variety-talk shows in daytime history. His co-host for the week when Tiffin guested was singer-actress Leslie Uggams. Also joining Pamela on the couch were Jan Peerce and his wife, comedian George Kirby, and Dr. Edward Annis.

ASSIGNMENT HOLLYWOOD
Talk Radio Program
Air date: June 22, 1966

Pamela discussed her career with host Fred Robbins on his ABC Radio syndicated program.

THE MERV GRIFFIN SHOW
Syndicated Daytime TV Talk Show
Air date: July 25, 1966

Pamela was a guest on Griffin's talk show, *the* longest running in daytime, along with her future movie co-star Vittorio Gassman, Tony Randall, and comedian Sandy Baron.

GIRL TALK
Syndicated Daytime TV Talk Show
Air date: September 4, 1966

Pamela was again part of Virginia Graham's chatfest along with buxom blonde actress and pinup June Wilkinson and British actress April Olrich.

WHAT'S MY LINE?
Primetime TV Game Show
Air date: September 25, 1966

Pamela joined a number of her Broadway co-stars from *Dinner at Eight* including Robert Burr, June Havoc, Darren McGavin and Walter Pidgeon as Mystery Guests trying to stump the panel of Arlene Francis (another member of the play's cast), Jayne Meadows, Steve Allen, and publisher Bennett Cerf.

CASPER CITRON VIEWPOINT
Talk Radio Program
Air date: November 1, 1966

Pamela, Ruth Ford, and Robert Burr discussed their Broadway show *Dinner at Eight* with Casper Citron on his nationally syndicated radio show broadcast from New York's Algonquin Hotel on WRFM.

PASSWORD
Primetime TV Game Show
Air date: January 8, 1967

Pamela Tiffin and Larry Blyden were the celebrity guests on the primetime version of *Password* hosted by Allen Ludden. Each was paired with a contestant and the object of the game was to give a one-word clue to get your partner to guess the secret word. Each round began with the announcer whispering to the home audience, "The password is…."

MOTION PICTURE ASSOCIATION OF AMERICA
Trailer
U.S. release date: March 1967

In a one-minute trailer, Pamela explained to moviegoers the new production code created by the Motion Picture Association of America. The actress said that under this new voluntary motion picture rating system (put into place by its new president Jack Valenti), films would be rated G for General Audiences, M for Mature Audiences, R for Restricted to Persons under 16 unless accompanied by an adult, and X for Adults Only.

WHAT'S MY LINE?
Primetime TV Game Show
Air date: March 12, 1967

Shortly after *Dinner at Eight* closed on Broadway, Pamela made a return appearance on the TV game show *What's My Line?*, this time as one of the guest panelists along with Arlene Francis, Martin Gabel, and Bennett Cerf.

OUTRAGEOUS OPINIONS
Syndicated Daytime TV Talk Show
Air date: April 7, 1967

Pamela was one of popular feminist writer Helen Gurley Brown's first guests on her syndicated daytime talk show. Not surprising from the author of *Sex and the Single Girl*, Brown focused her interviews with celebrities on their sex lives and sex in general. Tiffin shared her thoughts on this episode and commented about having sex with your partner, but in a very G-rated way. She was quoted as saying, "When you [a man and a woman] do have an attraction for one another, whether it is seven times a week, or once a week, or once a month, you should be happy about it. If you want more, then you should find out how you can get more."[2]

Brown would go on to interview such stalwarts as David Susskind, Woody Allen, Erica Jong, Otto Preminger, Joanna Pettet, and Norman Mailer. Unfortunately, the stay-at-home-housewife had a hard time relating to the show and it was cancelled after a very brief run. It was hard to keep a show going with only one topic as its focus. The celebrities mostly talked about sex in a roundabout way with Pamela being a perfect example. Reportedly, Brown was very disappointed with its failure, but was not surprised.

THE TONIGHT SHOW STARRING JOHNNY CARSON
Late Night TV Talk Show
Air date: October 8, 1969

This was probably not Pamela Tiffin's first appearance on the king of late night's TV talk show, as it is speculated that she had appeared on his program when it broadcast from New York City. Other guests on this night were Lon Chaney, Jr., singer Melanie, and Shani Wallis.

THE DAVID FROST SHOW
Syndicated Daytime TV Talk Show
Air date: January 8, 1970

In August 1969, when Merv Griffin was given a CBS-TV late night talk show opposite the mighty *Tonight Show Starring Johnny Carson*, Englishman David Frost became his daytime replacement. Pamela was a guest on Frost's program along with Alejandro Rey from TV's *The Flying Nun*, comedians Jerry Stiller & Anne Meara, and Elvis Presley's on stage opening act Jackie Kahane.

SALUTE TO VIVA MAX
TV Special
Air date: February 4, 1970

Pamela appeared in this KCOP-TV special, hosted by Dick Strout, which took a behind-the-scenes look at the making of the Commonwealth United comedy *Viva Max*.

SEEING STARS WITH JOE QUIRINO
Filipino TV Talk Show
Air date: April 15, 1972

One of the Philippines' most popular talk shows during the seventies, *Seeing Stars* was hosted by entertainment columnist Joe Quirino. Pamela was a guest when she was in that country shooting the movie *Amore mio, uccidimi!* Also appearing were some of her movie castmates, the Pangkat Kawayan (a group of elementary school musicians), and sixteen beauty contestants vying to become Miss Republic of the Philippines.

LIVE FROM LINCOLN CENTER
"THE FILM SOCIETY OF LINCOLN CENTER: A TRIBUTE TO BILLY WILDER"
TV Special
Air date: May 3, 1982

Shortly after the birth of her second daughter, Pamela appeared on PBS in this salute to the famed director Billy Wilder, held in Avery Fisher Hall. The program featured a number of actors and friends sharing their memories of working with the esteemed Academy Award–winning director. Pamela appeared onstage with Horst Buchholz to talk about making their classic comedy *One, Two, Three*.

Chapter Notes

Preface

1. Tom Lisanti, "Pamela Tiffin: Last of the Contract Players," *Films of the Golden Age*, Summer 1997, 87.
2. Chris Strodder, *The Encyclopedia of Sixties Cool: A Celebration of the Grooviest People, Events, and Artifacts of the 1960's* (Santa Monica, CA: Santa Monica Press, 2007).

Chapter 1

1. Tiffin, Pamela, Interview by Sonia Wolfson, "Notes on Pamela Tiffin: 'Margy' in 20th Century–Fox CinemaScope Color Production of Rodgers and Hammerstein's 'State Fair,'" 1961, 3. Sidney Skolsky Papers, Margaret Herrick Library, Academy of Motion Picture Arts and Sciences.
2. Ibid, 6.
3. Ibid.
4. Ibid, 14.

Chapter 2

1. Tiffin, Interview by Sonia Wolfson, "Notes on Pamela Tiffin," 8.
2. Ibid.
3. Ibid, 9.
4. W. Kenneth Holditch, "Interview with Pamela Tiffin," *The Tennessee Williams Literary Journal.* Vol. 3 (1993): 64.
5. "Pamela's Progress," *Esquire,* Jan. 1962, 94.
6. Tiffin, Interview by Sonia Wolfson, "Notes on Pamela Tiffin," 11.
7. Holditch, "Interview with Pamela Tiffin," 64.
8. Ibid.
9. Ibid, 65.
10. Ibid.
11. Tiffin, Interview by Sonia Wolfson, "Notes on Pamela Tiffin," 11.
12. William Werneth, "Pamela Tiffin Calls Nation's Exhibitors Solid, Efficient Men," *Motion Picture Herald,* May 2, 1962, 9.
13. Holditch, "Interview with Pamela Tiffin," 65.
14. Tiffin, Interview by Sonia Wolfson, "Notes on Pamela Tiffin," 12.
15. Holditch, "Interview with Pamela Tiffin," 65.
16. Tiffin, Interview by Sonia Wolfson, "Notes on Pamela Tiffin," 12.

17. Ibid.
18. Associated Press, "Seldom Done Stunt Pulled By Actress," *The Hartford Courant*, Dec. 10, 1961.
19. Holditch, "Interview with Pamela Tiffin, 66, 67.
20. Ibid, 65.
21. Mother Dolores Hart and Richard DeNeut, *The Ear of the Heart: An Actress' Journey from Hollywood to Holy Vows* (San Francisco: Ignatius Press, 2013), 118.

Chapter 3

1. "Pamela's Progress," 95.
2. Associated Press, "Cagney a Fighter Only in Films," *Newsday*, Jul. 7, 1961.
3. Tiffin, Interview by Sonia Wolfson, "Notes on Pamela Tiffin," 15.
4. Ibid.
5. Ibid.
6. Ibid.
7. Thomas Wood, "In Wilder's Wild West: Director and Troupe Shoot as Usual Despite Russian Ruses in Berlin," *New York Times*, July 16, 1961.
8. Ibid.
9. Ibid.
10. Ibid.
11. Tiffin, Interview by Sonia Wolfson, "Notes on Pamela Tiffin," 16.
12. Ibid.
13. Irene Thirer, "Movie Spotlight: Pamela Tiffin—Beauty with Brains," *New York Post*, Apr. 11, 1962: 90.
14. Cameron Crowe, *Conversations with Wilder*, (London: Faber and Faber, 1999), 16.
15. Tiffin, Interview by Sonia Wolfson, "Notes on Pamela Tiffin," 16.
16. James Cagney, *Cagney by Cagney*, (Garden City, NY: Doubleday, 1976), 157, 158.
17. Ibid, 158.
18. Ibid.
19. Ibid.
20. John Crosby, "Comedy Is Grim Business: Cagney Blows His Lines 51 Times for a Record," *Boston Globe*, Sept. 24, 1961.
21. Ibid.
22. Crowe, *Conversations with Wilder*, 165.
23. Tiffin, Interview by Sonia Wolfson, "Notes on Pamela Tiffin," 16.

24. Hedda Hopper, "Star Rising, A: Pamela Sure to Find It a Bright Christmas," *The Washington Post*, July 21, 1961.

25. Liza Wilson, "Time for Tiffin: She, Pamela, Is What Hollywood Is Ever Searching for—an Original," *Los Angeles Herald-Examiner*, Mar. 4, 1962.

26. Priscilla Tucker, "Young Star Solves the Clothes Problem," *New York Herald Tribune*, Dec. 13, 1961.

27. "Pamela's Progress," 92.

28. Marika Aba, "Billy Wilder: He Chose Hollywood," *Los Angeles Times*, Mar. 3, 1968.

29. Crowe, Conversations with Wilder, 15.

30. Ibid., 15, 16.

31. Arlene Dahl, "Arlene Dahl Selects Tomorrow's Leading Ladies," *Chicago Tribune*, Oct. 13, 1963.

32. Charles Champlin, "James Cagney at 70: Retired but Not Retiring," *Los Angeles Times*, May 6, 1973.

33. I.A.L. Diamond, "'One, Two, Three': Timetable Test," *New York Times*, Dec. 17, 1961.

34. Wilson, "Time for Tiffin."

35. Hedda Hopper, "I Pick These to Star in 1962," *Chicago Tribune*, Dec. 31, 1961.

36. "People on the Way Up: Pamela Tiffin," *Saturday Evening Post*, Dec. 2, 1961.

Chapter 4

1. Joe Hyams, "The Hogs and Cast Are New," *New York Herald Tribune*, Oct. 29, 1961, 4.

2. Tiffin, Interview by Sonia Wolfson, "Notes on Pamela Tiffin," 17.

3. Ibid.

4. Ibid., 18.

5. Ibid.

6. Werneth, "Pamela Tiffin Calls Nation's Exhibitors Solid, Efficient Men," 9.

7. Tiffin, Interview by Sonia Wolfson, "Notes on Pamela Tiffin," 19.

8. Richard D. Kibbey, *Pat Boone: The Hollywood Years*, (Tate Publishing & Enterprises, L.L.C., 2011), 239.

9. William Peper, "Pictures, Plays and Players: Acting Is Minor to Pam Tiffin," *New York World-Telegraph & Sun*, Dec. 6, 1961.

10. Tiffin, Interview by Sonia Wolfson, "Notes on Pamela Tiffin," 19.

11. Tom Lisanti, *Fantasy Femmes of Sixties Cinema: Interviews with Twenty Actresses from Biker, Beach, and Elvis Movies*, (Jefferson, NC: McFarland, 2001), 81.

12. Tiffin, Interview by Sonia Wolfson, "Notes on Pamela Tiffin," 18.

13. Ibid., 19.

14. Earl Wilson, "It Happened Last Night," *Newsday*, Nov. 20, 1961.

15. Hedda Hopper, "Faye's Knees Shaky (at First) in Return: After 15 Years, Star Resumes Career in New 'State Fair,'" *Los Angeles Times*, Sept. 29, 1961.

16. Telex from David I. Zeitlin to Carmichael for Prideaux and Stanton Life New York, September 26, 1961, David I. Zeitlin Papers, 1955–1968, Margaret Herrick Library, Academy of Motion Picture Arts and Sciences.

17. Ibid.

18. Telex from Guerin (Entertainment) New York to David I. Zeitlin, October 2, 1961, David I. Zeitlin Papers, 1955–1968, Margaret Herrick Library, Academy of Motion Picture Arts and Sciences.

19. Ibid.

20. Lisanti, "Pamela Tiffin: Last of the Contract Players," 90, 91.

21. Mike McGrady, "After 7 Movies, Pamela Is Learning to Act," *Newsday*, Jan. 15, 1965.

22. Ibid.

23. Bill Marshall and Robynn Stilwell, eds., *Musicals: Hollywood & Beyond* (Exeter, England; Portland, OR: Intellect, 2000), 40.

Chapter 5

1. Earl Wilson, "It Happened Last Night," *Newsday*, Apr. 17, 1962.

2. Hart and DeNeut, *The Ear of the Heart*, 164.

3. Richard L. Coe, "One on the Aisle: Come Fly with Freud," *The Washington Post*, Apr. 5, 1963.

4. Ibid.

5. John L. Scott, "Hollywood Calendar: One Minute Interview Covers Lots of Ground," *Los Angeles Times*, Apr. 7, 1963.

6. Letter from Hugh O'Brian to Hedda Hopper, July 5, 1962, 1, Sidney Skolsky Papers, Margaret Herrick Library, Academy of Motion Picture Arts and Sciences.

7. Ibid.

8. O'Brian, Hugh. Telephone interview with author, July 2013.

9. Ibid.

10. Hart and DeNeut, *The Ear of the Heart*, 164.

11. Ibid.

12. Erskine Johnson, "Hollywood Abroad: For Pamela Tiffin, the Eyes Have 'It,'" *The Evening Independent*, Sept. 25, 1962, 5-B.

13. Tiffin, Pamela, Interview by Sonia Wolfson, "Recent Notes on Pamela Tiffin, Currently Co-Starring in Metro-Goldwyn-Mayer's *Come Fly with Me*," Mar. 14, 1963, 2. Sidney Skolsky Papers, Margaret Herrick Library, Academy of Motion Picture Arts and Sciences.

14. Tom Wolfe, "A City Built of Clay," *New York*, July 6, 2008.

15. Hart and DeNeut, *The Ear of the Heart*, 213.

Chapter 6

1. Ed Robertson, *The Fugitive Recaptured: The 30th Anniversary Companion to a Television Classic*, (Los Angeles: Pomegranate Press, LTD, 1993).

2. Ibid.

3. Ed Robertson, Email interview with author, Jan. 23, 2013.

4. Harold Stern, "Screen Actress Finds TV 'Terrifying': Pace Too Exhausting, Moans Pamela Tiffin," *The Hartford Courant*, Jan. 31, 1965.

5. Robertson, *The Fugitive Recaptured*, 56.

6. Pamela Tiffin, Interview by Hedda Hopper, Transcription, November 27, 1963, 2. Hedda Hopper Papers, Margaret Herrick Library, Academy of Motion Picture Arts and Sciences.

7. Ibid., 2–3.

8. Ibid., 4.

9. Tom Lisanti, *Glamour Girls of Sixties Hollywood: Seventy-Five Profiles,* (Jefferson, NC: McFarland, 2008), 182.

10. Tiffin, Interview by Hedda Hopper, 2–4.

11. Stern, "Screen Actress Finds TV 'Terrifying.'"

Chapter 7

1. Keith Monroe, "Inside the Magazines: New Teen Publication Succeeds Without Sex or Sensationalism," *Los Angeles Times*, June 30, 1963.

2. Tiffin, Interview by Sonia Wolfson, "Notes on Pamela Tiffin," 20.

3. "Is Tiffin Different?" *Show Business Illustrated*, Apr. 1962, 73.

4. Werneth, "New Faces: Pamela Tiffin Calls Nation's Exhibitors Solid, Efficient Men," 10.

5. Art Seidenbaum, "Spectator 1963: 'For Those Who Think Young' Going all Out with Tie-Ins," *Los Angeles Times*, Oct. 25, 1963.

6. Edwin Miller, "The Hollywood Scene," *Seventeen*, Sept. 1964, 26.

7. Tom Lisanti, *Hollywood Surf and Beach Movies: The First Wave, 1959–1969,* (Jefferson, NC: McFarland, 2005), 104, 105.

8. Ibid., 105.

9. The Hollywood Kids, "Q&A: Tina Louise," *Movieline*, April 1992.

10. Lisanti, *Fantasy Femmes of Sixties Cinema*, 81.

11. Tom Lisanti, "Lada Edmund, Jr. Is *Out of It*."

12. Ibid.

13. Lisanti, *Hollywood Surf and Beach Movies*, 105, 106.

14. McGrady, "After 7 Movies."

Chapter 8

1. Tiffin, Interview by Hedda Hopper, 3.

2. McGrady, "After 7 Movies."

3. Earl Wilson, "It Happened Last Night," *Newsday*, Mar. 12, 1964.

4. Louella Parsons and Harriet Parsons, "Pamela's a Talker, But Beautiful," *Los Angeles Herald-Examiner*, June 13, 1965, 8.

5. Tom Lisanti, *Drive-in Dream Girls: A Galaxy of B-Movie Starlets of the Sixties*, (Jefferson, NC: McFarland, 2003), 198.

6. Letter from Robert L. Bratton to Academy of Motion Pictures Arts & Sciences, December 21, 1964.

Chapter 9

1. Philip K. Scheuer, "Murray Plans Life of Nathan Leopold," *Los Angeles Times*, June 2, 1964.

2. Hedda Hopper, "Looking at Hollywood: MacArthur Story to Be Made Into Movie," *Chicago Tribune*, Apr. 11, 1964.

3. "Appearance of Yank 'Pleasure' Unit a Reassuring Omen for Spaniards," *Variety*, June 3, 1964, 1.

4. Ibid., 18.

5. Scheuer, "Murray Plans Life of Nathan Leopold."

6. Email from George Chakiris, May 25, 2014.

7. Louella Parsons, Editorial, *Los Angeles Herald-Examiner*, Sept. 9, 1963.

8. "Appearance of Yank 'Pleasure' Unit," *Variety*.

9. Pamela Tiffin, "My Days in Spain," July 1964, 1–3. Hedda Hopper Papers, Margaret Herrick Library, Academy of Motion Picture Arts and Sciences.

10. Ibid., 4, 5.

11. Ibid., 5, 6.

12. Hedda Hopper, "Hollywood: Ann-Margret Knows How to Make Enemies," *The Hartford Courant*, Mar. 6, 1961.

13. Ann-Margret, *Ann-Margret: My Story* (New York: Putnam, 1994), 124.

14. Diane McBain and Michael Gregg Michaud, *Famous Enough: A Hollywood Memoir* (Duncan, Oklahoma: BearManor Media, 2014), 217.

15. Tiffin, "My Days in Spain," 3.

16. "You've Met Mrs. Lee: She's a Beauty; 'Hobby' Is Acting," *Humboldt Standard*, July 20, 1964: 2.

17. Sheilah Graham, "Twosomes," *Hollywood Citizen-News*, May 15, 1964.

18. "Miss Pamela Tiffin Is World Traveler," *Hollywood Citizen-News*, Aug. 28, 1964.

19. John Sherlock, "Skipper without a Ship," *TV Guide*, July 28, 1962.

20. "Distaff Side Spotlighted in New Film," *Los Angeles Times*, Jan. 21, 1965.

21. McGrady, "After 7 Movies."

Chapter 10

1. McGrady, "After 7 Movies."

2. Ibid.

3. Ibid.

4. Glenn Lovell, *Escape Artist: The Life and Films of John Sturges*, (Madison, Wis.: University of Wisconsin Press, 2008), 251.

5. Tiffin, "My Days in Spain," 7, 8.

6. Lovell, *Escape Artist*, 252.

7. Tim Zinnemann, Email interview with author, Jan. 27, 2013.

8. Ibid.

9. "Miss Pamela Tiffin Is World Traveler."

10. Zinnemann, Email interview with author.

11. Ibid.

12. Tom Lisanti, *Dueling Harlows: Race to the Silver Screen*, (Washington: CreateSpace, 2011), 141.

13. Zinnemann, Email interview with author.

14. Ibid.

15. Ibid.

16. Ibid.

17. "Tiffin Changes Slogan," *Los Angeles Herald-Examiner*, June 4, 1965, B-6.

18. Zinnemann, Email interview with author.

Chapter 11

1. Gay Pauley, "Pamela Tiffin a Busy Actress, Model, Student and Housewife," *Chicago Tribune*, Dec. 9, 1963.

2. Tiffin, Interview by Hedda Hopper, 3.

3. Paul Gardner, "Kate Smith Plans to Perform on TV Six Times Next Season," *New York Times,* Jul. 6, 1965.

4. Tiffin, Interview by Sonia Wolfson, "Notes on Pamela Tiffin," 21.

5. "Study in Beauty, A," *New York Daily News*, Aug. 9, 1965.

6. Daphne Kraft, "Pamela Tiffin No Harlow: Escapes the Shadow," *Newark Evening News*, Oct. 9, 1966.

7. Martin West, Email interview with author, July 24, 2014.

8. "No Flat Fee for Private-Eye 'Harper,'" Letter from the Warner Bros. Pictures, Inc. New Department, [1966]. Margaret Herrick Library, Academy of Motion Picture Arts and Sciences.

9. Joe Morella and Edward Z. Epstein, *Paul and Joanne: A Biography of Paul Newman and Joanne Woodward,* (New York: Delacorte Press, 1988), 110.

10. Ibid.

11. Sheilah Graham, "Pamela Tiffin Feels Better As a Blonde," *Hollywood Citizen-News*, Dec. 2, 1965.

12. Morella and Epstein, *Paul and Joanne*, 111.

13. West, Email interview with author.

14. Ibid.

15. Earl Wilson, "It Happened Last Night," *Newsday,* Apr. 4, 1966.

16. "Study in Beauty, A."

17. Morella and Epstein, *Paul and Joanne*, 111.

18. John L. Scott, "Hollywood Calendar: Good Old Days in Filmland Good to All," *Los Angeles Times*, July 18, 1965.

19. Morella and Epstein, *Paul and Joanne*, 110.

20. West, Email interview with author.

21. Ibid.

22. Dean Brierly, Email interview with author, Dec. 2, 2013.

Chapter 12

1. Saul Kahan, "Blondes, Bullets and Bathtubs," *Films and Filming*, July 1966.

2. "Study in Beauty, A."

3. Ibid.

4. Graham, "Pamela Tiffin Feels Better As a Blonde."

5. Ibid.

6. Robert Wahls, "Footlight: Over-Stimulated Pam," *New York Daily News*, Oct. 16, 1966.

7. Kahan, "Blondes, Bullets and Bathtubs."

8. "Leading Man," *Newsweek*, Nov. 29, 1965.

9. Jose A. Quirino, *Like Dew in April and Other Stories* (Philippines: Navotas Press, 1973), 144.

10. Graham, "Pamela Tiffin Feels Better As a Blonde."

11. A.V. Henderson, "What Can Mastroianni Learn from Valentino?" *The Hartford Courant*, Feb. 22, 1966.

12. Israel Shenker, "Faye's Knees Shaky (at First) in Return," *Los Angeles Times*, Sept. 29, 1961.

13. Earl Wilson, "Girl in a Petticoat," *New York Post*, July 23, 1961.

14. Earl Wilson, "Pamela Cooks Italian Style…," *New York Post*, Mar. 27, 1966, 5.

15. Graham, "Pamela Tiffin Feels Better As a Blonde."

16. Arlene Dahl, "It's O.K. with Pamela to Be Blonde—and Eat!," *Chicago Tribune*, Dec. 5, 1966.

17. Tom Lisanti, "Pamela Tiffin: An American Sexpot in Rome," *European Trash Cinema* 16 (1998): 25.

18. Roberto Curti, Email interview with author, October 2013.

Chapter 13

1. Joseph Gelmis, *The Film Director as Superstar* (Garden City: Doubleday, 1970), 24.

2. Kraft, "Pamela Tiffin No Harlow."

3. Nikki Flacks, Telephone interview with author, June 9, 2014.

4. Ibid.

5. Ibid.

6. Ibid.

7. Kraft, "Pamela Tiffin No Harlow."

8. "Actress' Room Reflects Earlier Era," *The News-Palladium, Benton Harbor, Michigan*, Dec. 15, 1966, 5.

9. Flacks, Telephone interview with author.

10. Wahls, "Footlight: Over-Stimulated Pam."

11. Whitney Bolton, "Pamela Tiffin Is One Blonde with Brain," *New York Morning Telegraph*, Oct. 22, 1966, 3.

12. Ibid.

13. Flacks, Telephone interview with author.

14. Harvey Aronson, "Sex … & the Single Exposure." *Newsday*, Nov. 19, 1966.

15. Tiffin, Interview by Hedda Hopper, 4.

Chapter 14

1. Curti, Email interview with author.

2. Ibid.

Chapter 15

1. Lisanti, *Drive-in Dream Girls*, 198.

2. Tom Lisanti, "Mimsy Farmer: From *Spencer's Mountain* to *More*," *Sixties Cinema*, http://sixtiescinema.com/2014/04/06/mimsy-farmer-from-spencers-mountain-to-more/, 2014.

Chapter 16

1. "'Protagonists' Pick Puzzles Italians; Showmen-from-Rome Fill Cannes," *Variety*, May 8, 1968, 90.
2. Paolo Mereghetti, Email interview with author, April 28, 2014.
3. Curti, Email interview with author.
4. Lisanti, "American Sexpot in Rome," 25.
5. Jed Curtis, Telephone interview with author, May 1, 2014.
6. Ibid.
7. Ibid.
8. Ibid.
9. Ibid.
10. Ibid.
11. Ibid.
12. Ibid.
13. Ibid.
14. Lisanti, "American Sexpot in Rome," 25.
15. Curti, Email interview with author.
16. Enrico Lancia and Fabio Melelli, *Le Straniere del nostro Cinema* (Rome, Italy: Gremese Editore, 2005), 107.
17. Ibid.
18. Mereghetti, Email interview with author.
19. Curti, Email interview with author.
20. Curtis, Telephone interview with author.
21. Curti, Email interview with author.
22. Lancia and Melelli, *Le Straniere del nostro Cinema*, 107.
23. Lisanti, "American Sexpot in Rome," 25.
24. Ibid.

Chapter 17

1. Les Brown, *Televi$ion: The Business Behind the Box.* (New York: Harcourt Brace Jovanovich, 1971), 38.
2. John Wilder, Email interview with author, Jul. 9, 2014.
3. Stephen Bowie, "Richard DeRoy," *Classic TV History*, http://www.classictvhistory.com/OralHistories/richard_deroy.html, 2007.
4. Ibid.
5. Percy Shain, "George Hamilton: Some Candid Views on the Good Life," *Boston Globe*, Sept. 7, 1969.
6. Wilder, Email interview with author.
7. Tom Lisanti, "Pamela Tiffin: From Hollywood Ingénue to Italian Bombshell," *Outré the World of UltraMedia,* No. 19, 2000, 72.
8. Bowie, "Richard DeRoy."
9. Ibid.
10. Ibid.
11. Lisanti, "Pamela Tiffin: From Hollywood Ingénue to Italian Bombshell," 72.
12. Wilder, Email interview with author.
13. Ibid.
14. Ibid.

Chapter 18

1. Michael Etchison, "Remember the Alamo? It's Being Retaken," *Los Angeles Herald-Examiner*, Apr. 6, 1969, E-1.
2. Norma Lee Browning, "Hollywood Today: Is 'Coco' for Kate?" *Chicago Tribune*, June 23, 1969.
3. Marika Aba, "Pamela Tiffin—American Sex Queen in Exile," *Los Angeles Times*, July 6, 1969.
4. Peter Gonzales Falcon, Telephone interview with author, Aug. 19, 2014.
5. UPI, "'Viva Max!' Wins Alamo Film Battle," *Los Angeles Times*, Mar. 29, 1969.
6. Ibid.
7. UPI, "Alamo '69 Pits 'Max' Against Texas Ladies," *Newsday*, Apr. 2, 1969.
8. Ibid.
9. Gonzales Falcon, Telephone interview with author.
10. UPI, "Alamo '69 Pits 'Max' Against Texas Ladies."
11. UPI, "Texans Up in Arms Over Alamo Movie," *Los Angeles Times*, Apr. 11, 1969.
12. Eldon Quick, Email interview with author, Sept. 13, 2013.
13. Larry Hankin, Email interview with author, Sept. 18, 2013.
14. Etchison, "Remember the Alamo? It's Being Retaken," E-10.
15. Ibid.
16. Gonzales Falcon, Telephone interview with author.
17. Hankin, Email interview with author.
18. Gonzales Falcon, Telephone interview with author.
19. Quick, Email interview with author.
20. Bob Rose, "Food for Thought—after 'Candy,'" *Boston Globe*, Aug. 31, 1969.
21. Aba, "Pamela Tiffin—American Sex Queen in Exile."
22. Hankin, Email interview with author.
23. Quick, Email interview with author.
24. Wayne Warga, "Film Students Put Director in Spotlight," *Los Angeles Times*, Feb. 25, 1970.
25. Ibid.
26. Lisanti, "Pamela Tiffin: From Hollywood Ingénue to Italian Bombshell," 72.
27. Gonzales Falcon, Telephone interview with author.
28. Ibid.
29. Quick, Email interview with author.
30. Aba, "Pamela Tiffin—American Sex Queen in Exile."
31. Lydia Lane, "She Has Beauty, Brains," *Los Angeles Times*, Sept. 16, 1969.
32. Aba, "Pamela Tiffin—American Sex Queen in Exile."
33. Earl Wilson, "Panthers, Yes; Playboy, No: Pamela Tiffin Reacts to Chicago," *The Hartford Courant*, Jan. 7, 1970.
34. Lisanti, "American Sexpot in Rome," 25.

Chapter 19

1. Gonzales Falcon, Telephone interview with author.

Chapter 20

1. Curti, Email interview with author.
2. Lisanti, "American Sexpot in Rome," 25.
3. Mereghetti, Email interview with author.
4. Lisanti, "American Sexpot in Rome," 25.

Chapter 21

1. Earl Wilson, "Panthers, Yes; Playboy, No: Pamela Tiffin Reacts to Chicago," *The Hartford Courant*, Jan. 7, 1970.
2. Franco Nero, Telephone interview with author, July 18, 2015.
3. Ibid.
4. Ibid.
5. Lisanti, *Fantasy Femmes of Sixties Cinema*, 90.
6. Ibid.
7. Danny Shipka, *Perverse Titillation: The Exploitation Cinema of Italy, Spain and France, 1960–1980*, (Jefferson, NC: McFarland, 2011), 104.
8. Ibid.
9. Curti, Email interview with author.
10. Howard Hughes, Email interview with author, Aug. 22, 2013.
11. Curti, Email interview with author.
12. Hughes, Email interview with author.
13. Ibid.
14. Nero, Telephone interview with author.
15. Hughes, Email interview with author.
16. Nero, Telephone interview with author.
17. Lisanti, "American Sexpot in Rome," 25.
18. Curti, Email interview with author.
19. Hughes, Email interview with author.
20. Curti, Email interview with author.
21. Hughes, Email interview with author.

Chapter 22

1. Nero, Telephone interview with author.
2. Ibid.
3. Hughes, Email interview with author.
4. Army Archerd, "Just for Variety," *Variety*, October 18, 1972, 2.
5. Ibid.
6. *MGM Pressbook: Deaf Smith and Johnny Ears*. Los Angeles: Metro-Goldwyn-Mayer, Inc., 1973.
7. Ibid.
8. Nero, Telephone interview with author.
9. *MGM Pressbook: Deaf Smith and Johnny Ears*.
10. Ibid.
11. Ibid.
12. Nero, Telephone interview with author.
13. Lisanti, *Fantasy Femmes of Sixties Cinema*, 89.

14. Nero, Telephone interview with author.
15. *MGM Pressbook: Deaf Smith and Johnny Ears*.
16. Lisanti, *Fantasy Femmes of Sixties Cinema*, 89.
17. Nero, Telephone interview with author.
18. *MGM Pressbook: Deaf Smith and Johnny Ears*.
19. Archerd, "Just for Variety."
20. Hughes, Email interview with author.
21. Curti, Email interview with author.
22. Hughes, Email interview with author.

Chapter 23

1. Curti, Email interview with author.
2. Lisanti, "American Sexpot in Rome," 26.
3. Ibid.
4. Ibid., 25.
5. Quirino, *Like Dew in April and Other Stories*, 141.
6. Ibid.
7. Ibid.
8. Ibid., 143.
9. Ibid.
10. Ibid., 145.
11. Ibid.
12. Ibid.
13. Lisanti, "American Sexpot in Rome," 25.
14. Farley Granger with Robert Calhoun, *Include Me Out: My Life from Goldwyn to Broadway*, (New York: St. Martin's Griffin, 2007), 229.
15. Lisanti, "American Sexpot in Rome," 25.
16. Curti, Email interview with author.
17. Ibid.
18. Ibid.

Chapter 24

1. Holditch, "Interview with Pamela Tiffin," 69.
2. Ibid.
3. Lisanti, "Pamela Tiffin: From Hollywood Ingénue to Italian Bombshell," 70.
4. Lisanti, "Pamela Tiffin: An American Sexpot in Rome," 26.
5. Liz Smith, "Gilda Radner's 'Something' Is a Devastatingly Good Book," *Orange County Register*, June 26, 1989.
6. Lisanti, *Fantasy Femmes of Sixties Cinema*, 90.
7. Brierly, Email interview with author.
8. Curti, Email interview with author.
9. Mereghetti, Email interview with author.
10. Hughes, Email interview with author.
11. Nero, Telephone interview with author.
12. Cagney, *Cagney by Cagney*, 155.

Pamela Tiffin as Herself

1. Stern, "Screen Actress Finds TV 'Terrifying.'"
2. Judy Klemesrud, "Mrs. Brown, Your Subject Is Showing," *New York Times*, Dec. 31, 1967.

Bibliography

Aba, Marika. "Billy Wilder: He Chose Hollywood." *Los Angeles Times*, Mar. 3, 1968.

_____. "Pamela Loses Self to Find Identity." *Pacific Stars & Stripes*, July 10, 1969: 14.

_____. "Pamela Tiffin—American Sex Queen in Exile." *Los Angeles Times*, July 6, 1969.

"Actress' Room Reflects Earlier Era." *The News-Palladium, Benton Harbor, Michigan*, Dec. 15, 1966: 5.

Amory, Cleveland. "Headliners: Pamela Tiffin." *The National Sunday Magazine*, Feb. 12, 1967.

Ann-Margret. *Ann-Margret: My Story*. New York: Putnam, 1994.

"Appearance of Yank 'Pleasure' Unit a Reassuring Omen for Spaniards." *Variety*, June 3, 1964: 1, 18.

Archerd, Army. "Just for Variety." *Variety*, Oct. 18, 1972: 2.

Aronson, Harvey. "Sex … & the Single Exposure." *Newsday*, Nov. 19, 1966.

Associated Press. "Cagney a Fighter Only in Films." *Newsday*, Jul. 7, 1961.

_____. "Seldom Done Stunt Pulled By Actress." *The Hartford Courant*, Dec. 10, 1961.

_____. "'Viva Max!' Wins Alamo Film Battle. *Los Angeles Times*, Mar. 29, 1969.

Bacon, James. "Pretty Model Snapped Up By Wallis." *The Hartford Courant*, Mar. 5, 1961.

Bernardini, Aldo. *Nino Manfredi*. Roma: Grenese, 1999.

Bolton, Whitney. "Pamela Tiffin Is One Blonde with Brain." *New York Morning Telegraph*, Oct. 22, 1966: 3, 14.

Boone, Pat. *State Fair* DVD audio commentary track. *60th Anniversary Edition Rodgers & Hammerstein State Fair*. Nov. 15, 2005.

Bowie, Stephen. "Richard DeRoy." *Classic TV History*, http://www.classictvhistory.com/Oral Histories/richard_deroy.html, 2007.

Bratton, Robert L. Letter to Academy of Motion Picture Arts & Sciences. Dec. 21, 1964. Margaret Herrick Library, Academy of Motion Picture Arts and Sciences.

Brown, Les. *Televi$ion: The Business Behind the Box*. New York: Harcourt Brace Jovanovich, 1971.

Brown, Vivian. "Degree-Minded Star: Pamela Tiffin Goes Back to College." *Newark Evening News*, Mar. 18, 1963: 26.

_____. "Newlywed Actress: Back to College." *The Sun*, Apr. 5, 1963.

Browning, Norma Lee. "Hollywood Today: Series On or Off?" *Chicago Tribune*, June 10, 1969.

_____. "Hollywood Today: Is 'Coco' for Kate?" *Chicago Tribune*, June 23, 1969.

_____. "Lana Gets Out of the Frye Pan." *Chicago Tribune*, Oct. 18, 1968.

Cagney, James. *Cagney by Cagney*. Garden City, NY: Doubleday, 1976.

Calta, Louis. "Play's the Thing, Film Stars Agree: Hollywood Actors Tell Why They Are Stage-Struck." *New York Times*, Dec. 3, 1966.

Cameron, Kate. "Western Epic with a Grin." *New York Daily News*, June 27, 1965.

"Carliner Producing 'Viva Max' for MGM." *The Hollywood Reporter*, Sept. 25, 1967.

Carroll, Harrison. "Behind the Scenes in Hollywood: Actresses in Hotel 'Bombed' in Madrid." *The New Tribune, Fort Pierce, Florida*, June 2, 1964: 8.

Cartwright, Gary. "Remember the Alamo, Please." *Life*, Apr. 24, 1969: 62–64.

"Cast Dances in Booties." *Los Angeles Times*, Sept. 12, 1964.

Champlin, Charles. "James Cagney at 70: Retired but Not Retiring." *Los Angeles Times*, May 6, 1973.

Chandler, Charlotte. *Nobody's Perfect: Billy Wilder: A Personal Biography*. New York; London: Simon & Schuster, 2002.

Clymer, Adam. "India's Erotic Art Has Lots of Style." *The Baltimore Sun*, May 3, 1970.

Coe, Richard L. "One on the Aisle: Come Fly with Freud." *The Washington Post*, Apr. 5, 1963.

"Contract OKd for Young Film Beauty." *Los Angeles Times*, May 13, 1961.

Counts, Kyle. "A Time to Remember." *Starlog*, July 1992.

Crosby, John. "Comedy Is Grim Business: Cagney Blows His Lines 51 Times for a Record." *Boston Globe*, Sept. 24, 1961.

Crowe, Cameron. *Conversations with Wilder*. London: Faber and Faber, 1999.

261

Dahl, Arlene. "Arlene Dahl Selects Tomorrow's Leading Ladies." *Chicago Tribune*, Oct. 13, 1963.

_____. "It's O.K. with Pamela to Be Blonde—and Eat!" *Chicago Tribune*, Dec. 5, 1966.

_____. "Model Turned Actress Now Dresses the Part." *Chicago Tribune*, Apr. 13, 1964: 2.

Del Amo, G. Andre. "Film Star Faces Odd Situation: Miss Pamela Tiffin Finds Herself Being 'Sold' in New Movie." *The Cumberland Sunday Times,* Oct. 17, 1965: 32.

"Designer Sketchbook: *State Fair*." *Entertainment Design*, Oct. 1995.

Diamond, I.A.L. "*One, Two, Three*: Timetable Test." *New York Times*, Dec. 17, 1961.

DiLeo, John. *Tennessee Williams and Company: His Essential Screen Actors*. East Brunswick, NJ: Hansen Pub. Group, 2010.

"Distaff Side Spotlighted in New Film." *Los Angeles Times*, Jan. 21, 1965.

"Embassy Refuses Ponti's 'Paranoia': Rumored Alienation Unconfirmed." *Variety*, Mar. 16, 1966: 4.

Etchison, Michael. "Remember the Alamo? It's Being Retaken." *Los Angeles Herald-Examiner*, Apr. 6, 1969: E-1, E-7.

Evans, Peter. "She's Got Subliminal Sex Appeal." *New York World-Telegram*, Nov. 13, 1963: 41.

"Film Aided by Spanish Government." *Los Angeles Times*, Feb. 16, 1965.

"Film Shot in Madrid Museum." *Los Angeles Times*, Feb. 2, 1965.

Freeman, Alex. "TV Close-Up: Husband Says 'No' to Star's Junket." *The Hartford Courant*, Mar. 15, 1965.

_____. "TV Close-Up: 'Iguana' Feud Still Going Strong." *The Hartford Courant*, June 10, 1965.

Fridlund, Bert. *The Spaghetti Western: A Thematic Analysis*. Jefferson, NC: McFarland, 2006.

Gardner, Paul. "Kate Smith Plans to Perform on TV Six Times Next Season." *New York Times,* Jul. 6, 1965.

Gelmis, Joseph. *The Film Director as Superstar*. Garden City: Doubleday, 1970.

Gerber, Gail with Tom Lisanti. *Trippin' with Terry Southern: What I Think I Remember*. Jefferson, NC: McFarland, 2009.

Glover, William. "Guthrie Back on Broadway." *Oakland Tribune*, Oct. 16, 1966: 7.

Goetz, Rick PFC. "Far East Film Fare." *Pacific Stars & Stripes*, Apr. 26, 1969.

Gorman, Mary Jo. "'Viva Max!' (CUE) Receives February Blue Ribbon Award." *Boxoffice*, Mar. 16, 1970: 43.

Graham, Sheilah. "Pamela Tiffin Feels Better As a Blonde." *Hollywood Citizen-News*, Dec. 2, 1965.

_____. "Twosomes." *Hollywood Citizen-News*, May 15, 1964.

Granger, Farley with Robert Calhoun. *Include Me Out: My Life from Goldwyn to Broadway.* New York: St. Martin's Griffin, 2007.

Hart, Mother Dolores and Richard DeNeut. *The Ear of the Heart: An Actress' Journey from Hollywood to Holy Vows*. San Francisco: Ignatius Press, 2013.

"Helen Gurley Brown Touch on TV, The." *Variety*, Apr. 10, 1967.

Henderson, A.V. "What Can Mastroianni Learn from Valentino?" *The Hartford Courant*, Feb. 22, 1966.

Hischak, Thomas S. *The Rodgers and Hammerstein Encyclopedia*. Westport, Conn.: Greenwood Press, 2007.

Hoberman, J. "Wilder at Heart: Cola versus Communism in Cagney's Good-Natured Cold War Comedy." *The Village Voice*, Jan. 17, 2006: C59.

Holditch, W. Kenneth. "Interview with Pamela Tiffin." *The Tennessee Williams Literary Journal*. Vol. 3 (1993): 62–72.

Hollywood Kids, The. "Q&A: Tina Louise." *Movieline*. April 1992.

Hopper, Hedda. "Faye's Knees Shaky (at First) in Return: After 15 Years, Star Resumes Career in New 'State Fair.'" *Los Angeles Times*, Sept. 29, 1961.

_____. "Hollywood: Ann-Margret Knows How to Make Enemies." *The Hartford Courant*, Mar. 6, 1961.

_____. "I Pick These to Star in 1962." *Chicago Tribune*, Dec. 31, 1961.

_____. "'Lilo Vivacious, Gay, and the Man Is Boss!'" *Los Angeles Times*, Sept. 17, 1961.

_____. "Looking at Hollywood: Carol Lynley Reports That There Are No Kidnappers in Spain." *Chicago Tribune*, June 22, 1964.

_____. "Looking at Hollywood: MacArthur Story to Be Made Into Movie." *Chicago Tribune*, Apr. 11, 1964.

_____. "Looking at Hollywood: Pat Boone, Minister Pal Building Plane." *Chicago Tribune*, July 17, 1962.

_____. "New Billy Wilder Film Pokes Fun at Russians." *Chicago Tribune*, July 14, 1961.

_____. Hugh O'Brian interview. Oct. 27, 1962. Hedda Hopper Papers, Margaret Herrick Library, Academy of Motion Picture Arts and Sciences.

_____. "Star Rising, A: Pamela Sure to Find It a Bright Christmas." *The Washington Post*, July 21, 1961.

_____. "'State Fair' Set Hums with Action." *Los Angeles Times*, Oct. 24, 1961.

_____. "Pamela Tiffin New Film Cinderella." *Los Angeles Times*, July 18, 1961.

_____. "Under Hedda's Hat: Pamela Tiffin, a Onetime Teen Model from Chicago, After Scoring a Success Thru Films in Hollywood, Is Working on a Television Series About Manhattan." *Chicago Tribune Magazine*, Feb. 9, 1964.

Hyams, Joe. "Hogs and Cast Are New, The." *New York Herald Tribune*, Oct. 29, 1961: 4.

_____. "Joe Hyams in Hollywood: Latin Isn't All to Pamela Tiffin." *New York Herald Tribune*, Dec. 6, 1961.

"Is Tiffin Different?" *Show Business Illustrated*, Apr. 1962: 32, 33, 73.

Johnson, Erskine. "Eyes of Texas Are on Pamela." *Los Angeles Mirror*, Oct. 7, 1961.

_____. "Hollywood Abroad: For Pamela Tiffin, the Eyes Have 'It.'" *The Evening Independent*, Sept. 25, 1962: 5-B.

_____. "In Hollywood: Sees Censorship as 'Kid Stuff.'" *Redlands Daily Facts*, July 18, 1961: 10.

_____. "Pamela Tiffin's Secret Eyes." *Los Angeles Mirror*, July 4, 1961: 8.

Kahan, Saul. "Blondes, Bullets and Bathtubs." *Films and Filming*, July 1966.

Kibbey, Richard D. *Pat Boone: The Hollywood Years.* Tate Publishing & Enterprises, L.L.C., 2011.

Kilgallen, Dorothy. "Broadway: Guaranteed Income Union Goal." *The Lowell Sun*, Oct. 17, 1964: 10.

_____. "Jose's Smitten with Pamela Tiffin." *The Washington Post*, Mar. 14, 1962.

Klemesrud, Judy. "Mrs. Brown, Your Subject Is Showing." *New York Times*, Dec. 31, 1967.

Koven, Mikel J. *La Dolce Morte: Vernacular Crime and the Italian Giallo Film.* Lanham, Md.: Scarecrow Press, 2006.

Kraft, Daphne. "Pamela Tiffin No Harlow: Escapes the Shadow." *Newark Evening News*, Oct. 9, 1966.

Lancia, Enrico and Fabio Melelli. *Le Straniere del nostro Cinema.* Rome, Italy: Gremese Editore, 2005.

Lane, Lydia. "She Has Beauty, Brains." *Los Angeles Times*, Sept. 16, 1969.

"Leading Man." *Newsweek*, Nov. 29, 1965.

Levin, Martin. "Reader's Report." *New York Times*, Mar. 27, 1966.

Lieber, Leslie. "Most Beautiful Coed." *Los Angeles Times*, Dec. 29, 1963.

Lisanti, Thomas. *Hollywood Surf and Beach Movies: The First Wave, 1959–1969.* Jefferson, NC: McFarland, 2005.

Lisanti, Tom. *Drive-in Dream Girls: A Galaxy of B-Movie Starlets of the Sixties.* Jefferson, NC: McFarland, 2003.

_____. *Dueling Harlows: Race to the Silver Screen.* Washington: CreateSpace, 2011.

_____. *Fantasy Femmes of Sixties Cinema: Interviews with 20 Actresses from Biker, Beach and Elvis Movies.* Jefferson, NC: McFarland, 2001.

_____. *Glamour Girls of Sixties Hollywood: Seventy-Five Profiles.* Jefferson, NC: McFarland, 2008.

_____. "Lada Edmund, Jr. Is *Out of It*." *Sixties Cinema.*

_____. "Mimsy Farmer: From *Spencer's Mountain* to *More*." *Sixties Cinema. http://sixtiescinema.*

com/2014/04/06/mimsy-farmer-from-spencers-mountain-to-more/ 2014.

_____. "Pamela Tiffin: An American Sexpot in Rome." *European Trash Cinema,* No. 16, 1998: 24–26.

_____. "Pamela Tiffin: From Hollywood Ingénue to Italian Bombshell." *Outré the World of Ultra-Media,* No. 19, 2000: 68–72.

_____. "Pamela Tiffin: Last of the Contract Players." *Films of the Golden Age,* Summer 1997: 87–94.

Lovell, Glenn. *Escape Artist: The Life and Films of John Sturges.* Madison, Wis.: University of Wisconsin Press, 2008.

Lyons, Leonard. "The Lyons Den: Of Place and People." *The Times, San Mateo,* Aug. 19, 1961: 12.

_____. "The Lyons Den: Star May Retire." *The Sun,* Nov. 24, 1966.

"Males All 40 or Up: Italy's Strange Young Actor Gap." *Variety,* Sept. 10, 1969: 32.

Marshall, Bill and Robynn Stilwell, ed. *Musicals: Hollywood and Beyond.* Exeter, England; Portland, OR: Intellect, 2000.

McBain, Diane and Michael Gregg Michaud. *Famous Enough: A Hollywood Memoir.* Duncan, Oklahoma: BearManor Media, 2014.

McGrady, Mike. "After 7 Movies, Pamela Is Learning to Act." *Newsday*, Jan. 15, 1965.

MGM Pressbook: Deaf Smith and Johnny Ears. Los Angeles: Metro-Goldwyn-Mayer, Inc., 1973.

Miller, Edwin. "The Hollywood Scene." *Seventeen,* Sept. 1964: 26.

"Miss Pamela Tiffin Is World Traveler." *Hollywood Citizen-News,* Aug. 28, 1964.

Monroe, Keith. "Inside the Magazines: New Teen Publication Succeeds Without Sex or Sensationalism." *Los Angeles Times*, June 30, 1963.

Morella, Joe and Edward Z. Epstein. *Paul and Joanne: A Biography of Paul Newman and Joanne Woodward.* New York: Delacorte Press, 1988.

Morris, Bruce M. *Prime Time Network Serials: Episode Guides, Casts and Credits for 37 Continuing Television Dramas, 1964–1993, Vol. 2.* Jefferson, NC: McFarland, 1997.

"Movie Star Picks Up Her Bonds." *Hollywood Citizen-News,* July 2, 1963.

Negulesco, Jean. *Things I Did—And Things I Think I Did.* New York: Linden Press/Simon & Schuster, 1984.

Nelson, Don. "She Set Her Mind to Acting: Pamela Tiffin Adds Up to a Young Film Star Whose Beauty of Coloring Outside Is Matched by Plenty of Gray Matter Inside." *New York Sunday News*, Feb. 25, 1962: 5.

Nero, Franco. DVD interview. *Giornata Nera. The Fifth Cord.* Mar. 28, 2006.

"No Flat Fee for Private-Eye 'Harper.'" Letter from the Warner Bros. Pictures, Inc. New Department.

[1966]. Margaret Herrick Library, Academy of Motion Picture Arts and Sciences.

O'Brian, Hugh. Letter to Hedda Hopper. July 5, 1962. Hedda Hopper Papers, Margaret Herrick Library, Academy of Motion Picture Arts and Sciences.

"Old Fashioned Is Word for Pamela—When She Sews." *Van Nuys (Calif.) News*, Apr. 21, 1961: 23-A.

"Pamela Tiffin Films Italo, But in Manila." *Variety*, Apr. 5, 1972: 1.

"Pamela's Progress." *Esquire*, Jan. 1962: 92–95.

Parker, Jerry. "At the Alamo: Remember Winters." *Newsday*, Feb. 18, 1970.

Parsons, Louella. Editorial. *Los Angeles Herald-Examiner*. Sept. 9, 1963.

Parsons, Louella and Harriet Parsons. "Pamela's a Talker, But Beautiful." *Los Angeles Herald-Examiner*, June 13, 1965: 1, 8.

Pauley, Gay. "Pamela Tiffin a Busy Actress, Model, Student and Housewife." *Chicago Tribune*, Dec. 9, 1963.

"People on the Way Up: Pamela Tiffin." *Saturday Evening Post*, Dec. 2, 1961.

Peper, William. "Pictures, Plays and Players: Acting Is Minor to Pam Tiffin." *New York World-Telegraph & Sun*, Dec. 6, 1961.

"Person of Promise: Pamela Tiffin." *Films and Filming*, Jan. 1962: 21.

"Ponti Again Rolls 'Paranoia' in Bid to Recoup Loss." *Variety*, June 21, 1967: 1.

"Private Life of Pamela Tiffin, The." *Glamour Girls of the Silver Screen. http://www.glamourgirlsof thesilverscreen.com/show/474/Pamela+Tiffin/ index.html*

"'Protagonists' Pick Puzzles Italians; Showmen-from-Rome Fill Cannes." *Variety*, May 8, 1968: 90.

Quirino, Jose A. *Like Dew in April and Other Stories*. Philippines: Navotas Press, 1973.

"Racing Cars Get Stellar Treatment." *Los Angeles Times*, Sept. 16, 1964.

Reemes, Dana M. *Directed by Jack Arnold*. Jefferson, N.C.: McFarland, 1988.

Rice, Charles D. "Success Stories You Won't Believe..." *New York Herald Tribune*, Sept. 24, 1961.

Robertson, Ed. *The Fugitive Recaptured: The 30th Anniversary Companion to a Television Classic*. Los Angeles: Pomegranate Press, LTD, 1993.

Rose, Bob. "Food for Thought—after 'Candy.'" *Boston Globe*, Aug. 31, 1969.

Saber, Joyce. "Sharif Featured in Love Triangles." *Los Angeles Times*, Jan. 22, 1969.

Scanlon, Jennifer. *Bad Girls Go Everywhere: The Life of Helen Gurley Brown, the Woman Behind Cosmopolitan Magazine*. New York: Penguin Group, 2010.

Scheuer, Philip K. "'Day Before Spring' Dawns for Debbie." *Los Angeles Times*, Feb. 21, 1964.

_____. "The Man Who Made Apathy: Irresistible Marcello Mastroianni." *Los Angeles Times*, Dec. 12, 1965.

_____. "Murray Plans Life of Nathan Leopold." *Los Angeles Times*, June 2, 1964.

Schumach, Murray. "Wilder to Adapt Molnar Comedy." *New York Times*, Jan. 12, 1961.

Scott, John L. "Hollywood: A Lesson in Larceny." *Los Angeles Times*, June 28, 1964.

_____. "Hollywood Calendar: Good Old Days in Filmland Good to All." *Los Angeles Times*, July 18, 1965.

_____. "Hollywood Calendar: One Minute Interview Covers Lots of Ground." *Los Angeles Times*, Apr. 7, 1963.

_____. "Hollywood Calendar: Star Is Born by Changing His Name." *Los Angeles Times*, Feb. 23, 1964.

Scott, Vernon. "Pamela Is Worth Second-Third Look." *The Brownsville Herald*, Aug. 6, 1961.

Seidenbaum, Art. "Indian Spoof Makes the Scalp Tingle." *Los Angeles Times*, Nov. 1, 1964.

_____. "Spectator 1963: 'For Those Who Think Young' Going all Out with Tie-Ins." *Los Angeles Times*, Oct. 25, 1963.

"Setting for a Western: Outdoor Barbeque Followed Premier of 'The Hallelujah Trail.'" *New York Sunday News*, Sept. 5, 1965: 13, 14.

Shain, Percy. "George Hamilton: Some Candid Views on the Good Life." *Boston Globe*, Sept. 7, 1969.

_____. "Upheaval Galore for 'Survivors.'" *Boston Globe*, May 8, 1969.

Shenker, Israel. "Faye's Knees Shaky (at First) in Return." *Los Angeles Times*, Sept. 29, 1961.

_____. "The Man Who Made Apathy." *New York Times*, Dec. 12, 1965: 54, 55, 58,60, 62, 65, 67, 70.

Sherlock, John. "Skipper without a Ship." *TV Guide*, July 28, 1962.

"'Sheik' Is Silly Comedy." *The Post-Standard*, Dec. 19, 1968: 16.

Shipka, Danny. *Perverse Titillation: The Exploitation Cinema of Italy, Spain and France, 1960–1980*. Jefferson, NC: McFarland, 2011.

Skolsky, Sidney. "Pam, Rising Young Star, Is Tintyped." *Hollywood Citizen-News*, Feb. 8, 1962.

Smith, Liz. "Gilda Radner's 'Something' Is a Devastatingly Good Book." *Orange County Register*, June 26, 1989.

Solomon, Aubrey. *Twentieth Century-Fox: A Corporate and Financial History*. Metuchen, N.J.: Scarecrow Press, 1988.

"Spotlight: Pamela Tiffin." *Life*, Apr. 13, 1962: 120.

"Star Commutes by Ambulance." *Los Angeles Times*, July 13, 1964.

"Star Dust." *Hollywood Citizen-News*, July 28, 1964.

"Star Is Made—In Detroit, A." *McCall's*, June 1964.

Stein, Percy. "Last *Survivors* Zeroes into Surprising Focus." *Boston Globe*, Jan. 13, 1970.

Stern, Harold. "Screen Actress Finds TV 'Terrifying': Pace Too Exhausting, Moans Pamela Tiffin." *The Hartford Courant*, Jan. 31, 1965.

Storaro, Vittorio. DVD interview. *Giornata Nera. The Fifth Cord.* Mar. 28, 2006.

Strodder, Chris. *The Encyclopedia of Sixties Cool: A Celebration of the Grooviest People, Events, and Artifacts of the 1960's.* Santa Monica, CA: Santa Monica Press, 2007.

"Study in Beauty, A." *NY Daily News.* Aug. 9, 1965.

"Sweet—And Not So Sweet." *Show*, March 1964.

Tatara, Paul. "One, Two, Three." *Turner Classic Movies*, http://www.tcm.com/tcmdb/title/17693/One-Two-Three/articles.html

Thirer, Irene. "Movie Spotlight: Pamela Tiffin—Beauty with Brains." *New York Post*, Apr. 11, 1962: 90.

Thomas, Bob. "Oscar Race Safe and Sane This Year." *Chicago Daily Tribune*, Feb. 11, 1962.

"Tiffin Changes Slogan." *Los Angeles Herald-Examiner.* June 4, 1965: B-6.

Tiffin, Pamela. Interview by Hedda Hopper "Pamela Tiffin." Transcription. November 27, 1963: 1–4. Hedda Hopper Papers, Margaret Herrick Library, Academy of Motion Picture Arts and Sciences.

_____. Interview by Sonia Wolfson. "Notes on Pamela Tiffin: 'Margy' in 20th Century–Fox CinemaScope Color Production of Rodgers and Hammerstein's 'State Fair.'" Transcription. 1961: 1–24. Sidney Skolsky Papers, Margaret Herrick Library, Academy of Motion Picture Arts and Sciences.

_____. Interview by Sonia Wolfson. "Recent Notes on Pamela Tiffin, Currently Co-Starring in Metro-Goldwyn-Mayer's *Come Fly with Me*. Transcription. Mar. 14, 1963: 1–8. Sidney Skolsky Papers, Margaret Herrick Library, Academy of Motion Picture Arts and Sciences.

_____. "My Days in Spain." July 1964: 1–8. Hedda Hopper Papers, Margaret Herrick Library, Academy of Motion Picture Arts and Sciences.

"Toast to Tiffin, A." *Playboy Magazine*, Feb. 1969.

Tomasson, Robert E. "Fox Loses Movie on Film Opening: 'Goldfarb' Appeal Scheduled for Hearing Jan. 5." *New York Times*, Dec. 19, 1964.

"Tommy Powers Had a Flair for Promoting His Movies." *San Antonio Express-News* [San Antonio, Texas], Jan. 23, 1990: 5.

Tucker, Priscilla. "Young Star Solves the Clothes Problem." *New York Herald Tribune*, Dec. 13, 1961.

UPI. "Alamo '69 Pits 'Max' Against Texas Ladies." *Newsday*, Apr. 2, 1969.

_____. "Texans Up in Arms Over Alamo Movie." *Los Angeles Times*, Apr. 11, 1969.

_____. "'Viva Max!' Wins Alamo Film Battle." *Los Angeles Times*, Mar. 29, 1969.

Wagner, Ruth. "*Summer and Smoke* Puts Her in the Limelight: Model Turned Actress Tells Secret of Success." *The Washington Post*, Jan. 2, 1962.

Wahls, Robert. "Footlight: Over-Stimulated Pam." *New York Daily News*, Oct. 16, 1966.

Warga, Wayne. "Film Students Put Director in Spotlight." *Los Angeles Times*, Feb. 25, 1970.

Warren, James. "Straight Shooter Jim Lehrer: Anchor, Author, Trailways Ticket Agent Extraordinaire." *Chicago Tribune*, Mar. 31, 1991: 2.

Weisser, Thomas. *Spaghetti Westerns: The Good, the Bad, and the Violent.* Jefferson, NC: McFarland, 1992.

Werba, Hank. "Sardinia's Banditry Provides Almost Too Much Realism for 3 Locations." *Variety,* Oct. 18, 1967: 2, 61.

Werneth, William. "New Faces: Pamela Tiffin Calls Nation's Exhibitors Solid, Efficient Men." *Motion Picture Herald*, May 2, 1962: 9, 10.

Wilson, Earl. "Girl in a Petticoat." *New York Post*, July 23, 1961.

_____. "It Happened Last Night." *Newsday,* Apr. 4, 1966.

_____. "It Happened Last Night." *Newsday,* Apr. 17, 1962.

_____. "It Happened Last Night." *Newsday,* Mar. 12, 1964.

_____. "It Happened Last Night." *Newsday,* May 17, 1963.

_____. "It Happened Last Night." *Newsday,* Oct. 29, 1964.

_____. "It Happened Last Night." *Newsday,* Nov. 20, 1961.

_____. "It Happened Last Night: Pamela Tiffin Worried About Being Compared to MM." *Sarasota Herald-Tribune*, Apr. 25, 1967: 16.

_____. "Pamela Cooks Italian Style..." *New York Post*, Mar. 27, 1966: 5.

_____. "Panthers, Yes; Playboy, No: Pamela Tiffin Reacts to Chicago." *The Hartford Courant*, Jan. 7, 1970.

Wilson, Liza. "Time for Tiffin: She, Pamela, Is What Hollywood Is Ever Searching for—an Original." *Los Angeles Herald-Examiner*, Mar. 4, 1962.

Winsten, Archer. "Rages and Outrages." *New York Post*, Nov. 8, 1965: 22.

Wolfe, Tom. "A City Built of Clay." *New York*, July 6, 2008.

Wood, Thomas. "In Wilder's Wild West: Director and Troupe Shoot as Usual Despite Russian Ruses in Berlin." *New York Times*, July 16, 1961.

"You've Met Mrs. Lee: She's a Beauty; 'Hobby' Is Acting." *Humboldt Standard*, July 20, 1964: 2.

Zolotow, Sam. "The End Is Near for Dinner at 8: 10-Star Revival Will Close on Saturday Evening." *New York Times*, Jan. 10, 1967.

Index